"In this exciting and extraordinarily important work, Gerald McDermott and his contributors point us toward a fresh way of understanding the relationship between Christianity and Judaism—one in which Israel is not regarded merely as a voice from the past or a transitional entity consigned to a passing dispensational role, but regarded instead as an essential and enduring presence at the heart of the church's ongoing life. In their view, the 'scandal of Zionism' is an instance of the 'scandal of particularity' at the very core of the gospel—the paradox that the biblical God has conveyed a universal message by means of a particular people and a particular land whose particularity is never to be effaced or superseded. If they are right, the implications are enormous for Christians and Jews alike."

Wilfred M. McClay, G. T. and Libby Blankenship Chair in the History of Liberty, University of Oklahoma

"This book is rigorous in its scholarship and speaks with thoughtfulness and passion about an understudied and widely misunderstood subject. This important book is both learned and provocative. It is clearly written and argued throughout and displays a wealth of historical understanding, theological richness and exegetical savvy. This book is a must-read for all who are interested in the truly big questions of our day."

Byron R. Johnson, Institute for Studies of Religion, Baylor University

"The essays here offer a fresh perspective on Christian Zionism, one based on careful biblical exegesis and in dialogue with the historic traditions of the church. A paradigm-challenging volume."

Timothy George, founding dean, Beeson Divinity School, Samford University, general editor of the Reformation Commentary on Scripture

THE NEW CHRISTIAN ZIONISM

FRESH PERSPECTIVES ON ISRAEL & THE LAND

EDITED BY
GERALD R. McDERMOTT

An imprint of InterVarsity Press
Downers Grove, Illinois

InterVarsity Press
P.O. Box 1400, Downers Grove, IL 60515-1426
ivpress.com
email@ivpress.com

©2016 by Gerald R. McDermott

All rights reserved. No part of this book may be reproduced in any form without written permission from InterVarsity Press.

InterVarsity Press® is the book-publishing division of InterVarsity Christian Fellowship/USA®, a movement of students and faculty active on campus at hundreds of universities, colleges and schools of nursing in the United States of America, and a member movement of the International Fellowship of Evangelical Students. For information about local and regional activities, visit intervarsity.org.

Scripture quotations, unless otherwise noted, are from the New Revised Standard Version of the Bible, copyright 1989 by the Division of Christian Education of the National Council of the Churches of Christ in the USA. Used by permission. All rights reserved.

Cover design: Cindy Kiple
Interior design: Beth McGill
Images: Landscape: suprunvitaly / iStockphoto
       Necklace: Lisalson / iStockphoto

ISBN 978-0-8308-5138-6 (print)
ISBN 978-0-8308-9438-3 (digital)

Printed in the United States of America ∞

 As a member of the Green Press Initiative, InterVarsity Press is committed to protecting the environment and to the responsible use of natural resources. To learn more, visit greenpressinitiative.org.

Library of Congress Cataloging-in-Publication Data
Names: McDermott, Gerald R. (Gerald Robert), editor.
Title: The new Christian Zionism : fresh perspectives on Israel and the land / edited by Gerald R. McDermott.
Description: Downers Grove : InterVarsity Press, 2016. | Includes bibliographical references and index.
Identifiers: LCCN 2016011844 (print) | LCCN 2016019816 (ebook) | ISBN 9780830851386 (pbk. : alk. paper) | ISBN 9780830894383 (eBook)
Subjects: LCSH: Christian Zionism.
Classification: LCC DS150.5 .N48 2016 (print) | LCC DS150.5 (ebook) | DDC 261.2/6--dc23
LC record available at https://lccn.loc.gov/2016011844

P	24	23	22	21	20	19	18	17	16	15	14	13	12	11	10	9	8	7	6	5	4	3
Y	34	33	32	31	30	29	28	27	26	25	24	23	22	21	20	19	18	17				

To Baruch Kvasnica,

who first planted the seed that eventually became

this book and whose teaching and correspondence

have taught me much ever since

CONTENTS

Acknowledgments.. 9

Introduction: What Is the New Christian Zionism?
    Gerald R. McDermott.. 11

PART ONE: THEOLOGY AND HISTORY

  1 A History of Supersessionism: Getting the Big Story Wrong
      Gerald R. McDermott.. 33

  2 A History of Christian Zionism: Is Christian Zionism Rooted Primarily
    in Premillennial Dispensationalism?
      Gerald R. McDermott.. 45

PART TWO: THEOLOGY AND THE BIBLE

  3 Biblical Hermeneutics: How Are We to Interpret the Relation Between
    the Tanak and the New Testament on This Question?
      Craig Blaising... 79

  4 Zionism in the Gospel of Matthew: Do the People of Israel and
    the Land of Israel Persist as Abiding Concerns for Matthew?
      Joel Willitts.. 107

  5 Zionism in Luke–Acts: Do the People of Israel and the Land of Israel
    Persist as Abiding Concerns in Luke's Two Volumes?
      Mark S. Kinzer.. 141

  6 Zionism in Pauline Literature: Does Paul Eliminate
    Particularity for Israel and the Land in His Portrayal
    of Salvation Available for All the World?
      David Rudolph.. 167

PART THREE: THEOLOGY AND ITS IMPLICATIONS

7 Theology and the Churches: Mainline Protestant Zionism and Anti-Zionism
   Mark Tooley... 197

8 Theology and Politics: Reinhold Niebuhr's Christian Zionism
   Robert Benne... 221

9 Theology and Law: Does the Modern State of Israel Violate Its Call to Justice in the Covenant by Its Relation to International Law?
   Robert Nicholson.. 249

10 Theology and Morality: Is Modern Israel Faithful to the Moral Demands of the Covenant in Its Treatment of Minorities?
   Shadi Khalloul... 281

PART FOUR: THEOLOGY AND THE FUTURE

11 How Should the New Christian Zionism Proceed?
   Darrell Bock... 305

12 Implications and Propositions
   Gerald R. McDermott.. 319

List of Contributors 335

Name Index.. 337

Subject Index... 341

Scripture and Ancient Writings Index 343

ACKNOWLEDGMENTS

I am most appreciative of my wife, Jean, who provides all kinds of support and ideas. I am also grateful to Andy Le Peau, who was willing to entertain and support this sensitive proposal. Drew Blankman has been encouraging, speedy and helpful throughout the editing process. Thanks to Robert Nicholson and Mark Tooley for helping organize this project, and to Robert Benne—who has been a wise adviser throughout. Finally, I am grateful to Yannick Christos-Wahab who prepared the Scripture index.

INTRODUCTION

What Is the New Christian Zionism?

Gerald R. McDermott

◆

Most scholars have assumed that all Christian Zionism is an outgrowth of premillennial dispensationalist theology. Originating in the nineteenth century, this school of thought became popular because it was taught in the notes of the Scofield version of the King James Bible and then developed by Hal Lindsey's *The Late Great Planet Earth* and the best-selling Left Behind series.

The traditional dispensationalist version of Christian Zionism puts Israel and the church on two different tracks, neither of which runs at the same time. This version is attached to an elaborate schedule of end-time events dominated by the great tribulation and a rapture of the church that leaves Jews and the rest of the world behind.

The Christian Zionism that this book proposes is not connected to the dispensationalism described in the previous paragraph. It looks to a long history of Christian Zionists who lived long before the rise of dispensationalism and to other thinkers in the last two centuries who have had nothing to do with dispensationalism—theologians such as Karl Barth, Reinhold Niebuhr, Robert Jenson and the Catholic Old Testament scholar Gary Anderson, as well as President Harry Truman. More on this in the first chapter.

So what do the scholars and experts in this book mean by "the New Christian Zionism"? The best answer to this question, we think, is the rest of the book. This introduction will telegraph, as it were, the basic implications of what we mean by this term. The first is that the people and land of Israel are central to the story of the Bible. This might seem obvious. But Israel has not been central to the church's traditional way of telling the story of salvation. Typically the story has moved from creation and fall to Christ's death and resurrection, with Israel as an illustration of false paths.[1] We believe that the Bible claims that God saves the world *through* Israel and the perfect Israelite; thus the Bible is incoherent and salvation impossible without Israel. We propose that the history of salvation is ongoing: the people of Israel and their land continue to have theological significance. I will return to Israel and salvation in the next section of this introduction.

We are also convinced that the return of Jews from all over the world to their land, and their efforts to establish a nation-state after two millennia of being separated from controlling the land, is *part* of the fulfillment of biblical prophecy. Further, we believe that Jews need and deserve a homeland in Israel—not to displace others but to accept and develop what the family of nations—the United Nations—ratified in 1948. We would add that this startling event climaxed a history of continual Jewish presence in the land going back at least three thousand years.

We should explain what we do *not* mean by the New Christian Zionism. We do not mean that the state of Israel is a perfect country. Or that it should not be criticized for its failures. Or that it is necessarily the last Jewish state we will see before the end of days. Or that we know the particular timetable or political schema that will come *before* or *in* the final days.

But we *do* know that the state of Israel, which includes more than two million non-Jews, is what protects the people of Israel. Support for this state and its people is eroding all over the world. Israel lies in a region of movements and governments bent on its destruction. Mainline Protestants have withdrawn their support. Many evangelicals are now starting to withdraw their support, using the same faulty arguments proffered by the Protestant mainline.[2] Those arguments will be reviewed in chapter seven. For these and other reasons, it is time for Christians, not just Jews, to make a case for the Jewish people and their land.

The goal of this book, however, is not simply to make a prudential argument that the state of Israel is needed to provide a shelter for its covenant people. Some of the chapters that follow will make some of those arguments, and some

---

[1]Christians also mine the Old Testament for prophecies of the Messiah.
[2]See Gerald McDermott, "A One-Sided Attack on Zionism: The Many Problems with the Documentary 'With God on Our Side,'" blog posted on Gleanings, *Christianity Today*, January 18, 2011, www.christianitytoday.com/gleanings/2011/january/one-sided-attack-on-zionism.html.

Introduction

of them need to be made, now more than ever. For example, Shadi Khalloul, a leader of the Aramean community in Israel, argues that the rights of his non-Jewish community and other minority communities will be protected only in the Jewish state. Attorney Robert Nicholson probes and refutes the charge that Israel violates international law. Lutheran ethicist Robert Benne considers the political ethics of Zionism by revisiting the work of Reinhold Niebuhr. Historian Mark Tooley weighs the arguments made by mainline Protestant churches against Israel.

But the purpose of these prudential arguments—political and legal and moral—is to undergird a new *theological* argument for the twenty-first century. So the center of this book is made up of chapters three through six, which focus first on theological history and biblical hermeneutics and then on authors of the New Testament. The burden of these chapters is to show *theologically* that the people of Israel *continue* to be significant for the history of redemption and that the land of Israel, which is at the heart of the covenantal promises, *continues* to be important to God's providential purposes.

This introduction will do two things to clarify further what the New Christian Zionism means. First, I explain here what the New Christian Zionism is *not*. It is neither dispensationalism nor mere nationalism, nor land theft, nor merely Christian eschatology, nor theocracy. Then I will outline the shape of our argument as it proceeds through the remaining chapters.

Not Dispensationalism

Many Christians today resist the idea that the land could have any theological significance, even if they grant that God's covenant with Jews is ongoing. They are not sure how that covenant relates to Jesus' "new" or "renewed"[3] covenant, but they have come to think, especially if they are Catholics or mainline Protestants, that Christian Zionism is a fundamentalist fantasy associated with old-style dispensationalism.

We do not wish to disparage the whole dispensationalist tradition. For a century before the Holocaust, dispensationalists were among the few Christians

---

[3]The latter may be a better translation of the famous passage in Jeremiah 31:31-34, for the Hebrew word for "new" and "renewed" is the same, and the latter better fits the Jewish tradition in Tanak (or TaNaKh, an acronym using the first Hebrew letter of each of the Masoretic text's three traditional subdivisions: Torah ["Teaching," also known as the Five Books of Moses], Nevi'im ["Prophets"] and Ketuvim ["Writings"]) of covenant renewals, such as under Joshua, Josiah, Ezra and Nehemiah.

who recognized that God's covenant with Israel did not stop in AD 33 or 30 (scholars differ on the date of the passion and resurrection of Jesus). That took both theological ingenuity and professional courage for the scholars among them. We also recognize that there is a new "progressive dispensationalism" that rejects the strict bifurcation maintained by traditional dispensationalists between God's work with Israel and his work in the church. It departs from other dispensationalist schools that are more concerned with date setting and less interested in contemporary engagement.[4]

The authors of this book reject those dispensationalist approaches that are confident they can plot the sequence or chronology of end-time events. We also disagree with many of the political beliefs associated with dispensationalism at the popular level (most of these are not embraced by dispensationalist scholars), such as the idea that the present state of Israel is never to be criticized because it is God's chosen people, or that any concessions of land are forbidden on theological grounds.

In contrast, the New Christian Zionism holds that the schedule of events leading up to and including the eschaton are in God's secret providence. We believe that the return of Jews to the land and their establishment of the state of Israel are partial fulfillments of biblical prophecy and so are part of God's design for what might be a long era of eschatological fulfillment. As Mark Kinzer puts it, today's state of Israel both awaits redemption and is a means to it.[5] It is a proleptic sign of the eschaton, which means that it is a provisional sign of the not-yet-actualized consummation. While a sign of God's final redemption, perhaps a type (divine prefiguration) of the new earth with Israel at its center, the state of Israel is still only a pointer to a far greater consummation to come.[6]

---

[4]See Craig A. Blaising and Darrell L. Bock, *Progressive Dispensationalism* (Grand Rapids: Baker Academic, 2000), esp. 377-94. For a survey of dispensational approaches to Israel, see Richard Harvey, *Mapping Messianic Jewish Theology: A Constructive Approach* (Milton Keynes, UK: Paternoster, 2009), 223-61.

[5]Mark S. Kinzer, *Israel's Messiah and the People of God: A Vision for Messianic Jewish Covenant Fidelity*, ed. Jennifer M. Rosner (Eugene, OR: Cascade, 2011), 94-102.

[6]Gary A. Anderson argues that "the eschatological end promised by God" should not be confused with the return after the second exile or the return in our day, even though those returns are partial fulfillments of biblical prophecy. Robert W. Jenson asserts that the present return of Jews to the land is "an anticipatory presence" or sacrament of the final Jerusalem. Anderson, "The Return to Zion as the Fulfillment and Non-Fulfillment of Biblical Promises," in *Returning to Zion: Christian and Jewish Perspectives*, ed. Robert W. Jenson and Eugene Korn (Efrat, Israel: Center for Jewish-Christian Understanding and Cooperation, 2015), 24; Jenson, "The Prophet's Double Vision of the Return to Zion," in Jenson and Korn, *Returning to Zion*, 34, 37.

Introduction

As I mentioned in the beginning of this introduction, this book is not connected to traditional dispensationalism. Chapter two traces the history of Christian Zionism over eighteen hundred years before the rise of dispensationalism and then discusses Christian Zionists in the last two centuries who had nothing to do with dispensationalism. The other chapters make no appeal to traditional dispensationalist frameworks in order to make their cases.[7] That is a major (but not the only) reason why this is a *New* Christian Zionism.

Not Merely Nationalism

Another reason why many Christians, including some scholars, dismiss Christian (and Jewish!) Zionism is that they think it is one example of many nationalisms that arose in the nineteenth century, when romanticism and European democratic movements were inspiring many peoples of common culture to form nation-states. This implies that Zionism is therefore recent and political, and cannot be essentially related to ancient times and religion, as religious Zionists claim it is.

The first problem with this charge is that there is plenty of evidence, as I show in chapter one, that Christian Zionism goes back two thousand years to the New Testament, and has been sustained with varying intensity ever since. In the next section of this introduction I show that the same can be said for Jewish Zionism: that it is even older, stretching back at least three thousand years.

But what of Zionism's relation to nineteenth-century nationalist movements? It is true that the rise of political Zionism in the nineteenth century followed, and to a degree benefited from, the romantic nationalism that was inspired by Jean-Jacques Rousseau (1712–1778) and Johann Gottfried Herder (1744–1803), who suggested that a people is formed by geography, language, customs and (for some) race. These new cultural winds helped form Germany, Italy and Romania by unifying what had been regional states and helped wars of independence to create Greece, Bulgaria and Poland.[8]

Yet four of these nationalisms—Germany, Romania, Bulgaria and Poland—were unable to go back more than a few centuries to a previous unity of culture or language or religion. Germany had no common language before the sixteenth century. Only Greece and Italy could point to ancient civilizations on

---

[7]Of course every biblical theologian is a dispensationalist insofar as she recognizes that God works in different eras or dispensations in history. Two of our authors, Craig Blaising and Darrell Bock, are originators of the "progressive dispensationalist" school.
[8]Eric J. Hobsbawm, *Nations and Nationalism Since 1780: Programme, Myth, Reality*, 2nd ed. (Cambridge: Cambridge University Press, 1992).

the same land, yet the religion (and therefore culture) of each in the nineteenth century was dramatically different from what obtained in their ancient predecessors. Israel alone can point to an ancient civilization on the same land with the same religion and language.[9] Nineteenth-century nationalism might have assisted the rise of Zionism, but the heightened anti-Semitism in Europe (which ironically was strengthened by the new race consciousness in that same nineteenth-century romantic nationalism) and vicious pogroms in Russia did far more than romantic nationalism to allow the ancient Zionist idea to blossom into Theodor Herzl's political Zionism in the late nineteenth century.[10]

Besides, a growing number of scholars are saying that the notion of European nationalism arising from Rousseau and Herder is more myth than fact, or at best grossly incomplete. These scholars argue that European nationalism had its source in the Hebrew Bible and in the adoption by European peoples of national identities consciously modeled on the national identity of biblical Israel—a modern phenomenon greatly accelerated by the vernacular Bible and Protestantism. By the late sixteenth century, for example, England and Holland were already European nations with self-understandings based on the Bible's division of the world into nations as God-given, and the independence of nations as a biblical ideal.[11]

No matter the character of modern nationalism, Jews have lived in the land of Israel for three thousand years, all the while thinking of themselves as Jews in the homeland for Jewish culture. This means that Jews thought of Israel as their natural home for millennia before the nineteenth century. Besides the continual residence—which most historians acknowledge—of Jews in the land from Joshua's conquests in the thirteenth century BC to the Bar Kokhba revolt in AD 135, four times in the last two thousand years the land of Israel served as the refuge for, and rebuilding of, Jewish culture.[12]

---

[9]From the second century AD until the revival of Hebrew as a spoken language circa 1880, Hebrew was employed as a literary and official language and the language of prayer. Chaim Rabin, *A Short History of the Hebrew Language* (Jerusalem: Jewish Agency and Alpha Press, 1973).

[10]Léon Poliakov, *The History of Anti-Semitism*, vol. 3, *From Voltaire to Wagner*, trans. Miriam Kochan (Philadelphia: University of Pennsylvania Press, 2003).

[11]See, for example, Adrian Hastings, *The Construction of Nationhood: Ethnicity, Religion and Nationalism* (Cambridge: Cambridge University Press, 1997).

[12]James Parkes, *End of an Exile: Israel, the Jews and the Gentile World*, ed. Eugene B. Korn and Roberta Kalechofsky (Marblehead, MA: Micah, 2004), 26-34.

Introduction

The first time that Jews regrouped in the land was after the two wars with Rome in 66–70 and 132–135. The rabbis were driven out of Jerusalem up to Galilee, where they compiled the Mishnah, a creative reinterpretation of the Torah after the destruction of the temple forced Jews to see Torah study as the new sacrifice. The northernmost land of Israel, Galilee, served as a center of Jewish culture for the next five hundred years.[13]

Later, after Jews fled Baghdad (where they had flourished for a time) in the eighth century when Turkish invasions destroyed the stability of the Abbasid Caliphate, Tiberias in Galilee once again became a center for Jewish culture. It was here that the Masoretic text of the Tanak (the Christian "Old Testament") was produced. From the eighth through the tenth centuries Galilee once again was a center of Jewish religious thought and life.[14]

A third time was after a century of Jewish martyrdom at the hand of Christian Europeans, a century that included the Fourth Lateran Council (1215), the compulsion of Jews to wear a badge, and the expulsion of Jews from Spain (1492) and Portugal (1496). When the Ottoman sultan Selim the Terrible in 1517 ousted the Mamelukes from Jerusalem, he opened the doors of Palestine to Jewish immigration once more. Small numbers of Jews had been living on the land all along, but now the Jewish population grew in numbers and prosperity. Safed in Galilee became the new center of rabbinic culture and produced two of its greatest sages in the sixteenth century, Joseph Caro and Isaac Luria. There they developed kabbalah, the mystical Judaism that brought life and hope to Jews in later centuries. Safed became a pilgrimage site for Polish Hasidim (lit., "the pious ones"; Jewish mystics) from the sixteenth through the nineteenth centuries.[15] In addition, many students of Rabbi Elijah of Vilna emigrated from Lithuania to Israel at the end of the eighteenth century to found what became known as the "old Yishuv" ("the original community") outside the ancient city walls of Jerusalem.

---

[13]"Despite the negative factors at work [persecution of Jews during the Byzantine period], it can be stated that most of Galilee retained its Jewish character through the sixth century." Gedaliah Alon, *The Jews in Their Land in the Talmudic Age*, trans. and ed. Gershon Levi (Cambridge, MA: Harvard University Press, 1996), 755.

[14]See "The Masoretes and the Punctuation of Biblical Hebrew," Machine Assisted Translation Team, *British & Foreign Bible Society*, May 2, 2002, http://lc.bfbs.org.uk/e107_files/downloads/masoretes.pdf; Elvira Martín Contreras, "Masora and Masoretic Interpretation," in *The Oxford Encyclopedia of Biblical Interpretation*, ed. Steven L. McKenzie, 2 vols., forthcoming; and Paul Johnson, *A History of the Jews* (New York: Harper & Row, 1987), 151-52.

[15]Johnson, *History of the Jews*, 260-61.

Finally, when czarist pogroms drove Jews from Russia and modern anti-Semitism in Europe started boiling over in the nineteenth century, Jews once again came to Israel for a refuge and cultural homeland. But they started coming long before the rise of what we now call Zionism, led by Theodor Herzl (1860–1904). For example, three hundred rabbis and their families moved to Ottoman Palestine in the eighteenth century, pursuing their vision of redemption in the Promised Land.[16] Others followed. The first wave of Jewish refugees from Europe came in 1882 to join the Sephardic Jews who had lived in Palestine for generations. Herzl did not organize the first Zionist Congress until 1897.[17]

So Zionism can rightly be called a nationalism because it has a sense of unity based on common customs, language and religious culture. But limiting its origins to the late nineteenth century contradicts its actual history.[18] Jews have been on the land for more than three thousand years and have always regarded it as their cultural and religious home. Indeed, it has been a place of pilgrimage for Jews in the diaspora for more than two thousand years.

Not Merely Christian

Some critics have pointed to Herzl's Zionist movement as proof that Zionism is more Christian than Jewish. They charge that this movement is relatively new to Judaism and is more secular than religious. Herzl himself was not an observant Jew, and he cast his movement in secular not religious terms.[19]

 It is true that the Babylonian Talmud contains an oath not to "go as one to the Holy Land" because it would suggest failure to trust that God alone would establish Zion.[20] It is also true that some rabbis criticized modern Zionism from its beginning because it was "not founded on Torah and religious repentance and [was] not the result of supernatural intervention."[21] At the turn of the twentieth century, a distinguished rabbi of the time, Elyakum Shlomo Shapira of Grodno (now in Belarus), complained that the new Zionists' "valor in the land

---

[16]Shalom Goldman, *Zeal for Zion: Christians, Jews, and the Idea of the Promised Land* (Chapel Hill: University of North Carolina Press, 2009), 10.
[17]Parkes, *End of an Exile*, 24; Johnson, *History of the Jews*, 357-65.
[18]Johnson, *History of the Jews*, 374-75.
[19]Goldman, *Zeal for Zion*, 88-136.
[20]Ibid., 5-6.
[21]Aviezer Ravitsky, *Messianism, Zionism, and Jewish Religious Radicalism* (Chicago: University of Chicago Press, 1996), 2.

Introduction

is not for the sake of the true faith. . . . How can I bear that something be called 'the state of Israel' without the Torah and the commandments (heaven forbid)?"[22]

But this is only a small part of the truth. The talmudic "oaths" were never considered law or even normative ideas in Judaism. Moreover, religious Jews were involved in modern Zionism from its beginnings, and a number of rabbis of that period gave wholehearted religious support for modern Zionism.[23] More importantly, religious Zionism has been a Jewish aspiration for thousands of years. For fifteen hundred years Jews have prayed the Amidah in the morning, afternoon and night, ending with these words: "May it be your will, Lord our God and God of our fathers, that the *beit Hamikdash* [holy temple] be speedily rebuilt in our days, and grant us our portion in Your Torah." The siddur, the Jewish prayer book, is full of references like this, creating a yearning for Zion in Jewish hearts for the last fifteen centuries.

While there were warnings in the Talmud against presumptuous attempts to rebuild Zion without divine openings, there were other parts of the Babylonian Talmud that instructed Jews to live in the land:

> You shall inherit the land and settle in it (Deuteronomy 11:31). A story of R. Judah b. Bathyra and R. Matthia b. Harash and R. Hanania the nephew of R. Joshua and R. Jonathan who were leaving the country and arrived at Ptolemais and remembered the land of Israel. They looked up and cried and they rent their clothes, and read this verse: "And you shall inherit [the land] and dwell in it, and you shall keep and observe all these laws" ([Deut] 11:31-32). They said: the dwelling in the land of Israel is equal to all commandments in the Torah.[24]

Another talmudic passage values living in the land of Israel so highly that it proclaims that it is better to live in the land of Israel with idolaters than to live with Jews outside the land and that one who lives in the land of Israel worships God, while someone who lives outside the land is similar to one who has no God.[25] Moreover, Jewish law prohibited a Jew from leaving the land of Israel, except to save one's life or when one cannot find means of support in Israel.[26]

---

[22]Quoted in ibid., 4.
[23]See Goldman, *Zeal for Zion*, 274-77, 297; and Ravitsky, *Messianism, Zionism, and Jewish Religious Radicalism*, 5, 79-144.
[24]Midrash Sifre, Re'eh 80, cited in R. Shai Held, "Living in the Land of Israel: Obligation, Option, or Sin?," 1, 4, http://mechonhadar.s3.amazonaws.com/mh_torah_source_sheets/Shai%20Held.pdf. Thanks to the Talmud scholar Carl Kinbar for pointing me to the Held essay.
[25]Babyonian Talmud Ketubbot 110b.
[26]Maimonides, *Mishneh Torah*, Laws of Kings 5:9.

Over the past millennium a rabbinic consensus has formed around the conviction that living in the land is one of the 613 commandments of the Torah that Jews should obey unless prevented by danger or lack of means. The consensus is based on, among other things, Numbers 33:53: "You shall take possession of the land and settle in it, for I have given you the land to possess."

There have been exceptions to this consensus. Maimonides (ca. 1135–1204) and some Hasidic sects have insisted that the Messiah must return first and bring all Jews back from exile. But Nahmanides (1194–1270), one of Judaism's most revered scholars, disagreed: "It is a positive [Torah] commandment applying to every generation, binding on each one of us, even during the period of exile, as is clear from many passages in the Talmud." Rabbi Israel of Shklov added, "The plain sense inclines toward the [idea], that the mitzvah [commandment] to live in the Land of Israel is a mitzvah like all the positive precepts in the Torah."[27]

In the early twentieth century Rabbi Abraham Isaac Kook (1865–1935), the legendary Torah scholar and chief rabbi during the British Mandate, believed that this Nahmanidean law applied to all generations.[28] Perhaps the most important rabbi of the twentieth century, Rabbi Moshe Feinstein (1895–1986), agreed: "There is no obligation to actively move [to the land]; but living there is a *mitzvah*."[29]

It is not accurate to say, then, that Zionism is a recent invention. Nor can anyone rightly say that Jews have never held a religious conviction about it. There have indeed been religiously Jewish opponents of Zionism, but they have never been the only religious Jewish voices on the question of going to the land. For a thousand years most rabbinic opinion has held that Jews have a religious obligation to live in the land of Israel.

Not Land Theft

If Jews are obligated to support the Jewish people in the land, and perhaps even to live there, did they make a mockery of that religious obligation by taking the

---

[27] Nahmanides, "Criticisms of the Rambam's Sefer HaMitzvot, Positive Commandment #4," cited in R. Shai Held, "Living in the Land of Israel," 4; Rabbi Israel of Shklov (1770–1839), Pe'at Hashulkhan, Beit Yisrael l:14, cited in Held, "Living in the Land of Israel," 5.

[28] R. Zvi Yehudah Kook (1891–1982), *Sichot HaRav Zvi Yehudah*, Eretz Yisrael, 62-63, cited in Held, "Living in the Land of Israel," 6-7, 9.

[29] Rabbi Moshe Feinstein, *Responsa Iggerot Moshe*, Even HaEzer, I, cited in Held, "Living in the Land of Israel," 10.

Introduction 21

land in the wrong way? In other words, did they steal the land from Arabs? This has been a common allegation by Arabs in the last few decades.[30]

Many critics think the creation of the state of Israel in 1948 was a kind of theft because there was no attempt to create two states at that point. Instead, Israel wound up with territory that had been owned by Arabs. So we need to start with 1948. Was there no attempt to create two states then?

There was. The United Nations partitioned Palestine in 1947, offering part to Jews and part to Arabs, with the intention that each part would become either a state or part of a state. The Arab state of Jordan already existed. Already home to many Palestinians, it was in position to annex the West Bank portion of the land partitioned for Arabs.

Critics allege that the United Nations partition was unfair to Arabs because non-Jews made up 93 percent of the population of Palestine and 78 percent of the land was left in Jewish hands. But here is what is commonly forgotten: the part of Palestine allotted to Jews was home to a substantial Jewish majority—538,000 Jews to 397,000 Arabs, according to official United Nations estimates. Besides, the "Jewish national home," mandated by the League of Nations in 1920, originally included what is now the state of Jordan. Eighty percent of this was given to Arabs in what was then called Transjordan. The remaining 20 percent was divided in the 1947 partition, which means Jews received only 17.5 percent of what was originally designated to be theirs.[31]

Jews were unhappy because the land they were given did not include Jerusalem, where Jews composed the largest religious population since the middle of the nineteenth century and constituted an absolute majority in the city from the end of the nineteenth century. Moreover, 60 percent of the Jewish state was the Negev, an arid desert then thought to be useless.[32] Yet the Jews accepted the United Nations Partition Plan. The Arabs did not.

Although they were unhappy with the partition, Jews did not rob land from poor Arab peasants, as many of today's critics suggest. By 1948 Britain had allocated 187,500 acres of cultivable land to Arabs and only 4,250 acres to Jews. So Jews

---

[30]For example, Mohammed Abu Laila, professor of comparative religion at Al-Azhar University in Cairo, reportedly claimed, "The Jews stole our land." Kenneth R. Timmerman, "Top Egyptian Cleric Justifies terrorism," *Insight on the News*, November 26, 2002. http://archive.frontpagemag.com/readArticle.aspx?ARTID=21111.

[31]Historic Palestine comprised what is today's Jordan (approximately 35,640 square miles), Israel (8,019 square miles), Gaza (139 square miles) and the West Bank (2,263 square miles).

[32]Aharon Cohen, *Israel and the Arab World* (Boston: Beacon Press, 1976), 238.

were forced to pay exorbitant prices for arid land to wealthy, often absentee landlords—$1,000 per acre, when rich black soil in Iowa was selling for $110 per acre.[33]

By 1947, 73 percent of land purchased by Jews came from large landowners, including Arab mayors of Gaza, Jerusalem and Jaffa and leaders of the Arab nationalist movement.[34] In his memoir, King Abdullah of Jordan said the story of Jewish displacement of Arabs from their land was a fiction: "Arabs are as prodigal in selling their land as they are in . . . weeping [about it]."[35]

It is true that hundreds of thousands of Arabs felt compelled to abandon their homes during the 1948 Arab-Israeli War. They fled the violence of war, which was begun by the Arab nations, not Israel. The majority simply wanted to get out of the line of fire. The Syrian prime minister, Haled al Azm, wrote in his memoirs, "Since 1948 we have been demanding the return of the refugees to their homes. But we ourselves are the ones who encouraged them to leave."[36] The *Economist*, a frequent critic of Zionists, reported in the October 2, 1948, issue that "the Higher Arab Executive . . . clearly intimated that those Arabs who remained in Haifa and accepted Jewish protection would be regarded as renegades."

Is It Racism?

Another charge by critics of Israel is that the modern state of Israel is organized on racist principles. This charge was broadcast around the world in 1975 when the United Nations General Assembly adopted a resolution equating Zionism with racism. Viewed charitably, the resolution assumed that Judaism is a *race* of people and that the Jewish state was therefore equivalent to the apartheid regime of South Africa before 1994.

The problem is that none of this is true. Israel has always been a people defined by religion, even for those who don't believe. The religious identity of Israel—not their race—defines the people, even those who say they don't believe in the God of Israel but identify with the people who do. We need to be reminded that there are Chinese Jews, African Jews, European Jews and even Arab Jews.

---

[33]Benny Morris, *Righteous Victims* (New York: Vintage, 2001), 111; and Abraham Granott, *The Land System in Palestine: History and Structure* (London: Eyre & Spottiswoode, 1952), 278.

[34]Hillel Cohen, *Army of Shadows: Palestinian Collaboration with Zionism, 1917–1948* (Oakland: University of California Press, 2009), 205-6, 214-22, 224-29.

[35]King Abdullah of Jordan, *My Memoirs Completed*, trans. Harold W. Glidden (London: Longman, 1978), 88-89.

[36]Haled al Azm, *The Memoirs of Haled al Azm* (Beirut, 1973), 1:386-87.

Furthermore, Israel has always accepted people of different religions who join themselves to Israel and are willing to do what that requires—religious or otherwise. In biblical times Rahab and her family and Ruth were Gentiles who were attracted to the God of Israel and assimilated. Many of David's men were foreigners from today's Lebanon, Syria, Jordan and Turkey who fought as soldiers and leaders in his army. Some became his trusted advisers (2 Sam 23:8-39; 1 Chron 11:10-47). Many probably became assimilated to Israel.

The best way to disabuse oneself of this myth of racism is to go to Israel today and see the thousands of handsome young Ethiopian men and women serving in the IDF (Israel Defense Forces). One will also notice the racial differences between white Ashkenazi Jews of European descent and the darker-complexioned Sephardic Jews from North Africa. There are complaints of racism toward Ethiopian Jews in Israel, but there are also open discussions in the Israeli media and government about how to put an end to racist attitudes. We Americans should remember our own history and continuing problems with race and be loathe to point the finger.

Importantly, as a democracy Israel has almost two million Muslim and Christian Arabs, Druze, Baháʼís, Circassians and other ethnic groups as citizens with full rights. Despite all this, some speak of "Israeli apartheid." This accusation is not only inaccurate and inflammatory but egregiously unfair. South African apartheid was based on race. "Blacks" and "coloureds" could not vote and had no representation in the South African parliament. But Israeli citizens of all races—Arabs and Jews alike—can vote, can be represented in the Knesset and have recourse to the courts.

Apartheid was also a legal system that restricted participation to a minority that had control over a majority. In Israel, the majority give equal legal rights and protection to Arab citizens, who make up 20 percent of the population of Israel. Irshad Manji, a Muslim author, has written:

> At only 20% of the population, would Arabs even be eligible for election if they squirmed under the thumb of apartheid? Would an apartheid state extend voting rights to women and the poor in local elections, which Israel did for the first time in the history of Palestinian Arabs?[37]

---

[37] Irshad Manji, *The Trouble with Islam Today: A Muslim's Call for Reform in Her Faith* (New York: St. Martin's Griffin, 2003), 108.

Of course, what is given by legal right is not always given in actual practice. Israeli newspapers debate whether Arabs get a fair shake, and many Israelis concede that racism is a problem. But the emotionally charged comparison of Israel to South Africa under apartheid is false.

Not Theocracy

But if Israel is organized on the basis of religion rather than race, does this make Israel a theocracy? This question took on new currency in 2015 when the Knesset (parliament) considered a bill that would define the state of Israel's identity as "the nation-state of the Jewish people." That would mean not only that the country's national holidays would be Jewish religious holidays and that the flag would be the Magen David; it would also mean that Jewish law would be the inspiration for Israel's legal system and that it would enshrine the automatic citizenship granted by the law of return.

The bill did not pass in 2015 and at the time of writing was no longer being debated. But we must clear up one thing about the charge of theocracy: a theocracy is by definition a polity run by clerics and religious law, and restricted in participation to one religion. This has never been the policy of the Jewish state, and it would contradict Israel's declaration of independence.[38] Israel has always been understood by the majority of its people as a homeland for the Jewish people—a broad civilization consisting of diverse ethnicities, cultural expression in all its forms, religion, history, philosophy, ethics and law—with participation open to a vast array and large number of non-Jews (as well as nonbelieving Jews).

Part of the difficulty in Christians understanding this is that most Protestants assume that because being Protestant is an exclusively religious category and because Protestant states in previous centuries restricted participation to Protestants, that must be the way a Jewish state would operate. They think a Jewish state must be a state run by the Jewish religion.

But this is not what Israeli (other than some ultra-Orthodox) Jews mean when they talk about a Jewish state. They mean a state that is a haven for the

---

[38]"THE STATE OF ISRAEL will be open for Jewish immigration and for the Ingathering of the Exiles; it will foster the development of the country for the benefit of all its inhabitants; it will be based on freedom, justice and peace as envisaged by the prophets of Israel; it will ensure complete equality of social and political rights to all its inhabitants irrespective of religion, race or sex; it will guarantee freedom of religion, conscience, language, education and culture; it will safeguard the Holy Places of all religions; and it will be faithful to the principles of the Charter of the United Nations." For the complete declaration, see www.mfa.gov.il/mfa/foreignpolicy/peace/guide/pages/declaration%20of%20establishment%20of%20state%20of%20israel.aspx.

Jewish people and institutionally fosters their Jewishness, but also a state that protects the religious and civil rights of its minorities. Often Zionism's modern founder Theodor Herzl is said to have been a secularist who wanted Israel to be a secular state. But in fact he envisioned a government that would be "Jewish in character" and would set up "laws and regulations adopted for the well-being of the Jewish people," while protecting the well-being of non-Jewish neighbors. He supported the revival of the Hebrew language, Jewish art, Jewish literature and a Jewish academy. He even hoped to write a biblical drama, to be titled *Moses*. David Ben-Gurion, the first prime minister, repeatedly referred to Zionism as a messianic movement. But neither Herzl nor Ben-Gurion wanted a theocracy *ruled* by religious leaders or a state without Gentiles or Gentiles lacking political and religious freedoms.[39]

This is still true today. When the prime minister of Israel speaks of the need to recognize Israel as a Jewish state, he has in mind a democracy, not a theocracy, in which the majority (but not all) of its citizens are Jewish and feel that Israel is their political and cultural home.

Is it wrong for Israel to have a law of return that grants automatic citizenship to Jews? Other countries such as Germany, Greece, Ireland and Finland also designate special categories of people who are entitled to citizenship. For example, Greece grants citizenship to broad categories of people of ethnic Greek ancestry who are members of the Greek diaspora, including individuals and families whose ancestors have been resident in diaspora communities outside the modern state of Greece for centuries or millennia.

In Israel, non-Jews are eligible to become citizens under naturalization procedures similar to those in other countries outside the Middle East. But the Arab states define citizenship by native parentage. It is almost impossible to become a naturalized citizen in many Arab states, especially Algeria, Saudi Arabia and Kuwait. Several Arab states have laws that allow for the naturalization of other Arabs, but with the exception of Palestinians. Jordan, on the other hand, instituted its own law of return in 1954 for all former residents of Palestine—*except Jews*.

So Israel, like other states outside the Middle East, is populated by a majority from one community but, like other democracies, protects the rights of minorities. Sweden is a good example of this kind of state. A majority of its citizens

---

[39] Yoram Hazony, "Did Herzl Want a 'Jewish' State?," *Azure* 9 (Spring 2000): 37-73; quotes from 59, 63.

have a similar cultural background, but the state protects the rights of those from other cultures. India and Pakistan, on the other hand, are also democracies reflecting the cultures of the majority, but their record on enforcing laws to protect minorities is weaker.

In the Middle East, however, Israel is unique. No other state protects the religious and political freedoms of minorities as does the Jewish state of Israel. Its democracy is open to citizenship to non-Jews, and it enforces religious and political freedoms for non-Jewish minorities. These practices prove that it is not a theocracy.

A Look Ahead

Where does this book go from here? It moves in what we think is a rhetorically logical order.

The purpose of this introduction has been to clear away underbrush so that we can look at the real olive tree, so to speak. I use that image purposely because it is the one Paul uses in Romans 11 to describe the relation of Gentile believers in Jesus to Israel.

The underbrush consists of a paradigm and objections. This introduction examined the most common objections to Christian Zionism. The first was that Christian Zionism is always dispensationalist and fundamentalist. This is why we have distinguished the New Christian Zionism from older, dispensationalist Zionisms.

Then there are the modern myths. I examined the claim that Zionism is simply another one of the many nationalisms that arose in the nineteenth century. Then I looked at the charge that Zionism is more Christian than Jewish—that for Jews it is a new cause and promoted more by Christians than Jews. Next I investigated the recurring indictment that Zionism is simply theft, having stolen land from Arabs before and after 1948. Finally, I responded to accusations that Zionism is racist and that Israel is a theocracy.

I imagine I have not convinced all my readers of our position on all these questions, but I hope you can see that there are plausible objections to all these claims, which means the claims might be more mythical than actual. If you get that far, you might then consider the principal argument of this book, which is theological.

The first two chapters (part one) make historical arguments. Chapter one depicts briefly the dominant paradigm that our new model seeks to displace—

Introduction

supersessionism. This is the view that the Christian church has superseded or replaced Israel as the locus of the covenant that God has made with his people. While *supersede* means to "replace what is old and no longer useful," *fulfill* means to "succeed in doing something or make something true and real."[40] Jesus said he did not come to "abolish" the Torah or the prophets but to "fulfill" them (Mt 5:17). The Greek word (*plērōsai*) that Matthew uses means to confirm or implement, or "make actual what was previously spoken" or "authoritatively interpret."[41] Jesus' words suggest epochal change from one form of the covenant to another but without denying or denigrating God's covenant with Israel. Jesus fulfilled the Tanak (the Hebrew acronym for what Christians call the Old Testament) in the English sense of the word by making the promise of the Messiah true and real, and gave form to the kingdom of God in a provisional and proleptic (anticipating the future) way by confirming and implementing the Torah and the kingdom and by prophesying their final earthly embodiment in a new world to come. The New Christian Zionism asserts that the people and land of Israel represent a provisional and proleptic fulfillment of the promises of that new world to come. So Jesus brought a new era to the history of Israel but without abolishing what came before, and he predicted that his people and land would be central to that new world.[42] This is why the New Christian Zionism speaks of fulfillment and not supersessionism.

Chapter two starts by showing how recent scholars have tagged Christian Zionism with the dispensationalist label, suggesting that Christian Zionism is a recent invention. In that chapter I try to show (1) that the history of Christian Zionism is long, going back two thousand years, and (2) that for all those centuries before the nineteenth it had nothing to do with dispensationalism. Furthermore, I try to show that in the last two centuries there have been important Christian Zionists whose arguments did not hang on a dispensationalist framework.

The next four chapters (part 2) are the heart of the book. Because all good theology is reflection on the biblical witness, we tangle in these chapters with the meaning of Scripture. The first problem that arises whenever Christianity and Israel are discussed is the relation of the Hebrew Bible to the New Testament. They are both canonical for Christians, and in some sense the latter fulfills the

---

[40]Both definitions are from Merriam-Webster.
[41]Noel Rabinowitz, "Yes, the Torah Is Fulfilled, But What Does This Mean?," *Kesher: A Journal of Messianic Judaism* 11 (Summer 2000): 19-44.
[42]See chaps. 3 and 4 for arguments to this effect.

first. But how? And what does that mean for the church's understanding of Israel? Craig Blaising engages these questions in chapter three.

The next three chapters are devoted to three of the principal authors of the New Testament. Joel Willitts shows (chap. 4) that the restoration of Eretz Israel (the land of Israel) is a fundamental presumption of Matthew's story of Jesus. Willitts insists that the first Gospel has "an abiding land consciousness" in line with the traditional Jewish territorial hope.

Mark Kinzer argues (chap. 5), against Gary Burge (perhaps the leading evangelical anti-Zionist), that Luke–Acts views the Holy Land as a locus of divine activity, promotes the Holy Land as a vital aspect of faith, possesses what could be called a territorial theology, is intensely concerned about a Jewish eschatology devoted to the restoration of the land, and is tethered to a material realization of the kingdom in the Holy Land.

David Rudolph (chap. 6) shows that Paul, who has most often been thought to have devalued Israel, in fact did the opposite. Paul kept both the people and the land of Israel at the center of his soteriology and eschatology. He taught that Jesus brings salvation to all the world, but only by keeping Israel at the center of that world. Gentiles will be saved, for Paul, only by being attached to Israel. They are to look forward to a renewed earth that is centered in Israel.

Part three deals not with the underbrush but with the other trees clogging the growth of the olive tree. They keep many from seeing the olive tree and stunt the growth of the tree by soaking up rainwater and stealing sunshine. They are the necessary implications of Christian Zionism, which when left unaddressed prevent proper understanding and encourage misdirected attacks.

The first is the recent history of attacks on Israel from mainline Protestant churches. Mark Tooley (chap. 7) rehearses their arguments, supersessionist and pragmatic, against Israel in the last forty-five years. He explains that it was only after 1970 that the Protestant mainline started to make arguments and proposals that would undermine support for the people and state of Israel. Along the way Tooley points to flaws in the reasoning of these new approaches.

Perhaps the most potent case against Christian Zionism on the world stage today is political. Opposition to Israel in recent decades has focused on the supposed injustice of a political state that is run by Jews in an Arab neighborhood. This of course includes the question of political justice for Palestinians. In chapter eight Robert Benne takes up eerily similar arguments and counterarguments in Reinhold Niebuhr's era and suggests that Niebuhr's approach is helpful for political questions today. Benne then adds his own take on Niebuhr's Christian Zionism.

The legal questions about Israel fall not too far behind the political ones. Is Israel violating international law by its control of the West Bank? Is it occupation? Is it illegal? If it is, does that not call into question the claim of Zionists that Israel is somehow connected to the biblical covenant that calls for justice? Robert Nicholson takes up these questions in chapter nine, arguing that international law is notoriously unclear but that, where it is clear, Israel is not in violation. In fact, Israel holds itself, albeit imperfectly, to legal standards that are higher than those of all its neighbors and indeed higher than in leading countries of the West.

In chapter ten Shadi Khalloul gives testimony from within the land of Israel that Israel, with all of its imperfections, nevertheless exemplifies some of the best that one could expect of morality from a modern state in this messy world. Khalloul is a leader of the Aramean community in Israel and what the outside world would call a Palestinian (though strictly speaking he is not, for Palestinians are typically Arabs, and his community predated the Arab invasions of the seventh century AD). He argues that while the state of Israel is far from perfect, it is not fundamentally unjust in the ways that it treats its minorities. From its founding nearly seventy years ago, Israel has been committed, legally and in other ways, to just treatment of its minorities.

In chapter eleven Darrell Bock plots a way forward for Christian Zionism. He says the New Christian Zionism must distinguish between individual Jews and corporate Israel and must never give carte blanche to Israel's conduct. Instead, future academic work by those who support this New Christian Zionism must stress five themes.

Finally, in chapter twelve I discuss how this new Christian Zionism will bring changes to biblical hermeneutics and exegesis, historical theology, systematic theology, political theology and Jewish-Christian dialogue.

In short, the New Christian Zionism hopes to alert scholars and other Christians to beware of the geographical-docetic temptation that anti-Zionism proffers. Supersessionist anti-Zionism proposes theology divorced from embodiment and physicality—a people without a land, a Jesus without his people and land and tradition, and the early church living, as it were, suspended in air above the Palestinian ground. It suggests that land, earth and territory do not matter to embodied human existence. It would not be stretching too much to say that it is ecclesiology and eschatology without incarnation.

- PART ONE -

THEOLOGY

AND

HISTORY

1

A HISTORY OF SUPERSESSIONISM

Getting the Big Story Wrong

Gerald R. McDermott

◆

The Bible is extraordinarily complex. While the sixteenth-century Protestant Reformers rightly insisted that its basic message of salvation could be understood by the simplest of sinners, they also believed that its preachers needed extensive training to be able to understand its many subtleties and profundities. They also knew that it is impossible to interpret the Bible rightly without having the right framework or lens through which to read it. The little stories could not be understood without knowing the Big Story into which they fit. Using the wrong Big Story would cause Christians to misinterpret the hundreds of little stories in the Bible, not to mention the meaning of the myriads of details from ancient cultures in ancient times.

For this reason it is essential that we get the big picture right. As I mentioned at the beginning of the introduction, the New Christian Zionism insists that the story of Israel is central to the story of salvation. The latter is fundamentally misunderstood and distorted when it omits Israel and her story with God. The sheer size of the Hebrew Scriptures, which dwarf the New Testament, should have signaled this to the historic church. But so does the gospel story in the New Testament, which portrays Israel at the center.

The very first Gospel—Matthew—opens with a genealogy that proves that Jesus is descended from Abraham, the first Jew, through forty-two generations of Jews. Luke's Gospel also contains a genealogy (Lk 3:23-38) that proves Jesus came from a long line of Jews going back to Abraham, and then all the way back to Adam. Apparently both Matthew and Luke believed it important to show that Jesus was connected to the history of Israel.

In her Magnificat, Mary suggests that the birth of the Messiah will be significant not only for all future "generations" but particularly for the history of Israel: this will show that God

> has helped his servant Israel,
>   in remembrance of his mercy,
> according to the *promise* he made to our ancestors,
>   to Abraham and to his descendants forever. (Lk 1:54-55, emphasis added)

If the incarnation was supposed to turn the focus away from Israel, as the supersessionist story has suggested, Mary did not get the text message. Her son would fulfill God's promise—which was made not to the whole human race but to the first Jew and all his Jewish descendants. Of course we know that this fulfillment brought the promise of salvation to the *world*, but Mary here mentioned only the promise to the Jews.

Paul, long cast as the apostle to the Gentiles, supposedly took the focus off Judaism and showed that the gospel was really a universal message for all. It has often been claimed that Paul believed the days of Jewish particularity were over and the days of non-Jewish universalism had begun. God's covenant with the Jews was done; he had transferred that covenant to the church. No longer would God be concerned with the Jews. They had forfeited their covenant because they had rejected the Messiah, Jesus.

This is what Christian theologian Kendall Soulen has termed the "punitive" version of supersessionism, the idea that God made a new covenant with the church that supersedes his old covenant with Israel because God was punishing Israel for not accepting her Messiah. Soulen's two other kinds of supersessionism are "economic" (in God's economy or administration of the history of salvation, Israel's purpose was to prepare for the Messiah, so once he came, Israel had no more purpose) and "structural" (the history of salvation is structured so as not to need Israel in any integral way, except to serve as a negative example).[1]

Although Paul has been been read this way for centuries, his letters tell a different story. In Romans 9 and 11 he laments his fellow Jews who have not accepted Jesus as Messiah. He says that they cause him "great sorrow and unceasing anguish" (Rom 9:2). Yet he says "the covenants" still "belong" to them

---

[1] R. Kendall Soulen, *The God of Israel and Christian Theology* (Minneapolis: Fortress, 1996), 29-32.

(Rom 9:4), and even though, "as regards the gospel," they have become "enemies of God," they still "*are* beloved" because of their "election," which is "irrevocable" (Rom 11:28-29, my emphasis).

Galatians is the letter that is most often used to prove that Paul has dispensed with Jewish law in favor of a church that has left Israel behind. Yet even here he says the gospel is all about "the blessing of Abraham . . . com[ing] to the Gentiles" (Gal 3:14) because "the promises [of blessing] were made to Abraham and to his offspring" (Gal 3:16) so that getting saved means being in Abraham's family: "If you belong to Christ, then you are Abraham's offspring, heirs according to the promise" (Gal 3:29).[2] In other words, the gospel means getting connected to Israel's history, not getting away from it. In contrast, supersessionism—the idea that the church has superseded Israel because God's covenant with Israel has been transferred to others—suggests that Israel has been left behind. Galatians says otherwise.

As chapters two through five will show, the New Testament develops what we have just seen in the genealogies and the Magnificat and Galatians—the intimate connection between Israel and the gospel. This is the constellation of connections that shows that Israel is essential not only to eschatology (the message of the old Christian Zionism) but to soteriology (in the New Christian Zionism). Israel is critical not only to the future (the old Christian Zionism) but also to our past and present (the New Christian Zionism). Not only to *where* Christians will be (the old Christian Zionism) but to what they *are* (the New Christian Zionism).

This constellation of connections is vivid in the New Testament, especially in its last book, Revelation. In that book, usually dated near the end of the first century, the new earth is centered in Jerusalem, whose twelve gates are inscribed with the names of the twelve tribes of Israel (Rev 21:12). So we can be confident that this Zionist vision, which the middle chapters of this book will show to have been prevalent in the New Testament, continued through at least the end of the first century.

In the mid-second century, when the synagogue was still very attractive to many Jesus-believing Jews and Gentiles, some of the former were tempted to

---

[2]In Romans 15:8-9 (emphasis added), Paul expands the promise to Abraham to mean more generally the promises to the patriarchs: "For I tell you that Christ *has become* [perfect passive] a servant of the circumcised on behalf of the truth of God in order that he might confirm the promises given to the patriarchs, and in order that the Gentiles might glorify God for his mercy." "Promises to the patriarchs" probably refers to the oaths God made to Abraham (Gen 22), Isaac (Gen 26) and Jacob (Gen 28). These are an increase in numbers, possession of the land, and being a source of blessing to the nations. The verb Paul uses (*gegenēsthai*) suggests that he thought that (a) Christ continued to be a servant of Israel and (b) the promise of the land was still to be upheld.

jettison their new devotion to Jesus, and some of the latter were drawn to nonmessianic Judaism. Early church leaders responded by stressing the superiority of Jesus' law to the Mosaic law. Their apologetic against the synagogue was so successful that their new version of salvation history—which declared that God had transferred the covenant from Israel to the church—became dominant.

Scholars as diverse as the Christian theologian Soulen and the Jewish historian/theologian Daniel Boyarin have agreed that second-century apologist Justin Martyr (100–ca. 165) played a key role in this transition of thinking among Jesus followers.[3] They also agree that Justin was not the only early Christian thinker who proposed supersessionism,[4] that the reasons for this transition were many and complex[5] and that this comparison of Jewish law versus Christian law was only one of many factors involved. But most historians agree that Justin's version of the biblical story caught on, and it was he who first applied to the church the term "true Israel."[6] The real story of salvation for Justin

---

[3] See Daniel Boyarin, *Border Lines: The Partition of Judaeo-Christianity* (Philadelphia: University of Pennsylvania Press, 200); and Soulen, *God of Israel and Christian Theology*, chap. 2.

[4] The Epistle of Barnabas (dated between 70 and 131) goes to great lengths to explain that all the ceremonial laws of the Torah were given as figures of the Christian dispensation and asserts that while the Jews possessed the covenant at one time, "their sins disqualified them for the possession of it" (Barn. 14). *Early Christian Writings*, trans. Maxwell Staniforth, ed. Andrew Louth (New York: Penguin, 1987), 176.

[5] The churches started to fill with Gentiles who did not understand that the quarrels between the apostles and "the Jews" was an in-house debate, so that criticism of "the Jews" in the Gospels referred usually not to all Jews but to the Jewish leaders in Jerusalem. According to some scholars, the churches in the second century and later were angered by the *Birkat ha-Minim* (lit., "blessing on the heretics"), which they took to be Jewish curses directed against Jesus followers and other "heretics," originating probably at the end of the first century. Nonmessianic Jews were angry that Jewish Christians abandoned the fight against Rome for the besieged city of Jerusalem in 68 and fled to Pella, and then refused to identify with the Jewish side during the Roman occupation in the Bar Kokhba revolt in 135. Furthermore, between 117 and 138 there was nonmessianic Jewish persecution of Jesus followers, encouraged by Hadrian's accession in 117 and his lenient policy toward Jews—which encouraged Jesus followers to return to the nonmessianic synagogues. Then after Rome brutally suppressed the Bar Kokhba revolt and Jews were driven out of Jerusalem, Gentile Christians had less contact with Judaism, which hardened the lines of supersessionism. Oskar Skarsaune believes that a good part of the mutual hostility came from "missionary competition" because both messianic and nonmessianic Jews were seeking Gentile converts. See Marcel Simon, *Verus Israel: A Study of the Relations Between Christians and Jews in the Roman Empire AD 135–425* (London: Littman Library, 1996); Oskar Skarsaune, *In the Shadow of the Temple: Jewish Influences on Early Christianity* (Downers Grove, IL: IVP Academic, 2002), 197-201, 260-61; and Gedaliah Alon, *The Jews in Their Land in the Talmudic Age* (Cambridge: Harvard University Press, 1996), 305-7. Boyarin argues that the second- and third-century debates between Jesus followers and their Jewish opponents were more about defining their own orthodoxies and heresies than anything else; Boyarin, *Border Lines*.

[6] *Dialogue with Trypho* 11.5; Peter Richardson, *Israel in the Apostolic Church* (Cambridge: Cambridge University Press, 1969), 1. My rendition of the *Dialogue* and Justin's *Second Apology* are

was the story of the Logos or eternal Word, which spoke to Jews in one way but in other ways to other cultures, especially the Greeks. Just as the Jews had their prophets, so too did the Greeks, Plato and Socrates among their foremost. Justin thought that Socrates had as much of the Logos as Moses. In fact, Christ "was and is the Logos who is in every man" and inspires whatever truth we find in the world (Justin, *2 Apol.* 10). The Old Testament was important not because it was the revelation of the true God but because it predicted the true Logos. The law given at Horeb was already "old" and belonged to Jews alone; the new one from Christ has made the old one cease, and now the new one belongs to "all men absolutely." God's relationship to Israel therefore was physical and temporary, but his new relationship to the church was spiritual and permanent. As Oskar Skarsaune observes, Justin fell prey to exactly what Paul warned against: "Do not boast over the branches" (Rom 11:18).[7]

Irenaeus (ca. 145–202) is another early father of the church who helped make supersessionism the dominant model for later centuries. He is famous for having contributed the church's first theology of history. Writing against Gnostics, who regarded matter as the creation of an evil god, he explained how the true God created matter and in fact took human matter onto himself in order to restore the broken image of his human creatures.

Irenaeus's grand metaphor was God as pedagogue. He gave the Mosaic law to the "headstrong" Jews because they needed it for their spiritual education; it was not for all times and all places. Their prescriptions were "temporal," "carnal" and "earthly," calling their users to another law that is "eternal," "spiritual" and "heavenly." Many precepts were included in the old law because of the Jews' "hardness of heart."[8]

After the Jewish law, the incarnation was the next stage in God's pedagogy of the human race. God used it to bring us into his very being, by what Irenaeus called "recapitulation." By this he meant that God started over again on the creation. Because Adam's sin significantly marred the divine image in humanity and prevented the Father from being able to bring human beings into

---

based on *The Writings of Justin Martyr and Athenagoras*, ed. Marcus Dods (Edinburgh: T&T Clark, 1879).

[7]Justin Martyr, *Second Apology* 10, 13: *Dialogue with Trypho* 24.1, 33.1, 43.1; Skarsaune, *In the Shadow of the Temple*, 263.

[8]Irenaeus, *Against Heresies*, in Philip Schaff, *Apostolic Fathers with Justin Martyr and Irenaeus*, vol. 1 of *The Ante-Nicene Fathers*, ed. Alexander Roberts and James Donaldson (Grand Rapids: Eerdmans; Edinburgh: T&T Clark, 1993), 4.14.3, 4.15.1-2.

communion with himself, he created the perfect man in Jesus—the man Adam was intended to be. Because Jesus was perfect, without sin, the Father could have communion with him. And because Jesus' human nature was *human*, like ours, *we* could have communion with God—because Jesus' human nature was the go-between that now linked us with God.

This was all very elegant. But it made the history of Israel, which made up most of the Bible, functionally and theologically unnecessary. It suggested that the story of Israel was simply educational, teaching the Gentiles how *not* to proceed, thus preparing the rest of us for the Second Adam. Hence it was economic supersessionism. Because it made Israel unnecessary, skipping from the first Adam directly to the Second, it was also structural supersessionism. Irenaeus also made use of punitive supersessionism by arguing that because the Jews repudiated their Messiah, they were "disinherited from the grace of God."[9]

Later church fathers perpetuated this pattern. As we will see in the next chapter, Origen reasoned that if the Messiah with his covenant had come, then the covenant with the Jews had ended—or true Israel is the spiritual band that follows Jesus as Messiah.[10] The fourth century and later brought new ill feeling into what had been, at least for Justin and Irenaeus, more of a reasoned debate.[11] Chrysostom (ca. 349–407), for example, preached that he thought Jews murdered their own children to offer as sacrifices to the devil, and exclaimed, "I hate the Jews."[12] Augustine was far milder, acknowledging that strictly speaking the church is the new Israel, but that for clarity's sake it was best to leave the name Israel to Jews.[13]

---

[9]Ibid., 4.21.3, 3.21.1.

[10]See Origen, *On First Principles*, trans. G. W. Butterworth (Gloucester, MA: Peter Smith, 1973), bk. 4. Origen attributes only typological meaning to the Jewish story, which he believed offered significance only by pointing to Christ and to his church. In his commentary on John's Gospel, Origen wrote that "the Jews . . . are images of those who approve sound doctrines. . . . The whole people of Christ, entitled Jewish in secret (see Rom. 2:29) and circumcised in secret, has . . . the properties of the tribes." For Origen, the Jewish Passover is not Christ's Passion but our passage into a transformed life in Christ. "Commentary on John," 13.81, 1.1, in Joseph W. Trigg, *Origen* (New York: Routledge, 1998), 161, 104, 40.

[11]Justin, for example, has Trypho the Jew say that in the dialogue "we have found more than we expected" and bids Justin "to think of us as your friends." *Dialogue with Trypho* in Dods, *Writings of Justin Martyr and Athenagoras*, 277.

[12]John Chrysostom, Homily 6, "Against the Jews," 6.11, accessed January 4, 2016, www.today-scatholicworld.com/homily-vi.htm.

[13]Paula Fredriksen, "*Secundem Carnem*: History and Israel in the Theology of St. Augustine," in *Augustine and World Religions*, ed. Brian Brown, John A. Doody and Kim Paffenroth (Lanham, MD: Lexington Books, 2008), 29-30.

A History of Supersessionism 39

Much later, Martin Luther (1483–1546) in his last years was as vitriolic as Chrysostom. Earlier he had shown deep appreciation for the Jewish tradition and wrote a number of philosemitic essays, including "That Jesus Christ Was Born a Jew" (1523). But toward the end of his life he snapped when considering Jewish refusal to accept Jesus as Messiah. In an effort to "save some from the flames and embers . . . their synagogues should be set on fire. . . . [Jewish homes should] be broken down or destroyed . . . [and Jews themselves should be] put under one roof, or in a stable, like Gypsies, in order that they may realize that they are not masters in our land."[14] Luther seems to have agreed with his predecessors that God's covenant with the Jews had long since been broken. Some Luther scholars think that these frightening words were motivated by Luther's apocalypticism—his belief that the world would end in his lifetime and that all enemies of the gospel were driven by the devil. And to be fair, we should recall that Luther demonized not only the Jews but also the Turks, the peasants (who started revolts in 1524–1526) and the papacy.[15]

Calvin (1509–1564) showed less invective, but he too was a supersessionist, and a punitive supersessionist at that. In his *Institutes* he wrote that "while the Jews *seemed* to be God's people, they not only rejected the teaching of the gospel but also persecuted it." So "God denies that he is bound to [their] wicked priests by the fact that he covenanted with their father Levi to be His angel or interpreter. . . . God willingly admits this and disputes with them on the ground that he is ready to keep the covenant, but that when they do not reciprocate, they deserve to be repudiated."[16] For Calvin and so many of the Fathers before him, God put an end to his covenant with Israel because her leaders rejected Jesus.[17]

---

[14] Luther, "On the Jews and Their Lies" (1543), quoted in Dennis Bielfeldt, Mickey L. Mattox and Paul Hinlicky, *The Substance of the Faith: Luther's Doctrinal Theology for Today* (Minneapolis: Fortress, 2008), 176.

[15] For more on Luther and the Jews, see Avihu Zakai, "Reformation, History, and Eschatology in English Protestantism," *History and Theory* 26 (October 1987): 300-318; and Paul Hinlicky, *Beloved Community: Critical Dogmatics After Christendom* (Grand Rapids: Eerdmans, 2015), 416-17, 49n, 50n.

[16] John Calvin, *Institutes of the Christian Religion*, ed. John T. McNeill, trans. Ford Lewis Battles (Philadelphia: Westminster, 1960), 4.2.3 (emphasis added).

[17] As Scott Bader-Saye has pointed out, Calvin refused to say that the church replaces Israel, the new covenant superseding the old, because there is only one covenant for Calvin. Calvin even says "the promise of the covenant is to be fulfilled, not only allegorically but literally, for Abraham's physical offspring." *Institutes* 4.16.15. But he also argued that "the general election of a people is not always firm and effectual," and so resorted to individual election alone, thus missing the Jewish sense of corporate election that persists despite the disobedience of a majority.

Supersessionism took an important step forward with the deists at the end of the seventeenth and beginning of the eighteenth centuries. Deists were the first moderns to make popular what has been called "the scandal of particularity." This is the idea that a just God would never restrict his revelation to particular places and times in history because that would be unfair. This was one of many reasons that deists repudiated the idea that the Jews were the chosen people. But, as Frank E. Manuel has chronicled, there were plenty of other reasons. Deists taught that Judaism was an outlandish example of the heavy encrustation of man-made ceremonials and priestly imposture. One of the cruelest religions ever, its miracles were frauds and its prophecies superstitious. In deist hands, Jews were transformed from a nation with a special religious identity to an isolated and irrelevant remnant of barbarian tribes, who still preserved the tribes' bizarre and fanatical customs. They worshiped dead, soulless animals rather than a spiritual divinity, and their sacrificial rites were like those of East Indians, American Indians and West Africans.[18]

Thomas Chubb (1679–1747), for example, said the Jewish law was completely unrelated to the gospel and argued that the preservation of the Jews over the centuries was not miraculous; they were preserved because their leaders instructed them not to mix with the Gentiles. Their belief that they are God's chosen people is egotistical, and arbitrariness (a word always used by deists with contempt) is the Jewish principle. Anthony Collins called the Jews an "illiterate, Barbarous and Ridiculous People," whom God picked only to show his patience with the world. Thomas Morgan (d. 1743) explained that the Jewish God was a cheat and an idol, and the Jewish religion a foul source of everything in Christianity that is contrary to a pure, simple and reasonable natural religion. The deist newspaper *The Independent Whig* broadcast to its readers that Moses gave the Jews a "Law of Bondage . . . [with] statutes which were not good, and Judgments by which they could not live."[19]

According to Manuel, the deists were the leaders of the Enlightenment's radical reevaluation of Judaism. Voltaire learned from them when he was in

---

Institutes 3.21.6; 3.21.1; 3.24.15; Bader-Saye, *Church and Israel After Christendom* (Eugene, OR: Wipf & Stock, 2005), 71-72.
[18]Frank E. Manuel, *The Broken Staff: Judaism Through Christian Eyes* (Cambridge, MA: Harvard University Press, 1992), 191, 179.
[19]Chubb, *The Author's Farewell to His Readers*, in *The Posthumous Works of Mr. Thomas Chubb* (London, 1748), 2:111, 161-67, 203, 307, 314, 121; Thomas Morgan, *The Moral Philosopher*, 2nd ed. (London, 1738), 19; Thomas Gordon and John Trenchard, eds., *The Independent Whig* [*IW*], 7th ed. (London, 1736), 1:328.

A History of Supersessionism 41

London in the 1720s. He eventually became an obsessive anti-Semite, always calling them the "execrable Jews," and once wrote that a Jew is someone who should have engraved on his forehead "Fit to be hanged." His *philosophe* confreres attacked the Hebrew Bible with zeal, reasoning that if Christianity is as old as creation, there was no need for Judaism. It simply serves as an illustration of detested "priestcraft."[20] In the mid- and late-eighteenth century the Holbachians still made it a practice to adapt the deist writings of the early eighteenth century for their own anticlerical and anti-Semitic crusades.[21]

Manuel concludes that the emergence of anti-Semitism as a "scientific doctrine" at the end of the nineteenth century can be traced to these deist sources.[22] It is no wonder that we find anti-Semitism and supersessionism in the thinking of Immanuel Kant (1724–1804), perhaps the most influential philosopher in the modern age. For Kant was influenced by the deists and David Hume, who himself was partly shaped by the deist critique of Judaism and orthodox Christianity.[23] As Soulen has vividly put it, Kant's *Religion Within the Limits of Reason Alone* (1793) stripped the "Christian divinity" of "Jewish flesh."[24] For the German philosopher, the Christian God is interested in moral perfection alone, so the kingdom of God is the supremacy of moral law. Judaism is about arbitrary law, not rational morality. Israel's chosenness is exclusive and therefore "shows enmity toward all other peoples."[25] The remaining existence of Jewish thought in Christian faith is "the original sin of Christian history."[26] The inevitable conclusion is that there is no connection whatsoever between Judaism and true Christianity.

Schleiermacher (1768–1834) took Kant's supersessionism a step further by calling, as a church theologian, for the elimination of the Hebrew Scriptures from the church's Sunday lectionary. The German theologian's attitude toward

---

[20]Frank E. Manuel, *Changing of the Gods* (Lebanon, NH: University Press of New England for Brown University, 1983), 112-16.

[21]The Holbachians were disciples of Baron d'Holbach, a genial atheist, militant against both Christianity and deism (because it was theistic). "He and his aristocratic atheist circle" were influential in Paris in the 1760s. Henry F. May, *The Enlightenment in America* (Oxford: Oxford University Press, 1976), 118.

[22]Manuel, *Broken Staff*, 166.

[23]Kant's favorite teacher wrote a book-length attack on the deists, which suggests that Kant was familiar with their arguments. Manfred Kuehn, *Kant: A Biography* (Cambridge: Cambridge University Press, 2002), 80-81.

[24]Soulen, *God of Israel and Christian Theology*, 57.

[25]Immanuel Kant, *Religion Within the Limits of Reason Alone*, trans. Theodore M. Greene and Hoyt H. Hudson (New York: Harper Torchbooks, 1960), 117.

[26]Soulen's phrase, in *God of Israel and Christian Theology*, 67.

the Old Testament was almost contemptuous. He wrote that if a doctrine appears only in the Old Testament and not also the New, it is not Christian. He declared that the Old Testament has neither the dignity nor the inspiration of the New, and that it contains instead the "spirit of the [Jewish] people . . . not the Christian Spirit." Therefore we are not to use the Old Testament to support Christian doctrines.[27]

Liberal Christians today, who often appeal to the Psalms and Prophets for moral teaching and consider Schleiermacher their mentor, might be surprised to hear their theological father saying, "It is only after *deluding* ourselves by unconscious additions and subtractions that we can suppose we are able to gather a Christian doctrine of God out of the Prophets and the Psalms." The following statement is still more alarming, and makes one wonder if there is a line from Schleiermacher to the German Christians of the 1930s who ripped the Old Testament out of their Bibles: The only reason why earlier eras read the Old Testament was because of its "historical connexions" to the Christian faith, so that its "gradual retirement into the background" of Christian reading and worship is not to be regretted.[28] This is structural supersessionism on steroids.

Of course most modern Christians did not follow the path of liberal theology. Yet most Catholic and mainline Protestant churches held to their own versions of supersessionism through the mid-twentieth century, when the Holocaust made them reexamine their attitudes toward Israel. A rereading of Scripture and particularly of Paul led to a new vision for Israel's future (and hence the land) among some theologians and New Testament scholars, such as Karl and Marcus Barth, C. E. B. Cranfield, Peter Stuhlmacher, Krister Stendahl and numerous evangelical scholars. Cranfield, for example, concluded that an impartial reading of Paul's epistle to the Romans demanded a revision of supersessionism: "These three chapters [Rom 9–11] emphatically forbid us to speak of the church as having once and for all taken the place of the Jewish people."[29] Like Cranfield, scholars began to notice that Paul seemed to believe that Jewish rejection of Jesus as Messiah did not abrogate God's covenant with them, for in Romans 11 he says explicitly that "God has not rejected his people whom he foreknew" (Rom 11:2). As W. D. Davies noted in his landmark work on the biblical concept

---

[27]Friedrich Schleiermacher, *The Christian Faith*, ed. H. R. Mackintosh (Philadelphia: Fortress, 1976), 116, 609, 610.

[28]Ibid., 609, 610 (my emphasis).

[29]C. E. B. Cranfield, *A Critical and Exegetical Commentary on the Epistle to the Romans* (Edinburgh: T&T Clark, 1979), 2:448.

A History of Supersessionism

of land, "Paul never calls the Church the New Israel or the Jewish people the Old Israel."[30] Elsewhere in Romans 11 Paul suggests the same theme of the continuance of the covenant: "The gifts and the calling of God are irrevocable" (Rom 11:29). "What will their acceptance [by God] be but life from the dead?" (Rom 11:15). "All Israel will be saved (Rom 11:26) . . . [and] receive mercy" (Rom 11:31). Craig Blaising notes that Paul bases this reading of Israel's future on Isaiah 59:20-21, where the prophet forecasts the return of divine favor on Zion and follows this promise with another: "Your people shall all be righteous; they shall possess the land forever" (Is 60:21).[31]

If Pauline research has shown new hope for the future of Israel and its land, so too has research into the historical Jesus, with E. P. Sanders, N. T. Wright, John P. Meier and Ben F. Meyer among the most important scholars showing that Jesus was far more interested in Israel than scholars had previously imagined.[32] Evangelical scholar Scot McKnight has pushed this further by arguing that Jesus intended to renew Israel's national covenant, not found a new religion. He wanted to restore the twelve tribes, which would bring the kingdom of God in and through Israel. By his death, Jesus believed the whole Jewish nation was being nailed to the cross, and God was restoring the nation and renewing its people. Hence, salvation was first and foremost for Israel; if the nations wanted salvation, they would need to assimilate themselves to saved Israel. Because of his claim to dispense forgiveness of sins and create a new community of restored Israel that would inherit the kingdom of God, his disciples saw Jesus as the savior of Israel, as God coming to them through Jesus, leading the nation out of exile to regain control of the land.[33] Roman Catholic historian Robert Wilken observes that "hopes of restoration and the establishment of a kingdom in Jerusalem were not, it seems, foreign to early Christian tradition." The angel tells Mary that "the Lord God will give to [Jesus] the throne of his ancestor David. He will reign over the house of Jacob forever" (Lk 1:32-33). Jesus himself antici-

---

[30]W. D. Davies, *The Gospel and the Land: Early Christianity and Jewish Territorial Doctrine* (Berkeley: University of California Press, 1974), 182.

[31]Craig A. Blaising, "The Future of Israel as a Theological Question," paper presented to the annual meeting of the Evangelical Theological Society, Nashville, November 19, 2000.

[32]E. P. Sanders, *Jesus and Judaism* (Philadelphia: Fortress, 1985); N. T. Wright, *Jesus and the Victory of God* (Minneapolis: Fortress, 1996); John P. Meier, *A Marginal Jew: Rethinking the Historical Jesus*, Anchor Bible Reference Library, 4 vols. (New York: Doubleday, 1991–2009); Ben F. Meyer, *The Aims of Jesus* (London: SCM Press, 1979).

[33]Scot McKnight, *A New Vision for Israel: The Teachings of Jesus in National Context* (Grand Rapids: Eerdmans, 1999).

pates the day when Jerusalem will welcome him: "Jerusalem, Jerusalem, . . . I tell you, you will not see me again until you say, 'Blessed is the one who comes in the name of the Lord'" (Mt 23:37, 39).[34]

But while Paul and Jesus scholarship has eroded support for one sort of supersessionism, most Protestant and Catholic scholars have not embraced the countervailing notion that God has a present and future role for Jews in the *land of Israel*. That is, while most Protestant and Catholic scholars since the Holocaust fall over each other reaffirming God's eternal covenant with Israel, for the most part they ignore what for most Jews is absolutely integral to that covenant: the land. Jews appreciate Roman Catholic and mainline Protestant affirmations that God's covenant with Israel is eternal but wonder why they ignore or deny what they believe is an indispensable manifestation of the covenant. As the authors of "*Dabru Emet*: A Jewish Statement on Christians and Christianity" put it, "The most important event for Jews since the Holocaust has been the reestablishment of a Jewish state in the Promised Land." They add, "Israel was promised—and given—to Jews as the physical center of the covenant between them and God." Yet most Protestant and Catholic affirmations of the Jewish covenant ignore this central component. A letter writer to the *Christian Century* complained that the editor's approach to the land of Israel "is roughly equivalent to a Jew asking a Protestant teenager: 'Hey, what's up with the resurrection thing?' A Judaism without the [covenantal] component of the land of Israel is a faith shorn of most of its power." This is in part because, as the National Council of Synagogues argues, "God wants the nations to see the redemption of Israel and be impressed. . . . They will therefore learn, if they had not learned before, that the Lord, God of Israel, restores His people to His land."[35]

---

[34]Robert Wilken, *A Land Called Holy* (New Haven, CT: Yale University Press, 1992), 49, 52, 48.
[35]"A Symposium on *Dabru Emet*: A Jewish Statement on Christians and Christianity," *Pro Ecclesia* 11, no. 1 (2002): 6; Jeffrey K. Salkin, letter to the editor, *Christian Century* 119, no. 22 (2002): 52; and "Reflections On Covenant and Mission," issued by the National Council of Synagogues and Delegates of the Bishops' Committee on Ecumenical and Interreligious Affairs (12 August 2002), 8.

2

A HISTORY OF CHRISTIAN ZIONISM

*Is Christian Zionism Rooted Primarily
in Premillennial Dispensationalism?*

Gerald R. McDermott

◆

*We can read in the newspapers,
"God keeps his promise."*

KARL BARTH, AFTER THE 1967 WAR

Most of us are familiar with the standard narrative about Christian Zionism. It is allegedly a result of bad exegesis and zany theology. While most scholars will concede that the Hebrew Bible is clearly Zionist (that is, that its primary focus is on a covenant with a particular people and land, both called Israel, and the land sometimes called Zion), they will typically insist that the New Testament drops this focus on a particular land and people, and replaces it with a universal vision for all peoples across the globe. *Eretz Yisrael* (Hebrew for "the land of Israel") is said to be replaced by *gē* (Greek for "land" or "earth"), the latter of which is usually translated the whole "earth." Concern with Jews as Jews is thought to be absent from the New Testament—except to insist that there is no longer any significant difference between Jew and Greek (Gal 3:28). Hence neither the people nor the land of Israel has any special significance after the resurrection of Jesus Christ.

According to this narrative, the only ones who have advocated for the idea that the New Testament maintains concern for the particular land and people of Israel are (traditional) premillennial dispensationalists. As we saw in the introduction, their theology—which puts Israel and the church on two different tracks, neither of which runs at the same time, and which often holds to elaborate and detailed schedules of end-time events, including a rapture—is thought to be the origin and essence of all Christian Zionism.

The burden of this chapter is to show that Christian Zionism is at least eighteen centuries older than dispensationalism. Its vision is rooted in the Hebrew Bible, where covenant is the central story, and at the heart of the covenant is the promise of a land. God takes the initiative to adopt a people and then to promise and eventually deliver a land to this people. God drove this people off their land twice, but even in exile his prophets declared that the land was still theirs. The Jews who wrote the New Testament continued with this vision. Just as the Hebrew Bible envisioned blessings going to the whole world through the people of this land, so too the New Testament proclaimed a blessing for the whole world coming through the Jewish Messiah, whose kingdom started in Israel and would eventually be centered once again in Israel. These New Testament writers held on to the prophets' promises that the Jews of the diaspora would one day return to the land from all over the world and establish there a *politeia* (a political entity), which one day would be transformed into a center of blessing for the world.

In this chapter we will trace the long history of Christian Zionism, from the early church into the first few centuries of the common era, then picking up new vitality in the sixteenth through the nineteenth centuries. We will see that the vast majority of Christian Zionists came long before the rise of dispensationalism in the nineteenth century and that many of the most prominent Christian Zionists of the last two centuries had nothing to do with dispensationalism.

After reviewing briefly what recent critics have said about Christian Zionism's supposed origins in dispensationalism, we will examine the Zionist vision in the Hebrew Bible. Then we will look very briefly at some of the oft-overlooked traces of that same vision in the New Testament. Next we will trace the history of Christian Zionism *before* the rise of dispensationalism and conclude with a look at other Christian Zionist leaders who were innocent of dispensationalism.

A Question of Origins

Most work on Christian Zionism in the last few decades has suggested that Christian Zionism is either the functional equivalent of dispensationalism or indebted primarily to dispensationalism. For example, Gary Burge does not name dispensationalists but seems to have them in mind as the only "Christian Zionists." For he says that Christian Zionists generally do not have "genuine sympathy for the Jews" and do not desire "to see a restoration and preservation of a biblical people to a biblical land for its own sake." No, their only desire is "to accelerate an eschatological crisis that will deliver the world to Armageddon and bring Christ back." These "evangelicals" (the word he uses for these Christian Zionists) are dispensationalists.[1]

Stephen Sizer acknowledges that Christian Zionism has its roots far earlier than the nineteenth century when dispensationalism began and that there is a "covenantal" form of Christian Zionism besides a dispensationalist form. But when he describes "the distinctive theology of Christian Zionism," four of the seven theological tenets are taken from what he says is dispensationalist, not covenantal, Zionism: that "Israel is elevated to a status above the church,"[2] that Eretz Israel extends all the way from the Nile to the Euphrates, that "the temple must be rebuilt and sacrifices re-instituted in order that it can be desecrated by the Antichrist before Jesus returns" and that the battle of Armageddon will lead to the death of two-thirds of the Jewish people.[3]

While Timothy P. Weber does not claim that all of Christian Zionism derives from dispensationalism, his book on evangelicals and Israel is devoted exclusively to the history and beliefs of dispensationalism. One gets the impression from his book that dispensationalism and Christian Zionism are two terms for the same phenomenon.[4] Shalom Goldman has traced the story of Christian Zionists in the last two centuries, ranging from Theodor Herzl's evangelical friends to Catholic thinkers and recent popes and then to recent evangelicals such as John Hagee and Jerry Falwell—both dispensationalists.[5] In his study of historic relationships between evangelicals and Jews, Yaakov Ariel focuses most particularly on dispensationalists.[6]

---

[1]Gary M. Burge, *Jesus and the Land: The New Testament Challenge to "Holy Land" Theology* (Grand Rapids: Baker Academic, 2010), 121-22.

[2]Many dispensationalists would disagree with this and say that Sizer has caricatured their views here.

[3]Stephen Sizer, *Christian Zionism: Roadmap to Armageddon?* (Downers Grove, IL: IVP Academic, 2005), 202-3.

[4]Timothy P. Weber, *On the Road to Armageddon: How Evangelicals Became Israel's Best Friend* (Grand Rapids: Baker Academic, 2004).

[5]Shalom L. Goldman, *Zeal for Zion: Christian, Jews, and the Idea of the Promised Land* (Chapel Hill: University of North Carolina Press, 2009).

[6]Yaakov Ariel, *On Behalf of Israel: American Fundamentalist Attitudes Toward Jews, Judaism, and Zionism, 1865–1945* (Brooklyn, NY: Carlson, 1991); idem, *Evangelizing the Chosen People: Missions*

Robert O. Smith's recent work on the "roots of Christian Zionism" helpfully shows that those roots are not primarily in dispensationalism. He points instead to Reformation and Puritan roots and argues that "popular American Christian support for the State of Israel is not grounded in popular adherence to dispensational doctrine." Yet he also maintains that "Christian Zionism is an imperial theology" that is dedicated to "American military and economic superiority" in order to "construct Jews for explicitly Christian purposes." These observations come from his discussion of dispensationalism.[7]

Only Donald Lewis has been able to break this near obsession with dispensationalism in his new study of Lord Shaftesbury, the nineteenth-century British Christian Zionist whose interest in Israel was indispensable to the movement that led eventually to the Balfour Declaration. Shaftesbury was influenced by historicist premillennialism, not the futurist premillennialism of dispensationalism.[8]

ZION IN THE TORAH

Not even the most virulent anti-Zionists deny that Zionism is in what Christians call the Old Testament. They acknowledge that the people of Israel are front and center in most of what Jews call the Tanak and that there is a great deal of concern for the land in these forty-odd books (thirty-nine for Protestants, forty-six for Catholics). But few realize how central the land is to these Scriptures. As Gerhard von Rad put it, "Of all the promises made to the patriarchs it was that of the land that was the most prominent and decisive."[9]

By one scholar's count, *land* is the fourth most frequent noun or substantive in the Tanak. He notes that it is more dominant statistically than the idea of covenant.[10]

---

to the Jews in America, 1880–2000 (Chapel Hill: University of North Carolina Press, 2000); idem, *An Unusual Relationship: Evangelical Christians and Jews* (New York: New York University Press, 2013).

[7]Robert O. Smith, *More Desired than Our Owne Salvation: The Roots of Christian Zionism* (New York: Oxford University Press, 2013), 160, 151-58, 181-82.

[8]Donald M. Lewis, *The Origins of Christian Zionism: Lord Shaftesbury and Evangelical Support for a Jewish Homeland* (Cambridge: Cambridge University Press, 2010), 318 passim. Historicist premillennialists believed the books of Daniel and Revelation were primarily about the *past* history of the church. Futurist premillennialists believed they were primarily about the *future* of the church and that Jews were destined to establish a Jewish state in Palestine so as to prepare for a return of the Messiah, but without Christian "responsibility to prioritize the conversion of the Jews." Lewis, *Origins of Christian Zionism*, 91, 318-19.

[9]Gerhard von Rad, *The Problem of the Hexateuch and Other Essays*, trans. E. W. Trueman Dicken (London: Oliver & Boyd, 1966), 79.

[10]Elmer A. Martens, *God's Design: A Focus on Old Testament Theology* (Grand Rapids: Baker Books, 1981), 97-98.

By my counting, more than one thousand times in the Tanak the land (*eretz*) of Israel is either stated or implied. Of the 250 times that *covenant* (*b'rît*) is mentioned, in 70 percent of those instances (177 times) *covenant* is either directly or indirectly connected to the land of Israel. Of the 74 times that *b'rît* appears in the Torah, 73 percent of those times (54) include the gift of the land, either explicitly or implicitly. In other words, when the biblical God calls out a people for himself, he does so in an earthly way, by making the gift of a particular land an integral aspect of that calling. See tables 2.1 and 2.2 for enumeration.

Table 2.1 Occurrences of *covenant* and *land* in the Torah and Ketuvim*

Book	Covenant+Land Explicit (Both Words)	C+L Explicit Total	C+L Implicit (Land Used, Covenant Implied)	Covenant Alone (God's Covenant with Israel)	Covenant Alone (total)
Genesis	5	6	70	13	17
Exodus	3	5	105	7	8
Leviticus	3	3	45	4	4
Numbers	0	0	98	3	5
Deuteronomy	3	3	129	13	23
Torah	14	17	447	40	57
Joshua	3	4	64	14	15
Judges	2	2	14	1	2
Ruth	0	0	0	0	0
1 Samuel	1	1	2	0	6
2 Samuel	0	1	9	1	2
1 Kings	2	2	19	3	8
2 Kings	0	0	28	9	10
1 Chronicles	0	0	12	6	11
2 Chronicles	1	1	29	6	14
Ezra	0	0	8	0	1
Nehemiah	1	1	13	2	2
Esther	0	0	0	0	0
Job	0	0	0	0	2
Psalms	2	2	67	18	19
Proverbs	0	0	15	0	1
Ecclesiastes	0	0	0	0	0
Song of Solomon	0	0	0	0	0
Other	12	14	280	60	93

*Table compiled by Benjamin Cowgill.

Table 2.2 Occurrences of *covenant* and *land* in the Prophets*

Book	Covenant+Land Explicit (Both Words)	C+L Explicit Total	C+L Implicit (Land Used, Covenant Implied)	Covenant Alone (God's Covenant with Israel)	Covenant Alone (total)
Isaiah	2	2	74	7	10
Jeremiah	4	4	104	11	17
Lamentations	0	0	0	0	0
Ezekiel	2	3	56	11	13
Daniel	1	1	4	3	5
Hosea	1	1	8	2	4
Joel	0	0	5	0	0
Amos	0	0	6	1	1
Obadiah	0	0	0	0	0
Jonah	0	0	0	0	0
Micah	0	0	4	0	0
Nahum	0	0	0	0	0
Habakkuk	0	0	2	0	0
Zephaniah	0	0	2	0	0
Haggai	0	0	0	0	0
Zechariah	0	0	13	1	2
Malachi	0	0	0	5	6
Prophets	10	11	278	41	58
Total	36	42	1005	141	208

*Table compiled by Benjamin Cowgill.

According to the *Dictionary of Biblical Imagery*, "Next to God himself, the longing for land dominates all others [in the Old Testament]." Land is presented by the Torah as a place of spiritual testing; its pollution by sin and Israel's consequent exiles are portrayed as analogous to humanity's fall from grace in Eden and consequent expulsion. Adam, formed from land, failed to protect it and therefore allowed the serpent (evil) access to it. Land also represents the human condition: "Good in principle, land is cursed as a result of humanity's sin, and people are alienated from it as well as being joined to it."[11]

It is this note of possible alienation that is often missed in both scholarly and nonscholarly treatments of biblical Zionism. From the very beginning of the compilation of the Torah it was recognized that the covenantal promise of the land did

---

[11] *Dictionary of Biblical Imagery*, ed. Leland Ryken, James C. Wilhoit and Tremper Longman III (Downers Grove, IL: InterVarsity Press, 1998), 487-88.

not guarantee possession of the land. The Torah itself specifies that possession of the land depends on moral and religious conditions. As Jack Schechter has shown in his study of Deuteronomy—which was probably written as Jews were repossessing the land after exile from the land—continued possession of the land was dependent on Israel's faithfulness to the covenant: the Lord "gives you all the land which he promised to give to your fathers—provided you are *careful to keep all this commandment*" (Deut 19:8-9 [added emphasis in Schechter's translation]).[12]

One line of conditions was the repeated commandment of the covenant to "love the alien as yourself." The Israelites were not to "oppress the alien," who "shall be to you as the citizen among you . . . for you were aliens in Egypt" (Lev 19:33-34).[13] Moses commanded that tithes be collected from Israelites to help poor aliens (Deut 14:28-29; 26:12); wages were not to be withheld from aliens (Deut 24:14); aliens were to use the same system of justice that was provided to Israelites (Deut 1:16; 24:17; 27:19).

This was remarkably demonstrated by biblical patriarchs and kings. For example, the Canaanites were not displaced when God promised the land to Abraham and his descendants. Instead, Abraham and the Canaanites became neighbors and trading partners. Abraham refused to accept parcels of that land as gifts from the natives but insisted on paying (Gen 23).[14]

Joshua included aliens in public recommittals to the covenant (Josh 8:33-35)[15] and kept his agreement with non-Israelites, even when that agreement had been made under false pretenses (Josh 9). Then he went so far as to risk the lives of his men to protect those non-Israelites in battle (Josh 10:6-8).[16]

So the Torah never guaranteed eternal possession of the land. It made possession conditional on faithfulness to God and justice to residents in the land.

---

[12]Jack Shechter, *The Land of Israel: Its Theological Dimensions* (Lanham, MD: University Press of America, 2010), 57.

[13]Gary M. Burge, *Who Are God's People in the Middle East?* (Grand Rapids: Zondervan, 1993), 74-75.

[14]Burge notes that in the Hexateuch the land is repeatedly called "Canaan" despite promises that Israel would inherit it. So Sarah "died at Kiriath-arba (that is, Hebron) in the land of Canaan" (Gen 23:2). Burge, *Who Are God's People in the Middle East?*, 65.

[15]When Hezekiah restored worship at the temple, he invited foreigners to participate (2 Chron 30:25).

[16]Burge points out that the analogy of modern Israel's occupation to Joshua's war against certain Canaanite cities is inappropriate. "The Canaanites promoted a religion utterly inimical to God's law. [But] modern Israel/Palestine is populated by people—Christians and Muslims—many of whom have a deep reverence for the Lord God of Abraham. In fact, Rahab's spiritual disposition was not unlike that of the Palestinians who acknowledge and worship the same God as the Jews but are not Jewish themselves." Burge, *Who Are God's People in the Middle East?*, 75.

The prophets, who wrote mostly from exile, prophesied that one day Jews from all over the world would return to the land. Isaiah, for example, predicted in the early seventh century BC that in some future day God

> will assemble the outcasts of Israel,
> and gather the dispersed of Judah
> from the four corners of the earth. (Is 11:12)

Roughly one century later Jeremiah wrote that "the days are coming" when it shall be said that the Lord "brought [the people of Israel] out of all the countries where he had driven them . . . back to their own land that [he] gave to their fathers . . . There they shall dwell in their own land" (Jer 16:14-15; 23:8). In the late sixth century BC Zechariah delivered God's promise that

> Though I scattered them among the nations,
> yet in far countries they shall remember me,
> and with their children they shall live and return. (Zech 10:9 RSV)

Similar promises are made throughout the prophets and over the course of different periods in Israel's later history—after the first exile to Assyria, during and after the second exile to Babylon and after the return of the exiles under Ezra and Nehemiah.

Zionism in the New Testament

Some scholars have suggested that these prophecies of return were fulfilled when some of the Babylonian exiles returned to rebuild Jerusalem toward the end of the sixth century BC. But Jesus and the apostles give evidence that they were still expecting a future return. When Jesus quotes Isaiah's prediction that the temple would become "a house of prayer for all the nations" (Mk 11:17; Is 56:7), he seems to concur, as Richard Hays suggests, with Isaiah's vision of "an eschatologically restored Jerusalem" where foreigners would come to God's holy mountain to join the "outcasts of Israel" whom God has "gathered" (Is 56:7-8).[17] Hays adds that John's figural reading of Jesus' body as the new temple (Jn 2:21) "should be read neither as flatly supersessionist nor as hostile to continuity with Israel."[18] It does not deny the literal sense of Israel's Scriptures—that the temple was God's house—"but completes it by linking it typologically with the narrative

---

[17] Richard Hays, *Reading Backwards: Figural Christology and the Fourfold Gospel Witness* (Waco, TX: Baylor University Press, 2014), 6-7.
[18] Ibid., 102.

of Jesus and disclosing a deeper prefigurative truth within the literal historical sense."[19] That the apostles saw the temple as both God's continuing house and *also* a figure for Jesus' body is shown by their participation in temple liturgies even after the temple's leaders had helped put their Messiah to death (Acts 2:46).

There is more evidence that Jesus looked to a future return of Jews and a restored Jerusalem. In Matthew 24 he says that when the Son of Man returns, "all the tribes of the earth will mourn" (Mt 24:30), quoting Zechariah's prophecy about the inhabitants of Jerusalem mourning when "the LORD will give salvation to the tents of Judah" (Zech 12:7, 10 ESV). Then in Matthew 19 Jesus tells his disciples that "in the new world, when the Son of Man will sit on his glorious throne, you who have followed me will also sit on twelve thrones, judging the twelve tribes of Israel" (Mt 19:28 ESV). James Sanders has observed that these repeated references to the twelve tribes imply restoration of Israel, particularly in Jerusalem.[20] Luke records Anna speaking of the baby Jesus "to all who were waiting for the redemption of Jerusalem" (Lk 2:38 ESV), and Jesus' expectation that when he returns Israel will welcome him: "You will not see me until the time comes when you say, 'Blessed is the one who comes in the name of the Lord'" (Lk 13:34-35; Mt 23:37-39). Luke suggests that the return will be in Jerusalem (Lk 21:24-28). And when his disciples asked Jesus just before his ascension, "Lord, is this the time when you will restore the kingdom to Israel?" (Acts 1:6), Jesus did not challenge their assumption that one day the kingdom would be restored to physical Israel. He simply said the Father had set the date, and they did not need to know it yet. It was these sorts of indications in the Gospels and Acts that caused Markus Bockmuehl to write that "the early Jesus movement evidently continued to focus upon the restoration of Israel's twelve tribes in a new messianic kingdom."[21]

Paul, Peter and the writer of the book of Revelation had similar expectations. Paul uses Isaiah's prophecy of restoration in Isaiah 59 to declare that "the deliverer will come from Zion; he will banish ungodliness from Jacob" (Rom 11:26). In Acts 3 Peter looks forward to "the times of restoration of all things which God spoke through the mouth of his holy prophets from ancient time" (Acts 3:21).[22]

---

[19] Ibid.
[20] James Sanders, *Jesus and Judaism* (Philadelphia: Fortress, 1985), 98.
[21] Markus Bockmuehl, *Jewish Law in Gentile Churches: Halakhah and the Beginning of Christian Public Ethics* (Grand Rapids: Baker Academic, 2000), xi.
[22] In this and other biblical quotations, I use my own translations from the Hebrew and Greek, unless otherwise noted.

The word Peter uses for "restoration" is the same word (*apokatastasis*) used in the Septuagint (which the early church used as its Bible) for God's future return of Jews from all over the world to Israel.[23] In Revelation the Lamb draws his followers to Zion in the final stage of history (Rev 14:1), and the new earth is centered in Jerusalem, which has twelve gates named after "the twelve tribes of the sons of Israel" (Rev 21:2, 12).

We will hear far more about these signs of Zion in the New Testament from the later chapters. Now let us move on to indications that early Christianity continued to expect a future for Israel as a people and land.

Zionism in Early and Medieval Christianity

Justin Martyr (100–165), one of the best-known second-century Christian writers, expected that the millennium would be centered in Jerusalem. Although he was one of the first replacement theologians, his vision of the church's future included a particular city in the particular land of Israel.

> But I and others, who are right-minded Christians on all points, are assured that there will be a resurrection of the dead, and a thousand years in Jerusalem, which will then be built, adorned and enlarged, [as] the prophets Ezekiel and Isaiah and others declare . . . [such as] John, one of the apostles of Christ, who prophesied, by a revelation that was made to him, that those who believed in our Christ would dwell a thousand years in Jerusalem.[24]

> Irenaeus (d. ca. 202) was similar. Like Justin, he believed "the church is the [true] seed of Abraham," and those who will return "from all the nations" will be Christians rather than Jews.[25] But he also believed there will be a future for Jerusalem in the end days. It will be "rebuilt after the pattern of the Jerusalem above," but not in allegorical fashion. Those who "allegorize [prophecies] of this kind . . . shall not be found consistent with themselves," for the new earth "cannot be understood in reference to super-celestial matters."[26]

---

[23]Jer 16:15: "I will bring them back [*apokatastēsō*] to their own land that I gave to their fathers"; Jer 24:6: "I will set my eyes on them for good, and I will bring them back [*apokatastēsō*] to this land"; Jer 50 [27 LXX]:19: "I will restore Israel [*apokatastēsō*] to his pasture"; Hos 11:11: "They shall come trembling like birds from Egypt, and like doves from the land of Assyria, and I will return [*apokatastēsō*] them to their homes, declares the Lord" (author's translations).

[24]Justin Martyr, *Dialogue with Trypho*, chaps. 80 and 81, in *Christian Classics Ethereal Library*, www.ccel.org/ccel/schaff/anf01.viii.iv.lxxx.html.

[25]Irenaeus, *Against Heresies* 5.34.1, www.newadvent.org/fathers/0103534.htm.

[26]Irenaeus, *Against Heresies* 5.35.1, 2, www.newadvent.org/fathers/0103535.htm.

Tertullian (160–ca. 225) also saw a future for the people and land of Israel. Although he decried "Jews" for their ignorance in putting Jesus to death, and thought that God punished them by tearing "from [their] throat[s] . . . the very land of promise," he believed that they would one day be returned to their land.

> It will be fitting for the Christian to rejoice, and not to grieve, at the restoration of Israel, if it be true, (as it is), that the whole of our hope is intimately united with the remaining expectation of Israel.[27]

A bit later in the third century, the Egyptian bishop Nepos, who "was a respected and admired Christian leader," foresaw a restoration of Jerusalem and rebuilding of the temple. Millennial teaching was prevalent in that area of third-century Egypt and had been so for a long time, along with, presumably, faith in a restored Israel.[28]

But this early church Zionism came screeching to a halt with Origen (184–254). He possessed a brilliant mind and was called by Jerome the greatest teacher of the church after the apostles. However, when it came to the Jewish Messiah and the promise of the land, Origen regarded their relationship as a zero-sum game. Either one or the other could be fulfilled, not both. As Robert Wilken puts it, "If Jesus of Nazareth was the Messiah, the prophecies about the messianic age had already been fulfilled, and it was the task of biblical interpreters to discover what the spiritual promises meant in light of this new 'fact.' For Origen the essential feature of the holy land was not its location but its quality and character." In Origen's words,

> Therefore the prophecies relating to Judaea and Jerusalem, and to Israel, Judah and Jacob indicate to us, because we do not interpret them in a fleshly sense, various divine mysteries.[29]

Therefore prophecies about the land of Israel and the future of the Jewish people on the land would be "emptied of their spiritual content" if they were permitted to refer in any literal sense to Jerusalem or the land. So Jerusalem "does not designate a future political center but a spiritual vision of heavenly bliss." When

---

[27]Tertullian, *On Modesty*, chap. 8, www.newadvent.org/fathers/0407.htm.
[28]Robert L. Wilken, *The Land Called Holy: Palestine in Christian History and Thought* (New Haven, CT: Yale University Press, 1992), 76-77, drawing on Eusebius, *The History of the Church* 7.24, and other sources.
[29]Origen, *On First Principles* (Gloucester, MA: Peter Smith, 1973), 301-2 (4.3.9).

the psalmist says "the meek shall possess the land," he means the "pure land in the pure heaven," not somewhere on planet earth.[30]

Augustine was willing to call soil taken from Israel "holy land,"[31] but he spiritualized the promises of land in a way similar to Origen. Once Augustine's amillennial eschatology became accepted in the medieval church, with its assertion that the millennium is simply the rule of Christ through the existing church, few medieval thinkers saw a future for the people or land of Israel. All Old Testament prophecies of future Israel were interpreted to be predictions of the Christian church that came after the resurrection of Christ.

There were exceptions, however. Hildegard of Bingen forecast a period of peace and the conversion of the Jews before the return of Christ.[32] Joachim of Fiore (ca. 1135–1202) and many later theologians influenced by him predicted the mass conversion of Jews in a future age of the Spirit. In this way Jews regained theological importance as a distinct people with a future, even if it would lead to assimilation into Christendom.[33] Gerard of Borgo San Donnino (ca. 1255) said that some Jews would be blessed as Jews in the end time, and they would return to their homeland.[34] John of Rupescissa (ca. 1310–1366) said Jews would be converted and Jerusalem would be rebuilt to become the center of a renewed and purified faith.[35]

It was not until the Reformation and later, however, that renewed vision for a future Israel gained momentum. Calvin's amillennialism and replacement theology prevented him from imagining such a thing. Something similar is routinely said of Luther, and for good reason. Yet there is the curious remark by the great Reformation scholar Heiko Oberman that Luther once quipped that if the Jews were to reestablish themselves in the Holy Land, he would be the first to

---

[30] Wilken, *Land Called Holy*, 70, 72, 77-78.
[31] Ibid., 125.
[32] Hildegard, *Scivias sive visionum*, PL 197:713-15; *Liber divinarum operum*, PL 197:1020, cited in Marjorie Reeves, "The Originality and Influence of Joachim of Fiore," *Traditio* 36 (1980): 286.
[33] Marjorie Reeves, *The Influence of Prophecy in the Later Middle Ages* (London: Oxford University Press, 1969), 6n2, 47, 77, 222, 237, 249, 299, 305, 307, 322, 427, 437-38, 460, 466, 474, 482, 508.
[34] Carl F. Ehle Jr., "Prolegomena to Christian Zionism in America: The Views of Increase Mather and William E. Blackstone Concerning the Doctrine of the Restoration of Israel" (PhD diss., New York University, 1977), 41-42, cited in Thomas D. Ice, "Lovers of Zion: A History of Christian Zionism" (2009), *Article Archives*, paper 29, http://digitalcommons.liberty.edu/pretrib_arch/29.
[35] Robert E. Lerner, "Millennialism," in *The Encyclopedia of Apocalypticism*, ed. John J. Collins, Bernard McGinn and Stephen Stein (New York: Continuum, 2000), 2:356.

go there and have himself circumcised![36] Even if this was a sarcastic counterfactual,[37] it suggests that the return of Jews to their ancient land would have had theological significance to the great Reformer.

SIXTEENTH-CENTURY GROUNDWORK

The stimulus for a new kind of Zionism came from Britain, and as early as the sixteenth century. In part this was because of its cultural memory. By the sixteenth century the Bible had already become "the national epic of Britain," as Julian Huxley put it.[38] The earliest surviving essay from England's history is the Epistle of Gildas, which dates from AD 550. After every battle is an Old Testament analogy, and on every page are quotes from the Pentateuch, Prophets or Psalms. The Venerable Bede, author of the eighth-century *Ecclesiastical History of the English People*, linked the earliest Britons to the Cymbri of Scythia (near the Black Sea), believed to be descended from Noah's sons. Later English medieval tradition held that Joseph of Arimathea, an Israelite, was the founder of Christianity in England.[39]

Another reason for England's eschatological singularity was that "England enjoyed relative political and religious tranquility in contrast to Europe's constant wars," political intrigues, economic distress and growing spiritual despair in the sixteenth and seventeenth centuries. When the English looked across the Channel at the wars and counterreformations of Europe, it became easy for Englishmen to think they were providentially favored. This was, "to a people steeped in Scripture, analogous to that special place held by the ancient Israelites." It was also congruent with the prevailing Calvinism, which "suggested the idea of Divine Election as belonging to the privileged and faithful nation."[40] Thus their own sense of election helped English Christians imagine that God had elected Israel to a permanent role in redemptive history.

---

[36]David Burrell, "How Christians Share in the Destiny of Israel," in *Voices from Jerusalem: Jews and Christians Reflect on the Holy Land*, ed. David Burrell and Yehezkel Landau (New York: Paulist, 1992), 13. Burrell reports this from a lecture by Oberman in Jerusalem, May 24, 1982.

[37]In other words, it is not going to happen—something like the snowball in hell. This is Lutheran theologian Paul Hinlicky's surmise; private conversation, March 25, 2015.

[38]Barbara W. Tuchman, *The Bible and the Sword: England and Palestine from the Bronze Age to Balfour* (New York: Ballantine, 1956), xiv.

[39]Ibid., 3-4, 13-14.

[40]This and other quotes in this paragraph are from Douglas J. Culver, *Albion and Ariel: British Puritanism and the Birth of Political Zionism* (New York: Peter Lang, 1995), 30-31.

Three influential English books in the sixteenth century helped focus this cultural memory and sense of privilege in ways that would resemble Zionism. John Bale (1495–1563) was "one of the best-known polemicists in the first generation of English Protestantism."[41] He was a supersessionist but without the anti-Jewish polemics of a Martin Luther. His 1570 edition of *The Image of Both Churches* includes what was then innovative—hope for the national conversion of Jews to Protestantism and assigning to them a place at the throne of the Lamb at the end of history. This meant they would have a central role in Christian eschatology.[42]

Bale was building on what had been suggested just ten years before in the Geneva Bible, first published in 1560 and more popular than the King James Bible for generations, especially among Presbyterian Scots and English Puritans. The notes of the Geneva Bible at Romans 11 predict that one day Israel as a people "shall embrace Christ" and then "the worlde shal be restored to a newe life." When it speaks at Revelation 1:7 of "they whiche pearced him [Christ]," it "deliberately does not single Jews out for condemnation or persecution." Historian Donald Lewis suggests that it was the Geneva Bible's vision of Israel's spiritual "return" or "turning" that prepared its huge readership for the associated idea of a literal return of Jews to their ancestral homeland.[43]

The third book of sixteenth-century Britain that helped prepare the English mind for Christian Zionism was John Foxe's *Book of Martyrs* (1563). After the Bible and John Bunyan's *Pilgrim's Progress*, it was the most widely read book in English for several centuries.[44] Foxe's book is not without its own denunciations of Jews and Judaism, yet he assures his readers that God's promises to Jews are "remaining still in their force." God has decreed that the time of the Gentiles will end, and then "the Jewes also after that fulnes of time shall returne unto the faith."[45] Once again British readers were told that there is a future for the Jewish people that is distinct from that of Gentiles (even if Jews would eventually change their faith!) and that they would play a role in God's drama at the end.

---

[41]Smith, *More Desired than Our Owne Salvation*, 55.
[42]Ibid., 58-59.
[43]Ibid., 60; Lewis, *Origins of Christian Zionism*, 29.
[44]Lewis, *Origins of Christian Zionism*, 47.
[45]Smith, *More Desired than Our Owne Salvation*, 64, 65.

Seventeenth-Century Puritan Restorationism

Beginning in the seventeenth century British thinkers started connecting Jewish conversion to Jewish return to Zion. Most had some connection to the Puritan movement, and some thought Jews would return to Zion without converting to Christianity first. Thomas Draxe (d. 1618), a disciple of the Puritan theologian William Perkins, held a view of Jews that for his day was remarkably generous. Even if Jews' usury and rejection of Christianity was to be criticized, Gentiles were "in many respects inferior unto them" because they were still "God's chosen nation." Christians "must therefore acknowledge our selves debters unto the Iewes."[46] Draxe believed that Jesus would not come again until "the dispersed Jewes generally converted to Christianitie," but that in the meantime they "would be temporally restored into their owne Country, [would] rebuild Jerusalem, and have a most reformed, and flourishing, Church and Commonwealth." Their attempts to return will cause "the great Turke, the King of the North," to try to exterminate them, but "Michaell the great Prince" will defend them. Then they will reach their ancient homeland, become "an Exemplary Church of all the world, and all Nations shall flow unto it, and it shall bee, as it were, a visible heaven upon earth."[47]

Thomas Brightman (1562–1607) laid the foundation for much future thought about eschatology and Israel, particularly by Puritans. In his commentary on the book of Revelation, published posthumously in 1611, Brightman said that Jews were the "kings of the east" (Rev 16:12) who would destroy Islam. He was certain they would be restored to the land of Zion: "Shal they returne agayn to Jerusalem? There is nothing more sure: the Prophets plainly confirme it, and beat often upon it." Brightman rebuked Gentile hatred for Jews and "laid out a political program by which well-meaning Gentiles will seek to advance Jewish interests."[48]

We don't know if Patrick Forbes of Corse (1564–1635), the later bishop of Aberdeen was influenced by Brightman, but in his own commentary on Revelation just two years after Brightman's appeared (1613), Forbes predicted the

---

[46] Thomas Draxe, *The Worldes Resurrection, or The General Calling of the Iewes* (London: G. Eld and John Wright, 1608), 3, 63-64. The best analysis of seventeenth-century Zionism among Puritans is Smith, *More Desired than Our Owne Salvation*, 69-94. This section follows his lead.

[47] Thomas Draxe, *An Alarum to the Last Judgement* (London: Nicholas Oakes and Matthew Law, 1615), 22, 74-76, 76-77.

[48] Thomas Brightman, *A Revelation of the Apocalyps* (Amsterdam: Hondius & Laurenss, 1611), 440, quoted in Smith, *More Desired than Our Owne Salvation*, 75.

future mass conversion of the Jews and said his "heart inclineth to thinke" they would also one day "inhabite againe their owne Land" so that they could "brooke a state in the [eyes] of the world."[49] In another two years (1615) Thomas Cooper reasoned in print that the Jews would experience a "Finall Conuersion" and that turning would take place "at Ierusalem, the old place of their worship." Why? It would demonstrate God's redemptive purposes, not only spiritually but materially.[50]

Toward the beginning of the next decade Henry Finch (ca. 1558–1625) expanded the British imagination on Zion. Finch was a legal scholar, a member of Parliament and a strong advocate of Puritan causes. In *The Worlds Great Restauration, or, The Calling of the Iewes* (1621), Finch asserted that after the Jews defeated Gog and Magog (the forces of Islam), they would "sit as a Lady in the mount of comelenesse, that hill of beautie, the true *Tsion*." Then the Gentiles would be their servants, and their land would become more fertile and populous than ever before. Making explicit what Brightman and others had assumed, Finch argued against the supersessionist assumption that all references to Israel and Zion in the Bible could be interpreted as references to the Gentile church:

> Where *Israel, Iudah, Tsion, Ierusalem,* &c. are named in this argument, the Holy Ghost meaneth not the spirituall Israel, or Church of God collected of the Gentiles, no nor of the Iewes and Gentiles both (for each of these have their promises severally and apart) but Israel properly descended out of *Iacobs* loynes.[51]

The widely respected biblical scholar at Cambridge Joseph Mede (1586–1638) was another Puritan sympathizer who advanced these same Zionist themes of the Jews being restored to the land of Israel after the destruction of the Turkish Empire. One of Mede's students was John Milton, who in *Paradise Regained* wrote in 1670 of the return of the people of Israel to their ancient land:

> Yet He at length, time to himself best known,
> Remembering Abraham, by some wondrous call
> May bring them back, repentant and sincere,

---

[49]Patrick Forbes, *An Exquisite Commentarie upon the Revelation of St. John* (London: T. Creede and Richard Redmer, 1615), 53.
[50]Thomas Cooper, *The Blessing of Japheth, Prouing the Gathering in of the Gentiles, and Finall Conuersion of the Iewes* (London: T. Creede and Richard Redmer, 1615), 53.
[51]Henry Finch, *The Worlds Great Restauration, or, The Calling of the Iewes* (London: Edward Griffin and William Bladen, 1621), A2-A3, 5-6.

And at their passing cleave the Assyrian flood,
While to their native land with joy they haste,
As the Red Sea and Jordan once he cleft,
When to the Promised Land their fathers passed.
To his due time and providence I leave them.[52]

Between Mede and Milton was John Cotton, the Puritan who helped shepherd the adventurous souls of the Massachusetts Bay Colony. Cotton's 1642 commentary on Canticles (Song of Solomon) followed Brightman's suggestion that the armies of the Jews "shall bee terrible to the Turkes and Tartars," but goes further by urging Gentiles to prove their faithfulness by actively helping Jews return to Palestine. They should be willing "to convey the Jewes into their owne Countrie, with Charets, and horses, and dromedaries."[53]

Another Puritan development of Christian Zionism came in Increase Mather's *The Mystery of Israel's Salvation* (1669), which was "the most comprehensive work on the restoration of Israel published" in this period. Writing from Boston in the Bay Colony, Mather wrote that the future conversion of "the Jewish Nation" was "a truth of late [that] hath gained ground much throughout the world." This widespread acceptance was a sign that the times of the end were near, a time when "the *Israelites* shall again possesse . . . the Land promised unto their *Father Abraham*."[54]

One of Mather's innovations was to charge that the Jews would regain their ancient land *before* they would convert. It would be only "after the Israelites shall be returned to their own Land again" that the Holy Spirit would be poured out on them. Mather also warned against a supersessionist spiritualization of promises made to Israel: "Why should we unnecessarily refuse literal interpretations?" Like Finch, Mather insisted that promises about earthly inheritance should not be spiritualized away.[55]

EIGHTEENTH-CENTURY ZIONIST POSTMILLENNIALISTS

At the turn of the eighteenth century the Dutch Reformed theologian Wilhelmus à Brakel (1635–1711) published a four-volume systematic theology that

---

[52]John Milton, *Paradise Regained* (1671), chap. 3, cited in Lewis, *Origins of Christian Zionism*, 33.
[53]John Cotton, *A Brief Exposition of the Whole Book of Canticles, or, Song of Solomon* (London: Philip Nevil, 1642), 195, 196.
[54]Smith, *More Desired than Our Owne Salvation*, 124; Increase Mather, *Mystery of Israel's Salvation* (London: John Allen, 1669), 43-44, 53-54.
[55]Mather, *Mystery*, 54, 56-57.

decisively broke with Calvin's supersessionism and presented a Christian Zionism that was more nuanced than we have seen heretofore. Brakel insisted that the church was not a New Israel and that Paul's reference to "all Israel" in Romans 11:26 had in mind Jewish Israel as a people with a distinct future.[56] Brakel declared emphatically that Jews would return to the land.

> Will the Jewish nation be gathered together again from all the regions of the world and from all the nations of the earth among which they have been dispersed? Will they come to and dwell in Canaan and all the lands promised to Abraham, and will Jerusalem be rebuilt? We believe that these events will transpire.[57]

But while Brakel followed the Puritans in holding to a return to the land and establishment of a polity there, he disagreed that the temple would be rebuilt and declared that Israel would not have "dominion over the entire world." Instead, it would be "an independent republic," only a segment of the glorious state of the church during the millennium. He warned Gentiles not to "despise the Jewish nation," for "they have received more than enough contempt from the unconverted." And Christians have provided a poor example to them: "The life of so many so-called Christians offends them and keeps them from exercising faith in Christ." This concern for persecution of Jews did not prevent Brakel, however, from his own dismissive remark that Jewish "religion does not even resemble a religion."[58]

Jonathan Edwards (1703–1758) agreed with Brakel that Calvin's supersessionism used a hyperspiritualist hermeneutic that rode roughshod over Scripture's plain sense. Like Brakel, he felt that the development of rabbinic Judaism had departed from the Old Testament's soteriological trajectory, but Edwards waxed lyrical over the theological continuity between the Jewish Bible and the New Testament. He did so in the midst of his lifelong battle against deism, which he considered to be the greatest enemy to Christian orthodoxy.

For the first time since Marcion (d. ca. 160), in the eighteenth century Jews were regarded as religiously unrelated to Christians. Deists launched the attack,

---

[56] Willem A. VanGemeren, "Israel as the Hermeneutical Crux in the Interpretation of Prophecy," *WTJ* 45 (1983): 142-43.

[57] Wilhelmus à Brakel, *The Christian's Reasonable Service* (Ligonier, PA: Soli Deo Gloria, 1992), 4:530-31, accessed January 4, 2016, www.abrakel.com/p/christians-reasonable-service.html. I am grateful for Barry E. Horner's work on Brakel: *Future Israel: Why Christian Anti-Judaism Must Be Challenged* (Nashville: B&H Academic, 2007), 153-55.

[58] Brakel, *Christian's Reasonable Service*, 4:534-35.

charging that Judaism was essentially pagan, unspiritual, unnecessary to Christianity and in fact the source of all that was wrong with traditional Christianity.[59] Edwards argued strenuously against the deist severance of the religious link between Jews and Christians by positing one covenant binding the two religions. The Old Testament and New Testament covenants, he asserted, are different but integrally related modes of a single plan of redemption. The Old Testament covenant was the "cortex" or "shell" that "envelops" the "medulla" of the gospel or covenant of grace.

For Edwards, the two covenants were two phases or ways of performing the same one covenant. As Edwards put it early in his career, "The gospel was preached to the Jews under a veil."[60] The process of conversion was the same for Jews in the Old Testament as for Christians in the New. They were "convinced so much of their wickedness that they trusted to nothing but the mere mercy of God." This included the antediluvians, and indeed all those who lived since "the beginning of the world." Even the rate of conversion was the same. There were wicked and godly then, and conversions were just as frequent then as in Edwards's day. Christ saved the Old Testament saints just like their cohorts in the New, and they believed in Christ, but under the name of the "angel of the Lord" or "messenger of the covenant." In fact, Christ appeared to Old Testament Jews; Moses saw his back parts on Mount Sinai, and he appeared in human form to the seventy elders as well as to Joshua, Gideon and Manoah. For that matter, every time God was said to have manifested himself to humans in a voice or otherwise tangible form, it was always through the second person of the Trinity.[61]

Though the two covenants had two federal heads, Adam and Christ, and one was a "dead" way but the other "living." "In strictness of speech" they were not two but one. For they shared the same mediator, the same salvation (which

---

[59] Gerald R. McDermott, *Jonathan Edwards Confronts the Gods: Christian Theology, Enlightenment Religion, and Non-Christian Faiths* (New York: Oxford University Press, 2000), 9-11, 26-28, 150-52.

[60] Jonathan Edwards, "Profitable Hearers of the Word," in *Sermons and Discourses, 1720–1723*, ed. Kenneth P. Minkema, vol. 14 of *The Works of Jonathan Edwards* (New Haven, CT: Yale University Press, 1997), 247.

[61] Edwards, *The "Miscellanies," a–500*, ed. Thomas A. Schafer, vol. 13 of *The Works of Jonathan Edwards* (New Haven, CT: Yale University Press, 1994), 221-22; idem, *The "Miscellanies," 1153–1360*, ed. Douglas A. Sweeney, vol. 23 of *The Works of Jonathan Edwards* (New Haven, CT: Yale University Press, 2004), 229-30; idem, *Writings on the Trinity, Grace, and Faith*, ed. Sang Hyun Lee, vol. 21 of *The Works of Jonathan Edwards* (New Haven, CT: Yale University Press, 2003), 372-73; 375-76; idem, *History of the Work of Redemption*, ed. John F. Wilson, vol. 9 of *The Works of Jonathan Edwards* (New Haven, CT: Yale University Press, 1989), 197, 131.

means the same calling, justification, adoption, sanctification and glory) and the same medium of salvation: the incarnation, suffering, righteousness and intercession of Christ. The Holy Spirit was the same person applying Christ's redemption in both dispensations, and the method of obtaining salvation was the same—faith and repentance. The external means (the word of God and ordinances such as prayer and praise, sabbath and sacraments) were not different. Nor were the benefits (God's Spirit by God's mere mercy and by a divine person—the angel of the Lord or Mediator) and future blessings. For both the condition was faith in the Son of God as Mediator, expressed with the same spirit of repentance and humility. This is why all parts of the Old Testament point to the future coming of Christ. In sum, the religion of the church of Israel is "essentially the same religion with that of the Christian church."[62]

Edwards also determined that the Jews would return to their homeland. This would happen, he reasoned, because the prophecies of land being given to them had been only partially fulfilled. In the mid-eighteenth century the majority of Jews were still living in the diaspora. It was also necessary for God to make them a "visible monument" of his grace and power at their return and then conversion. Canaan once again would be a spiritual center of the world. Although Israel would again be a distinct nation, Christians would have free access to Jerusalem because Jews would look on Christians as their brethren.[63]

According to Arthur Hertzberg, this American linkage of Jewish conversion to the millennium was why "American intellectual anti-Semitism never became as virulent as its counterparts in Europe."[64] Christians in Europe believed the end time was in the indefinite future. But in America the end seemed near because of the influence of Puritan theology and its foregrounding of Israel, and according to these Puritans the end would not come without major changes in the fortunes of the Jews. So in the colonies, the Jewish question moved "to center stage."[65]

---

[62]Edwards, *"Miscellanies," a-500*, 219; idem, *The "Miscellanies," 833-1152*, ed. Amy Plantinga Pauw, vol. 20 of *The Works of Jonathan Edwards* (New Haven, CT: Yale University Press, 2002), 117-18; idem, *"Miscellanies," 1153-1360*, 502-3; idem, *History of the Work of Redemption*, 283, 443.

[63]Blank Bible, Edwards Papers, Beinecke Rare Book and Manuscript Library, Yale University, 806; Edwards, *Apocalyptic Writings*, ed. Stephen J. Stein, vol. 5 of *The Works of Jonathan Edwards* (New Haven, CT: Yale University Press, 1977), 135.

[64]Hertzberg, "The New England Puritans and the Jews," in *Hebrew and the Bible in America: The First Two Centuries*, ed. Shalom Goldman (Hanover, NH: New England University Press, 1993), 116.

[65]Ibid. This question is not settled, however. As Avihu Zakai has recently pointed out, many English thinkers in the sixteenth and seventeenth centuries also taught an imminent millennium, and there is no clear indication that such belief reduced anti-Semitism. See Zakai, "The

So Edwards declined the invitation of the intellectual elites to minimize Christianity's debt to Judaism. If Christianity was the logical end of Judaism, its meaning could be found only through Judaism. The antitype was to be fully understood only by reference to its types. Hence, tension in the Jewish-Christian relationship was a family quarrel. Edwards may have exercised a certain hubris by claiming that his Jewish brethren were less favored by their common Father, and indeed had been disowned. But he believed they would someday be reconciled to their divine Parent, regain their ancient homeland, establish a polity there and regain their status as children in full favor.

After Edwards, Anglo-American theologians continued their fascination with eschatology and what they took to be the promise of Jewish return to the land. Even Sir Isaac Newton was persuaded: In his *Observations upon the Prophecies of Daniel and the Revelation of St. John* (1733) he wrote about the duty of Jews to return and rebuild Jerusalem.[66] The Anglican bishop Thomas Newton wrote a three-volume *Dissertations on the Prophecies* (1754–1758) that went through nine editions in forty years in which he twice discussed the restoration of Jews to the land. Postmillennialist Thomas Scott's *Commentary on the Bible*, which appeared between 1788 and 1792, did more than anything else to make belief in Jewish restoration to the land a staple of British evangelicalism in the nineteenth century. But just as Scott's commentary was being released, Cambridge University sponsored an essay contest on the subject: "The grounds contained in Scripture for expecting a future restoration of the Jews."[67]

In that same decade a Baptist minister, James Bicheno, published in London what was to be an influential and systematic treatment of prophetic themes, *The Signs of the Times*. Bicheno there argued that the restoration of Jews to Palestine must be imminent. For had not the Jews been given the "promised land" as their possession forever? Had not they received the Law, the revelation of God? And had not Paul insisted that in the end "all Israel will be saved" (Rom 11:26)? Bicheno was the first to assert that it was in Britain's interest to use its foreign policy to promote the restoration of Israel as a means of ushering in the millennium.[68]

Poetics of History and the Destiny of Israel: The Role of the Jews in English Apocalyptic Thought During the Sixteenth and Seventeenth Centuries," *JJTP* 5 (1996): 313-50; and Frank Felsenstein, *Anti-Semitic Stereotypes: A Paradigm of Otherness in English Popular Culture, 1660–1830* (Baltimore: Johns Hopkins University Press, 1995).

[66]Cited in Lewis, *Origins of Christian Zionism*, 34.
[67]Ibid., 35, 41, 44.
[68]Ibid., 43, 45.

Postmillennialist Christian Zionism in the Nineteenth Century

Bicheno was a postmillennialist, as Edwards had been. His work inspired a raft of postmillennial English thinkers after the turn of the nineteenth century, well before the rise of premillennialism there in the 1820s and 1830s. Other English leaders such as Charles Simeon and William Wilberforce were also inspired by biblical prophecy to promote missions to Jews, but they were influenced more by Calvinist theology with its emphasis on God's election of a chosen people and by the philosemitism of Lutheran Pietists in German-speaking lands. All of these saw the significance of Jews to eschatology, but without concern for or belief in premillennialism. In his *Origins of Christian Zionism*, Donald Lewis explains that it was a return to a closer and more literal reading of the Bible after the Reformation that gave all these Protestants a new interest in eschatology and the role of the Jews within it. And in England especially, it was a shared Calvinism "that resonated with the idea of the divine 'election' of the Jews," not premillennialism or postmillennialism, that fired the imagination of the hordes of prophetically minded English Protestants in the nineteenth century.[69] Evangelicals in nineteenth-century England saw philosemitism as their distinctive calling card, distinguishing them from Catholics, who they claimed had persecuted Jews in the long history of Christianity, and from the Anglo-Catholicism of the Tractarian movement started by John Henry Newman. Both Catholics and Tractarians were asserting that they had the best historical claims to Christian faith; evangelicals used their philosemitism to proclaim that their claims were even more ancient—going back to biblical Israel itself.[70]

The most famous and powerful English philosemite in the nineteenth century was Lord Ashley, the seventh earl of Shaftesbury (1801–1885), ennobled in 1851. He "became the leading proponent of Christian Zionism in the nineteenth century and was the first politician of stature to prepare the way for Jews to establish a homeland in Palestine."[71] His advocacy for a Jewish homeland was critical to the intellectual development behind the Balfour Declaration (1917).

What in particular inspired Shaftesbury? Lewis points to a number of influences: (1) Shaftesbury was a social reformer interested in the underdog, and he saw Jews as victims of historic Christian persecution. He shared a general British

---
[69]Ibid., 44, 66, 156, 68.
[70]Ibid., 102-3.
[71]Ibid., 107.

alarm at the persecution of Jews in the Damascus Blood Libel of 1840 and the mistreatment of Jews on the island of Rhodes as part of a general pattern in the declining Ottoman Empire.[72]

(2) He became an evangelical in the 1820s and most likely was influenced by Scott's postmillennialist *Bible Commentary*, which popularized the idea of a Jewish return to the land.[73]

(3) He was ashamed that England was the first Western nation to banish Jews, setting a terrible example to be repeated by France and Spain. Now England had the opportunity to be the first Gentile nation to cease to "tread down Jerusalem." This would lead not only to creating Jewish allies to the empire all over the world, but it would also bring down the blessing of God on the empire.[74] Shaftesbury was convinced by Henry Hart Milman's *History of the Jews* (1829) that Jews are at the center of the story of the rise and fall of European nations:

> We may trace, in the pages of history, the vestiges of this never-slumbering Providence. No sooner had England given shelter to the Jews, under Cromwell and Charles, than she started forward in a commercial career of unrivalled and uninterrupted prosperity; Holland, embracing the principles of the Reformation, threw off the yoke of Philip, opened her cities to the Hebrew people, and obtained an importance far beyond her natural advantages; while Spain, in her furious and bloody expulsion of the race, sealed her own condemnation. "How deep a wound," says Mr. Milman, "was inflicted on the national prosperity by this act of the 'most Christian Sovereign,' cannot easily be calculated, but it may be reckoned among the most effective causes of the decline of Spanish greatness."[75]

This was Shaftesbury's understanding of how God applied Genesis 12:3 to European history: "I will bless those who bless you, and him who dishonors you I will curse, and in you all the families of the earth shall be blessed"(ESV).

CHRISTIAN ZIONISM IN THE LAST TWO CENTURIES

We have seen that while many scholars have treated Christian Zionism as a recent phenomenon arising from dispensationalist premillennialism, in reality

---

[72]Ibid., 111, 158-59.
[73]Ibid., 114.
[74]Ibid., 167-70.
[75]Anthony Ashley-Cooper, known as Lord Ashley and later Lord Shaftesbury, "State and Prospects of the Jews," in Lewis, *Origins of Christian Zionism*, 169.

this approach to Israel was present from the creation of the church, and gained new momentum in the sixteenth through the eighteenth centuries *before* the rise of premillennial dispensationalism. It is also the case that important Christian Zionists of the last two centuries have developed their theologies completely apart from the dispensationalist movement. There are far too many to discuss in this short space, so I shall limit myself to six representative figures: William Hechler, Lev Gillet, Harry Truman, Basilea Schlink, Karl Barth and Gary Anderson.

Anglican priest William Hechler (1845–1931) was Theodor Herzl's "first . . . most constant and most indefatigable . . . follower."[76] It was Hechler who helped open doors for Herzl to Europe's palaces and corporate boardrooms, and Hechler who helped Herzl formulate his vision for a Jewish state. In the decade before his 1931 death Hechler repeatedly warned his Jewish friends of an impending massacre of Jews in Europe that would make the Crusades and Spanish Inquisition look like "child's play."[77] Hechler's warnings were dismissed by all who heard them.

Hechler learned Christian Zionism from his Anglican missionary father, whose Zionism—and that of his son—came from the same sources that influenced the postmillennialist Shaftesbury. Hechler's pamphlet "The Restoration of the Jews According to the Prophets" (1883) argued that "the duty of every Christian is to pray earnestly and to long for the restoration of God's chosen race, and to love the Jews; for they are still beloved for their fathers' sake." It stated explicitly that restoration to the land will take place before most Jews ever contemplate conversion to Christian faith.[78]

Lev Gillet (1893–1980) was a French Catholic convert to Orthodoxy who became a Russian Orthodox priest after spending three years with Russians during World War I as a prisoner of war. Trained in philosophy, he became a chaplain to an Anglican-Orthodox ecumenical fellowship in London from 1948 to his death in 1980. But toward the beginning of World War II, when he was a refugee from Nazi-occupied France, he wrote *Communion in the Messiah* (1941), in which he urged Christians to realize that Israel has a "special claim" on the

---

[76]Paul Charles Merkley, *The Politics of Christian Zionism 1891–1948* (London: Frank Cass, 1998), 25. Hechler was an Anglican clergyman who studied theology in London and Tübingen but "retained a distinctly creedal, doctrinal, even literalist theology." Merkley, *Politics of Christian Zionism*, 12.

[77]Ibid., 34.

[78]Goldman, *Zeal for Zion*, 102.

goodwill of all Christians. The people of Israel have a "privilege" and "priority" to the "birthright" since they are the "elder sons" in God's family. They are the *corpus mysticum* into which Gentile Christians are grafted. If Paul is right about this (Romans 11), then the earthly problems of Israel are "not outside" for us. We should make them our own. Hence, to help a Jew is to help Israel fulfill the "mysterious identity" to which it is called. Zionism is therefore a theological question that no Christian can ignore.[79]

What is this mysterious identity? Gillet said Israel was to be called to the "sufferings of the servant" in Isaiah and to somehow reveal the divine power through those sufferings. At the same time, it was to await and help embody the messianic era, which is specially realized in the land. So Zionism "is neither a part of, nor an addition to, Judaism, but its concentration and fullness." In fact, because of the "sacramental" quality of the land, it is only there that a Jew can "feel himself entirely Hebrew." For there is a sacred quality to the land. Martin Buber said the land "is the visible and efficacious sign of a spiritual reality." This, Gillet wrote, is true for Christians also. "For the Christian, the whole of Palestine is not only the shrine of Jesus' life, death and resurrection; it is also the land of the Presence, the meeting-place of Yahweh and Israel, and the Shekinah may still be felt there." Even secular Jews sense this: "A mystical feeling touches assimilated and denationalized Jews when they come to Eretz."[80]

These mystical and theological understandings of the land are at the heart of what Gillet called "spiritual Zionism." Its "motive force . . . is not the striving of the politician or economist, but the vision of Isaiah and Amos." This is what Buber meant in his striking formula, "One can only reach Zion if one has passed through Zionism." In other words, the true meaning of the land is spiritual, not political. This represents the "messianic mission" of Judaism and can be seen even in the secular kibbutzim, where the socialist ideal was put into practice. It was what animated the founding of Hebrew University, whose mission was to rely on knowledge, not arms. It was swallowed up by political Zionism at the first Zionist Congress of Basel in 1897, but not obliterated. Even when Gillet wrote in 1941, this spiritual Zionism persisted; it was the "warm religious current, like a hidden gulf-stream" that runs through "the stormy waters of Zionism."[81]

---

[79]Lev Gillet, *Communion in the Messiah: Studies in the Relationship Between Judaism and Christianity* (Eugene, OR: Wipf & Stock, 1999), 158, 161.
[80]Ibid., 160, 161-62, 167.
[81]Ibid., 164-66.

Therefore, Gillet concluded, Christians should hope for the future glory of a spiritual Zion, "to be revealed when the mysterious design of God shall have raised up the tribes of Jacob and restored the preserved Israel." They should pray for "a fully Messianic Jerusalem which would become a light of salvation unto the ends of the earth."[82] If anything, Gillet became even more of a Christian Zionist after the establishment of the state of Israel in 1948. The restoration had come, and spiritual Zionism was once again competing openly with political Zionism.

President Harry Truman, an active Baptist who became a Zionist from his own reading of the Bible, defied the State Department and nearly all his advisers, both when he supported the American-led United Nations resolution to recognize the state of Israel in 1948 and when he declared American recognition of the fledgling state. When he was introduced at the Jewish Theological Seminary as "the man who helped create the state of Israel," Truman protested, "What do you mean 'helped to create'?! I am Cyrus! I am Cyrus!"[83]

Truman "never expressed his acceptance of premillennialism. It is even doubtful that he ever adequately understood it."[84] According to presidential attorney and friend Clark Clifford, Truman's

> own reading of ancient history and the Bible made him a supporter of the idea of a Jewish homeland in Palestine, even when others who were sympathetic to the plight of the Jews were talking of sending them to places like Brazil. He did not need to be convinced by Zionists.... All in all, he believed that the surviving Jews deserved some place that was historically their own. I remember him talking once about the problem of repatriating displaced persons. "Everyone else who's been dragged away from his country has someplace to get back to," he said. "But the Jews have no place to go."[85]

Mother Basilea Schlink (1904–2001) was the Lutheran founder of the Evangelical Sisterhood of Mary in Darmstadt, Germany, which was the first Protestant

---

[82] Ibid., 171.
[83] Paul Charles Merkley, *The Politics of Christian Zionism 1891-1948* (London: Frank Cass, 1998), 166, 191. Cyrus was the Persian king who defeated the Babylonians in 539 BC and then allowed the exiled Judeans to return home and restore the temple in Jerusalem (Ezra 1:1; 2 Chron 36:23). Second Isaiah refers to him as a divinely designated agent for the liberation of Israel.

In contrast to Truman's vigorous support, President Roosevelt had only "platonic love" or "uninvolved benignancy" for Zionism and "seemed to do nothing of substance for" Jews and the Zionist cause (Emanuel Neumann). Merkley, *Politics of Christian Zionism*, 154.

[84] James A. Saddington, "Prophecy and Politics: A History of Christian Zionism in the Anglo-American Experience, 1800–1948" (PhD diss., Bowling Green State University, 1996), 364.
[85] Ibid., 372-73.

women's cloister in Germany since the Reformation. Some of Schlink's teachers had been influenced by dispensationalism, but Schlink showed her differences with that school in a number of ways. She never made it clear, for example, that she expected Jews to become Christians explicitly, and in her treatise on the chosen nature of the Jewish people "she took great lengths to avoid speaking of Christ as such."[86] Second, she rejected all negative stereotypes of Jews and blamed Christian nations for causing the stereotypes to exist: "We were the ones who forced the Jews to become usurers and junk dealers and locked them into Ghettoes like tombs.... We, the 'Christian people,' were the ones who thus deprived the Jews of their rights."[87] Jews, she said, demonstrated admirable traits: "respectability, nobility of character, professional competence, holiness, uniqueness, and persistence."[88] She also suggested that Jewish suffering had atoned for whatever guilt Jews might have, and in her interpretation of Isaiah 53 asserted that "the Jews collectively embodied the sufferings of Christ."[89] Rather than being "Christ-killers," Jews actually had the blood of Christ on them—yet the blood of redemption rather than the blood of guilt.[90]

The establishment of the state of Israel, wrote Schlink, was one of the greatest miracles of human history, and Jewish persistence as a people throughout history despite horrendous persecution was a "tangible sign of God's presence."[91] Both Jewish persistence and the state of Israel exist because God always keeps his promises. This was the theological axiom that underwrote Schlink's Christian Zionism: God's covenant to the Jews was still valid, and the state of Israel illustrates his faithfulness to those covenant promises.[92]

Some might be surprised to learn that Karl Barth (1886–1968) held to these same two convictions, and so can be called a Christian Zionist. In a provocative study of nationhood and providence in modern Protestant theology, Carys Moseley argues that Barth is the only major modern theologian who "distinguishes properly between nationhood and statehood." In other words, Barth

---

[86] George Faithful, "Trust, Repentance, and Apocalyptic Zionism: Basilea Schlink and the Evangelical Sisterhood of Mary Respond to War," *Magistra: A Journal of Women's Spirituality in History* 17, no. 2 (2011): 28.

[87] George Faithful, "Inverting the Eagle to Embrace the Star of David: The Nationalist Roots of German Christian Zionism," in *Comprehending Christian Zionism: Perspectives in Comparison*, ed. Göran Gunner and Robert O. Smith (Minneapolis: Fortress, 2014), 279-80.

[88] Ibid., 282.

[89] Ibid., 284.

[90] Ibid., 283.

[91] Ibid.

[92] Faithful, "Trust, Repentance, and Apocalyptic Zionism," 29.

"allows for the possibility that the God of the Bible, the God of Israel and the nations, recognizes both nation-states *and* stateless nations as entities in which he has, with the witting or unwitting cooperation of human beings, placed human beings to live in order to seek him (Acts 17, recapitulating Genesis 10)."[93] It was precisely because Barth recognized the theological significance of nationhood that he could "support early Zionism."[94]

Although Barth rejected nearly every distinctive teaching of dispensationalism, he was deeply indebted to the German Pietist preacher Johann Christoph Blumhardt and his son Christoph Friedrich Blumhardt. The family believed in the millenarian eschatology of Johann Albrecht Bengel, a major biblical exegete of the nineteenth century. Barth repudiated the notion that the end of days was yet to come, insisting that it started with the coming of Jesus in the first century. He also refused the interpretation of biblical prophecies as straightforward predictions in a literalistic sense, such as the idea that a literal great tribulation was to be expected, or a military battle between particular nations and Israel.[95]

But at the same time Barth thought that these eschatological errors were "errors in the right direction."[96] He respected millenarian attempts to take seriously God's sovereignty over world events, including the appearance of Israel as a nation-state in 1948. This was a "secular parable," as was the rise of socialism in modern history. The sudden reappearance of Israel was a type of resurrection and the kingdom of God. It was a "little light" that bore witness to the Light of the World in Jesus Christ. The modern history of Israel "even now hurries relentlessly" toward the future of God's redemptive purposes. According to Barth, biblical revelation points to a threefold parousia of Jesus—the incarnation, Pentecost and Christ's eschatological coming in Israel and the church. This last coming is the meaning of a long string of Old Testament prophecies that speak of the return of Jews to the land, a time when Gentiles shall come to Israel to learn the Torah.[97]

---

[93]Carys Moseley, *Nationhood, Providence, and Witness: Israel in Protestant Theology and Social Theory* (Eugene, OR: Cascade, 2013), xx.
[94]Ibid., 235.
[95]Ibid., 229-31.
[96]Ibid., 234.
[97]Ibid., xxxii, 221-22. On Barth's notion of "secular parable," see *Church Dogmatics* 4.3.1, trans. G. W. Bromiley (1961, repr., Peabody, MA: Hendrickson, 2010), 126-31; on Israel as a "little light" Moseley cites *CD* 4.3.1, pp. 55-58; for "even now hurries relentlessly," ibid., 59; for the long string of Old Testament prophecies, she cites ibid., 58-59.

So Barth, according to Moseley, "was reluctant to dismiss nationalistic overtones in the prophets" and warned against our dismissal of the historical sense of those texts.[98] They refer to the history of the Jews "right up to our own day." Barth wrote that "the glory of the history of Israel in its totality [is] . . . an *unbroken* sequence of *new* events of divine faithfulness."[99] Ezekiel's prophecy of the dry bones coming to life was a picture of the restoration of Jews to the land. Other prophets point to a "final outpouring of the Holy Spirit" within history, which Barth took to be "a day of forgiveness." This is part of what would be a final crisis in history—not a military showdown with guns but "a kind of 'revival' or mass conversion."[100] Israel would be involved in a global spiritual renewal at the end of history, and in the meantime God's promise to Abraham that in him all the earth would be blessed meant that "*any* national regime set up in deliberate opposition to the existence of Israel as a nation will not fare very well in the long run."[101]

Gary A. Anderson is a distinguished Old Testament scholar who teaches at the University of Notre Dame. He is a Catholic and a Christian Zionist. His argument for this position starts with "the biblical claim that the land of Canaan was given by God to the people Israel."[102] The gift of the land was intended not just for Israel but ultimately for creation as a whole—"to rectify the created order that [had] spun so badly out of control" in the "growing rebellion of the human community" depicted in Genesis 1–11.

The promise "is both irrevocable and unfulfilled." It is irrevocable because it is a promise made by God. As Paul says, even Israel's apostasy cannot erase the promises: "Let God be true, and every human being a liar" (Rom 3:4 NIV).

But at the same time, says Anderson, the promise is unfulfilled. At the end of the Tanak, there is still the exhortation, "Whoever is among you of all his people, . . . let him go up [to Jerusalem]!" (2 Chron 36:23). Besides, the land vomits out whoever is not worthy of it (Lev 18:24-30). "Israel's right to the land, though the result of a divine grant, is not without its restrictions." Only in the messianic age, according to the Tanak, will Israel's settlement in the land be secure.

---

[98]Moseley, *Nationhood, Providence, and Witness*, 222-23.
[99]She cites this quote from *CD* 4.3.1, p. 53; I added the emphasis.
[100]Moseley, *Nationhood, Providence, and Witness*, 231. For "right up to our own day," she cites *CD* 4.1, p. 175.
[101]Moseley, *Nationhood, Providence, and Witness*, 226 (her emphasis).
[102]The following paragraph is based on Anderson's article in *First Things*. Gary Anderson, "How to Think About Zionism," *First Things* (April 2005), www.firstthings.com/article/2005/04/how-to-think-about-zionism.

Anderson reminds his readers that some rabbis in the Talmud and later (even in the late nineteenth and early twentieth centuries when political Zionism arose) opposed a new Zion on the land. They said it would be repeating the sin of the spies in Numbers 13 when they tried to take the land prematurely, and neglecting to heed Jeremiah's advice to "seek the welfare of the city to which [God] had exiled" his people (Jer 29:7). But Anderson points out that this was not the consensus of all the rabbis. The thirteenth-century Meir of Rothenberg, for example, made his own plans to settle in the land despite these theological reservations.

Anderson concludes that we should avoid "a false messianism" by remembering that the land is always "given conditionally." Yet we should also remind ourselves that "the miraculous appearance of the Israeli state just after the darkest moment in Jewish history is hard to interpret outside of a theological framework."

Conclusion

Let us recapitulate what we have seen. It has been something of a consensus in the academy that Christian Zionism is recent and dispensationalist. According to this consensus, it originated as late as the nineteenth century and derives from what most academics think is presumptuous exegesis and zany theology, wedded to a conservative political agenda. This chapter has tried to show that Christian Zionism is far older and is derived from theological roots that are radically different from premillennial dispensationalism.

My argument started with the observation that land is central to the fundamental Old Testament motif of covenant. It proceeded to the more recent realization that Christian Zionism is an underlying New Testament assumption that breaks out on the surface far more than has been recognized by most scholars. This is probably why it shows up in the first three centuries of Christianity, so that one third-century Egyptian bishop could say that belief in the restoration of Israel was widespread and had been so for a long time.

Then we saw that after Augustinian amillennialism dominated the medieval period (with the exception of a few medieval thinkers who looked to a restoration of Israel), the return to the plain sense of the Bible in the Reformation period helped restore belief in a literal millennium to come and a return of Jews to the land before or during that time. This was particularly true in England, and especially in the Puritan movement. So from the sixteenth to the early nineteenth centuries Christian Zionism flourished, most notably among Calvinists. Most of these Zionists were postmillennialists of one sort or another, and all of this was before the rise of premillennial dispensationalism.

Finally we saw that important and influential Christian Zionist thinkers in the last two centuries have formed and maintained their positions without any influence from dispensationalism.

It is time, then, to revise our view of the nature and sources of Christian Zionism.

- PART TWO -

THEOLOGY AND THE BIBLE

3

BIBLICAL HERMENEUTICS

How Are We to Interpret the Relation Between the Tanak and the New Testament on This Question?

Craig Blaising

◆

Common among various forms of Christian Zionism are two points: (1) there is an ethnic, national, territorial Israel in the consummate plan of God, and (2) what we are witnessing today in the nation of Israel is a preconsummate work of God in continuity with the divine plan for Israel and the nations.

In this chapter, I want to address the question of how these claims are based on a reading of the Tanak (the Old Testament) and the New Testament, specifically what hermeneutical or interpretive issues are involved in reading them in this way.

There are, of course, a number of methodological and theoretical issues that belong to the field of hermeneutics. For the most part, these are treated in standard textbooks.[1] It is not necessary to review them here. In light of the challenges of postmodernism, it would be best to note that this essay will affirm the integrity of the author-text-reader relationship. While avoiding the naiveté of purely objective interpretation, this essay assumes both the possibility and desirability of a reasonably demonstrative, objective, truthful interpretation of the meaning of a text, and in this case, the meaning of the text(s) of the Tanak and the New Testament. This is, in fact, a discussion about proper interpretation

---

[1]See for example William W. Klein, Craig L. Blomberg and Robert L. Hubbard Jr., *Introduction to Biblical Interpretation* (Dallas: Word, 1993); Walter C. Kaiser Jr. and Moisés Silva, *An Introduction to Biblical Hermeneutics: The Search for Meaning* (Grand Rapids: Zondervan, 1994); and Grant R. Osborne, *The Hermeneutical Spiral: A Comprehensive Introduction to Biblical Interpretation* (Downers Grove, IL: InterVarsity Press, 1991).

with those who believe proper interpretation is possible and achievable, who believe it is both possible and necessary to speak objectively of the story of the Bible, its narrative plot, its themes, its claims and its theology. The problem it sees with the alternative viewpoint is not that it is "their" view as opposed to "ours" or that it involves an illegitimate exercise of power, or any such thing. Rather the claim is that the view being presented here is a right reading of the text and that the alternative view is wrong.

There Is an Ethnic, National, Territorial Israel in the Consummate Plan of God

Of course, there are those who, while admitting that the Tanak predicts an ethnic, national, territorial Israel in the consummate plan of God, would nevertheless argue that the New Testament does not do so. They believe that the New Testament presents a different consummation. There are differences in exactly how this different consummation is to be understood, but there is general agreement on this point: it does not include Israel defined as a particular nation in a particular territory on earth. Rather, the New Testament predicts a new redeemed people in the consummation—the church—who are drawn from all nations and ethnicities and are transformed into a kind of new uni-(non- or trans-)ethnic, uni-(non- or trans-)national human reality so as to effectively eliminate ethnic and national particularity from human existence. Furthermore, such people are to be consummately situated in a heavenly location, not an earthly territorial location such as that envisioned in the Tanak for Israel and the nations. To the extent that those who view the New Testament in this way wish to, or are obliged to, read the Tanak and the New Testament together as a single narrative, they must harmonize what appears to them as conflicting interpretations of the two canons. The usual choice of harmonization is to see the Israel of the Tanak *redefined, spiritualized or transcendentalized as*, or sometimes *simply replaced as*, the church of the New Testament. A shift in the plot line of the story begun in the Tanak is required in this view in order to graft the New Testament onto it as a continuance of its story. However, this involves not just a change in the identity of a character of the story (as if a character introduced early in a narrative turns out to be someone other than what or who he had been thought to be) but a change in the entire narrative—the story itself—since the character at issue in the earlier story is *essentially embedded in the narrative*.[2]

---

[2]It is not just Israel that is transcendentalized in this view, but the entire narrative setting and worldview—the whole material, political reality of the narrative—is oriented toward a nonmate-

The view advocated in this article is that the New Testament is best read as the continuance and advancement of the plan and purpose of God presented in the Tanak *for Israel and the nations, Jews and Gentiles*. The New Testament affirms the expectation of the Tanak of an ethnic, national, territorial Israel in the consummation of the divine plan—a plan that includes both Israel and the nations as well as the individual human beings who populate them. The distinctive ethnic, national and territorial identity of Israel specified in the Tanak is not just a temporary feature of the story but is affirmed in the narrative consummation presented by the New Testament. Yet the New Testament reveals more clearly than the Tanak just how that plan is actually achieved. A key problem of the narrative plot within the Tanak is the conflict of sin on both the personal and corporate levels threatening human well-being and even the earth itself. This is the conflict that threatens the ethnic, national and territorial identity of Israel, and it is a conflict that continues in the New Testament. Although the Tanak speaks of an eventual resolution, the manner and means of resolution are revealed only in the New Testament continuance of the story line. What the New Testament reveals is the identity and work of the Messiah, predicted in the Tanak, who will overcome the conflict(s) in all its forms and bring the plan to consummation.

What are the hermeneutical principles by which this latter view would be commended over the former? It is important to recognize that these two views are not simply different interpretations of a basic unit of text such as would normally be the focus of most textbook discussions of hermeneutics (that is, the historical, lexical, grammatical, syntactical and literary interpretation of a set of words arranged in a basic meaning pattern). Rather, these are different ways of construing the entire canonical narrative—the plot line running through all of Scripture. Such a construal is itself a hermeneutical act. It is, as Charles Wood has stated, "a basic

---

rial, nonpolitical, transnational consummation. Recent works emphasizing the material continuity of the new creation modify this view somewhat. See for example the works of N. T. Wright, *Surprised by Hope: Rethinking Heaven, the Resurrection, and the Mission of the Church* (New York: HarperOne, 2008); and Greg Beale, *A New Testament Biblical Theology: The Unfolding of the Old Testament in the New* (Grand Rapids: Baker Books, 2011). However, there is an inconsistency in such works in their adoption of the view of W. D. Davies that the land promised to Israel is "Christified" in the New Testament. W. D. Davies, *The Gospel and the Land: Early Christianity and Jewish Territorial Doctrine* (Berkeley: University of California Press, 1974), 213. A mysticism characterizes Beale's identification of the new earth with the heavenly city and the person of Christ. As a result, even though a "new creation" is affirmed, it appears to be not much different from the "heavenly" conception against which he protests.

decision" necessary for "the canonical use of the Bible."[3] It entails a grasp of the whole canonical story line, "the chronological sweep of the whole, from creation to new creation, including the various events and developments of what has sometimes been called 'salvation history.'"[4] That grasp of the plot line then functions, in R. Kendall Soulen's words, as "an interpretive instrument that provides a framework for reading the Christian Bible as a theological and narrative unity."[5]

What must be evaluated hermeneutically is the proposed construal of the canonical narrative and its function in the interpretation of the canon of Scripture. David Wolfe, drawing on the work of Willard Van Orman Quine, has suggested four criteria for evaluating broad interpretive systems: comprehensiveness, congruency, consistency and coherence.[6] Applied to our concern, we may say that to the extent that one's reading of the canonical narrative meets these criteria, it strongly merits our consideration. To the extent that it fails these criteria, it is weak, requiring reformulation or abandonment in favor of a better reading. Two of the criteria, comprehensiveness and congruency, have to do with the way the proposed reading relates directly to the canonical text, how comprehensive it is to the totality of biblical textual material, and how congruent it is—that is, how well it "fits" hermeneutically with the individual texts that compose the canon. The other two criteria have to do with the feasibility or plausibility of the proposed reading: its interpretations should be consistent, not in conflict with one another, and coherent overall, which is to say that the proposed reading should make sense.

Typically, a proposed way of construing a narrative plot will be developed from a set of textual clues. These clues, interpretations of key textual elements, must be validated hermeneutically according to normal hermeneutical methods, and a rationale must be given for their importance as directional indicators of the overall narrative plot. The construal then acquires legitimacy through its perceived explanatory power and by its continued use. However, it may be challenged by other proposed readings. The success of one construal over the other will have to do with its ability to account for all of the details and elements of the text, as well as the variety of canonical texts and themes, in a comprehensive, congruent,

---

[3]Charles M. Wood, *The Formation of Christian Understanding: Theological Hermeneutics* (Valley Forge, PA: Trinity Press International, 1993), 109.
[4]Ibid., 100.
[5]R. Kendall Soulen, *The God of Israel and Christian Theology* (Minneapolis: Fortress, 1996), 13.
[6]David L. Wolfe, *Epistemology: The Justification of Belief*, Contours of Christian Philosophy (Downers Grove, IL: InterVarsity Press, 1982), 50-55.

consistent and coherent manner. Factors that would generally account for the rejection or replacement of a particular way of reading Scripture would be (1) perceived key or crucial textual inadequacy. In other words, the construal of the narrative was developed from an inadequate set of textual clues, which means it did not take into account textual clues that are demonstratively crucial to understanding the plan and purpose of God (by either ignoring or mishandling those texts). Another factor would be (2) failure with respect to the handling of its own proposed set of textual clues, which is to say that it is suspected of having misinterpreted the set of texts at the heart of its construal or misjudging its significance and bearing on the plot line. (3) Widespread inadequacy or inapplicability of a proposed reading, either by its failure to cover large portions of the narrative or give an explanation that actually fits those texts, would also be grounds for its reassessment. Finally, (4) incoherence or inconsistency in the interpretive results would also warrant its reformulation or replacement.

Let's examine a typical set of alleged textual clues offered in various publications today as justification for a supersessionist construal of the biblical narrative.[7] It is alleged that these clues indicate that the New Testament teaches a shift from the narrative plot line of the Tanak to a redefined, transcendentalized or spiritualized "Israel" in the New Testament. Consequently, the New Testament teaches, according to this view, that there is no ethnic, national, territorial Israel in the consummate plan of God. The ethnic, national, territorial Israel envisioned in the Tanak has been replaced by "a new Israel" which is multi-(trans- or non-)ethnic, multi-(trans- or non-)national, and multi-(trans- or non-)territorial, a "new Israel," which this view would identify as the church. In the typical presentation, four key lines of New Testament textual material are cited: the "fulfillment" declarations of Matthew, the "spiritual language" of John, typology in Hebrews and Paul's universalism.[8]

---

[7]Though it is becoming fashionable today for some to deny the label *supersessionism* while nevertheless reading the New Testament as redefining Israel, the term is used here in its widest sense of any reading of Scripture that argues for such redefinition. Soulen's analysis of supersessionism is still applicable today, perhaps more so since it exposes the different levels of supersessionist thinking, especially that which is not conscious of it. See Soulen, *God of Israel and Christian Theology*, 1-21.

[8]See for example, Gary M. Burge, *Whose Land? Whose Promise? What Christians Are Not Being Told About Israel and the Palestinians* (Boston: Pilgrim Press, 2013), 171-89; Peter W. L. Walker, "The Land in the Apostle's Writings" and "The Land and Jesus Himself," in *The Land of Promise: Biblical, Theological, and Contemporary Perspectives*, ed. Philip Johnston and Peter Walker (Downers Grove, IL: InterVarsity Press, 2000), 81-120. These collections are essentially dependent on the textual arguments advanced by Davies, *Gospel and the Land*.

The replacement/redefinition construal of the New Testament canonical narrative.

Fulfillment citations in Matthew. Matthew's "fulfillment" citations are unique to his Gospel and have been the object of much study. Clearly, Matthew sees a type correspondence between the history of the Christ and that of Israel in the Tanak. This certainly emphasizes the special work of God in the person, activity and experience of the Christ in such a way as should be familiar and recognizable to Israel. This underscores his importance for the nation in the outworking of the divine plan. But the claim that Matthew is thereby teaching that Israel's identity as an ethnic, national, territorial reality is ending as such and being replaced by the singular person of the Christ and/or a new mixed corporate body to be created by him reads too much into the text. It belongs to an anti-Semitic, anti-Judaic interpretation of Matthew that is generally rejected today. As Donald Hagner notes, "None of the Jewish Christians of the NT would have thought of Christianity as anti-Judaism. To believe in the gospel of the kingdom and Jesus as the messianic king was for them to enter into the beginning of the fulfillment of the Jewish hope (cf. Acts 28:20), to be true Jews, and to form the remnant of the true Israel."[9]

It is for this purpose that Matthew presents Jesus as the one who will "save his people from their sins" (Mt 1:21), who took the message of the kingdom to "the lost sheep of the house of Israel" (Mt 10:5-6; 15:24), who mourned over Jerusalem's impending desolation until that day when she will welcome him (Mt 23:37-39), who declares after his resurrection that he has been given authority over all nations (Mt 28:18) and who prophesies that he will rule them from his throne on earth after his return (Mt 25:31-36). All of this is in keeping with the narrative line of promise and future fulfillment in the Tanak. It is a mishandling of Matthew to claim that the "fulfillment citations" insinuate a radical shift in Matthew's extension of the canonical plot line.

The spiritual language of the Fourth Gospel. The Fourth Gospel is cited as evidence that Jesus intentionally redirected the narrative line away from earthly, particularly Israelitish, realities to the reality of his own person and the giving of the Holy Spirit. For example, he spoke of his body as the temple (Jn 2:19-21), of birth into the kingdom as reception of the Holy Spirit (Jn 3:3-8), of the Spirit and eternal life as water (Jn 4:13-14; 7:37-39), of worship in Spirit and truth as

---

[9]Donald A. Hagner, *Matthew 1–13*, Word Biblical Commentary 33a (Dallas: Word, 1993), lxxii.

opposed to worship in a specific place (Jn 4:21-24), of his own body and blood as food like manna (Jn 6:30-65) and of words, which he said were "spirit and life" (Jn 6:63). He portrayed himself as the true vine (Jn 15:1-17), exploiting an image for Israel in the prophets (see Is 5:1-7), and his kingdom, he told Pilate, is not of this world (Jn 18:36). All of this is supposed to support a reality shift in fulfillment of OT promise and hope.

What is clear in John's Gospel is the focus on the person and work of Jesus and the gift of the promised Holy Spirit. While much of the language is distinctive in accordance with John's unique account of the words of Jesus, the content fits with New Testament teaching elsewhere. What is new in the canonical story line is the extended revelation that the Gospels give of the person of the Christ and the salvation from sin that comes through him. This is not contrary to messianic expectation in the Tanak but is in continuity with and complementary to what was predicted by the prophets.

Jesus' teaching on the gift of the Holy Spirit in the Fourth Gospel connects to predictions by the prophets of the eschatological, new-covenant ministry of the Spirit. In his conversation with Nicodemus, Jesus noted that a teacher of Israel should have understood his teaching on birth by the Spirit as requisite for entrance into the kingdom (Jn 3:5). Jesus' metaphors of water and spirit provide a link to Ezekiel 36–37, a kingdom-fulfillment text positioning a resurrected and Spirit-indwelt Israel in the midst of the nations.

Metaphors and images from Israel's experience are used to present Jesus' message. But nowhere in John's Gospel is Israel ever said to be redefined. Rather than seeing Jesus' use of the vine imagery in John 15 as somehow transcendentalizing Israel, it would be better to see it as indicating how the prophecy that spoke of Israel eschatologically bearing fruit pleasing to God would be fulfilled. It has to be fulfilled through the Christ, in whom Israel and the nations would be blessed, the one who has now been revealed to be the dispenser of the Spirit. John presents Jesus as revealing what must take place soteriologically in order for the kingdom promises to be fulfilled. They indicate that the kingdom does not arise out from the world, as Jesus testified to Pilate. The kingdom comes from above—just as was revealed to Daniel, as recorded in the Tanak.

Typology in Hebrews. The book of Hebrews refers to the Lord's instruction to Moses in Exodus 25:40 to build the tabernacle according to a "type" that was revealed to him. The writer portrays the tabernacle itself (and, by extension, the temple) and the service performed there as "a sketch and shadow of the heavenly one" (Heb 8:5; cf. 9:24). He speaks of Christ's atonement and ascension into heaven in fulfillment of a different order of priestly ministry, one that is coordinate with a change from the old covenant to the new. The writer speaks of the soon removal of "created things" (Heb 12:27; cf. 9:11) in contrast to the permanence of the heavenly city. Even Abraham is said to have been looking for this heavenly city when he went to the land of promise.

These statements in Hebrews are often cited as evidence that the biblical story line has been shifted from an earthly to a heavenly fulfillment. The earthly particulars of the hopes of Israel, including its territorial location and national identity, are to be read typologically of heavenly realities. However, recent studies on Hebrews have pulled back from Platonic interpretations of its teaching.[10] Its vertical reference to Christ's position and ministry in heaven and to the heavenly city need to be understood within a futurist eschatology. He is speaking of a "world order to come" (Heb 2:5). The city which is in heaven now is also "the city which is to come" (Heb 13:14, my translations). Consequently, Abraham's search for a heavenly city is to be understood as his seeking not a heavenly *land* as opposed to an earthly one, but a *city* that will come from heaven to the land of promise.[11] The coming of the city from heaven—to earth— will replace the current order on earth (an order "made with hands") with one created by God. While new revelation is given about the Christ, his ministry in heaven and the heavenly Jerusalem, the future expectation of Hebrews is not inconsistent with the story line from the Tanak regarding a kingdom that God would establish upon the earth.

It is not the substance of promise that is characterized in Hebrews as type and shadow. It is the tabernacle and its associated ritual that are so designated. On the other hand, literal fulfillment of divine promise is absolutely critical for the writer as can be seen in his frequent appeal to Psalm 110:1, 4. Christ, the Lord, is seated at the right hand of the Lord God, his Father, in heaven and has been

---

[10] See for example the work of L. D. Hurst, "Eschatology and 'Platonism' in the Epistle to the Hebrews," SBLSP 23 (1984): 41-74; idem, "How 'Platonic' Are Heb. viii.5 and ix.23f?," *JTS* 34 (1983): 156-68; and idem, *The Epistle to the Hebrews: Its Background of Thought* (Cambridge: Cambridge University Press, 1990).

[11] Whereas *patris* might refer to "hometown" or "homeland," its use in Hebrews 11:14 is better understood contextually in relation to the "city" Abraham was looking for in Hebrews 11:10. Since this is the city "that is to come" (Heb 13:14), it is better to interpret Abraham's sojourn as anticipating the establishment in that land of that permanent city. That would certainly establish his hope for an everlasting inheritance "in the land he had been promised" (Heb 11:9), a promise which is characterized as "sure" (Heb 6:17-18) since the one who made the promise is faithful (11:11).

appointed by God a priest forever on the order of Melchizedek in accordance with divine oath! In the same way, he designates the promises made to Abraham and sworn to him by divine oath (which promises pertain to ethnic, national, territorial Israel and also to all Gentile nations) as *unchangeable, sure* and *steadfast*. This is what must be kept in mind as well when we read in Hebrews 11 that Abraham went to live *in the land of promise*; that Abraham, Isaac and Jacob were *heirs of the same promise*; and that they died "not having received the things promised, but *having seen them and greeted them from afar*" (Heb 11:9, 13 ESV). They saw them in the "world order to come" (Heb 2:5, my translation) in which a "city to come" (Heb 13:14) is established forever. Surely, in this way, the land promised in the Tanak is secured as an everlasting possession! While Hebrews, along with the rest of the New Testament, adds to the biblical story line the remarkable ministry and heavenly session of the Christ, it is clearly advancing the story line of the Tanak, not spiritualizing its substance or shifting the metaphysical reality of its components. With respect to our concern, it is entirely compatible with the expectation in the Tanak of a future unshakable kingdom (Heb 12:28) in which Israel's particular promises are secured forever.

Paul's universalism. Paul's universalism is also said to support the idea of a reality shift in plot fulfillment. It is alleged that Romans 4:13 reveals a universalization of the Abrahamic promise when Paul restates the promise to "Abraham and his offspring" in this way: "that he would be heir of the world" (NIV). It is assumed that this indicates that the "world" has replaced Israel in the consummation of the covenant promise. And this is thought to be consistent with the teaching in Ephesians 2:11–3:17 of the one new humanity composed of Jews and Gentiles who together are being built to be a temple for the dwelling of God. It is also thought to be the meaning of the teaching in Galatians 3:28 that there is neither Jew nor Greek in Christ, in whom all (Jew and Greek) are "Abraham's offspring, heirs according to promise."

There is more here than can be addressed in this brief essay. However, it is enough to point out here that there are several mistakes in this reading of the canonical narrative. It fails to consider the universal dimension of the Abrahamic promise already present in the Tanak from the Torah to the Prophets that is never in conflict with God's particular promises to Israel. It typically fails to note how the promise to "bless all nations in you" is developed in Genesis as a universal hegemonic rule, a rule that is then given specifically to the house of David in Psalm 2, characterized as a worldwide "inheritance." Nowhere in the

Tanak is this "inheritance of the world" ever thought to replace or redefine Israel! Why would one think that Paul is implying this in Romans 4?

Clearly a major revelation in the New Testament addition to the biblical story line is the giving of the Holy Spirit to the Gentiles who believe in Christ. There is no distinction between Jew and Gentile in this gift of the Spirit by which (1) direct access to Christ and his benefits is secured, (2) God indwells and sanctifies the recipient and (3) communion with other recipients of the Spirit, whether Jew or Gentile, is formed. When the church met to consider the matter theologically in Acts 15, it was determined that Gentiles did not need to convert to Judaism. They would remain Gentiles while Jews remained Jews. But the gift of the Spirit and the soteriological blessings that gift brings were seen to be given to both. This reveals how the kingdom predicted in the Tanak would actually be everlastingly stable. It would be such because the people of Israel and the peoples of the Gentiles would be equally indwelt by God! This is undoubtedly why Paul speaks of Jew and Gentile in Christ as a new *anthropos* indwelt by God! However, as will be seen below, it goes beyond Paul's thought to assume that such unity in Christ obliterates ethnic and national identity. It certainly did not do so at the Jerusalem Council, which saw Gentiles in Christ as Gentiles and Jews in Christ as Jews! Clearly, Paul did not mean by "neither male nor female" (Gal 3:28 NASB) that sexual identity was obliterated by conversion. The point is that such difference makes no difference in the gift and reception of the Spirit. There is nothing here to indicate that Israel as an ethnic, national reality has been removed or redefined by the extension of the gift of the Spirit to Gentiles.[12]

Clearly, there are problems with the claims made about these texts. From what has already been said, three primary conceptual failures of the replacement or redefinition construal can be identified.

First is a failure to appreciate the continuity in the Tanak and the New Testament of a new creation eschatology that features the renewal of creation, not its annihilation in favor of a transcendental realm. Appreciation of the theme of

---

[12] See the following paragraphs and the next note. The crucial issue here is grasping the point in the canonical narrative that redemption extends to corporate, ethnic identities. Along with this, one needs to note how the church fits into the canonical narrative. Rather than seeing the church as an identity alongside or in replacement of Israel (as in traditional dispensational or supersessionist theologies, respectively), it is better to see it as the Spirit-formed union of all believers in and with Christ regardless of ethnic or national identity. This union pervades the new creation order in which ethnic and national identities are affirmed and renewed. It is what makes the multinational kingdom order everlastingly stable.

creation's renewal is important for grasping the everlasting *territorial* aspect of Israel's identity. The covenant promises of an everlasting inheritance in the land early in the canonical narrative cohere with the later revelation in the Tanak that God will make all things new—renewing the heavens and the earth, as well as Jerusalem on the earth.

Second is a failure to appreciate the corporate dimensions of biblical anthropology—the tribal, ethnic, national and political features of human life—as positive features of creation, ones that will also be redeemed. Instead, many readers try to force the biblical narrative into a presupposed consummate single collective of individuals stripped of their real ethnic or national identities. The fact that these aspects of human reality are said to be redeemed in the canonical narrative allows one to appreciate in turn the constantly repeated theme of the redemption of corporate ethnic, national Israel along with the redemption of Gentile peoples in their corporate structures as well.

Third is a failure to comprehend that the future kingdom predicted in the Tanak and preached and predicted in turn in the New Testament is consistently a multinational kingdom. It is not a uninational kingdom made up of peoples drawn from multiple nations. Rather, it is a kingdom composed of multiple nations, one of which is Israel. Many read the canonical narrative as if the divine plan were to replace all nations with one nation, a universal "nation" that is transcendentalized into a single corporate body of spiritual beings. But nowhere in the Tanak or in the New Testament is that the case. It is a kingdom, to be sure, that is predicted to fill the earth, but one in which multiple nations are distinctively present. At the same time, it is one in which all inhabitants—Jews of Israel and Gentiles of the various Gentile nations—are equally redeemed by Christ and indwelt by the Holy Spirit. In this way, God dwells with and in his peoples (Is 25:6-8; Rev 21:3, 22–22:5). This is essential to grasp both the universality of the kingdom and the particularity of the divine promise to Israel.[13]

What is needed is a better set of textual clues from which a better grasp of the narrative can be obtained. I propose that the place to look would be those texts

---

[13]This point is crucial for understanding the canonical narrative. The theme of a multinational worldwide kingdom is rooted in the patriarchal covenant to bless all nations as that promise is repeated to Jacob (Gen 27:29) and to Judah (Gen 49:10) and then made a feature of divine promise to the house of David (Pss 2:1-12; 72:17-20). The prophets repeat the expectation that the nations will be submissive to the messianic king (Is 11:10; Amos 9:11-15; Mic 4:1-3; 5:4-5). Gentile nations will be the Lord's people in addition to, not in place of, Israel (Is 19:19-25; Zeph 3:20; Zech 2:10-12).

that explicitly relate Israel and her covenant promises to the central narrative of the New Testament. Absolutely key are Paul's comments in Romans 9–11, the text that has played a pivotal role through the history of the church in convincing Christians that God still has a future for Israel. Also key is the thematic role given to Israel in the narrative of Luke–Acts. These texts provide a construal of the New Testament canon that is consistent with the Tanak in the expectation of an ethnic, national, territorial Israel in the consummate plan of God.

A holistic construal of the New Testament canonical narrative.
Luke–Acts: The redemption of Israel, Jerusalem and the nations. The Gospel of Luke begins as a continuation of the canonical narrative of the Tanak. Gabriel, the angel who spoke to Daniel about the future of his people and of the city Jerusalem (Dan 9:20-27), appears to Mary in Luke 1:26-38 and announces to her that she will bear a son who "will be called the Son of the Most High," because "the Lord God will give to him the throne of his ancestor David. He will reign over the house of Jacob forever, and of his kingdom there will be no end" (Lk 1:32-33). This prophecy to Mary continues and advances the narrative of the Tanak, in which we find the covenant God made with David (2 Sam 7:8-16; 1 Chron 17:7-15) promising these very things and a history of prophecy based on that covenant anticipating a future Davidic king for whom they would be fulfilled (e.g., Is 9:6-7; 11:10; Jer 33:15-16; Amos 9:11-15). The fact that the kingdom is specifically said to be "over the house of Jacob" is clearly consistent with the identity of Israel in the Tanak.

The hymns of Mary and Zechariah that follow in Luke 1 continue in this same direction, proclaiming the coming of this son of David as the Lord's provision for "his servant Israel, in remembrance of his mercy, as he spoke to our fathers, to Abraham and to his offspring forever" (Lk 1:54-55 ESV). Through this one will come the mercy "promised to our fathers" in remembrance of "his holy covenant, the oath that he swore to our father Abraham" (Lk 1:72-73 ESV). The consummate end of this mercy is "that we, being delivered from the hand of our enemies, might serve him without fear, in holiness and righteousness before him all our days" (Lk 1:74-75 ESV). As the Lord's Christ he comes "for the consolation of Israel," "for glory to your people Israel," and as "a light for revelation to the Gentiles" (Lk 2:25, 31-32 ESV). The textual allusion here to Isaiah 49:6-7 resonates with the use of Psalm 2 at the baptism of Jesus—a psalm in which the nations are given as an inheritance to the Lord's Messiah (Ps 2:8). This connects again

Biblical Hermeneutics 91

with the theme of good news to the nations at the end of Luke's Gospel and in the book of Acts.[14]

As the Gospel continues, Luke, like the other Gospels, presents the ministry and teaching of Jesus, centered on the theme of the kingdom. The climax comes with the crucifixion and resurrection of the Christ. But as the Gospel ends, Luke raises again the question of what all this means for the hope of Israel and the nations, the object of great anticipation at the very beginning of the narrative. In Luke 24, the resurrected Jesus joins two disciples walking from Jerusalem to Emmaus unrecognized. They lament to him, "But we had hoped that he [Jesus who was crucified] was the one to redeem Israel" (Lk 24:21). Jesus responds, "O foolish ones, and slow of heart to believe *all* that the prophets have spoken!" (Lk 24:25 ESV, emphasis added). The point that these disciples, and subsequent readers of the Gospel, needed to understand was that the crucifixion and resurrection of the Christ did not stand contrary to the previously revealed consummate plan and purpose of God for Israel and the nations. It does not signal a redefinition or metaphysical shift in the story line. It is itself part, in fact *the crucial part*, of that same plan. What the disciples needed was a more comprehensive understanding of the Tanak (Lk 24:27 ESV: "all the prophets have spoken"; Lk 24:44 ESV: "everything written about me in the Law of Moses and the Prophets and the Psalms must be fulfilled"), not a resignification of a part of it. This fuller understanding would link the death and resurrection of the Christ to the future worldwide kingdom of nations expected in the Tanak (which included Israel and Jerusalem) through an intervening history of gospel proclamation of forgiveness (the means of everlasting shalom) to those nations, beginning in Jerusalem (Lk 24:44-49).

Acts records the ascension of Jesus into heaven and the beginning of the mission to the nations. In Acts 2, Peter declares to Israel that Jesus is Lord and Christ, who has been seated in heaven at the right hand of the Father in keeping with Psalm 110:1. But he will return from heaven to bring to consummation what was prophesied of old. Just before the ascension, Jesus himself affirms that the kingdom (Acts 1:3) includes the restoration of Israel (Acts 1:6-8) but at a future

---

[14] An excellent argument for the continuity of Luke–Acts with the theme of Israel's restoration in the Tanak is found in Richard Bauckham, "The Restoration of Israel in Luke-Acts," in *Restoration: Old Testament, Jewish, and Christian Perspectives*, ed. James M. Scott (Leiden: Brill, 2001), 435-87. Also see Darrell L. Bock, *A Theology of Luke and Acts* (Grand Rapids: Zondervan, 2012), 279-301.

time fixed by the Father—after the gospel mission to the nations.[15] In Acts 3:21, Peter preaches to Jerusalem that Jesus has been received into heaven "until the time for restoring all the things about which God spoke by the mouth of his holy prophets long ago" (ESV). Nothing could be clearer than this about continuity with prophetic expectation in the Tanak, which is now tied to the future return of Jesus. The key term here is *restoration*. The restoration that was spoken by the prophets was in fact the future restoration of ethnic, national, territorial Israel.[16] And, in Acts 3:25, Peter ties this expected restoration to the Abrahamic covenant promise. What has now been more clearly revealed in the story line is the salvation that God has provided through Jesus, the atonement by which "your sins may be blotted out" (Acts 3:19 ESV), by which they may be turned "every one of you from your wickedness" (Acts 3:26 ESV). This salvation is the means for bringing the previously revealed plan to completion.

From this beginning, Acts records the mission of preaching the message of salvation and of the kingdom to Israel and the nations—a mission that proceeds under the Lordship of Jesus in heaven. It begins in Jerusalem and significantly ends with Paul preaching the kingdom in Rome (Acts 28:14, 31). However, the mission proceeds with the expectation that Jesus will yet come from heaven to fully restore Israel and bring to fulfillment the kingdom consummation prophesied in the Tanak. There is nothing to indicate any shift in the narrative that redefines Israel or moves the expected consummation to a different order of reality.

The continuity with the Tanak can also be seen in the various sermons in Acts. However, many have overlooked the significance of Paul's reference to the gift of the land to Israel in his sermon to the synagogue in Pisidian Antioch. In Acts 13:19, Paul, recounting briefly the exodus, says, "And after destroying seven nations in the land of Canaan, *he gave them their land as an inheritance*" (ESV, emphasis added). Paul goes on to speak of Jesus as the Christ raised up by God in accordance with the promise to David. But his mention of the gift of the land is significant in light of many denials that the New Testament has any interest in the land. The statement "he gave them their land as an inheritance" is taken

---

[15]Jesus' response to his disciples is sometimes misinterpreted to mean that he was rejecting the premise of their question that the kingdom pertained to the ethnic, national, territorial identity of Israel. However, in the text Jesus clearly accepts the premise as he answers their question regarding the timing of the kingdom. Peter's comments in Acts 3 affirm that the disciple's premise was correct and is now set within the temporal framework given by Jesus.

[16]The restoration theme is found throughout the prophets. Note especially Jeremiah 29:14; 30:3, 17-18; 31:23; 32:37-44; 33:7-9, 11, 26; Ezekiel 39:25-29; Hosea 6:11; Joel 3:1; Amos 9:13-15; and Zephaniah 3:20. Note that in these texts the restoration is national and territorial.

from covenant language. It is repeatedly found in Deuteronomy (Deut 4:21, 37-40; 12:10; 15:4; 19:10, 14; 21:23; 24:4; 25:19) and is declared to be everlasting (Deut 4:40), as is the Abrahamic covenant (Ps 105:7-11; cf. Gen 13:14-18; 17:8). This reference to the gift of the land fits thematically with the restoration theme of Acts 1 and 3, especially Peter's proclamation that the future restoration would be in accord with the words of the prophets and the Abrahamic covenant (Acts 3:17-26). The fact that the land was given to Israel as an inheritance is taken as a given by Paul, as it was by Peter, and as it would have been by first-century Jews in general, believers in Yeshua and those who were not.[17]

The narrative of Luke–Acts traces the history of the Christ from his birth to his death, resurrection and ascension. It looks forward to his future return. It clearly presents itself as a continuance of the canonical narrative of the Tanak directed toward the same consummate goal—an everlasting kingdom inclusive of Israel and the Gentile nations ruled by a messiah, a Christ, from the house of David. Its additions to the story line—the coming of the Christ in the person of Jesus; his death, resurrection and ascension; and the worldwide gospel mission—are not in any way seen as redefining Israel or eliminating that nation from the anticipated consummation. Rather, the hope of Israel is affirmed and situated within the new extension of the story line.

With this in mind, we turn to Paul's comments in Romans 9–11 on the situation of Israel as he came to understand it in ministry. Romans 9–11 has been the object of many studies that acknowledge that Paul here teaches a future for national Israel. My purpose is to highlight those elements in the text that make precisely that point.

Romans 9–11. At the outset of this significant portion of Romans, Paul acknowledges that "Israelites," that is, Paul's own "kinsmen according to the flesh," possess "the adoption . . . the covenants . . . the promises." "To them belong the patriarchs [who were given covenant promises regarding the land and future physical descendants], and from their race, according to the flesh, is the Christ [the one who was prophesied to rule ethnic, national, territorial Israel together with the nations], who is God over all, blessed forever" (Rom 9:3-5 ESV).

This language is exactly in accordance with the story line of the Tanak and with the addition of the incarnation of God in the person of the Christ. The problem Paul traces in Romans 9–11 is an unexpected development in the plot:

---

[17]It fits as well with the repeated stress on *the land of promise* in Hebrews as noted above.

"a partial hardening has come upon Israel" (Rom 11:25 ESV), indicating that a large number of Jews have so far failed to come to faith in the Christ. Note that the term *Israel* here has not been resignified. Paul is speaking of ethnic Jews, "Israelites," his "kinsmen according to the flesh." *Israel* bears the same meaning as in the Tanak.

Even though many in Israel are hardened, God has not rejected "his people" (Rom 11:1-2; cf. "the adoption" in Rom 9:4) since a remnant of them have obtained grace through faith (Rom 11:1-10; esp. 11:1-2, 8). But while the majority of Israel has been hardened, a great number of Gentile peoples have come to faith. Why this is so is a mystery. But it is only a mystery of order and timing, not a mystery of the identity of Israel. There is a twist in the plot, but not a metaphysical shift in narrative reality. The mystery was that, although the gospel began to bear fruit in Israel, the majority has failed to come to faith, while at the same time, many Gentiles are now responding in greater numbers than Jews. This has led to a situation that is the reverse of the order of "hardening" and "faith" seen in the exodus, where it was the Gentiles who were hardened and Israel who responded in faith. Nevertheless, Paul is certain that Israel's hardness will be reversed. It has to be so, since Israel is prominently featured in the expected messianic kingdom. Consequently, Paul writes in Romans 11:12: "Now if their trespass means riches for the world, and if their failure means riches for the Gentiles, how much more will their full inclusion mean!" (ESV). "Full inclusion" or "fullness" indicates the reversal of the hardness that had come upon the majority in Israel so that Israel would be fully saved—that is, wholly in Christ, which condition accords with the prophesied consummate state of the kingdom.

This is repeated in Romans 11:15-16: "If their rejection means the reconciliation of the world, what will their acceptance mean but life from the dead? If the dough offered as firstfruits is holy, so is the whole lump, and if the root is holy, so are the branches" (ESV). Even though many in his day were hardened, according to Paul, and would personally fail to obtain the salvation of God, nevertheless God's plan for corporate Israel remains. The "whole" remains holy. It remains holy even though only a small part is presently being "offered" to God. That small offering is to be regarded as "firstfruits" of the greater harvest in which the whole of Israel will be presented to God. When that occurs, it will be like Israel rising from the dead.

In order to grasp this, one has to have anthropological categories beyond individual personhood. There are corporate dimensions to human existence that are part of the divine design. Israel is a corporate reality. The holiness of the corporate whole is not contradicted by the failure of a majority at any particular time to obtain salvation. Rather, because of that holiness, such a situation cannot persist. The present holiness of the whole means that God continues to deal with Jews corporately as well as personally until the plan and purpose of God for the future whole is accomplished. The consummation plan, revealed in the Tanak and reaffirmed here as well as elsewhere in the New Testament, envisions a whole Israel that is wholly (all of its constituents) saved. A lack of faith, a hardening, of even a majority of Israel in history will not prevent the consummation of God's plan for a future whole Israel rightly related to the Lord by faith, recipients of his salvation and situated within the everlasting shalom of the Christ.

Paul's metaphor of the olive tree compares the unbelieving Jews to branches broken out of an olive tree. "And even they, if they do not continue in their unbelief, will be grafted in, for God has the power to graft them in again" (Rom 11:23 ESV). There is no limitation on divine power to "graft" repentant Jews back into "the nourishing root" (Rom 11:17 ESV) since "contrary to nature" he has "grafted in" Gentiles (Rom 11:24 ESV). The illustration beautifully captures the story line from the Tanak, the story of God's careful "cultivating" work with Israel over time and a plan for one worldwide kingdom composed of Israel and numerous Gentile nations ruled by the Christ, all of whose inhabitants are rightly related to God. God has the power to create that kingdom, even to restore Israel to its fullness within it (a message consistent with the prophets who stressed the unlimited power of God to do exactly this; Is 40–66).

All of this leads to the key passage of Romans 11:25-29:

> Lest you be wise in your own conceits, I want you to understand this mystery, brothers. A partial hardening has come upon Israel, until the fullness of the Gentiles has come in. Then all Israel will be saved, as it is written,
>
> > "The Deliverer will come from Zion,
> > he will banish ungodliness from Jacob";
> > "and this will be my covenant with them
> > when I take away their sins."

> As regards the gospel, they are enemies of God for your sake. But as regards election, they are beloved for the sake of their forefathers. For the gifts and the calling of God are irrevocable.

In this passage, Paul clarifies the mystery of Jewish and Gentile responses to the gospel in the plan of God. Romans 11:25 makes the point that the partial hardening will continue in time "until the full number of the Gentiles has come in." The *achri hou* (until) usually expresses a temporal limit, often with the idea of a reversal, which fits the context here. Various interpretations have been offered for *kai houtōs* in Romans 11:26. In this context it properly and naturally conveys a temporal sense, parallel to *achri hou*, which I've translated above as "then." What happens *then*—that is, after the fullness of the Gentiles has come to Christ—is that "all Israel will be saved."[18]

The phrase "all Israel" throughout the Tanak and elsewhere in the New Testament means the whole, the fullness of Israel. All Israel will be saved, which means that the whole of it, the whole of its constituents, will be saved.[19] In other words, Paul is envisioning a future Israel that is wholly, fully made up of saved Jews. There is no change in Israel's identity in this passage. The "all Israel" that is fully saved in Romans 11:26 is the same kind of "Israel" as that which is partially hardened in Romans 11:25. He is speaking of a present versus a future ethnic, national Israel—a present time in which only a remnant are being saved versus a future time in which the whole constituency of ethnic, national Israel will be saved. The manner and means of that salvation is exactly the manner and means that Paul has spelled out in Romans, justification and sanctification by and through faith in Jesus Christ.

Note that Paul says that this expectation fully accords with what is written in the Scriptures. He offers language from Psalm 14:7; Isaiah 27:9; 59:20-21; and Jeremiah 31:33-34, which coordinate the forgiveness of Israel's sins with

---

[18] See the excellent article by James M. Scott, "'And Then All Israel Will Be Saved' (Rom 11:26)," in *Restoration: Old Testament, Jewish, and Christian Perspectives*, ed. James M. Scott (Brill: Leiden, 2001), 489-527. Scott refutes the claim that the temporal sense of *kai houtōs* is rare and argues for it as the most natural sense in Romans 11:26 and context (ibid., 490-96).

[19] This does not imply salvation apart from faith in Christ. It does not imply the salvation of every descendant of Israel who ever lived or even the conversion of every living Jew at the time of this national conversion. However, it does envision an Israel in the eschatological consummation wholly made up of saved Jews, a vision that fits as well with nations of saved Gentiles. Together the consummation entails a new creation with a saved humanity of various ethnicities in various nations, one of which is Israel—a fitting climax to the repeated promises and work of divine providence throughout the canonical story line.

her future restoration. Isaiah 59 and Jeremiah 31 speak of new covenant blessings on Jacob, the house of Jacob. The latter passage carries the promise that Israel will be a nation forever (Jer 31:35-37) and is situated within in the well-known section of Jeremiah 29–33 that repeats the refrain, "I will restore your (their) fortunes." The *salvation of all Israel* is coordinate in Scripture with the *restoration of all Israel*. Accordingly, the Isaiah 59 text ties this salvation of all Israel to the coming of a deliverer. Just as in Acts, Paul connects the future restoration of the nation to the return of Christ. But the plot has been thickened by the partial hardening that has become manifest since the beginning of the gospel mission. Romans 11 affirms that the consummation will be as expected, but this new plot conflict will be resolved at the coming of Jesus.

Romans 11:28 is a remarkable passage that designates the status of partially hardened corporate Israel: "They are enemies of God for your sake; but as regards election they are beloved, for the sake of their ancestors." This is the text from which Barry Horner developed the label "beloved enemy."[20] The phrase "beloved for the sake of the forefathers" is taken from the Tanak, where it is offered as the explanation for both the original gift of the land and for future restoration to it after divine judgment (e.g., Deut 4:29-31, 37-40); it recalls the covenant promised and sworn to Abraham, Isaac and Jacob as the ground for the entire ethnic, national and territorial existence of Israel. Romans 11:29 states why they are beloved for the sake of the forefathers: because "the gifts and the calling of God are irrevocable." The gift of the land (the primary use of the word *gift* in the Tanak; recall comments on Acts 13:19 above) and the calling to be a nation forever before the Lord (Is 41:8-10; 43:1-7; 45:3; 48:12; 54:6-8; cf. Jer 31:33-37) cannot be revoked.[21] All this is in accordance with a divine plan to show mercy to Israel and to the Gentiles (Rom 11:30-32).

The traditional construal of the New Testament narrative as constituting a reality shift in the canonical narrative line in which Israel is spiritualized or trancendentalized fails with respect to this textual core, which in harmony with the Tanak expects the salvation and restoration of the nation of Israel both in terms of its constituent individual members and in terms of the nation as a corporate whole.

---

[20]Barry E. Horner, *Future Israel: Why Christian Anti-Judaism Must Be Challenged*, NAC Studies in Bible and Theology (Nashville: B&H Academic, 2007), 291-309.

[21]This is consistent with a performative language analysis of covenant promises and oaths in the canonical narrative.

It is best to see the New Testament in continuity with the Tanak in presenting a narrative of the divine plan that includes an ethnic, national, territorial Israel, positioned within an expected worldwide kingdom of nations, all of whose inhabitants (of all nations including Israel) have received forgiveness of sins through the salvation provided by Jesus the Christ, a salvation that has already begun to be revealed but that will reach the level of national restoration and political order at the return of Jesus Christ. This construal of the New Testament canon (1) fits the textual data surveyed above, (2) fits better with the textual data offered by the replacement or redefinition paradigm and (3) offers a coherent and consistent reading of the canonical narrative of the Tanak and the New Testament together.

In conclusion, the New Testament is best read in continuity with the Tanak on this point: there is an ethnic, national, territorial Israel in the consummate plan of God.

What We Are Witnessing Today in the Present State of Israel Is a Preconsummate Work of God in Continuity with the Divine Plan for Israel and the Nations

How are we to interpret the relation of the Tanak and the New Testament with respect to this claim?

The reemergence of Israel as a nation after almost 2,000 years is truly remarkable. Not only did Israel become a nation recognized by other nations in 1948, but she has survived threats and wars to become a significant national power in the Middle East. This fact has been celebrated by Jews for theological and nontheological reasons. However, a significant level of international support has come from Christians convinced that the reemergence of Israel as a nation in the land of promise must be seen as an act of God.

Stirrings among Christian theologians for approximately four hundred years before 1948 prepared the ground for the modern reemergence of the nation.[22] In the nineteenth and twentieth centuries, first British (and to a lesser degree Prussian) and then later American political efforts were rallied by Christians who believed not only that the Jews were destined to be reconstituted nationally

---

[22] The post-Reformation recognition of a future for Israel among early Puritan authors has been documented in works such as Iain H. Murray, *The Puritan Hope: A Study in Revival and the Interpretation of Prophecy* (London: Banner of Truth Trust, 1971); and Peter Toon, *Puritans, the Millennium and the Future of Israel: Puritan Eschatology 1600–1660* (Cambridge: James Clarke, 1970).

Biblical Hermeneutics   99

but that they should be encouraged to do so.[23] The basis for this early or proto-Zionism was the conviction that the consummate plan of God included a place for ethnic, national, territorial Israel and that with Israel's consummate restoration would come "riches for the world" (Rom 11:12).

The restoration of Israel is connected to the restoration of the Davidic house in the Tanak and to the return of Jesus, son of David, in the New Testament. This fits the general pattern in Scripture in which a future reestablishment of the nation is spoken of in a *final, complete* or *consummate* sense. Accordingly, it is understandable that Gentile Zionists or proto-Zionists for many centuries believed that a return of the people to national sovereignty in the land would take place either after the parousia or as a part of the general eschatological pattern (see chapter two). In either case, the return of the people to the land was expected in relation to the second coming of Christ.

However, the modern state of Israel has come into existence in advance of the Lord's return and continues in troubled times that are certainly not the predicted consummation. Nevertheless, this writer and many others would see the modern nationalization of Israel as an act of God in keeping with the divine plan. It is a preconsummate act of God.

If this is the case, what hermeneutical basis is there in the Tanak and the New Testament for recognizing it as such? Scripture clearly shows that a return of the Jewish people to the land after a time of dispersion can occur prior to the consummation. The return from Babylon demonstrated that very fact.

Prior to the Babylonian exile, the prophets predicted both destruction and restoration. Jeremiah specifically prophesied a return after seventy years (e.g., Jer 25). But the predictions of restoration were typically framed in language descriptive of the consummate order—including, for example, the restoration of the Davidic throne and the establishment of the everlasting worldwide kingdom of righteousness and peace through the implementation of the new covenant. Companies of Jews began to return from Babylon in successive waves following the decree of Cyrus in 538. The temple was rebuilt and dedicated seventy years after the Babylonian destruction of 586, fulfilling the prophecy of Jeremiah 25. However, the return from Babylon was not the consummation. The

---

[23]See Donald M. Lewis, *The Origins of Christian Zionism: Lord Shaftesbury and Evangelical Support for a Jewish Homeland* (Cambridge: Cambridge University Press, 2010).

Davidic throne was not restored, the prophesied kingdom was not established and the new covenant remained a future promise.[24]

In order to understand the situation, some have suggested a peaks-and-valleys approach to interpreting prophecy. This would mean that biblical prophecies cast a vision of future events that is similar to the vision of a mountainous region from a mountain observatory.[25] The observer's location represents a point in history, and the peaks within his view are events in the future. These events appear to be proximate to one another like the mountain peaks within the view of our observer. However, what the observer does not see are the valleys that separate these peaks. In the same way, prophets may not record periods of history that separate the eschatological events that they predict.[26]

What this means is that in both the Tanak and the New Testament a rather simple prophetic pattern may, under divine providence, be taken up and fulfilled through a more complex historical sequence. We may speak of this as a divinely directed historical complexification of prophetic patterns. This is not spiritual interpretation. It does not suggest a metaphysical shift in the narrative movement from promise to fulfillment but the complexification of the plot (events, characters, subordinate story lines) as it advances toward its climax and conclusion.

Evidence for this can be found throughout the biblical narrative. For example, the Lord told Moses that he would bring the people of Israel out of Egypt and take them to the land he had promised their forefathers (Ex 3:16-17). But many of the events that happened along the way, including the forty-year wilderness wandering between Sinai and crossing the Jordan, were not mentioned in that prophecy.

Consider the promise to David that the Lord would raise up his descendant after him, establish him on David's throne and secure his kingdom forever (2 Sam 7:13-18; 1 Chron 17:11-14). Nothing was said about a line of kings, a later division of the kingdom, trouble with Gentile powers, the destruction of Jerusalem and the temple, and an interruption of Davidic rule for over four hundred

---

[24]Haggai 2:4-5 explicitly states that the postexilic covenantal condition remained that of the Sinai covenant. The New Testament sees the new covenant of Jeremiah 31:31-37 inaugurated in the death of Jesus (Lk 22:20; Heb 7:18–10:18).

[25]Not a view from the sky (such as from a satellite or airplane) but from another mountain.

[26]This explanation is typically used to explain the distribution of messianic prophecies between the first and second comings of Christ. G. B. Caird refers to this phenomenon as "prophetic camera technique." See his comments in *The Language and Imagery of the Bible* (Philadelphia: Westminster, 1980), 258-64.

years, after which a son of David, heir-designate, would appear as God Incarnate, go to the cross, rise from the dead and ascend into heaven for a further two thousand years and counting, still awaiting the consummation of all that the prophets had predicted. A simple predictive pattern became historically complexified by divine will. Note that throughout that history each of the Davidic kings found legitimacy in the original covenant promise, while subsequent prophecy spoke of one yet to come who would fulfill the promise forever.[27]

Returning to the matter of the restoration of Judeans from Babylon, we know that the preexilic prophecy of judgment, return and kingdom consummation was historically complexified by divine design. Daniel, praying over Jeremiah's prophecy of the return after seventy years (Jer 25; Dan 9), is told by a messenger from heaven that that return would not be the final consummation. An unforeseen period of seventy sevens of years between the reconstruction of the city and the temple and another, yet future, destruction of the same was now being revealed by God. The period covered what we refer to as the Second Temple era. Some, but not all, Jews returned to the land, and Judea was constituted first as a province under governors, later as a kingdom under Hasmonean and then Herodian rule, and then as a Roman province in the time of Jesus. While not the consummate national and territorial restoration envisioned by the preexilic prophets, the corporate and territorial experience of Israel in the Second Temple period was a divinely directed restoration in continuity with the divine plan for Israel and the nations.

The Tanak and the New Testament are clear that a reconstitution of Israel can occur prior to the eschatological consummation due to the phenomenon of a divinely directed historical complexification of previously revealed prophetic patterns. This happened with a not-yet consummate reconstitution of Israel in the Second Temple era after the Babylonian dispersion. It is just as possible for a not-yet consummate reconstitution of Israel under some kind of national polity to appear after the long dispersion begun in the Roman era.

Such a reconstitution would need to be seen as an act of God in accordance with the divine purpose for Israel. It would not be sufficient to see it simply as general providence, the providence that oversees all things and under which nations appear and disappear in history. Rather, according to the canonical narrative, there is a particular providence with respect to Israel's corporate and territorial existence, grounded in the particular covenantal promises going back

---

[27]Note 1 Kings 8:12-21, as well as the numerous references to Davidic legitimacy throughout the narratives of Kings and Chronicles.

to the patriarchs. Israel's presence in or out of the land, as a nation or without national sovereignty, is always in Scripture by divine act, whether by divine installment, deliverance or judgment.[28] Scripture is clear that the land is a gift, but to enjoy it in a corporate sense—as a nation—Israel has to be brought into the land. This is the pattern in the Tanak, and the New Testament appears to confirm this pattern. It is never the case that Israel might simply migrate into the land and self-constitute as a nation. Israel has to be brought into the land by God. This may be by immediate divine leading and miraculous intervention (as in the exodus), or it may be mediated by Gentile powers (as in the Babylonian return). Either way, Israel's constitution or reconstitution in the land is a divine act.

Such an act of particular providence with respect to the Jewish people is not in itself a divine attestation of the spiritual condition of the people but rather a basis of appeal to them to repent and be right with God. Ezekiel, anticipating the return after the exile, explained that the restoration would take place not because of Israel but because of God's own regard for his name. Zechariah and Malachi, after the return from Babylon, called upon the people to repent because of the favor of the return.

In light of these things, the modern restoration of Israel to national status after so long a dispersion—one lasting almost two thousand years—needs to be understood from the perspective of Scripture (Tanak and New Testament) as an act of God in continuity with the divine plan for (1) an ethnic, national, territorial Israel and (2) the nations of the world.

If this is so, how should Jews and Gentiles respond? First, we see from Scripture that Gentile nations are obliged to accept and accommodate the Jewish nation when it is formed. This does not mean that they extend to Israel blind moral approval. But it does mean that they do not take a posture of seeking to remove her national sovereignty; kill, capture or disperse her people; or take possession of her land. The warning in the patriarchal covenant, "I will curse those who curse you," is foundational in this regard (Gen 12:3 GNT). Just as was the case before the Babylonian exile, so afterwards, warnings were given that nations attempting to harm Israel will injure themselves (Zech 12:3).[29] By

---

[28]We are not speaking of the presence of a few living in the land (such as was the case during the Babylonian exile or at times during the long history between the first and the twentieth centuries) but of a significant presence of the people recognized by other nations as a people with some level of sovereignty.

[29]On principle this should not be a problem to nations in the modern world since generally by international law nations are to respect each other's sovereignty and territory. Aggression to-

virtue of pattern repetition, the principle carries over to the modern restoration as well.

More importantly, when such a reconstitution occurs, Israel and the nations are then obliged to recognize, know and submit to the Lord as Lord. Such an act, according to the Tanak, puts the world on notice that the Lord is YHWH.

In Exodus 3:13-17 and 6:2-8, God revealed his name to Moses, the name by which Israel was to know God "throughout all generations" (Ex 3:15 ESV). By that name, God is known as the One who made the covenant with Abraham, Isaac and Jacob, to give to them and to their descendants the land that he assigned to them. By that name, he is to be known as the one who acts to fulfill his covenant promise, the one who brings Israel into that land and establishes them there as a nation. The two characteristics of the name featured in the Exodus texts are *remembrance* and *act*: remembrance of his promise and action to fulfill it.

The restoration of Israel to her land from a dispersed condition occurs primarily because God has regard for his holy name (Ezek 39:25; 36:22-38). It is not because of Israel's righteousness. Rather, Israel, on her part, is thereby obliged by the restoration action to know that God is YHWH—the One who remembers his covenant with the forefathers and who acts in accordance with it. The reason for the dispersion in the first place is precisely Israel's failure to know YHWH. But the Lord restores them because he is in fact YHWH and intends for them to know him as YHWH. Consequently, prophecies of the consummation picture an Israel restored as a nation in the Promised Land, who also knows God as YHWH:

> And you shall know that I am the LORD, when I bring you into the land of Israel, the country that I swore to give your fathers. (Ezek 20:42 ESV)

> Then they shall know that I am the LORD their God, because I sent them into exile among the nations and then assembled them into their own land. (Ezek 39:28 ESV)

The nations are also to know YHWH by the restoration event as well.

> Then the nations that are left all around you shall know that I am the LORD; I have rebuilt the ruined places and replanted that which was desolate. I am the LORD; I have spoken, and I will do it. (Ezek 36:36 ESV)

---

ward a nation or state is generally condemned. Even in regime change, it is not the destruction of a nation or its people that is in view. Note Habakkuk's condemnation of the Chaldeans for gobbling up peoples and nations (Hab 1:12–3:16).

Ezekiel foresaw the consummation in which a restored Israel and Gentile nations know and worship the Lord in everlasting peace. However, the restoration of which he spoke was taken up into a more complex history in which the consummation was projected further into the future. A not-yet-consummate restoration opened as the Second Temple era. The restoration occurred precisely for the reason Ezekiel stated—the Lord is YHWH. However, it occurred with a renewed appeal to Israel to return to YHWH—the message of the postexilic prophets being reset to that of the prophets before the exile (Zech 1:1-6; Mal 3:7). Israel had been restored, in part, but the restoration carried an obligation of repentance and faith with the prospect of further judgment yet to come.

In our day, God has acted to restore Israel as a nation in the land promised to the patriarchs. But this is not yet the restoration of all the things spoken by the prophets. The consummation is still future. Why has the present restoration occurred? It is because the Lord is YHWH! The God of the Tanak is the God of the New Testament. He remembers his covenant, and he acts in accordance with it. He is the one who disperses his people in judgment. He is the one who brings them back into the land and bestows some measure of sovereignty on them. But the important point is this: *such an act obligates Israel and all nations to know the Lord*. This preconsummate restoration resets the call to repentance back to that which preceded the dispersion. In the case of the present restoration, that is the call to repentance that was preached in Jerusalem for over thirty years before AD 70, the call to repentance recorded in the New Testament. It is a call to "know for certain" that God has made Jesus "both Lord and Christ" (Acts 2:36 ESV). It is a call for repentance and faith in his name [Yeshua, "YHWH saves"] because "there is no other *name* under heaven given among men by which we must be saved" (Acts 4:12 ESV, emphasis added). And this applies to Jew and Gentile alike because "the same Lord is Lord of all, bestowing his riches on all who call on him. For 'everyone who calls on the name of the Lord will be saved'" (Rom 10:12-13 ESV, quoting Joel 2:32; cf. Acts 2:21; 4:12).

The two canons, the Tanak and the New Testament, give a progressive revelation of YHWH and of the Son of YHWH, who is YHWH incarnate in the house of David, the heir of all nations (Ps 2), including Israel, and heir of all things, because he, as YHWH, is the creator of all things (Heb 1). It is under his authority, seated at the right hand of his Father, that this preconsummate restoration has occurred. It is a sign that he is the Lord, the same yesterday and today. It carries an urgent message of repentance and faith in his name. For forgiveness of sins and everlasting life—qualifications for the kingdom of God—are granted by him to those who believe. The choice is the same as Moses said long ago—a choice between life and death (Deut 30). For, he is the Lord who is coming, at whose coming "all the things about which God spoke by the mouth of his holy prophets long ago" will be restored (Acts 3:21 ESV). It will be so, because the covenant is his. He remembers it, and he will act.

4

ZIONISM IN THE GOSPEL OF MATTHEW

*Do the People of Israel and the Land of Israel
Persist as Abiding Concerns for Matthew?*

Joel Willitts

◆

וּבָא לְאֶרֶץ יִשְׂרָאֵל

ûbā' lə'ereṣ yiśrā'ēl

And go to the land of Israel

MATTHEW 2:21 (MHNT)

In our time, the people of Israel has returned to its land. Was it justified in doing so? Does this return signal the beginning of the redemption? . . . These are difficult questions to answer and will ultimately be answered by history. But whatever the answer to these questions might be, they concern only the issue of whether we should have waited longer. But that sometime Israel will return to the land which it has been promised by God cannot be in question because God has so promised. . . . The people who have come to dwell in the land during the estrangement of Israel from its land have been drawn into the vortex of a theological drama not of their making. Their pain must be felt by Israel and the compassion that is the deepest dimension of the Jewish consciousness must be brought to bear on the problem. But none of this can obscure the eternal link between Israel and the land, a link that must, sooner or later, be reestablished.

MICHAEL WYSCHOGROD

I had not yet grown accustomed to presenting academic papers to audiences of experts in the field of Matthean studies. At the time, I was still a PhD student who lacked confidence but was convicted about what I was arguing. So after I presented my paper on the topic "Matthew's Hope for Territorial Restoration," which I had been working on as a chapter in my PhD thesis, I was intimidated by all the distinguished faces looking back at me. The conference, the annual Tyndale Fellowship New Testament Group, was focused on Matthew's Gospel and was attended by renowned Matthean scholars: Hagner, Deines, Noland, France and Gurtner, just to name a handful.[1]

After presenting my paper, Donald Hagner, whom I have now come to know as a very warm-hearted person but then I knew only as a scholar who had written a significant two-volume commentary on Matthew, raised his hand with the first question. Was he about to ask that one question that would unravel my thesis? No, in fact, he didn't. The question he asked, though, surprised me. "Are you a dispensationalist?" Immediately, one of my former professors at Dallas Seminary, the late Harold Hoehner, who happened to be attending, piped up: "Don, that's not a fair question. What does that have to do with his paper's argument?" Don smiled in his warm way—these two obviously had known each other forever—and responded, "I don't mean to undermine his argument by labeling him a dispensationalist. I just can't figure out why he is making this argument. Why are you interested in the land? Where is this coming from?"

It was in that moment that I realized how crazy my argument was sounding to those who had long labored in the field of Matthean studies. A concrete vision of people and land, in line with the prophetic expectations of Israel's restoration, was *not* something that Matthean scholars seriously considered. While the paper may have been only a bit more baked than half—it did become a chapter in my dissertation (chap. 6)—I realized how steep the incline would be to push the stone over the peak of the hill and win the argument. In hindsight, I realize I was perhaps overreaching, or at least susceptible to being read as overreaching. In a chapter on territorial restoration in my published dissertation I wrote:

---

[1] Many of the key conference papers were published in Daniel M. Gurtner and John Nolland, *Built upon the Rock: Studies in the Gospel of Matthew* (Grand Rapids: Eerdmans, 2008).

A proposal suggesting that Matthew not only preserved, but also promulgated, the traditional Jewish hope for territorial restoration will probably strike many as verging on the preposterous.[2]

At the outset of this chapter I want to diminish the potential for misunderstanding by stating an important qualification: Matthew's Gospel is *not about* the territorial restoration of the land of Israel. If Matthew is *about* something, it is *about* the identity and significance of Jesus of Nazareth as Israel's long-awaited Messiah ben David. Nevertheless, while the Gospel is not about Israel's territorial restoration, the author *assumes* it.

Eretz Israel (the land of Israel), when it is present, serves mostly as the *setting* of the story of Jesus and is not intentionally contemplated. This qualification, however true, is nowhere close to an answer to the question posed in the subtitle of this chapter, although it seems to have been enough for most recent scholars to think that the land is a "moot question for Matthew's Gospel" and look for reasons *why* Matthew was so unlike his Jewish contemporaries.[3]

To illustrate the present scholarly inclination of completely ignoring the theological theme of the land in Matthew, mention can be made of Charles Carlston and Craig A. Evans's recent theology of Matthew, *From Synagogue to Ecclesia*.[4] Nowhere in the 483 pages of text do the authors address the theme of the land. This is a rather curious omission given the authors' statement that the book "concentrates on Matthew's theology as a whole ... [and] is intended as a portrayal of the major Matthean themes" with special attention to its relation *to Judaism*.[5] While the land may not be a major theme, one wonders if it is so unimportant to Matthew to not receive even a mention. However, in light of the conventional wisdom one should not be surprised.

Matthean scholarship has generally overlooked two important facts that have recently been emphasized, while also severely downplaying Matthew's

---

[2] Joel Willitts, *Matthew's Messianic Shepherd-King: In Search of "The Lost Sheep of the House of Israel"* (Berlin: De Gruyter, 2008), 157.

[3] Richard C. Lux, "The Land of Israel (*Eretz Yisra'el*) in Jewish and Christian Understanding," *SCJR* 3, no. 1 (2008): 11-12, http://ejournals.bc.edu/ojs/index.php/scjr/article/view/1479/1332. Lux decides that the best explanation for why the land of promise is "at best ambiguous" in Matthew's theology is the post–AD 70 reality of "Roman rule, and new directions the Pharisees were beginning to take at Javneh."

[4] Charles E. Carlston and Craig A. Evans, *From Synagogue to Ecclesia: Matthew's Community at the Crossroads*, WUNT (Tübingen: Mohr Siebeck, 2014).

[5] Ibid., vii.

continuity with his early Jewish milieu:[6] (1) the place of the land in the structure of Matthew's story reveals his territorial interests[7] and (2) when compared with the other Gospels—particularly Mark—Matthew reveals a greater attention to Eretz Israel in his reporting of both Jesus' teaching and activity within the land.[8]

Nevertheless, whatever we are to discern about Matthew's theology of the land, it will have to be read between the lines, so to speak. While the restoration of the *people* of Israel has been largely recognized as a central theme of Matthew, overcoming the subtle supersessionistic tendencies of Matthean scholars in the late twentieth and early twenty-first century, the same cannot be said for the restoration of the land of Israel.[9] What's more, since the territorial restoration of Eretz Israel would presuppose a restoration of the people, this chapter will focus primarily on the land in Matthew's theology.

In this chapter I set out the falsifiable hypothesis that the restoration of Eretz Israel is a fundamental *presumption* of the chief theological implication of

---

[6]See my recent article where I make this point: Willitts, "Matthew and Psalms of Solomon's Messianism: A Comparative Study in First-Century Messianology," *BBR* 22, no. 1 (2012): 27-50.

[7]Jürgen K. Zangenberg has rightly noted, "Theology is not only expressed through intellectual and religious concepts or the adaptation and alteration of contemporaneous traditions, but also by putting themes and topics *on a map*." Zangenberg, "Pharisees, Villages and Synagogues: Observations on the Theological Significance of Matthew's Geography of Galilee," in *Logos—Logik—Lyrik: Engagierte exegetische Studien zum biblischen Reden Gottes; Festschrift für Klaus Haacker*, ed. Volker A. Lehnert and Ulrich Rüsen-Weinhold (Leipzig: Evangelische Verlagsanstalt, 2007), 152 (emphasis added). In addition, when we move past the earlier redactional assumption that because Matthew used tradition from Mark, he would not have also meant to claim the same for his own narrative, we can take Matthew's geographical plot structure as theologically motivated. For a discussion of the theological significance of Matthew's geographical structure, see point 2, "Matthew's Geographical Orientation," below, and Willitts, *Matthew's Messianic Shepherd-King*, 184.

[8]Zangenberg speaks of Matthew's particular geographic "focalization," which reveals his "own interests and contribution" ("Pharisees, Villages and Synagogues," 156).

[9]See the recent and important work of Matthew Konradt, who strongly argues for the continuation of the people of Israel in Matthew's theology (*Israel, Church, and the Gentiles in the Gospel of Matthew*, ed. Wayne Coppins and Simon Gathercole, trans. Kathleen Ess [Waco, TX: Baylor University Press, 2014]) but criticizes my work, which stresses the territorial-political implications of Matthew's kingdom theology throughout the book, and in his review of my book referred to my interpretation as an "unusual reading" (*ungewöhnliche Lesart*) (Matthias Konradt, review of *Matthew's Messianic Shepherd-King*, by Joel Willitts, *TLZ* 134, no. 5 [2009]: 569-71). I will publish a sympathetic but critical review of Konradt's book in a forthcoming issue of the *Journal for the Evangelical Theological Society*. For an alternative suggestion, see the recent Carlston and Evans, *From Synagogue to Ecclesia*, 394-95. They argue that the language of the "restoration of Israel" is to "oversimplify" Matthew's complex picture of the "Christian church": "the new Israel is quite different from the old."

Matthew's story of Jesus:[10] the protagonist is the resurrected Lord of heaven and earth and, therefore, is the agent of both Israel's full restoration and the Gentiles' Abrahamic blessing (Mt 1:1; 28:18-20). This essay will highlight Matthew's preoccupation with the land and argue for an affirmative answer to the question posed in the subtitle: Yes! The people of Israel and the land of Israel persist as abiding concerns in the Gospel of Matthew.

This specific attention to the land in Matthew will serve, at the very least, to correct the conventional wisdom that Matthew had *little interest* in the land of Israel.[11] More than that, however, I think his interest in Eretz Israel, both what he adds to his sources[12] and what he includes of them,[13] can be reasonably taken to mean that the author of the First Gospel, and thus the Gospel itself, had an *abiding land consciousness* in line with the traditional Jewish territorial hope.

This chapter will demonstrate the turf orientation[14] of Matthew's narrative theology—which implies the restoration of the Eretz Israel—by taking notice of several aspects of his narrative: Matthew's (1) relationship to his early Jewish context, (2) narrative-geographical orientation, (3) Davidic messianism, (4) turfed kingdom, (5) view of Jerusalem and temple, (6) atonement theology and (7) eschatology.

---

[10]Konradt's methodological reflection serves as an important reminder: "Matthew did not compose a systematic theological treatise but a multifaceted story of Jesus. Every attempt to derive a theological concept from this narrative text rests on textual phenomena (at times ambiguous by nature) that are interpreted, compared with one another, evaluated, and assembled like a mosaic." Konradt, *Israel, Church, and the Gentiles*, 6.

[11]Walter Brueggemann bucks conventional wisdom by asserting, "It will not do to treat the New Testament as though it is disinterested in the land . . . [, but] it will not do to treat the New Testament as though it contains a simple promise of land." Brueggemann, *The Land: Place as Gift, Promise, and Challenge in Biblical Faith*, 2nd ed., OBT (Minneapolis: Fortress, 2002), 164.

[12]See Martin Vahrenhorst, who writes, "If one compares the geographical outline of Matthew's Gospel with that of his Markan source, it is clear that Matthew's Jesus more strongly concentrates his ministry in the land of Israel." Vahrenhorst, "Land und Landverheißung im Neuen Testament," in *Heiliges Land*, ed. Martin Ebner, JBTh 23 (Neukirchen-Vluyn: Neukirchener Verlag, 2009), 131 (my translation).

[13]Zangenberg notes Matthew's geographical interests in his use of Mark: "But even then, the Galilean plot still carried enough meaning to be retold, and Matthew's generalizations and additions especially in the *Basistexte* refute the notion that this happened only because tradition forced him to do so. Matthew does not merely follow archival interests to enable others to envision the life of Jesus as a past event. . . . When Matthew explicitly takes recourse to the 'Land of Israel'-concept, it can further be assumed that he addressed an audience that was familiar with its theological connotations." Zangenberg, "Pharisees, Villages and Synagogues," 167.

[14]See Brueggemann, who says, alluding to Matthew 5:3, "Meekness leads to turf" (*Land*, 166).

1. Matthew's Early Jewish Context

> *The land of Israel.*
>
> MATTHEW 2:21

Matthew is a Jewish text of the late Second Temple period. This is something of a beginning presupposition with which I approach the text, but it can also be easily demonstrated. Dorothy Jean Weaver, for example, recently highlighted the "intensely Jewish" character of Matthew's narrative:

> To read the Gospel of Matthew within its 1st century religious context is to read an *intensely Jewish narrative*. This narrative opens with a Jewish genealogy ([Mt] 1:1, 2-16, 17), beginning with Abraham, the "father" of the Jewish people ([Mt] 1:1, 2, 17; cf. 3:9), and coming to its climax in the birth of Jesus the Jewish Messiah ([Mt] 1:1, 16, 17; cf. 1:18). The narrative which follows, an account of the birth, childhood, ministry, death, and resurrection of Jesus Messiah, takes place against the backdrop of the Jewish religious world of 1st century Palestine. This is a world prominently peopled with Jewish leaders (Pharisees, Sadducees, scribes, priests/chief priests, and elders), closely associated with Jewish meeting places (synagogue, temple/house of God) and Jewish feasts (Passover/Unleavened Bread, feast), and regularly focused on Jewish scripture, the commandments, and what is lawful. This is likewise a world pervaded by the memory of the Jewish prophets of ancient days and history shaped by their prophetic pronouncements. The conflict which drives the plot of Matthew's narrative is a quintessentially Jewish conflict, the ongoing and ultimately deadly confrontation between Jesus Messiah and the Jewish leadership, who repeatedly contest his messianic status and "authority" and who persistently seek to "destroy" him, "kill" him, or "put him to death." Matthew's narrative retains its Jewish character and context up to its conclusion ([Mt] 28:20) and on into the world of Matthew's first readers with a reference by the narrator to a story which "is still told among the Jews to this day" ([Mt] 28:15b).[15]

---

[15] Dorothy Jean Weaver, "'What Is That to Us? See to It Yourself' (Mt 27:4): Making Atonement and the Matthean Portrait of the Jewish Chief Priests," *TS* 70, no. 1 (2014): 1-2 (emphasis added), www.hts.org.za/index.php/HTS/article/view/2703.

Zionism in the Gospel of Matthew

While not attempting to put it any better myself, let me add a list of some of the more obvious narrative elements that reveal Matthew's Jewish character:

1. A genealogy that begins and ends with Jewish concerns (Mt 1:1; 17)
2. The significant use of Jewish Scripture, most notably the so-called formula citations in the first two chapters (e.g., Mt 1:22; 2:6, 15, 17, 23)
3. The presentation of Jesus' mission to the "lost sheep of the house of Israel" (Mt 10:5-6; 15:24)
4. References to biblical details such as the ancient tribal areas of Zebulun and Naphtali and designation of Mark's Syrophoenician Woman as a "Canaanite" (Mt 15:22)
5. Jesus' statements about the abiding nature of the Law (Mt 5:21)
6. The presumption of the continuation of Jewish practices (alms, prayer and fasting [Mt 6:1-18]; sabbath [Mt 24:20])
7. Eschatological expectations concerning the twelve tribes (Mt 19:28)
8. The direct reference to the "land of Israel" (Mt 2:20-21)

More subtle elements are:

1. Scripture typologies such as David, Moses, Isaac and Joshua
2. Structure of the Gospel with five discourse sections suggesting an intentional allusion to the Mosaic Torah composed of five books
3. Sophisticated presentation of the law with its awareness of halakic (that is, legal interpretation) debates (Mt 19:1-9)
4. Jesus' ministry contained within Jewish lands (cf. Mt 8:28-34 and Mk 5:1-17)
5. Preoccupation with the Pharisees (e.g., Mt 23; 27:62-66)
6. References to Jerusalem as the "holy city" (Mt 4:5; 27:53)
7. Less critical of the temple and hopeful for its renewal (Mt 21:18-22; cf. Mk 11:11-19; Mt 23:37-39)
8. Awareness of the Jewish rumor to which Matthew refers after the resurrection (Mt 28:11-15)

If this is the case, and these days the Jewish character of Matthew is something nearing a consensus among Matthean scholars, we should expect that whatever Matthew's Jesus means for the author and whatever the author wishes to communicate about Jesus' significance to his audience, it should fit within the diverse world of late Second Temple Judaism. The late Anthony Saldarini wrote, "The gospel of Matthew should be read *along with* other Jewish postdestruction literature, such as the apocalyptic works 2 Baruch, 4 Ezra and Apocalypse of Abraham, early strata of the Mishnah and Josephus."[16]

So we take as our starting point that Matthew is a Jewish text.[17] This does not settle much, to be sure, since the exact relationship of Matthew's Jewish identity within the Judaism at the beginning of the Jewish revolt or in the post-70 aftermath must still be determined. While this question continues to be a fiercely debated aspect of contemporary Matthean studies, it does provide a horizon for interpretation.

What's more, for our interests, it means that we should assume that Matthew's outlook on the restoration of Israel—both its people and its land—would reflect the perspectives of Jews in the period. He may very well revise them in the light of the significance of Jesus, but they must be something a Jew could have believed. So what do our sources reveal about what Jews thought about the restoration of the land at the time of Jesus and Matthew?

It appears that the land promise was something that was largely taken for granted by most first-century Jews. Scholars have noted that there is not much evidence of Jewish authors writing on the question of the land in the Second Temple period. This is probably because Israel's land promise was a presupposition that rarely arose to the level of conscious reflection. When it did, the theme always retained its concrete territorial element, but at times was simultaneously spiritualized, idealized and allegorized.

In summarizing the Second Temple evidence for the Jewish hope for territorial restoration, we can conclude that among observant Jews in the first century there existed a widespread belief in the territorial restoration of Israel.[18] It is true that beliefs about Eretz Israel were diverse and first-century writers did not always make explicit reference to Israel's land promise. However, even Betsy Amaru, whose work Gary Burge uses to argue falsely for

---

[16] Anthony Saldarini, "The Gospel of Matthew and Jewish-Christian Conflict in Galilee," in *The Galilee in Late Antiquity*, ed. Lee I. Levine (New York: Jewish Theological Seminary of America, 1992), 24 (emphasis added).

[17] In addition, I am on the side of those who surmise that the geographical location of the author is Galilee and not Syrian Antioch, although the latter is the more conventional assumption. For discussion of the Galilean historical and geographical setting, see Saldarini, "Gospel of Matthew," and Aaron M. Gale, *Redefining Ancient Borders: The Jewish Scribal Framework of Matthew's Gospel* (New York: T&T Clark, 2005).

[18] See my earlier discussion in chap. 6 of Willitts, *Matthew's Messianic Shepherd-King*, 157-76.

an entire "redefinition" of Judaism's land theology in Second Temple Judaism, was not able to conclude that either Philo or Josephus abandoned their commitment to Eretz Israel.[19] No such wholesale revision of the land promise ever took place.

There is, therefore, absolutely no evidence to suggest that these beliefs, however universally and ethically they were expressed (Philo), or however much Jewish nationalism was sought to be mitigated before a Roman readership (Josephus), were ever untethered from the abiding conviction that God had "granted" a particular territory to Israel[20]—a territory whose parameters extended to encompass not only the dimensions of the former Davidic kingdom but also the entire "land of Canaan." This was a territory that was believed—universally—to have been promised by God to Israel.[21]

Walter Brueggemann, going very much against the grain, says much the same about the New Testament when he writes, "No matter how much it is spiritualized, it is probable that the image [of the land] is never robbed of its original, historical referent."[22] George Wesley Buchanan over four decades ago said it so well:

---

[19]Gary M. Burge, *Jesus and the Land: The New Testament Challenge to 'Holy Land' Theology* (Grand Rapids: SPCK, 2010), 21-24; and Betsy Halpern Amaru, "Land Theology in Philo and Josephus," in *The Land of Israel: Jewish Perspectives*, ed. Lawrence A. Hoffman (Notre Dame, IN: University of Notre Dame Press, 1986), 65-93. In an earlier work, Amaru says of Josephus: "Josephus is not unpatriotic or antinationalistic in the sense of landlessness. He retains land in his prophecies of the future, even to the possible displeasure of his Roman readers. He simply does not portray the land as the heart of the Jewish experience." Amaru, "Land Theology in Josephus' 'Jewish Antiquities,'" *JQR* 71, no. 4 (1981): 229.

[20]Note that Philo, while no doubt understanding the land as a symbol of a transcendent order, retained the messianic hope for Israel. This particular and universal dimension to his thinking about the eschaton is reflected in his royal eschatological figure in *On the Life of Moses* 1.289-291; *On Rewards and Punishments*, 93-97, 163-172. It implies a return to the land and a national-political empire for Israel. See Peder Borgen, "'There Shall Come Forth a Man': Reflections on Messianic Ideas in Philo," in *The Messiah*, ed. James H. Charlesworth (Minneapolis: Fortress, 1992), 567-69; W. D. Davies, *The Territorial Dimension of Judaism: With a Symposium and Further Reflections* (Minneapolis: Fortress, 1991), 53; Peder Borgen, *Philo of Alexandria: An Exegete for His Time*, NovTSup 86 (Leiden: Brill, 1997), 265-81; James M. Scott, "Philo and the Restoration of Israel," in *Society of Biblical Literature 1995 Seminar Papers*, ed. Eugene H. Lovering (Atlanta: Scholars Press, 1995); and Vahrenhorst, "Land," 143.

[21]Willitts, *Matthew's Messianic Shepherd-King*, 167-68.

[22]Brueggemann, *Land*, 160. See also J. Cornelis de Vos's contrast between the terms *Spiritualisierung* and *Metaphorisierung* ("Die Bedeutung des Landes Israel in den jüdischen Schriften der hellenistisch-römischen Zeit," in *Heiliges Land*, ed. Martin Ebner, JBTh 23 [Neukirchen-Vluyn: Neukirchener Verlag, 2009], 97). De Vos borrowed the *Metaphorisierung* concept from Frank-Lothar Hossfeld ("Die Metaphorisierung der Beziehung Israels zum Land im Frühjudentum und im Christentum," in *Zion: Ort der Begegnung: Festschrift*

The kingdom in the OT usually referred to Judah, Israel, or the United Kingdom. The United Kingdom was called the Kingdom of the Lord and Solomon was called the Son of God. The understanding that the Kingdom of God was also the kingdom of Israel continued into later Jewish documents.... With such long, continuous, and consistent relationship between militarism and religion, the nation of Israel and the Kingdom of God in earlier Israelite and later Jewish thought, it would be strange indeed if the Christianity, which arose from this environment, accepted the expressions of the major tenets of Israel's faith with a completely spiritual meaning.... It is sound scholarship to expect that people who lived on the same land at the same time with the same religious background had the same meanings for the same terms unless distinctions were shown.[23]

Matthew's Gospel resembles its Jewish contemporaries with its lack of much direct reflection on the land promise in its story about Jesus. Furthermore, as will be seen in the ensuing discussion, Matthew gives plenty of indications that he also maintains a conviction of the concrete territorial restoration of Israel in line with its Jewish contemporaries.

---

für Laurentius Klein zur Vollendung des 65. Lebensjahres, ed. Ferdinand Hahn et al. [Bodenheim: Athenäum, 1993], 19-33); it is a German way of naming the tendency of some Second Temple Jewish authors to "metaphorize" concrete elements of Scripture in their reuse of them. De Vos argues for the great advantage of the metaphorical concept over the more common way of referring to the practice as spiritualizing. De Vos believes that the metaphorization concept captures the practice of ancient Jews much more accurately than the spiritualization concept since it implies that "both poles, the concrete and the spiritual, can be intertwined in a metaphor" (my translation). This *Metaphorisierung* category has recently been pursued more fully by interpreters working in this field (see, e.g., Richard B. Hays, *Reading Backwards: Figural Christology and the Fourfold Gospel Witness* [Waco, TX: Baylor University Press, 2014]). I have some concern about Hays's figural reading, not least that the movement of influence of the OT goes *not only* backwards toward the OT, *but also* forwards from OT the toward the NT. This notwithstanding, I am sympathetic with his project.

[23]George W. Buchanan, *The Consequences of the Covenant*, NovTSup 20 (Leiden: Brill, 1970), 69.

2. Matthew's Geographical Orientation

> *The land of Israel.*
>
> **Matthew 2:20-21**

> *Land of Zebulun and land of Naphtali.*
>
> **Matthew 4:13**

> *He left Galilee and went into the region of Judea.*
>
> **Matthew 19:1**

For the longest time in modern scholarship, the geographical dimensions of Matthew's narrative were ignored. This was a response to the attempt in the middle of the nineteenth century to write "Life[s] of Jesus." Scholars in the late nineteenth and early twentieth centuries recognized that the Evangelists, particularly Mark, were *constructing* narratives from sources that represented *their* interpreted presentation of Jesus in storied form. They also assumed then that the chronological and geographical elements of Mark's narrative were irrelevant for understanding the historical person and work of Jesus. Since then, these aspects of the narrative structures of the Synoptic Gospels, which were assumed to have depended on the creativity of Mark, were essentially ignored. This tendency began to change with the emergence of redaction criticism in the middle- and late-twentieth century. In recent years, scholars have taken further steps toward a full narratological assessment of the Gospel of Matthew (studying the shape of its story), showing little interest in questions related to Matthew's use of sources.

Today some scholars, like Leroy Huizenga, have totally rejected redaction criticism for a narratological reading, informed by the work of Umberto Eco, which is, nevertheless, not dismissive of or disinterested in history like some earlier narrative criticism.[24] Of course later redaction critics, like my late professor Graham Stanton, noted that in assessing Matthew's theology one could not simply focus on Matthew's revisions and additions to the text of Mark to the

---

[24]Leroy Andrew Huizenga, *The New Isaac: Tradition and Intertextuality in the Gospel of Matthew*, NovTSup (Leiden: Brill, 2009).

exclusion of what Matthew included from it.[25] Presumably, Matthew borrowed from Mark what he agreed with.

This development in the field has allowed scholars to once again consider the theological importance of geography in Matthew.[26] Jürgen Zangenberg, for example, suggests that geography for Matthew is much more than simply the faithful handing down of tradition by an archivist: it is "theology in spatial form."[27] Zangenberg states, "Jesus' territorial context is not (yet!) 'Holy Land,' but it is a land with a distinct theological character and with a divine promise which is, in the person of Jesus himself, just being fulfilled."[28] He further argues that Matthew establishes

> a new, Jesus-centered affiliation with the land.... Matthew's picture of the past has a meaning for his present and pursues a deeply pedagogical agenda. When Matthew explicitly takes recourse to the "Land of Israel" concept, it can further be assumed that he addressed an audience that was familiar with its theological connotations.[29]

In a similar vein, Matthias Konradt recently suggested that Matthew's summary of the extent of Jesus' geographical influence reflects intentional reference to the twelve tribal areas of settlement in order to "allude to the motif of the reconstitution of Israel."[30] An audience that shared an interest in the land of Israel would have picked up this subtle and creative allusion.

Additionally, a study of Matthew's narrative with a focus on its geographical dimensions reveals a definitive geographical interest to Jesus' mission to the "lost sheep of the house of Israel." This interest expresses a unique (in comparison to the other Gospels) territorial consciousness and confirms Zangenberg's comment that "geography is integral" to Matthew's message.[31] After a lengthy introduction of nearly three and a half chapters, Matthew's narrative divides Jesus' mission into three parts (see table 4.1): (1) the ministry of Jesus in "Greater-Galilee" in the northern territory of Eretz Israel (Mt 4:12–19:1); (2) the Judean ministry, death, resurrection (Mt 19:1–28:15); and (3) the commission from a mountain in Galilee (Mt 28:16-20).

---

[25] Graham Stanton, *A Gospel for a New People: Studies in Matthew* (Louisville, KY: Westminster John Knox, 1993), 41.
[26] See Zangenberg, "Pharisees, Villages and Synagogues."
[27] Ibid., 166.
[28] Ibid., 159.
[29] Ibid., 167.
[30] Konradt, *Israel, Church, and the Gentiles*, 51.
[31] Zangenberg, "Pharisees, Villages and Synagogues," 156. See also Konradt, *Israel, Church, and the Gentiles*, 78.

Table 4.1 The geographical locations of Jesus' ministry as depicted by Matthew

Mt 1:1–4:11	Mt 4:12–18:35							Mt 19:1–28:15			Mt 28:16-20
Jesus Messiah's Origin and Preparation for Ministry	Jesus Messiah's Activity in Galilee and Environs							Jesus Messiah's Activity in Judea and Jerusalem			Jesus Messiah's Universal Kingship and Commission
	Mt 4:12 – 4:25 Narrative	Mt 5:1 – 7:29 Discourse	Mt 8:1 – 9:37 Narrative	Mt 10:1 – 10:42 Discourse	Mt 11:1 – 12:50 Narrative	Mt 13:1 – 13:52 Discourse	Mt 13:53 – 17:27 Narrative	Mt 18:1 – 18:35 Discourse	Mt 19:1 – 23:39 Narrative	Mt 24:1 – 25:46 Discourse	Mt 26:1 – 28:15 Narrative	

Having established the importance of the land of Israel in the introductory section of his narrative (Mt 2:20-21), Matthew depicts Jesus' ministry in Galilee, continuing the emphasis on the land in the mission of Jesus, Matthew 4:12–18:35.

Matthew 4:12-17 is a transition between the material of Matthew 1:1–4:11 (Jesus' early life and preparation for ministry) and what follows, Matthew 4:18–18:35 (Jesus' activity in Galilee). Matthew 19:1 presents another transitional statement also stressing geography: "When Jesus had finished saying these things, he left Galilee and went to the region of Judea beyond the Jordan."[32] The departure toward Judea here provides a seam in the narrative structure, and a new phase of the story begins. So Matthew 4:12-17 serves as the narrative introduction for the unit Matthew 4:18–18:35 and provides the framework within which the interpretation of the whole narrative section should be conducted. Zangenberg notes, "Ultimately, the reference to these traditional territories [Mt 4:12ff.] serves a similar purpose as the reference to the 'land of Israel' in [Mt] 2:22ff: Matthew sees Jesus' activity as fulfillment of divine promises."[33]

The focus of Matthew's Gospel on the messianic activity in the northern territory of the Promised Land is reminiscent of the Jewish traditions concerning the appearance of the Messiah in the north as well the general expectation of a new united Davidic kingdom of the twelve tribes in a restored territory.[34] Richard Beaton points in this direction in his exegesis of Matthew 4:15-16 and the reuse of Isaiah 8:23–9:1. Beaton's investigation considered both Matthew's text-type and the function of the quotation in Matthew's Gospel. With respect to the text-form of the citation, Beaton observed that the quotation's relationship to known ancient versions, though complex, suggests a *geographical* emphasis: "Matthew appears to draw upon the geographical specificity of the MT in support of Jesus' movements and messianic ministry."[35] It is quite clear, then, that the surface-level purpose of the citation is "to demonstrate how Jesus of Nazareth's geographical movements fulfilled Scripture."[36] Yet, Beaton adds that the

---

[32] See likewise Konradt, *Israel, Church, and the Gentiles*, 79.
[33] Zangenberg, "Pharisees, Villages and Synagogues," 161.
[34] See Willitts, *Matthew's Messianic Shepherd-King*, 162-68.
[35] Richard Beaton, *Isaiah's Christ in Matthew's Gospel*, SNTSMS 123 (Cambridge: Cambridge University Press, 2002), 104. The abbreviation stands for the Masoretic Text, the name given to the medieval manuscript upon which most of our modern English translations depend. This manuscript tradition has a history that dates to the early first century. Masoretes were scribes who preserved and copied the Hebrew text.
[36] Ibid., 102.

inclusion of Isaiah 9:1 as a mere "geographical validation" does not exhaust the import of the citation. He points to the quotation's importance for Israel and the land: "Matthew's emphasis upon Jesus' move to Capernaum and the mention of Zebulun and Naphtalai [sic] may suggest a desire to demonstrate that the messiah went initially to the tribes of Israel who were the first to be taken into captivity (cf. [Mt] 10:5-6; 15:24)."[37]

Beaton's observation provides the eschatological basis for the Galilean ministry: the restoration of the tribes of Israel. According to Konradt, "Matthew has composed these verses on the basis of his scriptural exposition of Galilee as the predetermined location for divine attendance to the 'lost sheep of the house of Israel.'"[38]

Significantly, then, the geographical structure of the narrative suggests that bound up in Matthew's portrayal of Jesus' ministry in Galilee may be a concern for the restoration of Eretz Israel and the twelve-tribe league of national-political Israel consonant with his Jewish contemporaries.[39]

3. MATTHEW'S DAVIDIC MESSIANISM

A ruler who is to shepherd my people Israel.

MATTHEW 2:6

A third piece of evidence in support of Matthew's land consciousness, and particularly one with a more obvious political interest, is his use of the Davidic Shepherd-King motif. Matthew uses a number of Old Testament figures as paradigms to illuminate the significance of Jesus for his Jewish audience. The most prominent, encompassing the whole sweep of his narrative, is Jesus as a Davidic Shepherd-King. Unlike other figural patterns that serve narrower purposes within segments of his narrative, such as Moses, Isaac and Joshua, David is a controlling figure throughout the narrative from beginning to end.

While there is little debate among scholars that Matthew employs this figure, its meaning and significance are up for grabs. Elsewhere I have argued

---

[37] Ibid., 106.
[38] Konradt, *Israel, Church, and the Gentiles*, 78-79.
[39] Konradt notes, "The placement of the list of the twelve in [Mt] 10.1-4 underscores that the gathering of the 'lost sheep of the house of Israel' is situated within the theological horizon of the eschatological restitution of the twelve tribes" (ibid., 86).

extensively that the Davidic Shepherd-King motif carries real political-national freight.[40] And for this reason it implies the concrete elements of a land with borders, and a capital city. While these elements are not Matthew's most dominant themes, their presence is suggestive of an underlying presupposition. Let me draw three conclusions from my larger study of the Davidic Shepherd-King motif in Matthew.

First, the motif in the Old Testament and Second Temple period had a particular application. The image of a Davidic Shepherd in eschatological expectation was used (1) to criticize current political powers who inappropriately exercised authority over God's people in the land and (2) to foster hope for a just and merciful future in which a new government of God led by his Davidic king would replace the inept and oppressive leadership currently in power. So the image of a Davidic Shepherd-King had a dual political purpose: polemical and hopeful.

Second, Matthew uses the motif throughout his narrative: in its beginning, middle and end. In Konradt's words, "The metaphor of shepherd and sheep is introduced as a leitmotif through which Matthew unfolds his understanding of Jesus as the Davidic-Messianic king."[41] Here I simply list several examples of Matthew's use of the motif with brief descriptions:

- *Matthew 2:6*—"a ruler who is to shepherd my people Israel." This is a composite quotation of Micah 5:2 and 1 Chronicles 11:2 (2 Sam 5:2) under the clear influence of Jeremiah 23:1-7 and Ezekiel 34 and 37. Through his redaction in naming "the land of Judah," Matthew has intensified the territorial aspects of the citations.[42]

- *Matthew 9:36*—"sheep without a shepherd." The phrase, while not a direct quotation, has a strong Old Testament and early Jewish pedigree. It is used in contexts of military and political upheaval. See Numbers 27:17, 2 Chronicles 18:16 and Judith 11:19. The phrase culminates in a Davidic messianic expectation. As in these other cases, the phrase connotes the predicament of Israel in the absence of a royal political figure. It implies the inauguration of the restoration of a territorial kingdom of Israel over which God's Davidic Shepherd-King will reign with his under-shepherds (Mt 10:1-5; 19:28).[43]

---

[40]Willitts, *Matthew's Messianic Shepherd-King*.
[41]Konradt, *Israel, Church, and the Gentiles*, 31.
[42]See chap. 3 of Willitts, *Matthew's Messianic Shepherd-King*, 97-115.
[43]See chap. 4 of Willitts, *Matthew's Messianic Shepherd-King*, 117-34.

- *Matthew 10:6; 15:24*—"the lost sheep of the house of Israel." The phrase appears in two different contexts but similarly names the target of the first stage of Jesus' work. In my estimation, the phrase signals the restoration of the *whole* of Israel politically and spiritually, but by focusing on a *subset* within the whole—the exilic peoples of the former Northern Kingdom of Israel, who continued to reside in the northern region of the land. Jesus' announcement to *them* of the nearness of the kingdom implies the restoration of the whole. Matthew is unique among the four Gospels in presenting Jesus' mission in these terms.[44]
- *Matthew 25:31-32*—"as a shepherd separates the sheep from the goats." This unique Matthean parable presents Jesus as the Son of Man who will judge the nations as a shepherd. This is another example of the Davidic Shepherd-King motif. Not only because of its connection with Ezekiel 34, but also according to some recent research on the title "Son of Man" from Daniel 7, it is likely that Daniel, and the subsequent interpretive tradition at the very least, endued the title with Davidic significance. Matthew's Davidic Shepherd-King will judge the nations in the eschaton.[45]
- *Matthew 26:31-32; 28:16-20*—"I will strike the shepherd, and the sheep of the flock will be scattered. . . . I will go ahead of you to Galilee." This composite quotation of Zechariah 13:7 and Ezekiel 34:21 intensifies the territorial aspect of the expectation of the slain Shepherd-King of Zechariah. Matthew's redaction of the Scripture and his use of the Davidic Shepherd-King motif in the context of this narrative climax signifies the fulfillment of God's promise to restore the Davidic kingdom in the land and regather the dispersed at the end of the age. The connection between Matthew 26:31-32 and 28:16 signifies, in the words of Peter Stuhlmacher, "the eschatological restoration of Greater Israel."[46]

Third, Matthew intensifies the geographical elements in citations he used from the Old Testament by creating composite texts from different parts of the

---

[44] See chaps. 7–8 of Willitts, *Matthew's Messianic Shepherd-King*, 181-219.

[45] See discussion in Young Sam Chae, *Jesus as the Eschatological Davidic Shepherd: Studies in the Old Testament, Second Temple Judaism, and in the Gospel of Matthew*, WUNT (Tübingen: Mohr Siebeck, 2006), 219-33. See also the work of Daniel Boyarin, *The Jewish Gospels: The Story of the Jewish Christ* (New York: New Press, 2011).

[46] Peter Stuhlmacher, "Matt 28:16-20 and the Course of Mission in the Apostolic and Postapostolic Age," in *The Mission of the Early Church to Jews and Gentiles*, ed. Jostein Ådna and Hans Kvalbein, WUNT (Tübingen: Mohr Siebeck, 2000), 27; see also chap. 5 of Willitts, *Matthew's Messianic Shepherd-King*, 135-56.

Bible. Matthew used the Shepherd-King motif as both a political polemic and a way to foster hope for political-national rescue. The problem for which the Davidic messiah was the solution was then a geopolitical one, to use an anachronistic term. And the answer was a new Shepherd-King who would reconstitute—and rule over—the restored kingdom of God. This would be the renewed kingdom of Israel under a new David, a kingdom in the eschaton that encompasses the whole world.[47]

4. Matthew's Turfed Kingdom

On the land as it is in heaven.

Matthew 6:10 (author's translation)

Many will come from east and west and recline at table with Abraham, Isaac, and Jacob in the kingdom of heaven.

Matthew 8:11 (ESV)

What was sown on the good land.

Matthew 13:23 (author's translation)

The kingdom of God will be taken away from you and given to a people that produces the fruits of the kingdom.

Matthew 21:43 (NRSV)

Additional evidence for the land consciousness in the first Gospel is found in the "turfed" (concrete and territorial) nature of the kingdom of heaven. Four passages illustrate, first, that the kingdom is *somewhere* on earth. Second, on a more careful survey, one can see that the "somewhere" is most likely the land of Israel. In each case, the passage under consideration is either a more landed version in comparison with Mark and Luke, or it is unique to Matthew's Gospel.

The first passage is from the "Lord's Prayer" of Matthew 6:10:

---

[47] See 2 Chronicles 9:8 and 13:8 (also 1 Chron 17:14; 28:5; 29:23), where these three entities are equated: kingdom of God = kingdom of Israel = kingdom of David.

>Your kingdom come,
>Your will be done,
>>on the *land* as it is in heaven.

In this translation, I departed from the standard English translations and rendered the Greek word *gē* with "land" instead of "earth." There are two considerations here. First, notice should be taken of the relationship between kingdom and land/earth here. Even if one takes *gē* to be better rendered as "earth," there is still the link between the realm of heaven and earth/land. The prayer for the disciples is that what is true in heaven—where God is the unrivaled sovereign—would be equally true on earth/land, and that the realm of God and the realm of humanity/Israel would be in unity.[48]

Second, the translation of *gē* as "land" instead of "earth" is based on the earlier uses of the word in the context of the Gospel, beginning with Matthew 2:20-21, extending through Matthew 5:5 and 5:13. While it is not possible here to defend/explain this thread fully, scholars on both sides of the Atlantic are increasingly arguing that the meaning of *gē* in Matthew 5:5 is "land."[49] What's more, the context weighs in this direction in Matthew 5:13 as well, when one recognizes that *gē* ("land/earth") and *kosmos* ("world") in Matthew 5:14, on the one hand, and "salt" and "light" on the other, are not synonymous. Here Jesus is instructing the disciples on the role of the renewed Israel both within the land of Israel and outside among the Gentiles.[50] This reading is confirmed in Matthew 5:16, where Matthew describes the effect of the light shining among the Gentiles: they will glorify the Father in heaven. While of course the term *Gentile* or *non-Jew* is not used here, it seems unlikely that Matthew is speaking of Jews in light of the generic use of *anthrōpos* in conjunction with *kosmos*. What's more, presumably

---

[48]See Jonathan Pennington's important recent work (*Heaven and Earth in the Gospel of Matthew*, NovTSup [Leiden: Brill, 2007]), where he has convincingly argued—against conventional wisdom—that Matthew's "kingdom of heaven" is more than a circumlocution, a word or phrase standing in the place of another. Pennington states, "Inherent in this text is a consciousness that the kingdom of heaven needs to and will come upon the earth. This idea entails the fact that the present earthly order, including its kingdoms, empires, and current social and political realities, will be superseded and replaced when God's heavenly kingdom comes to earth [or land]" (*Heaven and Earth*, 318).

[49]Christoph Heil, "'Selig die Sanftmütigen, denn sie werden das Land besitzen' (Mt, 5,5): Das matthäische Verständnis der Landverheissung in seinen frühjüdischen und frühchristlichen Kontexten," in Donald Senior, *The Gospel of Matthew at the Crossroads of Early Christianity*, BETL 243 (Leuven: Peeters, 2011), 389-417; Vahrenhorst, "Land"; Scot McKnight, *Sermon on the Mount*, ed. Tremper Longman III and Scot McKnight, SGBC (Grand Rapids: Zondervan, 2013), 57-59; Zangenberg, "Pharisees, Villages and Synagogues."

[50]See similarly McKnight, *Sermon*, 57-59.

Matthew would already think that the Jews glorify Israel's God. It is the light of the renewed Israel that will shine among the nations and attract the worship of Israel's God.

These contextual considerations lend support for a more turfed and specific focus of this prayer for Matthew's first audience. It is the Jewish disciples who are in the land of Israel who are to pray that God's kingdom, once again, takes the concrete form of the Davidic kingdom on earth. The kingdom's tribal borders will be the Levant—that is, the eastern coast of the Mediterranean Sea north of the Arabian Peninsula and south of Turkey—but its sovereignty will extend over the whole earth (Ps 72).

The second example comes from Matthew 8:11 (ESV): "Many will come from east and west and recline at table with Abraham, Isaac, and Jacob in the kingdom of heaven." The turfed nature of the kingdom of heaven is evident in that "the many" will be coming *from somewhere* in the east and the west *to* feast with Israel's patriarchs in the kingdom of heaven. Key elements of this statement require brief mention. First, the reference to Israel's patriarchs is certainly pregnant with meaning. The land of the patriarchs is Canaan, Eretz Israel; it was to them that the land was promised (Gen 12; 15; 17; 26 and 28). The direction in question from the east and from the west is *to Israel and, specifically, to Jerusalem.*

Second, Matthew is echoing biblical prophecy and Jewish tradition related to the eschatological return of the exiles to Israel. It is also likely that included here are the righteous Gentiles who will accompany the returnees. Isaiah portrays the reconstitution of the nation of Israel in the land as facilitated by Gentile supporters (Is 49:22-23), and the event is pictured as a great feast (Is 25).[51]

A third passage serves as another example of Matthew's turfed kingdom: the parable of the sower in Matthew 13:3-9, 18-23. In this text the term *gē* is again used. In a narrow sense, the term simply refers to the soil into which seeds fall and take root. However, within the parable's narrative and as one of the parables of the kingdom, it is "about God's sowing his people in *the land* in fulfillment of his promises."[52] Jesus in a rather convoluted way mixes his metaphors so that the seed is both the people sown into the good land and also the message— which, when obeyed, creates the restored remnant sown. According to Klyne

---

[51]See Willitts, *Matthew's Messianic Shepherd-King*, 82.
[52]Klyne Snodgrass, *Stories with Intent: A Comprehensive Guide to the Parables of Jesus* (Grand Rapids: Eerdmans 2008), 156 (emphasis added).

Snodgrass, "Matthew intends the parables to warn readers not to repeat Israel's failure to respond to the kingdom message and also to help people understand why Israel rejected Jesus' message: hardness of heart, the efforts of the evil one, the world's cares and money, and the seeming insignificance of the kingdom."[53]

A fourth example of the landedness of the kingdom in Matthew is the parable of the tenants in Matthew 21:33-43. This is the second of a triad of parables contained in Matthew 21–22: two sons (Mt 21:28-32), tenants (Mt 21:33-46) and the wedding banquet (Mt 22:1-14). The vineyard and other elements, such as the tower, in the parable of the two sons make it clear that behind this parable is Isaiah 5:2. Current research on the parable has noted the connection with other Second Temple texts in the use of a vineyard and tower, with the vineyard denoting the land and the tower the temple.[54] The key statement for our purposes is Matthew 21:43: "Therefore I tell you, the kingdom of God will be taken away from you and given to a people that produces the fruits of the kingdom." Without getting mired down in the scholarly arguments on this statement—and they are legion—notice should be taken of the content of the exchange: the vineyard and the tower. The kingdom of God is the vineyard and the tower, the land and the temple. Jesus pronounced judgment on a particular people through the announcement of a replacement. Of course this has been used to argue for Christian replacement theories: the church of the Jew and Gentile replacing ethnic Israel. But it certainly does not require this interpretation. And furthermore, it seems that Matthew's focus is much more limited. Matthew 21:45 makes clear that the intended audience got the message: "When the chief priests and the Pharisees heard [Jesus'] parables, they realized that he was speaking about them." Jesus' judgment is not on ethnic Israel but on the inept and corrupt leadership. It is they whom God will replace in his kingdom, the land of Israel.

The four passages briefly surveyed here lead to the conclusion that the kingdom of God was not merely a spiritual, ethereal realm. But it was and is a *turfed kingdom*. In other words, it means a place that can be visited, inhabited, exchanged, planted and restored to be in sync with heaven. What's

---

[53]Ibid., 174.
[54]See Wesley G. Olmstead, *Matthew's Trilogy of Parables: The Nation, the Nations and the Reader in Matthew 21.28–22.14*, SNTSMS 127 (Cambridge: Cambridge University Press, 2003); George J. Brooke, "4Q500 1 and the Use of Scripture in the Parable of the Vineyard," *Dead Sea Discoveries* 2, no. 3 (1995): 268-94; and Craig A. Evans, "On the Vineyard Parables of Isaiah 5 and Mark 12," *BZ* 28 (1984): 82-86.

more, it seems that for Matthew the heart of that turfed kingdom was Eretz Israel.

5. Matthew's Jerusalem and Temple

The holy city

Matthew 4:5; 27:53

The city of the great King

Matthew 5:35

My house shall be called a house of prayer

Matthew 21:13

Jerusalem . . .
you will not see me again until . . .

Matthew 23:37-39

A fifth line of evidence in favor of Matthew's abiding hope for the restoration of the land of Israel is his affirmative posture toward Jerusalem and the temple in spite of his severe critique and prophetic word of destruction. Two times Matthew refers to Jerusalem as "the holy city." Some commentators overlook this phrase altogether. Others deny its relevance, claiming it to be simply a cultural holdover.[55] The phrase is used often in Jewish Scriptures and would certainly have represented the reverence Jews held for the city at the time of Jesus (see Is 48:2; 52:1; Dan 9:24; 2 Macc 3:1; Tob 13:9; Rev 11:2; 21:1-2; Pss. Sol. 8:4). Others see it as ironic, since it is the city that is holy that is rejecting the "holy one."[56] These readings are shortsighted. In the wider frame of Matthew's story, Matthew expresses ambivalence about Jerusalem and its temple to be sure, but on the whole it is a positive perspective.[57] Matthew shares a reverence for the

---

[55] See R. T. France, "Matthew and Jerusalem," in Gurtner and Nolland, *Built upon the Rock*, 109.
[56] See W. D. Davies and Dale C. Allison, *The Gospel According to Saint Matthew*, ICC (Edinburgh: T&T Clark, 1997), 3:635.
[57] See similarly Daniel M. Gurtner, who writes, "That the data seem so consistent suggests a concerted perspective on the part of the First Evangelist toward the Jerusalem Temple. The striking

city and presents a hope for its future.[58] Anders Runesson, in agreement, concludes: "The Gospel of Matthew indicates that its author and immediate audience acknowledged the Jerusalem temple and its cult while the temple still stood, and continued to revere both Jerusalem and the temple after AD 70."[59] This view, however, is disputed, and the dispute turns on the interpretation of Matthew 23:39. In the NIV we read: "For I tell you, you will not see me again until you say, 'Blessed is he who comes in the name of the Lord.'" Like most modern translations, the NIV takes the Greek phrase *ou mē . . . ap' arti heōs an* (not . . . until) to be a conditional clause. The condition indicates that any future seeing by the Jerusalemites is dependent on meeting a specific condition. The *ou mē* is an emphatic double negative, "by no means," and the conjunction *ap' arti heōs an* is taken as a temporal indicator with a strong element of uncertainty.

R. T. France agrees with the conditional rendering: "There is no prediction here, only a condition."[60] What's more, he argues that Matthew's Jesus was not at all optimistic that this would happen. For France, the statement is a pessimistic judgment against Jerusalem: "You won't see me again unless and until you say 'Blessed is he who comes in the name of the Lord,' and *that will never happen!*" France sees no hint of a future hope for Jerusalem in this statement. But is this correct?

John Nolland's interpretation seems more reasonable, based on the contexts of both this passage and the rest of Matthew's Gospel. He takes the clause in a way that sees a future time when the people of Jerusalem will receive their king— the Greek phrases thus indicating that seeing will resume at an indicated but uncertain future moment.[61] The possibility that this will happen in Jesus' "now" is cut off, but that is not the end of the story. The sense of this statement by Jesus is that there is a future scene to be enacted. And Jesus' statement has a hopeful tone, albeit full of present grief.

The statement therefore describes a future time when the "one in the name of the Lord" comes. This of course is referring to the return of Jesus at some

---

positive redactional and narrative portrayal of the temple raises important questions regarding Matthew's relationship to first-century Judaism" ("Matthew's Theology of the Temple and the 'Parting of the Ways': Christian Origins and the First Gospel," in Gurtner and Nolland, *Built upon the Rock*, 153).

[58] John Nolland, *The Gospel of Matthew*, NIGTC (Grand Rapids: Eerdmans, 2005), 165.
[59] Anders Runesson, "Rethinking Early Jewish-Christian Relations: Matthean Community History as Pharisaic Intragroup Conflict," *JBL* 127, no. 1 (2008): 116.
[60] R. T. France, *The Gospel of Matthew*, NICNT (Grand Rapids: Eerdmans, 2007), 884.
[61] Nolland, *Gospel of Matthew*, 952-53.

future point (see Mt 10:23; 24:29–25:13). But what is the posture of those who say "Blessed is he . . . ?" Is it in the terror of judgment or in the joy of reception? Ulrich Luz makes a case for the former and appeals to parallels within other Second Temple Jewish literature, specifically passages from 1 Enoch.[62] He writes, "At the parousia they will greet the World Judge as the one who comes in the name of the Lord, but then it will be too late."[63] Still, as convincing as Luz's logic might seem, he overlooks something that Nolland does not: the shed blood of Jesus for the forgiveness of sins.

Jesus envisages a day when there will be a conversion of heart and mind among the Jersualemites.[64] Whereas once they opposed and murdered their king, they will in the future rejoice and receive him. Nolland convincingly connects this change to the atoning work of Jesus. Nolland observes the great irony in the words of the people stirred up by the leaders ("chief priests and elders"): "His blood be on us and on our children" (Mt 27:11, 25). But far from this being a final word, it falls within the section framed by the Lord's Supper: "This is my blood of the covenant, which is poured out for many for the forgiveness of sins" (Mt 26:28). About the self-condemning statement of the crowd, Nolland perceptively comments: "The cross reveals the guilt of all, but in turn it offers forgiveness to all."[65] Catherine Sider Hamilton puts it eloquently: "Jesus' innocent blood is also the blood that saves."[66] This makes the latter, the joy of reception, the most appropriate interpretation, given the nature of the blessing and its parallel with Matthew 21:9.

There is an additional feature to take notice of in the passage. In Matthew 23:37 Jesus states: "Jerusalem, Jerusalem . . . How often have I desired to gather your children together as a hen gathers her brood." Here we have a strong allusion to Isaiah 54, with its depiction of a desolate and barren wife who will soon be redeemed and made fertile again. The two opposing conditions of the wife-mother Jerusalem symbolize the before and after of God's redemption of his people and his city. There should then be little doubt

---

[62]Ulrich Luz, *Matthew 21–28: A Commentary*, trans. James E. Crouch, Hermeneia (Minneapolis: Fortress, 2005), 163-64.
[63]Ibid., 163.
[64]Peter Fiedler, *Das Matthäusevangelium*, ThKNT 1 (Stuttgart: Kohlhammer, 2006), 358.
[65]John Nolland, "The Gospel of Matthew and Anti-Semitism," in Gurtner and Nolland, *Built upon the Rock*, 168.
[66]Catherine Sider Hamilton, "Innocent Blood Traditions in Early Judaism and the Death of Jesus in Matthew" (PhD thesis, University of Saint Michael's College, 2013), 342, https://tspace.library.utoronto.ca/bitstream/1807/43419/1/Hamilton_Catherine_MS_201311_PhD_thesis.pdf.

that Jesus, when he speaks of gathering Jerusalem's children with the image of a hen gathering her chicks, makes explicit reference to the reconstitution of God's exilic people in the land of Israel in a new Jerusalem. The similarity of expectation with Isaiah 54:1-2, 7 (NIV) is unmistakable, although the symbolism is a little different:

> "Sing, barren woman,
>   you who never bore a child;
> burst into song, shout for joy,
>   you who were never in labor;
> because more are the children of the desolate woman
>   than of her who has a husband,"
>   says the LORD.
> "Enlarge the place of your tent,
>   stretch your tent curtains wide,
>   do not hold back;
> lengthen your cords,
>   strengthen your stakes.
> For you will spread out to the right and to the left;
>   your descendants will dispossess nations
>   and settle in their desolate cities. . . .
> For a brief moment I abandoned you,
>   but with deep compassion I will bring you back."

This may even be the assumption behind the reference in Matthew 24:31 to the gathering of the "elect" from the four winds: at the parousia, Jesus will reconstitute Israel under a renewed "house" (Mt 23:38). The one that was once desolate will in the future be flourishing and fertile. The term translated "house" could refer to the nation of Israel, Jerusalem, the temple or the leadership. Commentators debate which is in view.[67] I think all are in play here for Matthew. Given the strong Davidic connotation of "house," all four options become important elements for understanding both the present devastating failure in the rejection of their Davidic king[68] and the glorious future, when God will "restore David's fallen shelter" (Amos 9:11 NIV). In Amos, the image of "shelter" is simply

---

[67] As an example see Nolland's discussion, *Gospel of Matthew*, 951.

[68] See Ulrich Luz, *Matthew 8–20: A Commentary*, trans. James E. Crouch, Hermeneia (Minneapolis: Fortress, 2001), 162.

another figure for the term "house" used for David's dynastic promise in 1 Chronicles 17:12 (2 Sam 7:11).

Matthew's treatment of the city of Jerusalem and the temple, then, strongly implies a conviction of both God's present judgment on them and their future restoration. This twofold judgment and restoration sequence is also important for the land element in Matthew's theology of innocent blood and atonement.

6. Matthew's Atonement Theology

> *And so upon you will come all the righteous blood that has been shed on the land.*
>
> **Matthew 23:35 (author's translation)**

> *This is my blood of the covenant, which is poured out for many for the forgiveness of sins.*
>
> **Matthew 26:28 (nrsv)**

> *I am innocent of this man's blood.*
> *... His blood be on us and on our children!*
>
> **Matthew 27:24-25 (nrsv)**

One surprising place to find evidence for a theology of land is Matthew's presentation of the significance of Jesus' death. But not only is this an element of Matthew's narrative about the meaning of Jesus' death; it may also be the aspect of Jesus' death that Matthew wants his readers to notice the most.

That for Matthew Jesus' death forgives sins is abundantly clear. The Matthean Jesus explicitly teaches this in instituting the Lord's Supper: "This is my blood of the covenant, which is poured out for many for the forgiveness of sins" (Mt 26:28). And the Evangelist at the beginning of the Gospel relates that Jesus is given his name because "he will save his people from their sins" (Mt 1:21).

Recently Catherine Sider Hamilton has elucidated the significance of the death of Jesus for the forgiveness of sins in her successfully defended doctoral thesis at the Toronto School of Theology (2013) titled "Innocent Blood Traditions in Early Judaism and the Death of Jesus in Matthew."[69] Hamilton has shown convincingly that Matthew's passion story is a narrative of innocent blood that is best read against the backdrop of traditions in the Old Testament and Second Temple literature, particularly in 1 Enoch, about Cain and Abel and the blood of Zechariah. In addition, she shows how Matthew combines this with a tradition found in Qumran's Damascus Document (CD 5) and later rabbinic texts about Uriah's innocent blood shed by King David, to which Matthew enigmatically makes reference in the genealogy (Mt 1:6). What these traditions have in common is the way the shedding of innocent blood, which was a major concern in the Torah (Deut 21:1-9), required purging. If innocent blood shed in the land went untreated, Israel would be summarily cast out of the land into exile.

> Innocent blood poured out upon the land becomes the problem par excellence, leading to the flood [in the Cain traditions] in a paradigmatic "wiping clean" of the land; leading in the Zechariah legends to the temple's destruction. In his focus on David and Uriah in the genealogy, in his insistence on the slaughter of the innocent children of Bethlehem, Matthew shares this way of seeing.... In Matthew [innocent blood] leads to exile.[70]

"Pollution," then, "is central and Israel . . . stands at the heart of the story; for innocent blood means defilement, and raises the question of the fate of the people in the land."[71] Thus, "the problem of innocent blood," Hamilton notes, "highlights the concreteness of that question in the perspective of the Gospel. It is a matter of the land and the life of the people in that land."[72] So exile was the consequence of innocent blood. Exile, however, would not be the final scene in Israel's story. Exile was the path to restoration, to return and reconstitution in the land. Again Hamilton states,

> If commentators have read the cry of the people as the end of Israel's story—in part because they see, correctly, that it is connected in the Gospel narrative to the destruction of Jerusalem—that is because they have not seen the logic of innocent blood that underlies the story. Innocent blood defiles, and so the

---

[69] The dissertation will be published in 2016 in the Society for New Testament Studies Monograph Series (SNTSMS) published by Cambridge University Press.
[70] Hamilton, "Innocent Blood Traditions," 315.
[71] Ibid., 290.
[72] Ibid., 291.

people are cast out. But innocent blood brings also (in the mercy of God) the cataclysm, and so the promise of new creation. Destruction is part of the history, but is not that history's end. Or rather, the cataclysm that, in the vision of Matthew (as in the Cain/blood-flood/judgement traditions) rises over Israel's history means both destruction and new beginning, new life rising out the purged land.[73]

Salvation for Matthew then involves at its very heart the question of Israel in its history as God's people and the problem of exile—the loss of the land.[74]

Hamilton shows how Matthew's Gospel from top to bottom exhibits this theme of innocent blood, exile and return.[75] At the beginning, Matthew's genealogy sets this narrative frame of exile. Then at the climax and resolution of the plot's conflict, Jesus' death is presented as bringing both the subsequent catastrophe for the shedding of innocent blood and restoration as holy ones are raised from the dead, echoing Ezekiel's vision (Ezek 37).

Hamilton's work on Jesus' death in Matthew, read within its cultural and religious context, shows that for Matthew Eretz Israel is still a centerpiece of eschatological hope. The purging of the land from the guilt of innocent blood through the death of Jesus is the God-ordained means by which the kingdom of God is realized concretely on earth in time and space. In the passion story of innocent blood, Matthew affirms that Jesus is the long-awaited Shepherd-King whose death was predicted by the prophets. And, far from tragic and unexpected, it is the way God purifies, atones and redeems Israel—its people *and* its place.

> In describing a salvation written upon the land and culminating in the entrance into the holy city, and in setting the story of salvation under the sign of exile, Matthew's Gospel makes it clear from the beginning that this is a narrative about Israel.... The whole narrative unfolds against the background of Israel's history and hope, defined in terms of exile and return.... In Matthew's history of innocent blood, Israel's thus stands at the centre of the story.[76]

The narrative presentation of Jesus' innocent death as the solution to the problem of the shedding of innocent blood represents a formidable indication

---
[73]Ibid., 345.
[74]Ibid., 315.
[75]Ibid., 308.
[76]Ibid., 345-46.

of the significance that the land and its future hold for the author of the First Gospel. As more scholars engage Hamilton's work, they will not be able any longer to sidestep the role of the land in Matthean theology. If the land is at the heart of the atonement, it is at the heart of Matthew's theology.

7. MATTHEW'S ESCHATOLOGY

> *For they will inherit the land.*
>
> **MATTHEW 5:5 (AUTHOR'S TRANSLATION)**
>
> *You who have followed me will also sit on twelve thrones, judging the twelve tribes of Israel.*
>
> **MATTHEW 19:28 (NRSV)**

The last line of evidence is in some ways the most obvious: eschatology. But let's first recap what we have already seen. Matthew's Jewish context assumed a future for the land as a first principle, and his Gospel reveals this assumption in its narrative structure (2), in its reverence for Jerusalem (5), in its Davidic messianism (3), in its conception of kingdom (4) and in its presentation of Jesus' death (6). In these ways, Matthew reveals a very high level of continuity with his social context (1). Now let us examine Matthew's conception of the future.

Matthew's record of Jesus' statement in the Sermon on the Mount about the meek is debated today. How should we translate the Matthean Jesus' Greek word *gē*? Should it be translated as "earth," a synonym for the world (NIV, ESV, NRSV, CEB, NJB, etc.)? Or are there good grounds to translate it as "land," with a much narrower reference to the land of Israel (see the Complete Jewish Bible translation)? For most interpreters of Matthew, the answer has been the former, based on Matthew's universal mission (Mt 28:19-20). But I would argue that, the universal mission notwithstanding, in light of the biblical background and postbiblical parallels within early first-century Jewish tradition and Matthew's focus on Israel, the better choice is the latter. It seems much more likely that on the lips of Jesus and in the report of Matthew, the narrower meaning of the term is intended, Eretz Israel.

Jesus' statement is adapted from and nearly identical to Psalm 37:11 (NIV): "But the meek will inherit the land and enjoy peace and prosperity." In the context of that psalm, the word is best rendered "land" and not "earth." It is the meek who receive the inheritance of the Promised Land, not the violent and evil. In later postbiblical usage, it retains this narrow meaning. Among the Dead Sea Scrolls, a pesher (ancient commentary on the text of the Bible) on Psalm 37 was discovered, 4Q171 (4QpPs^a] II, 9-12:

> [4Q171] Ps 37:11 ⁹And the poor shall possess the land and enjoy peace in plenty. Its interpretation concerns ¹⁰the congregation of the poor who will tough out the period of distress and will be rescued from all the snares of ¹¹Belial. Afterwards, all who shall po[sse]ss the land will enjoy and grow fat with everything enjoy[able to] ¹²the flesh. [Blank][77]

The interpretation developed the verse beyond its biblical context in two ways: (1) by placing it into an eschatological context: this is a promise for the future and (2) by applying it to the Scroll community. The question that concerned those who received the text among the Scroll community was "Who are the 'poor' who will eschatologically inherit the ʾereṣ (land)?" Their interpretation of the verse specified the "poor" as their *own* community; it provided a term of self-definition.[78] However, the pesherist left unchanged the fundamental meaning of ʾereṣ, which without question names the Promised Land, Eretz Israel. This evidence shows both that it was a popular text for Jews at the time of Jesus and that while the interpretations sought to define who were the truly "poor," the promise of inheritance of the land remained firmly in view.

For Matthew, the promise of the land of Israel remains intact, and he, like the pesherist, sees the fulfillment of the promise in the future and defines the community for whom the promise was made; it is to the "meek" ("meek" or "gentle" is how the LXX [*praeis*] translated the Hebrew term [ʿănāwîm], and Matthew's translation is in line with the LXX here). Matthew's narrative then unfolds the meaning of meek by giving it a christological definition. The meek are those who follow Jesus and who live in obedience to his word (Mt 11:29; 21:5).[79] Christoph

---
[77]Florentino García Martínez and Eibert J. C. Tigchelaar, *The Dead Sea Scrolls Study Edition* (Leiden: Brill, 1997), 343.
[78]See the discussion in Heil, "Selig die Sanftmütigen," 407-9.
[79]Jonathan T. Pennington overreaches when he suggests that Matthew's intention here is to make a point about the "Gentile-inclusive mission." Pennington interprets the beatitude to mean the

Heil is right then to observe the similarity between the pesher and Matthew on the meaning of the "land": "Both Matthew and the Qumran Commentary on Psalm 37 evidently agree in an expectation for their addressees of a concrete and this-worldly enjoyment of the land. So in Matthew 5:5 the Greek word *gē* is better translated as 'land,' not 'earth.'"[80] In his conclusion, Heil further sums it up:

> Matthew has understood the beatitude for the meek concretely; the meek are the disciples of the meek Jesus who will inherit the land. He has not spiritualized, cosmologized or universalized the land promise. Matthew has, rather like the Qumran community, ethicized the land promise and actualized it on the group who follow the ethic.[81]

In addition to the beatitude about the "meek," another promise of eschatological restoration of the Eretz Israel seems presupposed in the statement recorded in Matthew 19:28: "Jesus said to them, 'Truly I tell you, at the renewal of all things, when the Son of Man is seated on the throne of his glory, you who have followed me will also sit on twelve thrones, judging the twelve tribes of Israel.'" The context for the statement is a discussion of the cost and reward of discipleship.[82] In response to Peter's question about the Twelve's future reward for the sacrifice of the present, Matthew's Jesus declares that in the future renewal, *en tē palingenesia*,[83] they will be rewarded with governance over the

---

land promise is "not exclusively to those of Jewish descent.... Now this promise is made to *all* those who align themselves with Jesus" ("Heaven, Earth, and a New Genesis: Theological Cosmology in Matthew," in *Cosmology and New Testament Theology*, ed. Jonathan T. Pennington and Sean M. McDonough, LNTS [London: T&T Clark, 2008], 30 [emphasis mine]. It is true that Matthew has reconfigured the promise around Jesus. But his reconfiguration takes the promise in the *opposite* direction from what Pennington suggests: Jesus *restricts* its application; *he does not expand it*. Jesus does not universalize the promise of land to include Gentiles. He, like the pesher at Qumran, *limits the scope* of the promise of inheritance so that it cannot be simply a matter of ethnic prerogative. The recipients of the future inheritance of the land are only *those Jews* loyal to Jesus.

[80]Heil, "Selig die Sanftmütigen," 411 (translation mine).

[81]Ibid., 415-16 (translation mine).

[82]See the parallel in Luke 22:30. The saying is usually assigned to Q, although the nature of the logion is debated. See Davies and Allison, *Matthew*, 3:55; and Ulrich Luz, *The Theology of the Gospel of Matthew*, ed. James D. G. Dunn, trans. J. Bradford Robinson, New Testament Theology (Cambridge: Cambridge University Press, 1995), 121, for discussions concerning the relationship between Matthew's and Luke's use of the statement.

[83]Warren Carter's explanation of the phrase is assumed here. He understands the term to refer to "the new age and world, a new heaven and earth, both temporal and spatial ([Mt] 5:18; 24:35; cf. *1 En* 45:4-5; 91:16; *2 Bar* 44:12; 57:2), a new creation ([Mt] 1:1; 14:32; 19:4, 8), God's salvation and Empire, which ends the oppressive imperial world under the control of the devil ([Mt] 4:8),

twelve tribes of Israel.[84] Implicit in this eschatological promise is the political *reconstitution* of a twelve-tribe nation state. The prediction of tribal oversight alludes to and is based on the model of the administration of the Davidic and Solomonic empires by twelve tribal leaders (see 1 Kings 4:7-19; 1 Chron 27:16-22; Ezra 2:2; Neh 7:7). Matthew assumes, it appears, that in the future in the restored Davidic kingdom, the twelve disciples will govern over *restored* tribal territories. Matthew's assumption is in concert with the eschatological expectation, apparently in the air in the first century, that the tribal leaders of the Davidic empire would be restored in the messianic kingdom.[85]

These two passages (Mt 5:5; 19:28) clearly indicate that Matthew's eschatology included affirmation of Israel's land promise. What's more, they assume that in the future, the members of Israel of the Messiah Jesus will enjoy life in the land God promised in a reconstituted Davidic kingdom.

This chapter has discussed the *landedness* of Matthew's narrative theology by considering elements of his narrative that reveal a continuing concern for Eretz Israel. It is clear that Matthew continued to hold traditional assumptions about the people and land of Israel, although his assumptions have been reconfigured around the person of Jesus of Nazareth.

Matthew believed that Jesus was the long-awaited Davidic messiah whose appearance meant the eventual restoration of exilic Israel on the one hand, and on the other the worship of the God of Israel among all the nations. The two aspects of Jesus' significance stand side by side in Matthew. When rightly understood,

---

of Rome and its gods" (*Matthew and the Margins: A Sociopolitical and Religious Reading* [Sheffield: Sheffield Academic Press, 2000], 392). See also Fred W. Burnett, "Παλιγγενεσία in Matt. 19:28: A Window on the Matthean Community?," *JSNT* 17 (1983): 60-72; Davies and Allison, *Matthew*, 3:57; David C. Sim, "The Meaning of παλιγγενεσία in Matthew 19.28," *JSNT* 50 (1993): 3-12; and F. Büchsel, "παλιγγενεσία," *TDNT* 1.686-89, for discussions of the unusual term *palingenesia*. Recently Pennington ("Heaven, Earth, and a New Genesis," 41) noted that *palingenesia* was used by Josephus to refer to Israel's reestablishment after exile (*Jewish Antiquities* 11.66).

[84]See Davies and Allison, *Matthew*, 3:55-56, for a defense of the view that takes the term *krinontes* here to mean "to rule" or "to govern" over a period of time and not a one-time judgment.

[85]The political-constitutional importance of the twelve princes is clear in the LXX (e.g., Num 30:2; Deut 5:20 [23]; 1 Chron 27:16; Ezra 6:17, 8:35), Eupolemus (see Eusebius, *Praeparatio evangelica* 9.30.8), Qumran (4Q403 1 I, 1, 10, 21, 26; 4Q400 3 II, 2; 4QpIsad; 1QM II, 1-3; 11QT 57, 11-15) and the Testaments of the Twelve Patriarchs (T. Jud. 25:1-2; T. Benj. 10:7). For a discussion of this passage in the context of the eschatological expectation surrounding the twelve princes of Israel in the Second Temple period, see also the work of William Horbury, *Messianism Among Jews and Christians: Twelve Biblical and Historical Studies* (London: T&T Clark, 2003), 157-88.

they pose no contradiction. The one leads to the other without replacing or minimizing either. The structure of Matthew's story expresses it clearly.[86]

A Davidic restoration can and did presuppose Gentile inclusion. Not only did Matthew claim that Jesus was the key to the salvation of both the Israelite and the non-Israelite, but the early church also found (from the promises of Davidic restoration) the salvation and inclusion of the nations (see Acts 15:13-19; Amos 9:11). The Matthean Jesus did not redefine a concrete view of Israel's restoration into something else. The elements of a restored *turfed* Davidic kingdom remain present for Matthew and were expected in the indeterminate future. In this way, Matthew stood firmly within his late first-century Jewish historical and social context. Matthew held to the hope for Israel's territorial restoration and believed it would be realized as a consequence of Jesus' life, death and resurrection.

I read Matthew as a Gentile Christian at a time when Israel has returned to its land for some six decades now. A large part of this chapter, in fact, was written in Israel while I was taking a short study leave in Jerusalem at the historic *École Biblique et Archéologique Française*. The consequence of the state of Israel's existence is palpable when one is there—as anyone who has visited Israel can attest; and in my view its modern appearance has both positive and negative effects. Given the theology of Matthew, I must ask, what might he say about Israel's modern return? I think he would share Michael Wyschogrod's conviction with ambivalence expressed in the lengthy epigraph with which I opened the chapter. "That sometime Israel will return to the land which it has been promised by God cannot be in question because God has so promised."[87] Yet a judgment about the theological legitimacy of the modern state of Israel cannot be rendered with unqualified certainty.

In Wyschogrod's wise counsel, a full judgment in the present should be suspended because only history will ultimately answer the questions of legitimacy. But what is in question neither for Matthew nor for me is the eternal link between the land and people of Israel in God's eschatological purposes: the people as well as the land have a future.

---

[86]This is essentially Konradt's thesis: "Matthew represents Gentiles and Israel to a certain extent on equal footing, despite the abiding distinction between them. . . . Matthew emphasizes Israel's special position but also just as emphatically asserts that salvation is open to Gentiles and reconciles the two facets with one another. . . . The universal significance of Jesus' death and resurrection establishes equal access to salvation for Gentiles . . . but does not nullify Israel's special position." Konradt, *Israel, Church, and the Gentiles*, 377, 380.

[87]Michael Wyschogrod, "Judaism and the Land," in *Abraham's Promise: Judaism and Jewish-Christian Relations*, ed. R. Kendall Soulen (Grand Rapids: Eerdmans, 2004), 103.

So for me, in the present day, I have a cautious, critical but sympathetic posture toward the existence of the modern state of Israel. I believe this is in line with the teaching of Matthew's Gospel as well as the whole of the New Testament.

שָׁלוֹם עַל־יִשְׂרָאֵל

šālôm ʿal-yiśrāʾēl

Peace be upon Israel!

Psalm 128:6

5

ZIONISM IN LUKE–ACTS

*Do the People of Israel and the Land of Israel
Persist as Abiding Concerns in Luke's Two Volumes?*

Mark S. Kinzer

◆

> At no point do the earliest Christians view the Holy Land as a locus of divine activity to which the people of the Roman empire must be drawn. They do not promote the Holy Land either for the Jew or for the Christian as a vital aspect of faith. . . . The early Christians possessed no territorial theology. Early Christian preaching is utterly uninterested in a Jewish eschatology devoted to the restoration of the land. The kingdom of Christ began in Judea and is historically anchored there but it is not tethered to a political realization of that kingdom in the Holy Land.[1]

These words place their author, Gary Burge, in the mainstream of Christian scholars. It is commonplace for specialists in Christian theology and Scripture to assert that the land of Israel loses its theological significance in the New Testament. Minimally, it seems self-evident to most that the theme of the land as a particular geographical location (as opposed to an eschatological symbol representing the entire world) lacks prominence in the New Testament texts.

I will argue in this chapter that Luke–Acts displays an orientation to the city of Jerusalem that contradicts these standard conclusions. According to

---
[1]Gary M. Burge, *Jesus and the Land: The New Testament Challenge to "Holy Land" Theology* (Grand Rapids: Baker Books, 2010), 59 (emphasis original).

Luke–Acts, Jerusalem possesses a unique status not only because "the kingdom of Christ" is "historically anchored" there but even more because that kingdom will achieve its eschatological consummation within its walls. This means that the land of Israel also retains its unique status for Luke–Acts, for the city of Jerusalem functioned from the time of the postexilic prophets as a symbol for the land as a whole, as well as for the people destined to inherit it.[2] It is no accident that the modern movement to restore corporate Jewish life in the land took the name Zionism, for Zion (i.e., Jerusalem) represents the entire land of Israel.

Gary Burge recognizes the importance of Luke–Acts for any treatment of this topic and rightly highlights a set of verses from the first chapter of Acts:

> So when they had come together, they asked him, "Lord, is this the time when you will restore the kingdom to Israel?" He replied, "It is not for you to know the times or periods that the Father has set by his own authority. But you will receive power when the Holy Spirit has come upon you; and you will be my witnesses in Jerusalem, in all Judea and Samaria, and to the ends of the earth." (Acts 1:6-8)

Burge interprets these words of Jesus as a denial of the validity of the disciples' question: "Jesus' correction of the apostles should not be taken to mean that Jesus acknowledges the old Jewish worldview and that its timing is now hidden from the apostles. Instead Jesus is acknowledging their incomprehension. He in effect says, 'Yes, I will restore Israel—but in a way you cannot imagine.'"[3]

This reading of Acts 1 draws support from two structural features of the book of Acts. First, Acts 1:8 signals the geographical structure of the book as a whole. The volume begins in Jerusalem, moves on to Judea and Samaria, and then concludes in Rome (the "ends of the earth"). This structure suggests that Jerusalem is important only as the site of ecclesial origins; it represents the honored past but not the glorious future. In the words of Burge, "The work of this messianic era is not centripetal but centrifugal: moving away from the center, Jerusalem, while remembering where it came from."[4] Second, many commentators

---

[2] "Isaiah, like Ezekiel, reorients the blessing of Abraham so that it comes to center almost exclusively on Jerusalem, on Mount Zion.... What had formerly been attributed to the land as a whole is now transferred to the city and the holy mountain.... Like Ezekiel, Zechariah uses the traditional formulas associated with the promise of the land, but he has centered them solely on Jerusalem and Judah." Robert L. Wilken, *The Land Called Holy: Palestine in Christian History and Thought* (New Haven, CT: Yale University Press, 1992), 15-16, 18.
[3] Burge, *Jesus and the Land*, 61.
[4] Ibid., 62.

see the tone and content of the book's final scene in Rome as implying a definitive judgment on the Jewish people, a judgment that deprives them of their covenantal privileges. The destruction of Jerusalem, which will occur in the years immediately following this final scene, confirms the decisive nature of this judgment. Thus, for the author of Luke–Acts, Jerusalem and the Jewish people represent the *ekklēsia*'s past, but her future belongs with the nations of the world.

I will first examine these two structural features of the Lukan writings and argue that their significance has commonly been misunderstood. I will then return to Acts 1:6-8 and offer my own interpretation of these crucial verses.

"He Set His Face to Go to Jerusalem" (Lk 9:51)

Luke underlines the thematic centrality of Jerusalem for his two-volume work by structuring his narrative geographically, with Jerusalem as its pivot. No other book in the New Testament adheres to such a defined geographical pattern as a primary principle of organization. This author also gives more attention to the destiny of Jerusalem than does any other New Testament writer. An examination of the geographical structure of Luke–Acts, and of Luke's teaching concerning Jerusalem, will provide clues regarding the message that the two volumes convey.

The geographical structure of the Gospel of Luke. Among the four Gospels, only Luke begins in Jerusalem—and not merely in Jerusalem but at the heart of the city, the holy temple, where the future father of John the Baptist offers incense and receives an angelic visitation (Lk 1:5-23). While both Matthew and Luke describe Jesus' birth near Jerusalem in Bethlehem (Mt 2:1-12; Lk 2:1-20), only Luke depicts the presentation of the infant Jesus in the temple, accompanied by the prophetic blessings of Simeon and Anna (Lk 2:22-38). Only Luke among the canonical Gospels provides readers with a story of Jesus as a youth, and that story recounts the boy's visit to Jerusalem and his lingering in the courts of the temple (Lk 2:41-51). Thus, Luke's two-chapter introduction centers on the city of Jerusalem and its temple.

In Luke 3 the book shifts its focus to Galilee, and for the next seven chapters it follows generally the order of events recorded in the Gospel of Mark. Near the end of Luke 9 the Evangelist begins a new section of his narrative, which combines material from the double tradition (i.e., units shared by Luke and Matthew but not by Mark) with material unique to Luke. The new section begins in this way: "When the days drew near for him to be taken up, he set his face to go to

Jerusalem" (Lk 9:51). The next nine chapters of Luke's "Special Section" (Lk 9:51–18:14) take the form of an extended travel narrative relating Jesus' final journey to Jerusalem. The material itself is only loosely geographical in character, consisting of parables and stories that usually lack an intrinsic connection to the journey. Nevertheless, Luke has chosen to organize the material around this Passover pilgrimage, with occasional editorial reminders of the geographical context (e.g., Lk 13:22; 17:11). In this way the central section of Luke's narrative, which occurs outside Jerusalem, employs the holy city as its point of orientation and source of structural unity.

As in all four Gospels, the events of Luke's Passion narrative occur in Jerusalem and its immediate environs. However, only Luke restricts resurrection appearances to the Jerusalem region, and only Luke includes the dominical command requiring the disciples to remain in the city (Lk 24:49). The Gospel ends as it began—in the Jerusalem temple, with a community of Jews worshiping the God of Israel (Lk 24:53).

Among the canonical Gospels only Luke begins in Jerusalem, ends in Jerusalem and orients its central narrative around a journey *to* Jerusalem. This geographical structure underlines Luke's unique concern for the holy city and its enduring theological significance.

The geographical structure of the book of Acts. The book of Acts likewise orders its narrative according to a geographical pattern centered in Jerusalem, and, as already noted, that pattern finds explicit articulation in Acts 1:8: "You will be my witnesses in Jerusalem, in all Judea and Samaria, and to the ends of the earth."

Like the Gospel of Luke, the book of Acts begins in Jerusalem, with a community centered on the temple (Acts 2:46; 3:1-10; 4:1-2; 5:12, 20-21, 42). The story develops as the message of Jesus radiates outward—first to the towns of Judea and Samaria, then with reference to Damascus.[5] In Acts 10 Peter proclaims the good news to Cornelius and his household in the coastal city of Caesarea. In Acts 11 the reader learns that persecution in Jerusalem has led some disciples to Phoenicia, Cyprus and Antioch (Acts 11:19). From Antioch Paul begins his travels (Acts 13:1-3), wending his way through Asia Minor (Acts 13:4–14:26) and eventually crossing over to Europe (Acts 16:9-10) and establishing Jesus-

---

[5]On the spread of the movement to Judea and Samaria, see Acts 8:1, 4-25; on the city of Damascus, see Acts 9:1-2, 10, 19.

believing communities in Greece. The story concludes with Paul in Rome, the capital of the empire.

The geographical outline of Acts 1:8 and this summary of the narrative of Acts leave out a particular detail that has profound implications for our interpretation of the geographical structure of Acts: while radiating steadily outward, *the story continually reverts back to Jerusalem*. Paul encounters Jesus on the road to Damascus, and then *returns to Jerusalem* (Acts 9:26-29). Peter proclaims Jesus to Cornelius in Caesarea, and then *returns to Jerusalem* (Acts 11:2). A congregation arises in Antioch, and then in a time of famine *sends aid to Jerusalem* (Acts 11:27-30). Paul and Barnabas journey from Antioch to Asia Minor, and then *return to Jerusalem* for the central event in the book—the Jerusalem Council (Acts 15:2). From Jerusalem Paul travels with Silas to Greece, and then *returns to Jerusalem* (Acts 18:22).[6] Paul completes his final missionary journey and then *returns to Jerusalem*, where he is arrested (Acts 21:17-23:11). While this feature of the geographical structure of Acts is often ignored by commentators, Robert Brawley is a notable exception:

> Although Acts begins in Jerusalem and ends in Rome, it is inaccurate to conclude that Jerusalem falls out in favor of Rome. The narrative in Acts actually reciprocates between Jerusalem and the extended mission.... Even when Paul is in Rome, his memory reverts to Jerusalem to reiterate his fate there ([Acts] 28:17). Hence, Acts does not delineate a movement away from Jerusalem, but *a constant return to Jerusalem*. In the geography of Acts emphasis repeatedly falls on Jerusalem from beginning to end.[7]

If indeed Acts 1:8 is a geographical outline of the book, then its language supports this conclusion, for it characterizes Rome as being located at "the ends of the earth." Given the city's overwhelming political, military, economic and cultural

---

[6]The Greek text of Acts 18:22 says merely that "Paul went up and greeted the church" (see KJV, RSV, NIV). However, commentators generally recognize that Luke is employing the traditional Jewish idiom ("to go up") for a journey to Jerusalem. The translators of the NRSV were so confident of this interpretation that they incorporated it into their English text: "When he had landed at Caesarea, he went up *to Jerusalem* and greeted the church, and then went down to Antioch" (emphasis added). I. Howard Marshall concurs with this understanding of the verse, and also notes its significance: "When he [Luke] goes on to say that *Paul went up and greeted the church*, this is usually understood as a reference to going up to Jerusalem and seeing the church there.... If this is a correct assumption, it means that each of Paul's missionary campaigns concluded with a visit to Jerusalem, so that Paul's work began from and ended in Jerusalem in each case." Marshall, *Acts* (Grand Rapids: Eerdmans, 1980), 301-2.

[7]Robert L. Brawley, *Luke-Acts and the Jews: Conflict, Apology, and Conciliation* (Atlanta: Scholars Press, 1987), 35-36 (emphasis added).

dominance within the first-century world inhabited by Luke, applying this phrase (even by implication) to Rome comes as a shock. For Luke, Rome may be the capital of a Gentile empire that rules much of the earth, but it was neither the center nor the true capital of the world.[8] That honor belonged to Jerusalem alone.

This assessment finds further confirmation in the geographical structure of the list of Jews gathered for the holiday of Pentecost (Acts 2:5, 9-11). Richard Bauckham has analyzed this list, and the results are striking:

> Luke's list of the nations and countries from which the pilgrims attending the festival of Pentecost had come (Acts 2:9-11) provides a much more authentically *Jerusalem* perspective on the Diaspora. The order in which the names occur has perplexed interpreters. In fact, if we take the trouble to plot the names on a map of the world as an ancient reader would have perceived it, we can see that Luke's list is carefully designed to depict the Jewish Diaspora with Jerusalem at its centre. . . . The names in Acts 2:9-11 are listed in four groups corresponding to the four points of the compass, beginning in the east and moving counterclockwise. . . . The first group of names in the list . . . *begins in the far east and moves in towards Judaea*, which is then named. Recognizing that Judaea is in the list because it is the centre of the pattern described by the names is the key to understanding the list. The second group of names . . . is of places to the north of Judaea, and follows *an order which moves out from and back to Judaea*, ending at the point from which one might sail to Judaea. The third group of names . . . moves west from Judaea through Egypt . . . and Libya to Rome, *and then back to Judaea* by a sea route calling at Crete. Finally, a single name (Arabs) represents the movement south from Judaea, presumably indicating Nabataea, immediately due south of Judaea.[9]

Not only does this list depict Jerusalem as the center of the world; it also follows the same rhythm of outward and inward movement that characterizes the entire narrative of Acts. Reading Acts 1:8 in light of Acts 2:9-11 and in light of the overall structure of Acts, we might say that the Pentecost list portrays the historical spread of the good news in accordance with Acts 1:8, whereas the

---

[8] "Luke rejoices that the word of God and the good news about the Jewish messiah and king Jesus flow out of Zion to the rest of the world, conquering even Rome, which, vis-à-vis Jerusalem, lies at the extremities of the earth, not at the center." Isaac W. Oliver, *Torah Praxis After 70 CE: Reading Matthew and Luke-Acts as Jewish Texts* (Tübingen: Mohr Siebeck, 2013), 28.

[9] Richard Bauckham, "James and the Jerusalem Church," in *The Book of Acts in Its Palestinian Setting*, vol. 1 of *The Book of Acts in Its First Century Setting*, ed. Richard Bauckham (Grand Rapids: Eerdmans, 1995), 419 (emphases added).

narrative of the book of Acts focuses on one particular strand of that greater story—the strand associated with the controversial figure of Paul. In both the greater story of the advance of the good news and the more circumscribed story of Paul, Jerusalem is the heart from which the blood flows and to which it invariably returns. Contrary to Burge's claim, the centrifugal movement of the narrative of Acts is continually balanced by a centripetal movement.

The judgment/redemption of Jerusalem and the puzzle of Luke-Acts. This movement of outward flow and inward return continues until we reach the final chapter of Acts, at which point the movement is cut off midcycle. The story concludes in Rome, at "the ends of the earth," with no return to Jerusalem. If Jerusalem had only functioned in the narrative as a point of origin, as Burge suggests, then an ending in Rome would be natural and fitting. However, as we have seen, Jerusalem plays a much more prominent role in the geographical structure of Acts than this simple linear scheme would suggest. It is Luke's center, and Rome is but the periphery. Has that center now forfeited its privileged status? Has the former periphery now taken its place?

To answer this question, we must return to the Gospel of Luke and reflect on a puzzling feature of its narrative that provides essential insight into the meaning of its companion volume. I refer to the Gospel of Luke's preoccupation with the destruction of Jerusalem in AD 70 and its hints of Jerusalem's future redemption. While the Jewish war with Rome looms in the background of each of the canonical Gospels, Luke's orientation to this event is unique among the four of them.

First, Luke is unique in his portrait of Jesus' sympathy for the suffering that Jerusalem will undergo. Like Matthew, Luke depicts Jesus' frustrated longing for Jerusalem's repentance: "Jerusalem, Jerusalem, the city that kills the prophets and stones those who are sent to it! How often have I desired to gather your children together as a hen gathers her brood under her wings, and you were not willing!" (Lk 13:34). But in Luke this verse follows a warning from the Pharisees to Jesus that Herod seeks to kill him (Lk 13:31-33)—a warning that distances these Pharisees from Herod's malicious intent and portrays them as quasi allies of Jesus.[10] In contrast, Matthew positions this saying (Mt 23:37-39) as the climax of a fierce denunciation of the Pharisees that holds them culpable for the blood

---

[10]See Peter J. Tomson, *'If This Be from Heaven . . .': Jesus and the New Testament Authors in Their Relationship to Judaism* (Sheffield: Sheffield Academic, 2001), 223; and Brawley, *Luke-Acts and the Jews*, 84, 102.

of the prophets (Mt 23:34-36); the Matthean context undercuts the pathos accentuated in the Lukan setting and inherent in the words themselves.[11]

Luke also emphasizes this pathos by including two incidents in his Gospel that are absent from Matthew, Mark and John—one describing Jesus' public entrance into Jerusalem and the other portraying his public departure. When Luke recounts Jesus' triumphal procession into the holy city, he alone among the Gospel writers informs us that Jesus wept as he contemplated the suffering the city would experience forty years later at the hands of the Romans (Lk 19:41-44). When Luke describes Jesus' humiliating exit from the city under the whip of Roman soldiers, he alone among the Gospel writers tells us of the women who follow along wailing for him (Lk 23:27) and of Jesus' response to them—a response that again anticipates the future suffering of Jerusalem:

> But Jesus turned to them and said, "Daughters of Jerusalem, do not weep for me, but weep for yourselves and for your children. For the days are surely coming when they will say, 'Blessed are the barren, and the wombs that never bore, and the breasts that never nursed.' Then they will begin to say to the mountains, 'Fall on us'; and to the hills, 'Cover us.' For if they do this when the wood is green, what will happen when it is dry?" (Lk 23:28-31)

Luke includes more of these proleptic flashes of impending judgment than the other Gospels, but in doing so the author evinces no sense of joy or vindication at Jerusalem's tragic fate. In pondering the city's day of judgment, the Lukan Jesus weeps.

A second unique feature of Luke's orientation to the destruction of Jerusalem in AD 70 appears in his account of Jesus' eschatological discourse (Lk 21:5-36). In Mark and Matthew this discourse so combines and compresses references to the *imminent* destruction of Jerusalem and the *ultimate* distress of the eschaton that the two events are inextricably entangled. This overlay of one event on the other is especially evident in Mark 13:14-20:

> But when you see the desolating sacrilege [*to bdelygma tēs erēmōseōs*] set up where it ought not to be (let the reader understand), then those in Judea must

---

[11]The Matthean version of this saying is typical of the book's polemical attitude toward the Pharisees. As I have argued elsewhere, Matthew's polemics derive in large part from the author's ideological proximity to Pharisaic thought (see Mark S. Kinzer, *Postmissionary Messianic Judaism: Redefining Christian Engagement with the Jewish People* [Grand Rapids: Brazos, 2005], 247-55). These polemics do not imply a view of the Jewish people or the land of Israel that diverges radically from what is found in Luke–Acts.

flee to the mountains; the one on the housetop must not go down or enter the house to take anything away; the one in the field must not turn back to get a coat. Woe to those who are pregnant and to those who are nursing infants in those days! Pray that it may not be in winter. For in those days there will be suffering, such as has not been from the beginning of the creation that God created until now, no, and never will be. And if the Lord had not cut short those days, no one would be saved; but for the sake of the elect, whom he chose, he has cut short those days.

The "desolating sacrilege"—or, more literally, "the detestable thing of desolation"—alludes to the apocalyptic prophecies of Daniel (Dan 9:27; 11:31; 12:11) and their description of an idolatrous altar or image erected in the temple; the phrase thus refers to an event immediately preceding the resurrection of the saints and the transformation of heaven and earth.

In contrast, Luke's version of these verses distinguishes clearly between what will happen in Jerusalem in AD 70 and what will happen when Jesus returns.[12]

> When you see Jerusalem surrounded by armies, then know that its desolation [*erēmōsis*] has come near. Then those in Judea must flee to the mountains, and those inside the city must leave it, and those out in the country must not enter it; for these are days of vengeance, as a fulfillment of all that is written. Woe to those who are pregnant and to those who are nursing infants in those days! For there will be great distress on the earth and wrath against this people [*laos*]; they will fall by the edge of the sword and be taken away as captives among all nations [*ethnē*]; and Jerusalem will be trampled on by the Gentiles [*ethnōn*], until the times of the Gentiles [*ethnōn*] are fulfilled. (Lk 21:20-24)

Luke transforms Mark's reference to the desecration of the temple (*to bdelygma tēs erēmōseōs*) so that it becomes a description of the "desolation" (*erēmōsis*) of the entire city. The sign that leads the disciples to flee is no longer an idolatrous altar but instead the sight of Jerusalem surrounded by Roman armies. The Markan text implies a cosmic distress, whereas the Lukan version speaks of "wrath against *this people*" (i.e., the Jewish people who inhabit Jerusalem). Most

---

[12]N. T. Wright famously interprets the entirety of Mark 13 as referring to the destruction of Jerusalem in AD 70 (see N. T. Wright, *Jesus and the Victory of God* [Minneapolis: Fortress, 1996], 339-68). His argument for this position has convinced few scholars. Dale Allison's trenchant critique of this reading of Mark 13 represents the trustworthy consensus of New Testament scholarship. See Dale C. Allison Jr., "Jesus and the Victory of Apocalyptic," in *Jesus and the Restoration of Israel*, ed. Carey C. Newman (Downers Grove, IL: InterVarsity Press, 1999), 126-41. Wright's response to this critique is found in the same volume (pp. 261-68).

significantly, *the world in its unredeemed form—and the Jewish people—remain in existence after this event*, for not all of the inhabitants of Jerusalem are slain but some are "taken away as captives among all the Gentiles [*ethnē*]," and "Jerusalem will be trampled on by the Gentiles [*ethnōn*], until the times of the Gentiles [*ethnōn*] are fulfilled."[13] This concluding statement about Jerusalem implies that an extended period of time will elapse between the destruction of the city by the Gentiles and the end of the age (which will occur only *after* "the times of the Gentiles are fulfilled").

This text from Luke 21 also displays the third unique feature of Luke's orientation to the destruction of Jerusalem. Robert Tannehill considers Luke 21:24 in light of other Jewish literature of the period, and draws the most reasonable conclusion:

> That Jerusalem or the sanctuary has been or will be "trampled on" is a repeated theme in ancient Jewish writings.... This trampling of Jerusalem will last only "until the times of the Gentiles are fulfilled." We are not told explicitly what will happen then, but if we return to the other texts that speak of this trampling, we find the expectation *that Jerusalem will be restored*.[14]

This interpretation of Luke 21:24 receives further support from a similar use of *achri* ("until") in Peter's temple speech in Acts 3:

> And now, brethren, I know that you acted in ignorance, just as your rulers did also. But the things which God announced beforehand by the mouth of all the prophets, that His Christ would suffer, He has thus fulfilled. Therefore repent and return, so that your sins may be wiped away, in order that times [*kairoi*] of refreshing may come from the presence of the Lord; and that He may send Jesus, the Christ appointed for you, whom heaven must receive until [*achri*] the period of restoration [*apokatastasis*] of all things about which God spoke by the mouth of His holy prophets from ancient time. (Acts 3:17-21 NASB)

I will comment further on this passage below, but at this point I only note its connection to Luke 21:24. The "times [*kairoi*] of the Gentiles"—referring to

---

[13]It is unfortunate that the NRSV translates *ethnē* in Lk 21:24a as "nations" and then renders the two uses of *ethnōn* in Lk 21:24b as "Gentiles." This obscures the connection between the two halves of the verse, which preserves throughout the distinction between the Jewish people (the *laos* of Lk 21:23b) and the Gentiles who are the agents and the locus of their exile.

[14]Robert C. Tannehill, *Luke* (Nashville: Abingdon, 1996), 305-6 (emphasis added). The "other texts" to which Tannehill refers include Zechariah 12:3 (LXX) and Psalms of Solomon 17:21-24.

exclusive Gentile sovereignty over Jerusalem resulting from Israel's rejection of the prophetic message—will give way to the "times [*kairoi*] of refreshing" when Israel repents and welcomes "the Christ [i.e., Messiah] appointed for you." The resurrected Messiah will remain in the heavenly sphere "*until* [*achri*] the period [*chronoi*] of restoration [*apokatastasis*] of all things about which God spoke by the mouth of His holy prophets"—which is apparently equivalent in meaning to "*until* [*achri*] the times [*kairioi*] of the Gentiles are fulfilled." According to Albrecht Oepke, the verbal form of *apokatastasis* becomes in the Septuagint and Josephus a technical term "for the restoration of Israel to its own land."[15] From its context, the noun form in Acts 3:21 evidently includes this meaning.

Luke is thus unique among the Gospels not only in its emphasis on Jerusalem's coming destruction but also in its anticipation of the city's future restoration. This theme occupies an especially prominent place in the Lukan infancy narrative, where Simeon and Anna's encounter with the child Jesus satisfies their longing to see the beginning of "the redemption of Jerusalem" (Lk 2:38) and the "consolation of Israel" (Lk 2:25). Since the hope for Jerusalem's redemption resounds at the beginning of the Gospel, but is not in fact attained in the course of the events recounted in Luke's two volumes, attentive readers recognize that Luke's story is incomplete.

Luke displays this sense of incompleteness—or, one might even say, of the temporary frustration of God's redemptive purpose—through the verbal connections linking two of his key texts. The first is the Song of Zechariah in Luke 1:68-79, uttered by the father of John the Baptist on the occasion of the child's circumcision. The song is a celebration of God's saving power at work in the fulfillment of God's promises to Israel. The object of praise is "the Lord God of Israel" (Lk 1:68), and God's redeeming act is in accordance with the oath sworn to Abraham (Lk 1:73) and the covenant established with the patriarchs (Lk 1:72). In the births of John the Baptist and Jesus, God has "looked favorably on ['visited,' *epeskepsato*] his people and redeemed them" (Lk 1:68), "to give knowledge [*gnosis*] of salvation to his people" (Lk 1:77) and "to guide our feet into the way of peace [*eirēnēs*]" (Lk 1:79). God's work through John and Jesus will result in Israel being "saved" and "rescued" from its enemies (*echthrōn*) (Lk 1:71, 73).

---

[15]Albrecht Oepke, "*apokathistemi*," *TDNT* 1:388. See Hosea 11:11; Jeremiah 16:15, 24:6; Josephus, *Jewish Antiquities* 11.2, 63.

The second text is Luke's account of Jesus' weeping over Jerusalem before his triumphal entry to the city:

> As he came near and saw the city, he wept over it, saying, "If you, even you, had only recognized [*egnōs*] on this day the things that make for peace [*eirēnēn*]! But now they are hidden from your eyes. Indeed, the days will come upon you, when your enemies [*echthroi*] will set up ramparts around you and surround you, and hem you in on every side. They will crush you to the ground, you and your children within you, and they will not leave within you one stone upon another; because you did not recognize [*egnōs*] the time of your visitation [*episcopē*] from God." (Lk 19:41-44)

While the language of these verses recalls that of the Song of Zechariah, the tone and content of the two texts are diametrically opposed. The ecstatic joy of the song has been transmuted into profound grief. John and Jesus came to bring Israel "the knowledge [*gnosis*] of salvation," but the people "did not recognize ["know," *egnōs*]" this salvation when it appeared. God has "visited" [*epeskepsato*] Israel for their good, but the people did not discern this "visitation" [*episcopē*]. God had wanted to bring Israel "peace" [*eirēnēs*] and rescue from "enemies" [*echthrōn*], but Israel did not recognize "the things that make for peace [*eirēnēs*]" and consequently will be surrounded and defeated by its "enemies" [*echthrōn*].[16]

The contradictory tone and content of these two texts represent in vivid fashion the puzzling and paradoxical character of Luke's geographical structure and message. As the Jewish people's longed-for Messiah, Jesus comes to bring redemption to Jerusalem and consolation to Israel. Nevertheless, his mission results in the destruction of Jerusalem and Israel's second exile. Luke highlights both themes and sets them in jarring juxtaposition, rather than accentuating one and downplaying the other. Luke then proceeds to treat this destruction and exile as the beginning of an era—associated with "the Gentiles"—which at some point in the future will come to an end. Finally, he implies in Acts 3:19-21 (and also in Lk 13:35) that Jesus will return in response to Jerusalem's repentance and corporate welcome. In this way the

---

[16]Robert C. Tannehill notes the link between these two texts and the literary effect it produces: "The narrator intends to connect the arrival in Jerusalem with the birth narrative in order to highlight the tragic turn which the narrative is now taking. The great expectations in the birth narrative for the redemption of Israel and Jerusalem are not being realized in the anticipated way and with the anticipated fullness, because Jerusalem is failing to recognize the time of its visitation." Tannehill, *The Narrative Unity of Luke-Acts*, vol. 1, *The Gospel According to Luke* (Philadelphia: Fortress, 1986), 160.

content of Luke and Acts supports our conclusion regarding the geographical structure of the latter book: the end of the book is not the end of the story. Luke intimates that the outward flow will once again be followed by an inward return, and Israel's second Babylonian exile will culminate in a final pilgrimage to Zion.

Traditional interpreters such as Gary Burge have looked to the geographical structure of Luke–Acts in order to support their reading of Acts 1:6-8. Our examination of that structure in the light of the Lukan teaching concerning the judgment and redemption of Jerusalem shows that the opposite is the case. Far from confirming the traditional view of Acts 1, the geographical structure of the book effectively undermines that view. Luke tells a story that remains unfinished, and that points forward to a day "when the times of the Gentiles are fulfilled." In that day Israel's Roman exile (anticipated by Acts 28:23-31) will come to an end, as did its earlier Babylonian exile.

> And the ransomed of the LORD shall return,
> and come to Zion with singing. (Is 35:10)

"THIS SALVATION OF GOD HAS BEEN SENT TO THE GENTILES" (ACTS 28:28)

The traditional reading. The ending of the book of Acts is significant not only because its scenes are set in Rome. Traditional commentators also underline the fact that the book ends with Paul's prophetic rebuke of the Jewish leaders of the city.

> The Holy Spirit was right in saying to your ancestors through the prophet Isaiah,
>
> "Go to this people and say,
> You will indeed listen, but never understand,
>   and you will indeed look, but never perceive.
> For this people's heart has grown dull,
>   and their ears are hard of hearing,
>   and they have shut their eyes;
>   so that they might not look with their eyes,
>   and listen with their ears,
>   and understand with their heart and turn—
>   and I would heal them."

Let it be known to you then that this salvation [*sōtērion*] of God has been sent to the Gentiles; they will listen. (Acts 28:25-28)

Paul's citation of Isaiah 6 has been taken as marking the definitive dissolution of the Jewish people's covenantal status. Thus, Hans Conzelmann asserts, "Israel's turning away from salvation is final, as is clear in Paul's concluding statement in Acts 28:28."[17] While Joseph Tyson considers Luke's view of Judaism to be conflicted and complex, his assessment of Acts 28:28 echoes that of Conzelmann: "The text that exhibits such profound ambivalence in regard to Jews and Judaism [i.e., Luke-Acts as a whole] moves toward a resolution without ambivalence or ambiguity: an image of Jewish people as rejecting the gospel and thus as a people without hope."[18] If that is the case, then Luke envisions no eventual "return to Jerusalem," and Burge is justified in reading Acts 1:6-8 as an instance of apostolic misunderstanding and dominical correction.[19]

This conclusion draws support from the way Luke structures his narrative of Paul's missionary expeditions. In his initial journey Paul delivers a lengthy speech in the synagogue of Antioch of Pisidia in Asia Minor (Acts 13:16-41). At first the Jewish audience welcomes Paul's message (Acts 13:42-43), but the following week they turn hostile. Paul's response anticipates his words to the Jewish elders of Rome, though here he cites Isaiah 49:6 rather than Isaiah 6:

It was necessary that the word of God should be spoken first to you. Since you reject it and judge yourselves to be unworthy of eternal life, we are now turning to the Gentiles. For so the Lord has commanded us, saying,

"I have set you to be a light for the Gentiles,
so that you may bring salvation to the ends of the earth." (Acts 13:46-47)

---

[17] Cited in Joseph B. Tyson, *Luke, Judaism, and the Scholars: Critical Approaches to Luke-Acts* (Columbia: University of South Carolina Press, 1999), 88.
[18] Ibid., 144-45.
[19] Like Burge, Conzelmann contends that Jesus *will* restore the kingdom to a *redefined* Israel, and the basis for his contention is Acts 28: "Acts i,6 speaks of the Kingdom being restored to Israel.... The emphatic passage, xxviii, 28 ... shows who now shares in this hope: salvation is passing to the Gentiles.... Luke thinks of the Christians, according to plan, taking over the privileges of the Jews as one epoch is succeeded by the next" (Hans Conzelmann, *The Theology of St. Luke*, trans. Geoffrey Buswell [1961; repr., Philadelphia: Fortress, 1982], 163). In other words, Conzelmann believes the question of the apostles in Acts 1:6 is not in itself misguided; they only misunderstand the meaning of the term "Israel," which in the new dispensation refers to the church of the Gentiles. Of course, this also implies a dramatic change in the nature of that kingdom (i.e., it will be nongeographical) and its restoration.

In his second missionary journey Paul receives a vision beckoning him to leave Asia Minor in order to begin a new work across the Aegean (Acts 16:9-10). Paul eventually makes his way to Corinth, a city situated on an isthmus and described by Strabo in 7 BC as "master of two harbors, of which the one leads straight to Asia, and the other to Italy."[20] Here Luke describes briefly a scene that resembles what occurred earlier in Antioch of Pisidia (in Asia) and what will occur later in Rome (in Italy):

> Paul was occupied with proclaiming the word, testifying to the Jews that the Messiah was Jesus. When they opposed and reviled him, in protest he shook the dust from his clothes and said to them, "Your blood be on your own heads! I am innocent. From now on I will go to the Gentiles." Then he left the synagogue and went to the house of a man named Titius Justus, a worshiper of God; his house was next door to the synagogue. (Acts 18:5-7)

Thus, Paul's declaration that he is "going to the Gentiles" is recounted three times in three geographical settings that represent the crucial stages of Paul's expanding apostolic sphere. As with the three accounts of Paul's vision on the road to Damascus (Acts 9:1-19; 22:6-16; 26:12-18) and the three accounts of Peter's encounter with Cornelius (Acts 10:1-48; 11:4-18; 15:7-9), the literary technique of threefold repetition emphasizes the importance of Paul's words in the eyes of the author.

Therefore, the traditional commentators have good reason to stress Paul's final words to the Jewish elders of Rome. But how does Luke understand these words, and what is he trying to say through them? And how might they help us understand the words of Jesus at the beginning of the book of Acts (i.e., Acts 1:6-8)?

To answer these questions, I will first examine the intertextual network underlying Acts 28:28 and Acts 13:47 and then reflect on the impact of social context on the prophetic rhetoric of Paul's speeches.

The intertextual network underlying Acts 28:28. Paul's concluding words to the Jewish elders of Rome are as follows: "Let it be known to you then that this salvation of God [*to sōtērion tou Theou*] has been sent to the Gentiles; they will listen" (Acts 28:28). The Greek word *sōtērion* (salvation) is rare in the New Testament, appearing only five times. Three of those occurrences are found in Luke–Acts. The most important of the three, which illuminates the others, is

---

[20]Cited by Richard B. Hays, *First Corinthians* (Louisville, KY: Westminster John Knox, 1997), 3.

Luke 3:4-6. Here Luke parallels Mark and Matthew by characterizing the mission of John the Baptist in terms of Isaiah 40:3, but then goes beyond Mark and Matthew by citing Isaiah 40:4-5 as well:

> As it is written in the book of the words of the prophet Isaiah,
>
> > "The voice of one crying out in the wilderness:
> > 'Prepare the way of the Lord,
> > > make his paths straight. [Citation of Is 40 in Mark and Matthew ends here.]
> > Every valley shall be filled,
> > > and every mountain and hill shall be made low,
> > and the crooked shall be made straight,
> > > and the rough ways made smooth;
> > and all flesh [*pasa sarx*] shall see the salvation of God [*to sōtērion tou Theou*].'"
> > (Lk 3:4-6)

In Acts 28:28 Paul states that "the salvation of God" [*to sōtērion tou Theou*], which Israel is now failing to receive, will be experienced by Gentiles. Yet, citing Isaiah 40:5, Luke 3 tells us that this "salvation" will be seen (i.e., experienced) by "all flesh." It thus appears that Acts 28:28 witnesses to only a partial fulfillment of Isaiah 40:5.

How does Luke understand the phrase "all flesh" (*pasa sarx*) in Isaiah 40:5 (LXX)? Who are those who are destined to "see the salvation of God"? Luke's intention becomes clear in the Song of Simeon, the remaining text in which the word *sōtērion* is found.[21]

> Master, now you are dismissing your servant in peace,
> > according to your word;
> for my eyes have seen your salvation [*sōtērion*],
> > which you have prepared in the presence of all peoples [*pantōn tōn laōn*],
> a light for revelation to the Gentiles
> > and for glory to your people Israel. (Lk 2:29-32)

---

[21] The importance of Isaiah 40 as an intertextual reference in the Song of Simeon is highlighted also by the way Luke introduces the figure of Simeon: "Now there was a man in Jerusalem whose name was Simeon; this man was righteous and devout, looking forward to the consolation [*paraklēsin*] of Israel" (Lk 2:25). The phrase "the consolation of Israel" alludes to the opening words of Isaiah 40: "Comfort, o comfort [*parakaleite, parakaleite*] my people" (Is 40:1).

Simeon's "all peoples" (*pantōn tōn laōn*) is equivalent to Isaiah's "all flesh" (*pasa sarx*), and the meaning of "all peoples" is then explained in the line that follows: the phrase refers to Israel and the Gentiles (i.e., the nations) together. Luke 2:32 alludes to Isaiah 49:5-6:

> And now the LORD says,
>   who formed me in the womb to be his servant,
> to bring Jacob back to him,
>   and that Israel might be gathered to him,
> for I am honored in the sight of the LORD,
>   and my God has become my strength—
> he says,
> "It is too light a thing that you should be my servant
>   to raise up the tribes of Jacob
>   and to restore the survivors of Israel;
> I will give you as a light to the nations,
>   that my salvation may reach to the end of the earth."

God sends the servant to accomplish a dual mission: he is to be a "light to the nations" (i.e., Gentiles) but also "to raise up the tribes of Jacob." Luke perceives these verses of Isaiah to be fundamental to the divine purpose, and they give shape to his overall narrative. When Paul bears witness before King Agrippa, Isaiah 49:5-6 underlies his formulation of the mission of the risen Messiah conducted through his *ekklēsia*: "To this day I have had help from God, and so I stand here, testifying to both small and great, saying nothing but what the prophets and Moses said would take place: that the Messiah must suffer, and that, by being the first to rise from the dead, *he would proclaim light both to our people and to the Gentiles*" (Acts 26:22-23, emphasis added). Even more telling is the explicit citation of Isaiah 49 in Paul's words to the Jewish community of Antioch in Pisidia, already noted above:

> It was necessary that the word of God should be spoken first to you. Since you reject it and judge yourselves to be unworthy of eternal life, we are now turning to the Gentiles. For so the Lord has commanded us, saying,
>
> "I have set you to be a light for the Gentiles,
>   so that you may bring salvation to the ends of the earth." (Acts 13:46-47)

While the Song of Simeon refers to both parts of the dual mission of the servant, and the reference to "all flesh" ("all peoples" in NRSV) in Luke's citation of Isaiah

40:5 likewise asserts a comprehensive salvific purpose in the work of the Messiah (i.e., including both Gentiles and the "tribes of Jacob"), Paul in Acts 13 ignores Isaiah 49:5-6a (which speaks of Israel) and mentions only Isaiah 49:6b (which speaks of the Gentiles). As we have seen, this anticipates the final scene of Acts 28, in which Paul rebukes the Jewish elders of Rome and announces his "going to the Gentiles."

The most reasonable conclusion to draw from this *intertextual* puzzle is identical to the one we reached regarding Luke's *geographical* puzzle: Luke never tires of asserting that the prophetic words of Scripture must be fulfilled, and Isaiah 40:5 ("*all flesh* will see the salvation of God")—understood in light of Isaiah 49:5-6 ("all flesh" = Israel + the nations)—takes a place of prominence in his reading of those prophetic words. Because of Israel's corporate resistance to the message of the Messiah, Jerusalem will be judged, and only the Gentile portion of Isaiah 49 will be realized in the immediate future. This is the significance of Paul's "going to the Gentiles." However, Jesus has come not only as "a light for revelation to the Gentiles"; he is also destined to bring "glory to your people Israel" (Lk 2:32). Isaiah 49:5-6 will come to pass, but only in a future beyond the events of AD 70 and Israel's second exile, when "the times of the Gentiles are fulfilled" (Lk 21:24).[22] Just as in its original context Isaiah 6 pronounced a judgment and exile whose goal and result was to purify Israel and lead to its ultimate restoration, so Paul in Acts 28 cites these words of Isaiah with the same intent and meaning.[23]

The social context of Paul's prophetic rhetoric in Acts. In order to understand Paul's rebuke of the Jewish leaders in Acts 28 and Luke's threefold description of Paul's "going to the Gentiles," it is necessary to notice the social

---

[22]Charles B. Puskas skillfully identifies the intertextual network discussed here and its relevance to the interpretation of Acts 28. Unfortunately, ignoring the evidence to the contrary, he thinks that Acts 28 indicates the fulfillment of the promises of Isaiah 40 for "all flesh," i.e., *both* Gentiles and Jews: "Paul at Rome brings the universal significance of God's salvation in the person of Jesus, to its completion." Puskas, *The Conclusion of Luke-Acts: The Significance of Acts 28:16-31* (Eugene, OR: Pickwick, 2009), 103. This reading of Acts 28 fails to attend to the *lack of completion* that Luke conveys by ending his narrative in Rome, with Israel about to fall under divine judgment.

[23]Justin Taylor takes a similar approach to Paul's use of Isaiah 6 in Acts 28: "As in the original context in the Book of Isaiah, it is a call to conversion [i.e., repentance] rather than a declaration of rejection." Taylor, "Paul and the Jewish Leaders of Rome: Acts 28:17-31," in *Paul's Jewish Matrix*, ed. Thomas G. Casey and Justin Taylor (Rome: Gregorian & Biblical Press, 2011), 323. Moreover, Taylor argues that the Lukan Paul "who meets with representatives of the Jewish community in Rome in Acts 28 is in substantial agreement in his attitude to Israel with the Paul of Romans 9-11" (ibid., 321).

context in which Paul speaks. In this regard, Acts 28 sheds light on the earlier narratives in the book.

Soon after Paul arrives in Rome, he invites the Jewish leaders of the city to visit him.

> Three days later [after arriving in Rome] he [Paul] called together the local leaders of the Jews. When they had assembled, he said to them, "Brothers, though I had done nothing against our people or the customs of our ancestors, yet I was arrested in Jerusalem and handed over to the Romans.... For this reason therefore I have asked to see you and speak with you, since it is for the sake of the hope of Israel that I am bound with this chain." (Acts 28:17, 20)

This is a formal gathering in which Paul addresses a set of communal representatives. His mode of address displays a rhetoric that emphasizes his relationship with these leaders as fellow members of the same people. He calls them his "brothers," refers to Israel as "*our* people" and to Judaism as "the customs of *our* ancestors," and speaks of his apostolic mission as oriented to "the hope of Israel." Luke then describes the discussion that ensued:

> From morning until evening he explained the matter to them, testifying to the kingdom of God and trying to convince them about Jesus both from the law of Moses and from the prophets. Some were convinced by what he had said, while others refused to believe. So they disagreed with each other. (Acts 28:23-25)

Luke stresses the division of opinion that exists among these Jewish leaders. Some accept Paul's message, while others reject it. From Luke's brief summary description, the reader may assume that there are as many Jewish leaders in the former group as in the latter.[24] This is the social context in which Paul rebukes his audience by citing Isaiah 6 (Acts 28:25-27) and announces his intention of going "to the Gentiles" (Acts 28:28).

Why does Paul respond so negatively to what Christians today might consider a rather successful evangelistic encounter? His fierce reaction appears disproportionate to the mixed attitudes of his audience. This scene makes little sense if we view Paul's audience as a collection of Jewish individuals and Paul's aim in addressing them as the "salvation" of as many of them as possible. Instead,

---

[24]As Taylor notes, "The text simply shows the group who heard Paul as divided: we are not even told that those who did not accept Paul's message were more numerous than those who did" (ibid., 315).

this assembly of prominent Roman Jews must have a corporate and representative function, and Paul's unattained goal in relation to them must likewise be defined in communal terms. Robert Tannehill interprets this scene in a way that takes account of these factors and explains the apparent disproportionality of Paul's response:

> The presence of disagreement among the Jews is enough to show that Paul has not achieved what he sought. He was seeking a communal decision, a recognition by the Jewish community as a whole that Jesus is the fulfillment of the Jewish hope. The presence of significant opposition shows that this is not going to happen.[25]

In other words, the point of the passage is not that these leaders, as individuals or as a group, are definitively saying no to Paul's apostolic message. Instead, the point is that they are failing to definitively say yes, that is, to offer a communal welcome to the announcement of Israel's risen Messiah. The significance of such a yes becomes clear if we interpret Acts 3:19-21 (and Lk 13:35) as a prophetic promise that Israel's corporate repentance and reception of the apostolic message would trigger the events that culminate in the Messiah's return. Paul's rebuke of this divided group of Jewish leaders should be taken then not as a sign that the Jewish people have forfeited their promised inheritance but as implying the exact opposite: the Jewish people retain their unique covenantal status, a fact that increases both their responsibility when they fail and the cosmic blessing that ensues when they succeed.

Tannehill applies this same insight to the previous two incidents in which Paul faults Jewish communal recalcitrance and declares that he will henceforth "go to the Gentiles":

> Paul's announcement that he is going to the Gentiles indicates a shift from a synagogue-based mission, addressed to Jews and to those Gentiles attracted to Judaism, to a mission in the city at large, where the population is predominantly Gentile. . . . Paul . . . has fulfilled his obligation to speak God's word to God's people. They are now responsible for their own fate. The pattern of speaking first to Jews and only later turning to the Gentiles testifies to Paul's sense of prophetic obligation to his own people. He is released from this obligation only when he meets strong public resistance within the Jewish com-

---

[25]Robert C. Tannehill, *The Narrative Unity of Luke-Acts*, vol. 2, *The Acts of the Apostles* (Minneapolis: Fortress, 1990), 347.

munity. Then he can begin the second phase of his mission within a city, a phase in which the conversion of individual Jews is still possible, although Paul is no longer preaching in the synagogue nor addressing Jews as a community.[26]

Paul must go to the Jewish community first, for they are the people of God, and the Messiah is in a unique way *their* Messiah. (Paul's commitment to this truth provides the theological rationale for the initial rhetoric of Acts 28:17-20 in which the apostle stresses his solidarity with the wider Jewish community and its leadership.) Once it becomes evident that the Jewish community in a region will fail to corporately acknowledge Jesus as the Messiah, Paul is free to speak to Jewish and Gentile individuals and to form a distinct ecclesial body in that location. The transition from the first to the second phase of Paul's apostolic strategy in Acts means not that Israel forfeits its status but that it exposes itself to divine judgment (as in past eras) and delays the ultimate arrival of both national and cosmic redemption.

By ending his two volumes with this scene in Rome, Luke signals that a new judgment—and a new exile—is about to befall the people of Israel. While individual Jews would continue to receive the message of Jesus, the Jewish community as a whole would for the immediate future withhold its corporate acclamation of Jesus as the one sent to be "the consolation of Israel." This does not, however, imply a definitive divorce of the Jesus movement from identification with that community or a surrendering of hope for an eschatological reversal of that official communal response.[27] Far from undermining the thesis we have argued based on the geographical structure of Luke-Acts and its treatment of Jerusalem's coming judgment and redemption, this reading of Acts 28 offers further support for that thesis.

---

[26]Ibid., 222-23.

[27]Tannehill adopts a view similar to that expressed here. Joseph Tyson endorses Tannehill's insight into the communal dimension of Paul's efforts among the Jewish people, but he disagrees with Tannehill's suggestion that Israel's future is still open. Tyson thinks that Luke sees Israel as "a people without hope." As my entire argument shows, I find Tyson's contention unconvincing. See Joseph B. Tyson, "The Problem of Jewish Rejection in Acts," in *Luke-Acts and the Jewish People: Eight Critical Perspectives*, ed. Joseph B. Tyson (Minneapolis: Augsburg, 1988), 126-27; and idem, *Luke, Judaism, and the Scholars*, 142-45.

"The Time When You Will Restore the Kingdom to Israel" (Acts 1:6)

We are now ready to analyze Acts 1:6-8 itself.

> So when they had come together, they asked him, "Lord, is this the time [*tō chronō*] when you will restore [*apokathistaneis*] the kingdom to Israel?" He replied, "It is not for you to know the times [*chronous*] or periods [*kairous*] that the Father has set by his own authority. But you will receive power when the Holy Spirit has come upon you; and you will be my witnesses in Jerusalem, in all Judea and Samaria, and to the ends of the earth." (Acts 1:6-8)

One of the most striking features of this text is the way its language and meaning coincide with two interrelated passages examined above—namely, Luke 21:24 and Acts 3:17-21. The first of these passages speaks of "the times [*kairous*] of the Gentiles" as a temporal period intervening between the destruction of Jerusalem and its restoration. The addition of the word *kairos* by Jesus in Acts 1:6 (the question of the apostles uses only the synonym *chronos*) may point the reader back to this crucial verse in the eschatological discourse and imply that the apostles have not yet understood that Jerusalem would be judged before being redeemed.

The second passage is found in Peter's speech in the Jerusalem temple:

> And now, brethren, I know that you acted in ignorance, just as your rulers did also. But the things which God announced beforehand by the mouth of all the prophets, that His Christ would suffer, He has thus fulfilled. Therefore repent and return, so that your sins may be wiped away, in order that times [*kairoi*] of refreshing may come from the presence of the Lord; and that He may send Jesus, the Christ appointed for you, whom heaven must receive until [*achri*] the period [*chronōn*, lit. "times"] of restoration [*apokatastaseōs*] of all things about which God spoke by the mouth of His holy prophets from ancient time. (Acts 3:17-21; NASB)

We have already noted the connection between the use of *achri* (until) in Acts 3:21 and the appearance of the same word in Luke 21:24 ("until [*achri*] the times of the Gentiles are fulfilled"). At this point we must attend to the parallels between these verses in Acts 3 and in our main text, Acts 1:6-8. In both passages the two roughly synonymous nouns, *chronoi* and *kairoi*, are paired. More significantly, Acts 1:6 employs the verb *apokathistēmi* (translated by the NRSV as "restore") while Acts 3:21 uses the cognate nominal form *apokatastasis* (translated by the NASB as "restoration"). As noted above, Albrecht Oepke views the verb as a technical term in wider Jewish use "for the restoration of Israel to its own land." The language of the apostles' question to Jesus in Acts 1:6 is thus echoed by Peter's speech to the people of Jerusalem in Acts 3, with the same meaning in both cases: Peter tells the Jerusalemites that the kingdom will be restored to Israel (as a central and essential element in the "restoration of all things about which God spoke by the mouth of His holy prophets") when they acknowledge Jesus as Israel's returning king. This echo implies that Peter has not interpreted Jesus' answer in Acts 1:7-8 as a rejection of the legitimacy of the question.

The verses immediately following the opening dialogue between Jesus and his disciples in Acts 1 provide further confirmation of our thesis:

> When he had said this, as they were watching, he was lifted up, and a cloud took him out of their sight. While he was going and they were gazing up toward heaven, suddenly two men in white robes stood by them. They said, "Men of Galilee, why do you stand looking up toward heaven? This Jesus, who has been taken up from you into heaven, will come in the same way as you saw him go into heaven."
>
> Then they returned to Jerusalem from the mount called Olivet, which is near Jerusalem, a sabbath day's journey away. (Acts 1:9-12)

What is meant by the revelation that Jesus "will come in the same way as you saw him go"? Acts 1:12 hints at the answer by telling us that the ascension occurred on the Mount of Olives. Luke's mention of the location points the reader to the eschatological prophecy of Zechariah 14:

> For I will gather all the nations against Jerusalem to battle.... Then the LORD will go forth and fight against those nations as when he fights on a day of battle. On that day *his feet shall stand on the Mount of Olives*, which lies before Jerusalem on the east; and the Mount of Olives shall be split in two from east to west by a very wide valley.... *Then the LORD my God will come, and all the holy ones with him.* (Zech 14:2-5, emphasis added)

In light of Zechariah 14 and Luke's Jerusalem-centered cartography, we should interpret the phrase "in the same way" (Acts 1:11) as including the physical site of the two events. Just as Jesus ascends now *from* the Mount of Olives, so he will descend at the end *to* the Mount of Olives. Just as he ascends now *from* Jerusalem, so he will descend at the end *to* Jerusalem. Jerusalem will suffer many things, just as Zechariah 12–14 foretells. But she will be consoled when her Lord comes to defend her at the end, his feet standing on the Mount of Olives. At that time the Lord will be welcomed by Jerusalem in a fitting manner, with her leaders and people taking up the cry uttered only by his disciples at Jesus' first coming: "Blessed is the king who comes in the name of the Lord!" (Lk 19:38; see Lk 13:35). This triumphal entry will be an occasion of messianic joy rather than lament (see again Lk 19:41-44).

Whether read in light of parallel verses in Luke and Acts, or in its own immediate context, or in relation to the ending or geographical structure of the books, or in connection to the wider Lukan teaching regarding Jerusalem's judgment and redemption, there is little evidence to suggest that Acts 1:6-8 should be read as anything but a dominical promise of the ultimate restoration of the kingdom to Israel in the holy city of Jerusalem. Moreover, there is likewise little evidence to suggest that the "Israel" that is spoken of is an entity separate from the Jewish people. With the prophet Simeon, Luke continues to await the "redemption of Jerusalem."

Conclusion

While necessary and richly suggestive, exegesis of Luke–Acts—or of any other New Testament texts—is not a sufficient ground for the cultivation of a twenty-first-century theological Zionism among the disciples of Jesus. The development of such a theological vision will also require (among other things) sustained and disciplined reflection on the identity of the *ekklēsia*, her relationship to the Jewish people and her vocation in the realm of worldly politics; in addition, it will demand a theological and ethical assessment of a multitude of contingent facts of history. The remaining chapters in the present volume address some of these essential matters, and take us further on the road to a new twenty-first-century theological Zionism.

The question I have addressed in this chapter (as expressed in its title) is more circumscribed in character: Do the people of Israel and the land of Israel persist as abiding concerns in Luke and Acts? My answer is a resounding yes. Exegesis of Luke–Acts *is* sufficient to undermine the arguments of those who assert that the New Testament delegitimizes the theological claims of the Jewish people in relation to the city of Jerusalem and the land of Israel. That is precisely the intent of the assertions of Gary Burge with which we began, and which we will again cite as we conclude:

> At no point do the earliest Christians view the Holy Land as a locus of divine activity to which the people of the Roman empire must be drawn. They do not promote the Holy Land either for the Jew or for the Christian as a vital aspect of faith. . . . The early Christians possessed no territorial theology. Early Christian preaching is utterly *uninterested* in a Jewish eschatology devoted to the restoration of the land. The kingdom of Christ began in Judea and is historically anchored there but it is not tethered to a political realization of that kingdom in the Holy Land.[28]

Luke–Acts refutes each of the above propositions: this two-volume work *does* "view the Holy Land as a locus of divine activity," *does* "promote the Holy Land . . . as a vital aspect of faith," *does* possess a "territorial theology," *is intensely concerned about* "a Jewish eschatology devoted to the restoration of the land" and—depending on the meaning assigned here to the word *political*—*is* "tethered to a political realization" of the "kingdom in the Holy Land."

The story told by Luke–Acts is unfinished. Its last *recorded* chapter is set in Rome, at the "ends of the earth." While yet unwritten, we know where the *final* chapter of the story will take place—and it will not be Washington, D.C., Beijing, Brussels or Moscow. When the outward flow of the apostolic mission has reached its appointed limit, the current will reverse and return to its center so that from there it might nurture the entire world. Then will be realized the words of the prophet:

> On that day living waters shall flow out from Jerusalem, half of them to the eastern sea and half of them to the western sea; it shall continue in summer as in winter.
>
> And the LORD will become king over all the earth; on that day the LORD will be one and his name one. (Zech 14:8-9)

---

[28] Burge, *Jesus and the Land*, 59.

6

ZIONISM IN PAULINE LITERATURE

Does Paul Eliminate Particularity for Israel and the Land in His Portrayal of Salvation Available for All the World?

David Rudolph

◆

About eighty-five years after Paul wrote his letter to the Romans, Justin Martyr wrote in his *Dialogue with Trypho*, "And hence you [Trypho] ought to understand that [the gifts] formerly among your nation [the Jewish people] have been *transferred* to us [Christians]."[1] Perhaps the most articulate proponent of this "*transference* theology" today is N. T. Wright, who has spent the last forty years writing about the relationship between the church and Israel in Paul's theology. Wright argues that through the coming of Christ, God's relationship with the Jewish people has been reconfigured so that Israel's covenant blessings, responsibilities and calling have all been "transferred" to the church as a whole, thus resulting in the erasure of divinely given Jewish boundary markers of identity. Or to put it in more politically correct language, these boundary markers have all been universalized:

> In Rom. 5–8 Paul develops the picture of the church in terms belonging to Israel. This transfer is achieved in two stages. First, Israel's calling, responsibilities

---

[1] Justin, *Dialogue with Trypho* 82. In the oldest extant commentary on Paul's letter to the Romans (ca. AD 246), Origen argues that Israel's blessings have been transferred from the Jews to the Gentiles: "Through the whole text of the epistle . . . the Apostle has taught how the highest religion has been *transferred* from the Jews to the Gentiles, from circumcision to faith, from the letter to the spirit, from shadow to truth, from carnal observance to spiritual observance." Origen, *Commentaire sur l'Épître aux Romains, tome 4: Livres IX—X*, trans. Caroline P. Hammond Bammel and Luc Bresard, *Sources chrétiennes*, 555 (Paris: Cerf, 2012) (emphasis added).

and privileges have been taken over by the Messiah himself, alone: second, what is true of the Messiah is reckoned to be true of his people. . . . In him all believers, without distinction of race, inherit all that was Israel's. . . . Paul, in line with Old Testament prophecy, claims that God's glory has been taken away from Israel according to the flesh and given to the community of the new covenant. . . . The Christian is the true Jew. . . . The first five verses of the chapter [Rom 5:1-5] thus set out the grounds of assurance in terms of the transfer of Israel's privileges to the church. . . . What Israel should have done, the Messiah has done alone. Having therefore taken Israel's task, he (and hence his people) inherit Israel's privileges. . . . We have seen that Paul explicitly and consciously transfers blessings from Israel according to the flesh to the Messiah, and thence to the church. . . . In the same way, Gal. 2–4 argues precisely that the worldwide believing church is the true family of Abraham, and that those who remain as "Israel according to the flesh" are in fact the theological descendants of Hagar and Ishmael, with no title to the promises. . . . It is not therefore without a touch of bitter irony, reminiscent of Phil. 3.2ff., that he [Paul] transfers the name "Israel" to the church.[2]

In line with this transference theology paradigm,[3] Wright argues that the temple, Jerusalem and the land of Israel are all covenantal blessings that were "superseded" (to use Wright's term!)[4] through the coming of Christ. Based on this supersessionist reading of Paul, Wright goes on to describe Christian

---

[2]N. T. Wright, "The Messiah and the People of God: A Study in Pauline Theology with Particular Reference to the Argument of the Epistle to the Romans" (PhD diss., University of Oxford, 1980), 135-37, 139-40, 193, 196. "In Romans 5–8 Paul argues that all of Israel's privileges have now been transferred, via the Messiah, to the worldwide people of God, the true family of Abraham. . . . Christians are the new humanity ([Rom] 5.12ff.), God's sons ([Rom] 8.12ff.), inheriting God's glory ([Rom] 8.18ff.), his covenants and law ([Rom] 7.1–8.11), his promises to the Patriarchs ([Rom] 4) and so offering to God the true worship of Israel (Phil. 3.2ff.). That this list fits so well with Rom. 9.3ff. is again indicative of the whole shape of Paul's argument." N. T. Wright, "Justification: Its Relevance for Contemporary Evangelicalism (1980)," in *Pauline Perspectives: Essays on Paul, 1978–2013* (Minneapolis: Fortress, 2013), 32, 32n59.

[3]Wright's brand of supersessionism is reviewed in Douglas Harink, *Paul Among the Postliberals: Pauline Theology Beyond Christendom and Modernity* (Grand Rapids: Brazos, 2003), 151-207, and in Michael G. Vanlaningham, "An Evaluation of N. T. Wright's View of Israel in Romans 11," *BSac* 170 (April-June 2013): 179-93.

[4]For a discussion of the history and definition of the term *supersessionism*, see Matthew A. Tapie, *Aquinas on Israel and the Church: The Question of Supersessionism in the Theology of Thomas Aquinas* (Eugene, OR: Pickwick, 2014), 9-24; R. Kendall Soulen, "Supersessionism," in *A Dictionary of Jewish-Christian Relations*, ed. Edward Kessler and Neil Wenborn (Cambridge: Cambridge University Press, 2008), 413-14; and Michael J. Vlach, *The Church as a Replacement of Israel: An Analysis of Supersessionism* (Frankfurt am Main: Peter Lang, 2009), 17-40.

Zionism as a "*soi-disant* 'Christian' apartheid" that should be rejected. He writes in his essay "Jerusalem in the New Testament":

> In Romans 4:13 Paul says, startlingly, "The promise to Abraham and his seed, that they should inherit the world." Surely the promises of inheritance were that Abraham's family would inherit the land of Israel, not the world? Paul's horizon, however, is bigger. The Land, like the Torah, was a temporary stage in the long purpose of the God of Abraham. It was not a bad thing now done away with, but a good and necessary thing now fulfilled in Christ and the Spirit. It is as though, in fact, the Land were a great advance metaphor for the design of God that his people should eventually bring the world into submission to his healing reign. God's whole purpose now goes beyond Jerusalem and the Land to the whole world. . . . The Temple had been superseded by the Church. If this is so for the Temple, and in Romans 4 for the Land, then it must *a fortiori* be the case for Jerusalem. . . . Jesus' whole claim is to do and be what the city and the temple were and did. As a result, both claims, the claim of Jesus and the claim of "holy land," can never be sustained simultaneously. . . . The only appropriate attitude in subsequent generations towards Jews, the Temple, the Land or Jerusalem must be one of sorrow or pity. . . . The responsibility of the church in the present age is to anticipate the age to come in acts of justice, mercy, beauty and truth; we are to live "now" as it will be "then." We can only do this, of course, insofar as we have got quite clear in our minds that there is no going back to the old lines that demarcate human beings (race, colour, gender, geography, etc.). That is to say, among other things, that there can and must be no "Christian" theology of "holy places" (on the model or analogy of the "holy places" of a religion that has an essentially geographical base), any more than there can be a "Christian" theology of racial superiority on the model or analogy of a religion that has an essentially racial base. To that extent, "Christian Zionism" is the geographical equivalent of a *soi-disant* "Christian" apartheid, and ought to be rejected as such.[5]

---

[5] N. T. Wright, "Jerusalem in the New Testament," in *Jerusalem Past and Present in the Purposes of God*, ed. P. W. L. Walker (Cambridge: Tyndale House, 1992), 67, 70, 73-75. Wright's polemic could be construed as an unintended Christian theology of ethnic cleansing that stigmatizes Jewish boundary markers of identity, including those that are mentioned in the Scriptures as God-ordained, leading ultimately to the elimination of Jewish presence in the church. This result is not mere theory but the historical footprint of Christian transference theology since the time of Justin Martyr. As Michael Wyschogrod puts it, "In fact, throughout the centuries, Jews who entered the Church very quickly lost their Jewish identity. . . . In short, if all Jews in past ages had followed the advice of the Church to become Christians, there would be no more Jews in the world today. The question we must ask is: Does the Church really want a world without Jews?

It is not an overstatement to say that a growing number of Christians are sympathetic to Wright's view. But is this transference reading of Paul correct? Would "the circumcised apostle"[6] nod approvingly at Wright's attempted synthesis of Paul's perspective on this subject? Or would Paul view the notion of a first-century expiration date on Jewish election as a distortion of his teachings? The bottom-line question is, does Paul eliminate particularity for Israel and the land in his portrayal of salvation available for all the world?

This essay maintains that Paul's gospel does *not* eliminate such particularity and that a compelling case can be made on the basis of Paul's writings for the perpetuity of Jewish particularity. I will begin by discussing several Pauline passages that are often quoted by transference theology proponents to contend that Paul opposed Jewish particularity. Then I will present arguments in support of the view that Paul upheld the continued election, gifts and calling of the Jewish people.

Does the Church believe that such a world is in accordance with the will of God? Or does the Church believe that it is God's will, even after the coming of Jesus, that there be a Jewish people in the world? . . . If, from the Christian point of view, Israel's election remains a contemporary reality, then the disappearance of the Jewish people from the world cannot be an acceptable development." Michael Wyschogrod, "A Letter to Cardinal Lustiger," in *Abraham's Promise: Judaism and Jewish-Christian Relations*, ed. R. Kendall Soulen (Grand Rapids: Eerdmans, 2004), 207-8.

William S. Campbell calls into question Christian attempts like Wright's to equate equality with sameness, and distinction with discrimination: "What Paul intended by differentiation between ethnic groups should, however, certainly not be construed as discrimination against any of the groups under discussion. Differentiation and discrimination are two very different activities and should not be confused. . . . Getting rid of human difference is often a cloak for a cultural imperialism. . . . The biblical understanding of the impartiality of God in Romans is in no sense an anti-Jewish perspective, but one that ensures the mercy of God equally for Jew and gentile. And the acknowledgment of this blessing, emanating from the house of Israel, requires two very specific responses from gentiles in Christ. The first is that they recognize that their election in Christ is secure only on the basis of the prior election of Israel and, secondly, that this status brings with it the obligation that gentiles learn what it means to be gentiles in Christ. . . . It is indeed ironic that the heritage of Paul in Judaism that stresses the impartiality of God should somehow become misconstrued to mean that Christ followers should discriminate against the very people whose heritage gave Paul the convictions to oppose all discrimination." William S. Campbell, "No Distinction or No Discrimination? The Translation of Διαστολή in Romans 3:22 and 10:12," *TZ* 4, no. 69 (2013): 353, 368, 370; see also William S. Campbell, "Differentiation and Discrimination in Paul's Ethnic Discourse," *Transformation* 30, no. 3 (2013): 157-68.

[6]In his magnum opus *History of the Jews*, Heinrich Graetz describes Paul as "the circumcised apostle," a sarcastic designation intended to highlight the Ebionite view that Paul, a circumcised Jew, purportedly taught first-century Jews not to circumcise their children or keep the Torah. See Graetz, *History of the Jews* (Philadelphia: Jewish Publication Society of America, 1893), 2:367.

Arguments Against Particularity

The Promised Land has been universalized in Christ. In his book *Jesus and the Land*, Gary Burge claims that Christ universalized the Promised Land and that this is explicitly stated in Paul's words, "For the promise that he would inherit the world did not come to Abraham or to his descendants through the law but through the righteousness of faith" (Rom 4:13). Burge, building on Wright,[7] reasons that Paul's use of the expression "inherit the world" rather than "inherit the land of Judea" indicates that the land promise was reconfigured and no longer in force: "The formula that linked Abraham to Jewish ethnic lineage and the right to possess the land has now been overturned in Christ. Paul's Christian theology links Abraham to children of faith, and to them belongs God's full domain, namely, the world."[8]

Transference theology proponents often consider Romans 4:13 to be the clearest statement in Paul's writings that the particularity of the land promise was voided after the coming of Christ.[9] The case for this, however, is surprisingly weak. First, Romans 4:13 does not say that the Jewish "right to possess the land has now been overturned in Christ" as Burge contends. To suggest this is to read into the text something that Paul does not actually say.

Second, Burge does not substantiate his assumption that for Paul the universal is better than the particular. The Pauline corpus does not support a Baurian view that Judaism is defective because of its particularism.[10] The fact of the matter is that there is much in Paul's letters (e.g., Rom 9–11; 15) that envisions the universal and particular coexisting in God's kingdom, a view consistent with

---

[7] Wright, "Jerusalem in the New Testament," 67.

[8] Gary M. Burge, *Jesus and the Land: The New Testament Challenge to "Holy Land" Theology* (Grand Rapids: Baker Books, 2010), 85-86.

[9] E.g., Oren R. Martin, *Bound for the Promised Land: The Land Promise in God's Redemptive Plan* (Downers Grove, IL: InterVarsity Press, 2015), 131.

[10] F. C. Baur viewed Christianity as a universal religion that transcended the particularism of Judaism: "What is it in Christianity that gives it its absolute character? The first and obvious answer to this question is that Christianity is elevated above the defects and limitations, the one-sidedness and finiteness, which constitute the particularism of other forms of religion. Here then we meet again the characteristic feature of the Christian principle. It looks beyond the outward, the accidental, the particular, and rises to the universal, the unconditioned, the essential . . . the all-commanding universalism of its spirit and aims. . . . [Paul was] the first to lay down expressly and distinctly the principle of Christian universalism as a thing essentially opposed to Jewish particularism." Baur, *The Church History of the First Three Centuries* (London: Williams & Norgate, 1878), 33, 43, 47. See James D. G. Dunn, "Was Judaism Particularist or Universalist?," in *Judaism in Late Antiquity*, part 3, vol. 2, *Where We Stand: Issues and Debates in Ancient Judaism*, ed. Jacob Neusner and Alan J. Avery-Peck (Leiden: Brill, 2001), 57-73.

the eschatological model in Paul's Jewish Bible (cf. Deut 32:43; Rom 15:10). Paul's ideal is not the erasure of Jewish distinctiveness but Jews and Gentiles relating to one another in a spirit of interdependence and mutual blessing, which leads to mutual humbling and praise to God (Rom 11:11-32; 15:7-27).

Third, Burge presumes that in Paul's thought when something takes on new or additional meaning in Christ that the "fulfillment" ipso facto cancels out the validity of the prior practice or institution. However, Burge offers no evidence to support this presupposition, and there are a number of texts that would call it into question. Consider the Pauline view that marriage points to the relationship between Christ and the church (2 Cor 11:2; Eph 5:21-33), and yet marriage is not overturned through the coming of Christ. God continues to call men and women to be married (1 Cor 7:1-40; Col 3:18-19). Or consider Paul's present-tense affirmation of temple worship in Romans 9:4 ("the glory . . . the worship") and Luke's account in Acts 21:17-26 that Paul entered the Jerusalem temple and participated in offerings,[11] or Paul's prophecy in 2 Thessalonians 2:4 about the man of lawlessness who "takes his seat in the temple of God," even while Paul considered his own body and the church to be temples of the Holy Spirit (1 Cor 3:16; 6:19; 2 Cor 6:16; Eph 2:21-22). Similarly, Romans 4:13 indicates that the Abrahamic promise ultimately points to Christ and the church, but this does not necessarily imply that the particular territorial dimension of the Abrahamic promise has been "overturned."

Fourth, Burge asserts that "Romans 4.13 is the only place where the apostle refers explicitly to the promises for the land given to Abraham."[12] However, Paul may not have the land specifically in view in this passage; he may be speaking

---

[11]"Rom 9:4 refers to the temple cultus as a central and continuing privilege of the Jews. . . . Since Paul's communities are gentile and the concerns of his letters are gentile, he has little opportunity to mention Jerusalem, the temple, and the Jewish situation. When he does refer to these institutions, however, he assumes their continuing validity." S. K. Stowers, *A Rereading of Romans: Justice, Jews, and Gentiles* (New Haven, CT: Yale University Press, 1994), 130-31. Cf. Bruce Longenecker, "On Israel's God and God's Israel: Assessing Supersessionism in Paul," *JTS* 58, no. 1 (2007): 27-29. For a discussion of Paul's possible motive(s) for participating in temple worship according to Acts 21, see David J. Rudolph, *A Jew to the Jews: Jewish Contours of Pauline Flexibility in 1 Corinthians 9:19-23* (Tübingen: Mohr Siebeck, 2011), 53-72.

[12]Burge, *Jesus and the Land*, 85. The land promise is reiterated hundreds of times in the Tanak, Paul's Bible, which the apostle regarded as "God-breathed" (2 Tim 3:16). "Arguing from the absence of the term 'land' . . . is a dubious argument from silence. One might just as well argue against the validity of repentance from the absence of the term in the Gospel of John, or against the importance of love from the term's absence in the Acts of the Apostles." Barry E. Horner, *Future Israel: Why Christian Anti-Judaism Must Be Challenged* (Nashville: B&H Academic, 2007), 225.

of people. In his article "Abraham as 'Heir of the World,'" Nelson Hsieh concludes that in Romans 4:13 Paul is focusing not on the land but on Abraham's descendants:

> I have shown that the context of Rom 4:13 is focused upon the OT promises of descendants ([Rom 4:]17-18, quoting Gen 17:5 and 15:5), not the OT promises of land (e.g. Gen 12:7; 13:15; 17:8). Finally, I have shown that κόσμος can refer to persons as well as land, and that κληρονόμος does not always refer to inheriting land, but can also refer to inheriting righteousness, life, persons, etc. This understanding of Rom 4:13 is appropriately called the "inheritance of many nations" view. Abraham is not inheriting land, but inheriting people—namely, his innumerable spiritual descendants from all the nations of the world. According to this view, Rom 4:13 has nothing to do with the OT land promises and thus neither affirms nor expands the OT land promises. It is about the worldwide nature of Abraham's descendants; it is not about the worldwide nature of Abraham's land promise. Thus, Rom 4:13 simply has nothing to say about the land promise.[13]

Boyd Luter concurs that "the flow of this entire passage is clearly about people and faith, not land. Thus, Romans 4 cannot be legitimately used to argue for the replacing of the Land Promise to Israel in the New Testament."[14]

Fifth, in Second Temple Jewish literature, there are numerous statements similar to Romans 4:13 that describe Abraham as heir of the world. Gerhard Visscher surveys these texts in his monograph *Romans 4 and the New Perspective on Paul*:

> In Hebrew scriptures, there is no statement to the effect that Abraham would be heir of the world. However, as Schreiner has pointed out (*Romans*, 227), both in the Hebrew scriptures (cf. Pss. 2, 22, 47, 72; Isa. 2:1-4; 19:18-25; 49:6-7; 52:7-10; 55:3-5; 66:23; Amos 9:11-12; Zeph. 3:9-10; Zech. 14:9) and in Second Temple Literature, the universal character of the promise to Abraham was stressed. In Sir 44:19, Abraham is described as "the great father of a multitude of nations . . . and Sir 44:21 speaks of how the Lord swore to give him offspring as numerous as the dust of the earth and the stars of the sky, and he would "give them an inheritance from sea to sea and from the Euphrates to the ends

---

[13]Nelson S. Hsieh, "Abraham as 'Heir of the World': Does Romans 4:13 Expand the Old Testament Abrahamic Land Promises?," *MSJ* 26, no. 1 (Spring 2015): 95-110.

[14]A. Boyd Luter, "The Continuation of Israel's Land Promise in the New Testament: A Fresh Approach," *Eruditio Ardescens* 1, no. 2 (2014): 13 (an expanded unpublished version of the article).

of the earth." It is especially in the extrabiblical literature that the idea seems to grow that Abraham would inherit the world. According to *Jub.* 22:14, Abraham gives a blessing to Jacob which includes the wish that he "inherit all of the earth." According to *Jub.* 32:19, Jacob receives the promise from God at Bethel: "And I shall give to your seed all of the land under heaven and they will rule in all nations as they have desired. And after this all of the earth will be gathered together and they will inherit it forever." In *2 Bar.* 14:13, the righteous are said to leave this world, confident "of the world promised to them" and in *2 Bar.* 51:3, the righteous will one day "acquire and receive the undying world which is promised to them." According to *1 En.* 5:7, the elect "shall inherit the earth." Given all these references, Paul does not seem to be sounding a note too far removed when he refers to Abraham and his offspring "inheriting the world."[15]

These first-century Jewish texts not only highlight the universal dimension of the Abrahamic promise but also assume the continuation of Jewish particularity in the eschaton.[16] For example, in Jubilees 22:14, Abraham blesses Jacob with the words, "May you inherit all of the earth." Notably this passage is located between Jubilees 22:11 and Jubilees 22:15, where Abraham says to Jacob, "May nations serve you, and all the nations bow themselves before your seed. . . . May He renew His covenant with you that you may be to Him a nation for His inheritance for all ages."[17] Given Paul's emphasis in Romans 2–3 and 9–11 on

---

[15]Gerhard H. Visscher, *Romans 4 and the New Perspective on Paul: Faith Embraces the Promises* (New York: Peter Lang, 2009), 198-99, 197n. Citing Thomas R. Schreiner, *Romans*, BECNT (Grand Rapids: Baker Books, 1998), 227.

[16]"Here we see once again the twin foci of the book [Jubilees]—particularism (the focus on Israel) and universalism (the focus on the world)—coming to expression in a harmonious way. The positive effects of Israel's restoration are expected to spill out over the borders of the Land to the rest of the world. . . . The universalistic strains in the book are completely subordinated to its particularistic emphasis on Israel and the Temple in the Land." James M. Scott, "The Land of Israel in the *Book of Jubilees*," in *On Earth as in Heaven: The Restoration of Sacred Time and Sacred Space in the Book of Jubilees* (Leiden: Brill, 2005), 208-9. Cf. Doron Mendels, *The Land of Israel as a Political Concept in Hasmonean Literature: Recourse to History in Second Century BC Claims to the Holy Land* (Tübingen: Mohr Siebeck, 1987), 57-88. This both/and emphasis in Second Temple Jewish literature with respect to the universal and particular is overlooked in Yohanna Katanacho, *The Land of Christ: A Palestinian Cry* (Eugene, OR: Pickwick, 2013), 41-42; Peter W. L. Walker, "The Land in the Apostles' Writings," in *The Land of Promise: Biblical, Theological and Contemporary Perspectives*, ed. Philip Johnston and Peter Walker (Downers Grove, IL: InterVarsity Press, 2000), 87; and Martin, *Bound for the Promised Land*, 134-35.

[17]At Qumran the land promise was viewed as having *both* a spiritual and a territorial meaning, "In a brief midrash on Psalm 37 found at Qumran the phrase 'possess the land' was interpreted to refer to the 'congregation of [God's] elect who do His will.' Here 'possess the land' seems to have become a metaphor for a good and holy life. Elsewhere in the commentary 'land' is taken

the present-tense election, gifts and calling of the Jewish people, it is reasonable to assume that in Romans 4:13 he echoes the normative view of his day that the Abrahamic promise included universal and particular elements. Mark Forman arrives at the same conclusion in his study *The Politics of Inheritance in Romans*:

> But how does all of this relate to the phrase Paul uses in Rom. 4:13, "inherit the world"? Within the tradition surveyed above, there does seem to be the implication that the Abrahamic promise was always intended for the entire world, not exclusively for Israel. As Scott observes, "The Abrahamic Promise sets in motion a trajectory whose ultimate fulfillment takes place in the time of Israel's Restoration, when Israel will again become a great nation, and all nations (i.e. all those listed in the Table of Nations) will be blessed in Abraham and his seed." . . .
>
> References to Israel's future "inheritance" of *the world* are scattered throughout the Intertestamental literature, as is the more general concept of Israel in relation to the nations. . . . Amidst these references, however, there is one book in particular, the *Book of Jubilees*, which has much to offer to an understanding of "inherit the world" in Rom. 4:13 and the tradition which this stems. There are several reasons why *Jubilees* is especially instructive. To begin with, there are three direct references to the inheritance of Israel: inherit "the land" ([Jub.] 17:3); "inherit the earth" ([Jub.] 22:14); and "gain the entire earth and inherit it forever" ([Jub.] 32:19). In itself, this makes these references particularly illuminating for a reading of Rom. 4:13. But what adds to the import of these phrases is the broader framework within which the word inheritance is used: the land of Israel, together with the role it fulfills within the purposes of God, is one of the primary concerns of *Jubilees*. In other words the concept of inheritance takes its place within the broader expectation of Israel's future. This is not to say that Rom. 4:13 should be understood exclusively in relation to *Jubilees* but that the use of inheritance here does bear close resemblance to Romans and is therefore instructive. . . .

---

to mean the entire earth. But then the midrash becomes very concrete; 'They shall possess the High Mountain of Israel [forever] and shall enjoy [everlasting delights] in His Sanctuary.' See 4QpPs 37.2 and 3. Also CD 1.7-8; 3.7, 10; 13.21 for *'ereṣ* as the Land of Israel. See also *War Scroll*, 1QM 19.4-5, 'Fill your land with glory and your inheritance with blessing.' The next line reads, 'Rejoice greatly O Zion, O Jerusalem show yourself with jubilation. Rejoice, all your cities of Judah.'" Robert Wilken, *The Land Called Holy: Palestine in Christian History and Thought* (New Haven, CT: Yale University Press, 1992), 278n10.

Similar to the OT tradition, *Jubilees* conveys the idea that first Zion will be renewed and then the rest of the earth will similarly be restored....

All of this suggests, therefore, that in using the phrase "inherit the world" Paul stands in continuity with this Intertestamental literature. In these texts the language of inheritance takes its place within a wider perspective of the descendants of Israel and the relationship which they will one day have with the whole earth.[18]

Sixth, the Second Temple Jewish concept that Abraham would be "heir of the world" is likely rooted in Genesis 22:17-18, where the Lord declares that Abraham's descendants will possess the cities of their enemies: "I will surely bless you and make your descendants as numerous as the stars in the sky and as the sand on the seashore. *Your descendants will take possession of the cities of their enemies,* and *through your offspring all nations on earth will be blessed,* because you have obeyed me" (NIV, emphasis added).[19] Similarly, Isaiah 54:1-3 (cf. Gal 4:27) states, "Sing, O barren one.... Your descendants will possess the nations." The LXX word for "possess" is κληρονομέω, a cognate of κληρονόμος—the term Paul uses in Romans 4:13 for "heir."

In using the expression "heir of the world," Paul may also have in mind Genesis 26, where the Lord says to Isaac, "I will give you *all these lands* [plural]":

> Do not go down to Egypt; settle in the land that I shall show you. Reside in this land as an alien, and I will be with you, and will bless you; for to you and to your descendants I will give *all these lands* [kāl-hā' ărāsōt], and I will fulfill the oath that I swore to your father Abraham. I will make your offspring as numerous as the stars of heaven, and will give to your offspring *all these lands* [kāl-hā' ărāsōt]; and all the nations of the earth shall gain blessing for themselves through your offspring, because Abraham obeyed my voice and kept my charge, my commandments, my statutes, and my laws. (Gen 26:2-5)

Later, the Lord confirms to Jacob that he will not only inherit the land promised to Abraham but that nations and kings will come from him:

> God said to him [Israel], "I am God Almighty: be fruitful and multiply; *a nation and a company of nations* [gôy ûqhal gôyim] shall come from you, and

---

[18]Mark Forman, *The Politics of Inheritance in Romans* (Cambridge: Cambridge University Press, 2011), 80-81, 84.
[19]For a study of the international aspect of the Abrahamic promise in the Torah, see Paul R. Williamson, *Abraham, Israel and the Nations: The Patriarchal Promise and Its Covenantal Development in Genesis* (Sheffield: Sheffield Academic Press, 2000), 151-70.

> kings shall spring from you. The land that I gave to Abraham and Isaac I will give *to you*, and I will give the land to your offspring after you." (Gen 35:11-12, emphasis added)

Note that the universal and particular are both present. All of this serves to underscore the point that Paul's portrayal of Abraham in Romans 4:13 as "heir of the world" is unspectacular. Paul did not make a startling statement, as Wright suggests.[20] The image of Abraham as "heir of the world" is strongly implied in the Torah, and this is why it was a familiar concept in Paul's day. In the Torah and in Second Temple Judaism, Abraham's call to be "heir of the world" and the particularity of the land promise were not seen as either-or trajectories but *both/and*.[21] If Paul had territory in view in Romans 4:13, he had one eye on the universal aspect of the promise and the other on the particular. Michael Vanlaningham concludes, "Rather than removing the privilege of the land from Israel, Paul appears to affirm it. . . . It is preferable, precisely because the OT and Early Judaism indicate that Israel will inherit the world, to place Paul in continuity with the OT teaching rather than in contrast to it."[22]

Jewish identity is a matter of indifference in Christ. Paul makes three statements that are often taken by transference theology proponents to be synopses of his view that Jewish identity is relativized to the point of indifference in Christ.[23] The similar language suggests to some scholars that they are variations of a slogan:[24]

> Circumcision is nothing, and uncircumcision is *nothing* (οὐδέν); but obeying the commandments of God is everything. (1 Cor 7:19, emphasis added)

> For in Christ Jesus neither circumcision nor uncircumcision counts for anything; the only thing that counts is faith working through love. (Gal 5:6)

---

[20] Wright, "Jerusalem in the New Testament," 67.
[21] Burge, *Jesus and the Land*, 21-24, argues that Philo and Josephus redefined the land promise in such a way that its particularity was undermined. However, this is an oversimplification. See William Horbury, "Jerusalem in Pre-Pauline and Pauline Hope," in *Messianism Among Jews and Christians: Twelve Biblical and Historical Studies* (London: T&T Clark, 2003), 190; and George Wesley Buchanan, *The Covenant: Its Replacement and Renewal in Judaism and Christianity* (Eugene, OR: Wipf & Stock, 2012), 100.
[22] Michael G. Vanlaningham, "The Jewish People According to the Book of Romans," in *The People, the Land, and the Future of Israel*, ed. Darrell L. Bock and Mitch Glaser (Grand Rapids: Kregel, 2014), 120-21.
[23] See Rudolph, *A Jew to the Jews*, 27-32.
[24] James D. G. Dunn, "Neither Circumcision nor Uncircumcision, but . . . (Gal 5.2-12; 6.12-16; cf. 1 Cor 7.17–20)," in *La Foi Agissant par L'amour (Galates 4,12–6,16)* (Rome: Benedictina, 1996), 80-81.

For neither circumcision nor uncircumcision is anything; but a new creation is everything! (Gal 6:15)

Did Paul consider Jewish identity to be a matter of indifference, as 1 Corinthians 7:19 and Galatians 5:6 and 6:15 seem to indicate? Horrell assumes that "nothing" or "not anything" points to unimportance.[25] But given the context, Paul is more likely saying that "neither circumcision nor the lack of circumcision has ultimate bearing on salvation."[26] With respect to status before God and eschatological blessing, being Jewish or Gentile is irrelevant.

I contend that Paul uses hyperbole in these passages to stress that being "in Christ" is *more important than* being Jewish.[27] This means that being Jewish could still be very important to Paul. He is simply relativizing A to B. In support of this possibility, there are several occasions when Paul uses "nothing" (οὐδέν) or "not anything" (οὔτε . . . τι) language in a clearly hyperbolic way. First, with respect to the work of planting the Corinthian congregation, Paul describes himself as nothing compared to the Lord:

> What then is Apollos? What is Paul? Servants through whom you came to believe, as the Lord assigned to each. I planted, Apollos watered, but God gave the growth. So neither the one who plants nor the one who waters is anything [οὔτε . . . ἐστίν τι οὔτε], but only God who gives the growth. (1 Cor 3:5-7)

Are Paul and Apollos truly nothing? Did they really do no work of any significance? On the contrary, their work was vital to the establishment of the Corinthian congregation. But *relative to* what God did, the miracle of changing lives, their work was nothing. Similarly, Paul writes in 2 Corinthians 12:11, "I am not at all inferior to these super-apostles, even though I am nothing [οὐδέν εἰμι]."

---

[25]David G. Horrell, "'No Longer Jew or Greek': Paul's Corporate Christology and the Construction of Christian Community," in *Christology, Controversy and Community: New Testament Essays in Honour of David R. Catchpole*, ed. David G. Horrell and Christopher M. Tuckett (Leiden: Brill, 2000), 343; and David G. Horrell, *Solidarity and Difference: A Contemporary Reading of Paul's Ethics* (London: T&T Clark, 2005), 18, 260n50.

[26]Raymond F. Collins, *First Corinthians* (Collegeville, MN: Liturgical, 1999), 284. Also Peter J. Tomson, "Paul's Jewish Background in View of His Law Teaching in 1 Cor 7," in *Paul and the Mosaic Law*, ed. James D. G. Dunn (Grand Rapids: Eerdmans, 2001), 266; and Anthony C Thiselton, *The First Epistle to the Corinthians: A Commentary on the Greek Text* (Grand Rapids: Eerdmans, 2000), 550.

[27]Cf. Caroline Johnson Hodge, *If Sons, Then Heirs: A Study of Kinship and Ethnicity in the Letters of Paul* (Oxford: Oxford University Press, 2007), 131-34; and Christopher Zoccali, *Whom God Has Called: The Relationship of Church and Israel in Pauline Interpretation, 1920 to the Present* (Eugene, OR: Pickwick, 2010), 129.

Again, was Paul—the apostle to the Gentiles—truly "nothing"? Or is he saying that, *relative to* the Lord, he is nothing, even as *relative to* the super-apostles he is something?

Another example of Paul relativizing two important works of God is 2 Corinthians 3:6-11. Here Paul contrasts the glory of Moses' ministry with the ministry of the Spirit. Though God performed miracles through Moses' ministry that were unparalleled in history, Paul refers to Moses' ministry as having no glory now, for "what once had splendor has come to have no splendor at all, because of the splendor that surpasses it" (RSV). It all pales in comparison. Moreover, three times Paul uses a *kal vachomer* (*a fortiori*) argument to compare old covenant and new covenant experiences of the presence and power of God (2 Cor 3:8, 9, 11). *Both* are truly glorious revelations of the God of Israel, but one is more glorious than the other. To emphasize the "splendor that surpasses," Paul uses language that downplays the Sinai revelation. But it is wrong to mistake this as trivialization of the old covenant glory.[28] It is instead a rhetorical device intended to highlight the greater glory. He refers to something genuinely important to emphasize what is *even more important*. It is likely that Paul used the same rhetorical device when he referred to circumcision and uncircumcision as "nothing."

Second, Paul's manner of expression (οὐδέν . . . ἀλλά and οὔτε . . . τι . . . ἀλλά) in 1 Corinthians 7:19 and Galatians 5:6 and 6:15 is consistent with the Jewish idiom of dialectic negation in which the "'not . . . but . . .' antithesis need not be understood as an 'either . . . or,' but rather with the force of 'more important than.'"[29] Consider, for example, how the prophet Hosea makes the same kind of hyperbolic comparison statement when he speaks in the name of the Lord,

> For I desire steadfast love and not sacrifice,
>   the knowledge of God rather than burnt offerings. (Hos 6:6)

Sacrifices were important, for the Lord commanded them, but "steadfast love" was *even more important*. To emphasize this, the Lord states that he does *not*

---

[28]Scott Hafemann, *Paul, Moses, and the History of Israel: The Letter/Spirit Contrast and the Argument from Scripture in 2 Corinthians 3* (Tübingen: Mohr Siebeck, 1995), 321-27.
[29]James D. G. Dunn, *Jesus, Paul and the Law: Studies in Mark and Galatians* (Louisville, KY: Westminster John Knox, 1990), 51. Cf. E. P. Sanders, *Jesus and Judaism* (Philadelphia: Fortress, 1985), 260-64; Roger P. Booth, *Jesus and the Laws of Purity: Tradition History and Legal History in Mark 7* (Sheffield: Sheffield Academic Press, 1986), 69-70; and Jonathan Klawans, *Impurity and Sin in Ancient Judaism* (Oxford: Oxford University Press, 2000), 147.

desire sacrifice. The negative statement should be taken as hyperbole; it is a Hebrew rhetorical device.[30]

Third, Paul's anti-circumcision language (directed at Gentiles) in Galatians can be understood as upholding Jew-Gentile distinction rather than collapsing it: "Circumcising Gentiles would have made Jews and Gentiles all the same. Paul's vehement rejection of circumcision demonstrates his commitment to maintaining Jews and Gentiles as different and distinct, and militates strongly against seeing Paul's goal as creating human homogeneity."[31]

There is no longer Jew or Gentile in Christ. Transference theology tends to place a lot of weight on Galatians 3:28 ("There is no longer Jew or Greek . . . ; for all of you are one in Christ Jesus"), viewing it as evidence that Paul considered Jewish particularity to be universalized in Christ.[32] But examined more closely, there are numerous holes in this argument.[33] First, the Galatians 3 context has more to do with the justification of Jesus-believing Jews and Gentiles in Christ and the community formed by these believers than the erasure of Jewish and Gentile identity in the present age.[34] Paul makes the same point in Romans 10:10-12, "For one believes with the heart and so is justified, and one confesses with the mouth and so is saved. . . . For there is no distinction between Jew and Greek."[35]

---

[30]A variation of this is found in the *Letter of Aristeas* 234. Cf. Mark 2:17; 7:15.
[31]Paula Fredriksen, "Judaizing the Nations: The Ritual Demands of Paul's Gospel," *NTS* 56 (2010): 249-50. Also Pamela Eisenbaum, "Paul as the New Abraham," in *Paul and Politics: Ekklesia, Israel, Imperium, Interpretation*, ed. Richard A. Horsley (Harrisburg, PA: Trinity Press International, 2000), 518; and Mark D. Nanos, *The Mystery of Romans: The Jewish Context of Paul's Letter* (Minneapolis: Fortress, 1996), 116n84.
[32]See Daniel Boyarin, *A Radical Jew: Paul and the Politics of Identity* (Berkeley: University of California Press, 1994), 19-23; and J. Louis Martyn, *Galatians: A New Translation with Introduction and Commentary* (New York: Doubleday, 1997), 376-77.
[33]See Rudolph, *A Jew to the Jews*, 27-32; Justin K. Hardin, "Equality in the Church," in *Introduction to Messianic Judaism: Its Ecclesial Context and Biblical Foundations*, ed. David Rudolph and Joel Willitts (Grand Rapids: Zondervan, 2013), 224-29.
[34]Judith M. Gundry-Volf, "Beyond Difference? Paul's Vision of a New Humanity in Galatians 3.28," in *Gospel and Gender: A Trinitarian Engagement with Being Male and Female in Christ*, ed. Douglas A. Campbell (London: T&T Clark, 2003), 18-19. Also Pamela Eisenbaum, "Is Paul the Father of Misogyny and Antisemitism?," *Cross Currents* 50, no. 4 (2000–2001): 515; and Troy W. Martin, "The Covenant of Circumcision (Genesis 17:9-14) and the Situational Antitheses in Galatians 3:28," *JBL* 122, no. 1 (2003): 121.
[35]See Campbell, "No Distinction or No Discrimination?," 353-71. For a discussion of Ephesians 2:14-18, see Hardin, "Equality in the Church," 229-32; David B. Woods, "Jew-Gentile Distinction in the One New Man of Ephesians 2:15," *Conspectus* 18 (September 2014): 1-41; and William S. Campbell, "Unity and Diversity in the Church: Transformed Identities and the Peace of Christ in Ephesians," *IBS* 27 (2007): 4-19.

Second, Paul states in Galatians 3:28 that "there is no longer male and female." But is the male-female distinction erased in Christ? On the contrary, Paul distinguishes between men and women in his congregations (1 Cor 11:1-16; 14:34; Eph 5:22-24; Col 3:18; 1 Tim 2:12). The created order with respect to "male and female" (Gen 1:27-28) is not overturned in Christ. This raises an important question: if in Paul's thought the third pair (male and female) is not erased, why should it be concluded that the first pair (Jew and Greek) is erased?

Third, the NA28 text of Galatians 3:28 includes the word ἐν ("one").[36] The NRSV translates Galatians 3:28 "for all of you are one in Christ Jesus." What is this oneness? Boyarin interprets it as a "universal human essence" where all distinction is eradicated.[37] But where is the direct evidence for this? If "male and female" in Galatians 3:28 alludes to Genesis 1:27-28, perhaps "one in Christ Jesus" is not unlike the ləbāśār ʾeḥād ("one flesh") between male and female in Genesis 2:24.[38] Here ʾeḥād describes a composite unity (two that are distinct but one). Might Paul have been thinking of a Genesis 2 ʾeḥād-like unity in Galatians 3:28?[39] The argument adds to the case that the relationship between Jew and Gentile in Galatians 3:28 is one of unity with distinction, sameness.

Fourth, Paul refers to Jews and Gentiles (Greeks) in his letters.[40] To Peter, who withdrew from eating with Jesus-believing "Gentiles" (Gal 2:12), he says, "you are a Jew" (Gal 2:14 NIV). The writer of Colossians 4:10-11 refers to Aristarchus, Mark and Justus as "the only ones of the circumcision among my co-workers for the kingdom of God." By contrast, Titus is a "Greek" (Gal 2:3). In Romans 11:13, Paul writes, "Now I am speaking to you Gentiles" (cf. Rom 4:11-12). All of this suggests that, for Paul, the Jew-Gentile distinction is preserved, not erased in Christ.[41] "He accepts, and even insists on retaining, the differences as ethnic-identity markers at the same time as he strips them of soteriological

---

[36]P46 omits ἐν.
[37]Boyarin, *Radical Jew* 7.
[38]Gundry-Volf, "Beyond Difference?," 31-34. Cf. Richard W. Hove, *Equality in Christ? Galatians 3:28 and the Gender Dispute* (Wheaton, IL: Crossway, 1999), 69-76, 107-9.
[39]Eisenbaum, "Is Paul the Father of Misogyny and Antisemitism?," 520-21.
[40]See Christopher D. Stanley, "'Neither Jew Nor Greek': Ethnic Conflict in Graeco-Roman Society," *JSNT* 64 (1996): 101-24, for a discussion of the term *Greeks*.
[41]Denise K. Buell, *Why This New Race: Ethnic Reasoning in Early Christianity* (New York: Columbia University Press, 2005), 76; Denise K. Buell and Caroline Johnson Hodge, "The Politics of Interpretation: The Rhetoric of Race and Ethnicity in Paul," *JBL* 123, no. 2 (2004): 247-50; and Kathy Ehrensperger, *Paul and the Dynamics of Power: Communication and Interaction in the Early Christ-Movement* (London: T&T Clark, 2007), 192-93.

significance.... 'There is neither Jew nor Greek' is not about erasure of differences but revalorization of differences."[42]

Arguments for Particularity

Having discussed several Pauline passages that are often quoted by transference theology proponents to demonstrate that Paul opposed Jewish particularity, I will now present arguments in support of the view that Paul upheld the continued election, gifts and calling of the Jewish people. The combination of these arguments is mnemonically represented in the acronym GUCCI.

> G The **Gifts** of Israel
> U The **Uniqueness** of Israel
> C The **Calling** of Israel
> C The **Confirmation** of Israel's promises
> I The **Irrevocability** of Israel's election

Figure 6.1 Arguments for particularity

The gifts of Israel. Paul writes in Romans 9:3-5:

> For I could wish that I myself were accursed and cut off from Christ for the sake of my people, my kindred according to the flesh. They are Israelites, and to them belong the adoption, the glory, the covenants, the giving of the law, the worship, and the promises; to them belong the patriarchs, and from them, according to the flesh, comes the Messiah.

Here Paul states that the covenants, the promises and the Torah remain (in the present tense) possessions of the Jewish people. In his essay "The Priority of the Present Tense for Jewish-Christian Relations," R. Kendall Soulen points up the significance of Paul's use of the present tense in this passage:

> The single most important element of Rom 9–11 for Jewish-Christian relations is its use of the *present tense* to characterize the Jewish people—Paul's kinsmen "according to the flesh"—as the heirs of God's covenant promises. We encounter this all-important present tense at two crucial points, near the very beginning: "They are Israelites ... and to them belong ... the covenants ... the promises ..." ([Rom] 9:4-5) and again near the very end (where the

---

[42]Gundry-Volf, "Beyond Difference?," 21. Also Hodge, *If Sons, Then Heirs*, 126-31.

Zionism in Pauline Literature

present tense is, to be sure, implied): "... as regards election they are beloved ... for the sake of their ancestors" ([Rom] 11:28). It is impossible to overstate the importance of these two present-tense passages for the structure of Paul's argument. They are the iron brackets which surround Paul's argument and ultimately contain its explosive force....

When Christians do not attend in a serious way to "the shock of the present tense" in Rom 9–11, they are prone to read the Scriptures in ways that lead them to conclude that God's election of the Jewish people was a phenomenon of the *ancient past*. Perhaps if they pay a little attention to Rom 11, they will also think of Israel's election as a phenomenon of the *eschatological future*, when "all Israel will be saved" ([Rom] 11:26). This traditional Christian view of Israel's election may remind us of the Queen's attitude toward tea in *Alice in Wonderland*: "Tea yesterday, and tea tomorrow, but never tea today!" Precisely here, the "shock of the present tense" in Rom 9–11 exerts its enduring, foundational importance for Christian-Jewish relations. To the degree that Christians submit themselves to this shock, they will turn to their Jewish neighbor and see one who is God's beloved—not *only* in the primordial past and eschatological future—but *also* and *above all* in the abiding now of covenant history.[43]

When Paul refers to Israel's "gifts" (χαρίσματα) in Romans 11:29 ("for the gifts and the calling of God [to Israel] are irrevocable"), he is likely pointing back to the list of national privileges of the Jewish people mentioned in Romans 9. Moreover, Paul's use of the term χαρίσματα in Romans 11 is informed by Second Temple Jewish literature where Israel is described as having been given national "gifts" from God. This is attested in Philo, Josephus (who relates the term "gifts" to the land of Israel) and Ezekiel the Tragedian (a Jewish dramatist who wrote in Alexandria at the end of the second century BC).[44] After surveying this Second Temple background, William Horbury concludes in his study "The Gifts of God in Ezekiel the Tragedian":

> By "gifts" were meant, as in line 35 [in *Ezekiel Tragicus*], the national privileges given by God through the patriarchal covenants; and the promises of increase and of the land were probably especially in view (cf. Exod. 32.13). Ezekiel

---

[43] R. Kendall Soulen, "The Priority of the Present Tense for Jewish-Christian Relations," in *Between Gospel and Election: Explorations in the Interpretation of Romans 9–11*, ed. Florian Wilk and J. Ross Wagner (Tübingen: Mohr Siebeck, 2010), 498-99. Cf. Richard H. Bell, *The Irrevocable Call of God: An Inquiry into Paul's Theology of Israel* (Tübingen: Mohr Siebeck, 2005), 198-213, 280-81.

[44] Philo, *On Rewards and Punishments* 79; Josephus, *On the Special Laws* 2.219 [cf. Deut 26:5-11]; *Ezekiel Tragicus* 35, 106.

Tragicus is an early witness to this application of words for "gift" to the covenantal privileges of Israel. The allusive character of his usage suggests that it was already traditional. This view of its age is consistent with its widespread attestation at the end of the Second Temple period, both among Greek-speaking Jews (see Philo and Josephus) and among those who used Hebrew or Aramaic (see the rabbinic texts). A wide currency is also suggested by its appearance, in Philo and Josephus, in summaries of prescribed prayers. This Jewish usage was reproduced by St. Paul (Rom. 11.29; cf. Rom. 9.4-5), and extended in 1 Clement.[45]

What is the takeaway from Horbury's findings? It is that the term "gifts" includes the land especially. Similarly, the terms "covenants" and "promises" in Romans 9:4 and 15:8 cannot be understood apart from their land aspect, because the origins of these covenants and promises are coterminous with the oath that God made to Abraham, Isaac and Jacob concerning the land (e.g., Ex 32:13).[46] This interconnection between covenant, promise and land is echoed hundreds of times in Israel's Scriptures, something that would have been as clear to Paul as the stars in the sky.[47] Along these lines, Richard Bell concludes in his monograph *The Irrevocable Call of God: An Inquiry into Paul's Theology of Israel*:

> The term τὰ χαρίσματα [in Rom 11:29] refers most likely to the election of and promise to Abraham and his descendants κατὰ χάριν (Rom 4:4, 16). Although Paul's argument is primarily concerned with salvation I wonder whether one can exclude the concrete promise of the land (and of "seed"). Further, one should add that the promise of the land is made more concrete through Jesus Christ. For by becoming a servant of the circumcision, he has confirmed the promises made to the patriarchs. Jesus Christ does not make the promises to

---

[45] William Horbury, "The Gifts of God in Ezekiel the Tragedian," in *Messianism Among Jews and Christians*, 79.

[46] "The stress upon Abraham as the paradigm for faith warns us against deciding too quickly that the land motif is absent (see Romans 4; Galatians 3–4). While the Abraham image undoubtedly is transformed, it is inconceivable that it should have been emptied of its reference to land. No matter how spiritualized, transcendentalized or existentialized, it has its primary focus undeniably on land. That is what is promised, not to the competent deserving or to the dutifully obedient, but freely given (as in the beginning) to one who had no claim." Walter Brueggemann, *The Land: Place as Gift, Promise, and Challenge in Biblical Faith* (Minneapolis: Fortress, 2002), 166. Cf. Richard C. Lux, "The Land of Israel (*Eretz Yisra'el*) in Jewish and Christian Understanding," *SCJR* 3 (2008): 15; and James D. G. Dunn, "Did Paul Have a Covenant Theology? Reflections on Romans 9.4 and 11.27," in *The Concept of Covenant in the Second Temple Period*, ed. Stanley E. Porter and Jacqueline C. R. de Roo (Leiden: Brill, 2003), 301-3.

[47] Cf. C. F. D. Moule, *The Epistle to the Romans* (Cambridge: Cambridge University Press, 1903), 164.

Israel less concrete; he makes them more concrete.... I therefore conclude that from a Pauline perspective God's promise to Israel of the land still stands. It is the gift of the electing God to his elected people.[48]

The uniqueness of Israel. The gifts of God to Israel made Israel unique. In his letters, Paul communicates this uniqueness (or "particularity") in various ways. For example, he divides the world (including the church) into two groups: Jews and Gentiles.[49] Jews are "the circumcised" as distinct from "the uncircumcised" (Rom 3:30; 4:9, 12). Jews are "natural branches" in contrast to "wild olive shoot[s]" (Rom 11:17, 21, 24).[50] Jews are "Israelites" in contrast to "the nations" (Rom 9:4; cf. Rom 10:1; 11:11, 25-26):

> Paul is convinced that the election and calling of Israel are irrevocable (Rom 11:28-29) and, by implication, that the distinctiveness and uniqueness of Israel among the nations persist. In other words, there can be no ironing out of the distinction between Jews and Gentiles.... The Christ event, instead of bringing about a binary opposition between old and new Israel, reveals and renews a nondivisive difference between Israel and the nations, Jews and Gentiles. This is the nondivisive difference of election, in which Israel is distinguished from the Gentiles in a way that includes them, and the Gentiles are united with Israel in a way that undergirds Israel's irreducible difference. Israel and the Gentiles share in the same God, but differently.[51]

---

[48]Bell, *Irrevocable Call of God*, 379-80.

[49]See Romans 11:13 and Galatians 2:15. When Paul refers to Jews and Gentiles as a pair, he typically lists Jews first, the exception being Colossians 3:11.

[50]"Although the NRSV [Rom 11:17] reflects traditional replacement theology, 'and you ... were grafted *in their place*,' the NASB and the KJV are closer to the Greek: 'you ... were grafted in *among* them [σὺ δὲ ... ἐν αὐτοῖς].'... In other words, the wild shoot is placed among the remaining branches as well as among the broken ones, which remain on the tree in an impaired state." Mark D. Nanos, "'Broken Branches': A Pauline Metaphor Gone Awry? (Romans 11:11-24)," in Wilk and Wagner, *Between Gospel and Election*, 342-43. Cf. Terence L. Donaldson, "'Riches for the Gentiles' (Rom 11:2): Israel's Rejection and Paul's Gentile Mission," *JBL* 112, no. 1 (1993): 84-85. For a discussion of other translations of Romans 11 that reflect transference theology, see Mark D. Nanos, "Romans 11 and Christian-Jewish Relations: Exegetical Options for Revisiting the Translation and Interpretation of This Central Text," *CTR* 9, no. 2 (2012): 3-21.

[51]Susannah Ticciati, "The Nondivisive Difference of Election: A Reading of Romans 9–11," *JTI* 6, no. 2 (2012): 271, 276. Cf. William S. Campbell, *Unity & Diversity in Christ: Interpreting Paul in Context* (Eugene, OR: Cascade, 2013), 91-145; and idem, *Paul and the Creation of Christian Identity* (London: T&T Clark, 2008), 86-158.

The relationship between Jews and Gentiles is one of interdependence and mutual blessing.[52] The salvation of Israel cannot happen without the faithful witness of Jesus-believing Gentiles to the Jewish people (Rom 11:11-14, 25-26, 30-31),[53] and world revival cannot take place until Israel becomes a messianic Jewish nation (Rom 11:12, 15).[54] Because Gentiles "share" in the nourishing sap of the Jewish olive tree (Rom 11:17), they are indebted to the Jewish people, "For if the Gentiles have shared in the Jews' spiritual blessings, they owe it to the Jews to share with them their material blessings" (Rom 15:27 NIV).[55]

The apostle writes that there is much "advantage" in being a Jew, and that there is significant "value" in circumcision if one keeps the Torah (Rom 2:25; 3:1-2). Paul even goes further and maintains that Jews (unlike Gentiles) are supposed to keep the whole Torah. He writes in Galatians 5:3 (NIV), "Again I declare to every man who lets himself be circumcised that he is obligated to obey the whole law."[56]

---

[52]See R. Kendall Soulen, *The God of Israel and Christian Theology* (Minneapolis: Fortress, 1996), 114-77.

[53]"An apt analogy likens Judaism to a ladder, with the sophistication of one's commitment a function of how high a rung one has attained. Most Jews are positioned on a rung high enough to discern Mount Sinai and the Law Moses received thereon. Yet Paul feels that he has achieved a still higher rung and vantage point enabling him to discern, *beyond* the giving of the Torah at Mount Sinai, the benefits of the far more marvelous revelation of Jesus as the Christ—i.e., as the Messiah. . . . Unbelieving Jews will not be in a position to share Paul's realization until they themselves venture higher on the self-same ladder that Paul *still* occupies. Since Paul anticipates their ultimately doing so, he now broadly lays out how he expects this development will unfold: the proliferation of Gentiles within the church, newly enjoying the fruits of God's promises tendered originally to Israel's own Patriarchs, will arouse within Jews a craving for the blessings they believe are properly *theirs*, mobilizing them, finally, to accept Christ Jesus after all!" Michael J. Cook, "Paul's Argument in Romans 9–11," *RevExp* 103 (Winter 2006): 101-2. Cf. Samuel Sandmel, *The Genius of Paul* (Philadelphia: Fortress, 1979), 36.

[54]For a survey of views on Romans 11:26 ("all Israel will be saved"), see Christopher Zoccali, "'And So All Israel Will Be Saved': Competing Interpretations of Romans 11.26 in Pauline Scholarship," *JSNT* 30, no. 3 (2008): 289-318; J. R. Daniel Kirk, "Why Does the Deliverer Come ἐκ Σιών (Romans 11.26)?," *JSNT* 33, no. 1 (2010): 91, 96-97; Reidar Hvalvik, "A 'Sonderveg' for Israel: A Critical Examination of a Current Interpretation," *JSNT* 38 (1990): 87-107; and Vanlaningham, "Jewish People According to the Book of Romans," 122-28.

[55]See Gerald Peterman, "Social Reciprocity and Gentile Debt to Jews in Romans 15:26-27," *JETS* 50, no. 4 (2007): 735-46.

[56]Paul's words appear to imply that he was living the circumcised life: "If the Galatians did not know Paul as a Torah-observant Jew, then the rhetoric of [Gal] 5:3 would have no bite: 'I testify again to every man who receives circumcision that he is bound to keep the whole law.' Otherwise, they might simply respond, 'but we want only what you have: Jewish identity, without obligation to observe "the whole law."'" Mark D. Nanos, "The Inter- and Intra-Jewish Political Context of Paul's Letter to the Galatians," in *The Galatians Debate: Contemporary Issues in Rhetorical and Historical Interpretation* (Peabody, MA: Hendrickson, 2002), 405. See also Mark D. Nanos, "Paul and Judaism: Why Not Paul's Judaism?," in *Paul Unbound: Other Perspectives on*

Paul writes in Romans 11:28 (NIV) that "as far as election is concerned, they [the Jewish people] are loved [by God] on account of the patriarchs." This is why Paul refers to fellow members of the tribe as "his [God's] people" (Rom 11:1) or "his inheritance [τὴν κληρονομίαν]" as the marginalized reading of Romans 11:1 puts it,[57] thus emphasizing the land and seed promises:

> In [Rom] 11:1-2 the word λαόν has a semantic range which includes not only the people of God but also, in line with its OT usage, the people who inhabit *a particular land*. There is thus no weakening of the geographical dimension of the inheritance concept when it is used in tandem with λαόν in [Rom] 11:1-2. The two words κληρονομία and λαόν are here used in parallel because together they convey (and this is what is distinct about the Romans 11 text) the *permanent nature* of God's relationship to Israel. Here the word explicitly expresses the concept of God's enduring faithfulness. It is a reminder that the original promise to Abraham and his descendants is one which God, at least ultimately, intends to keep.[58]

Because of Israel's election, Paul can say in Romans 1:16 (NIV) that the gospel is "first for the Jew, then for the Gentile."[59] Going first to the Jewish people was not mainly a matter of chronological order, ethnic loyalty or wise outreach strategy; it was primarily because the Jewish people remain elect,[60] and therefore

---

the Apostle, ed. Mark D. Given (Peabody, MA: Hendrickson, 2010), 151-52; Dieter Mitternacht, "Foolish Galatians?—A Recipient-Oriented Assessment of Paul's Letter," in *The Galatians Debate*, 409; and Markus Bockmuehl, *Jewish Law in Gentile Churches: Halakhah and the Beginning of Christian Public Ethics* (Edinburgh: T&T Clark, 2000), 171.

[57] Most notably P[46].

[58] Forman, *Politics of Inheritance in Romans*, 152. See Mark D. Given, "Restoring the Inheritance in Romans 11:1," *JBL* 118, no. 1 (1999): 89-96.

[59] Marcion removed the word πρῶτον from Romans 1:16 because it affirms Jewish particularity in Paul's thought. See A. G. Padgett, "Marcion," in *Dictionary of the Later New Testament and Its Developments*, ed. Ralph P. Martin and Peter Davids (Downers Grove, IL: InterVarsity Press, 1997), 706-8.

[60] In saying that the gospel is "first (πρῶτον) for the Jew," Paul may be following the example of the Messiah who said, "*First* (πρῶτον) let the children eat all they want" (Mk 7:27, [emphasis added]; cf. Mt 10:5-6; 15:24; Acts 3:25-26; 13:46). "Paul's phrase 'to the Jew first' is not simply a rhetorical device. It was designed not to deceive readers about his view of Israel, but to emphasize it. Paul's attitude toward Israel, though cautious because of their hardness of heart and constant rejection of the gospel, is based on a thoroughgoing conviction that Israel's election by God is permanent and determinate for salvation history. Nor does the phrase merely depict Paul's missionary pattern or the chronological precedence of Israel as the object of gospel preaching, since the context of Romans 1:16 is primarily theological and is designed to set the stage for Paul's consideration of the relevance of God's promises to both Jews and Gentiles throughout the epistle. Paul's emphasis on the justification of Gentiles by faith never overshadows his confidence that God's plan for Israel is still unfinished and that God's fulfillment of His

God's children in a unique sense, "adoption" through covenant being one of the national privileges of the Jewish people that Paul lists in the present tense in Romans 9:4.[61] That is why Paul can write in Romans 2:9-10 (NIV, emphases added): "There will be trouble and distress for every human being who does evil: *first* for the Jew, then for the Gentile; but glory, honor and peace for everyone who does good: *first* for the Jew, then for the Gentile." The Pauline principle here is theological and ethical: To whom much is given, much is expected. Because the Jewish people are in a unique filial relationship with God and have national privileges (including covenants, promises and the Torah), they will be judged by a different standard than the Gentile world.

The calling of Israel. In Romans 11:29 (emphasis added), Paul writes, "for the gifts and the *calling* of God [to Israel] are irrevocable." What does Paul mean by the "calling" of God to Israel? Notably, Paul uses the same term for "calling"—κλῆσις—in 1 Corinthians 7:17-20, where he refers to the "calling" of being circumcised. Paul writes, "This is my rule in all the congregations. Was anyone at the time of his call [to salvation] already circumcised? . . . In the calling in which he was called, in this let him remain" (1 Cor 7:17-18, 20, author's translation).[62]

The notion of a "Jewish calling," and the responsibility of Jews to remain in their particular calling, finds support in Paul's command to Jewish people in 1 Corinthians 7:18, where he says μὴ ἐπισπάσθω (literally: "do not put on foreskin" / metonymically: "do not assimilate or Gentilize yourself").[63] The language is a

---

covenant promises to Israel is just as significant in this age as His focus on worldwide Gentile salvation. For Paul, Christ's mission to fulfill God's covenants with Israel has theological priority and provides a paradigm for dealing with Jewish-Gentiles issues in the church." Wayne A. Brindle, "'To the Jew First': Rhetoric, Strategy, History, or Theology?," *BSac* 159 (April-June 2002): 221-33. See Reidar Hvalvik, "'To the Jew First and Also to the Greek': The Meaning of Romans 1:16b," *Mishkan* 10, no. 1 (1989): 1-8.

[61]Cf. Exodus 4:22-23, Jeremiah 31:9 and Hosea 11:1. "In the Bible, it is not Abraham who moves toward God but God who turns to Abraham with an election that is not explained because it is an act of love that requires no explanation. If God continues to love the people of Israel—and it is the faith of Israel that he does—it is because he sees the face of his beloved Abraham in each and every one of his children as a man sees the face of his beloved in the children of his union with his beloved." Michael Wyschogrod, *The Body of Faith: God in the People Israel* (Northvale, NJ: Jason Aronson, 2000), 64.

[62]For a fuller discussion of 1 Corinthians 7:17-24, see David J. Rudolph, "Paul's 'Rule in All the Churches' (1 Cor 7:17-24) and Torah-Defined Ecclesiological Variegation," *SCJR* 5 (2010): 1-23; idem, *A Jew to the Jews*, 75-88; J. Brian Tucker, "Particularistic Approach to 'in Christ' Social Identities," in *"Remain in Your Calling": Paul and the Continuation of Social Identities in 1 Corinthians* (Eugene, OR: Pickwick, 2011), 62-88; and Anders Runesson, "Paul's Rule in All the Ekklēsiai," in Rudolph and Willitts, *Introduction to Messianic Judaism*, 214-23.

[63]"*Let him not undo his circumcision*. . . . Paul is thinking of more than surgical operation, of one kind or another. The converted Jew continues to be a Jew, with his own appointed way of obedience."

likely allusion to 1 Maccabees 1:11-15, where the expression "removed the marks of circumcision" is linked to dejudaization and the adoption of Gentile customs that collapse Jew-Gentile distinction.

Why was Jewish assimilation so problematic for Paul? It is probably because Jewish particularity reflects Israel's divine calling. According to Exodus 19, the Lord elected Israel to be his "treasured possession [*səgullâ*] out of all the peoples." The text goes on to say that Israel was called to be a "priestly kingdom and a holy nation" [*mamleket cōhănîm wəgōy qādôs*] (Ex 19:5-6; cf. Deut 7:6; 14:2; 26:18). Philo, a Jewish contemporary of Paul, considered Israel's Exodus 19 calling to be fundamental to the nation's identity.[64] He compared Israel to a king's royal estate and to a priest who ministered on behalf of a city.[65] In other words, Philo viewed Israel as having a priestly calling to be different, and through that difference to minister to the nations.

Against this Second Temple Jewish backdrop, we can understand Paul's command in 1 Corinthians 7:18—μὴ ἐπισπάσθω (do not assimilate)—as an imperatival instruction to Jewish people, including Jesus-believing Jews, to remain faithful to their Jewish identity. This was ultimately so that, through their particularity, they might live out Israel's priestly calling to the nations, even as Paul was living out this "priestly service" (as he puts it in Rom 15:16) by being the "apostle to the Gentiles" (Rom 11:13).

The confirmation of Israel's promises. In Romans 15:8, Paul writes: "For I tell you that Christ has become a *servant of the circumcised* on behalf of the truth of God in order that he might *confirm the promises given to the patriarchs*."[66] Here

---

C. K. Barrett, *A Commentary on the First Epistle to the Corinthians*, 2nd ed. (London: A&C Black, 1971), 168. Contra Bruce W. Winter, *Seek the Welfare of the City: Christians as Benefactors and Citizens* (Grand Rapids: Eerdmans, 1994), 146-64, who argues that 1 Corinthians 7:20 refers to epispasm operations. Winter, however, offers no direct evidence that epispasm was common enough in the first century to warrant Paul making a "rule in all the churches" (1 Cor 7:17) banning the operation. It should be noted that the metonymic and nonmetonymic positions are not mutually exclusive. A metonymic interpretation of 1 Corinthians 7:20 would include epispasm among the diverse ways that Jews could assimilate into Gentile identity and lifestyle.

[64]Philo, *On the Life of Abraham* 56, 98. Cf. *On the Embassy to Gaius* 3; *On the Life of Moses* 1.149; *On Rewards and Punishments* 114; *On the Special Laws* 1.97, 168; *Questions and Answers on Exodus* 2.42.

[65]Philo, *On Planting* 54-60; *On the Special Laws* 2.163-67. See Martha Himmelfarb, *A Kingdom of Priests: Ancestry and Merit in Ancient Judaism* (Philadelphia: University of Pennsylvania Press, 2006), 158-59.

[66]"'Promises made to the patriarchs' reprises the theme of the gracious election of Israel ([Rom] 9:4) and, in particular, the story of Abraham ([Rom] 4:13, 14, 16, 20, 21; 9:8-9). 'Confirm' here has the sense not only of 'reaffirming' but also of 'realizing' the promises. . . . The primary issue Paul addresses in Romans in regard to God's truthfulness is God's faithfulness to his promises to Israel (e.g., [Rom] 3:4; 9:4, 6; 11:1, 11)." J. Ross Wagner, "The Christ, Servant of Jew and Gentile: A Fresh Approach to Romans 15:8-9," *JBL* 116, no. 3 (1997): 477-78.

"Paul's use of the perfect tense γεγενῆσθαι in [Rom 15:]8, over against the simple aorist γενέσθαι, indicates Christ's *continuing* to be a servant to the circumcision."[67] Paul goes on to quote the Septuagint version of Isaiah 11:10 to show how these promises to the patriarchs will come to ultimate fulfillment in the messianic kingdom.[68] Romans 15:12 states:

and again Isaiah says,

"The root of Jesse shall come,
    the one who rises to rule the Gentiles;
in him the Gentiles shall hope."

Notably, the context of this Isaiah passage includes fulfillment of the land promise. After the words "in him the Gentiles shall hope," Isaiah declares:

And it shall be in that day, *that* the Lord shall again show his hand, to be zealous for the remnant that is left of the people....

And he shall lift up a standard for the nations,
    and he shall gather the lost ones of Israel,
    and he shall gather the dispersed of Judah
        from the four corners of the earth. (Is 11:11-12 LXX)

In Isaiah 11 the universal dimension of the messianic kingdom is balanced by the particularity of Israel's king ("the root of Jesse," that is, the son of David) and the return of his people to their land. Though Paul does not quote Isaiah 11:11-12, we can reasonably assume that he was aware of the territorial context and that in keeping with contemporary Jewish practice his quotation served as more of a bookmark than a stand-alone comment.

Paul's Isaiah references (especially Isaiah 59 and 27) in the discourse leading up to Romans 15 and following also shore up the view that Paul understood the *ekklēsia* as a prolepsis of Israel and the nations in the eschaton. Contrary to Wright's transference view that Paul "subverts the Jewish story from within,"[69]

---

[67]Scott Hafemann, "Eschatology and Ethics: The Future of Israel and the Nations in Romans 15:1-13," *TynBul* 51, no. 2 (2000): 170.
[68]Cf. J. Ross Wagner, *Heralds of the Good News: Isaiah and Paul "in Concert" in the Letter to the Romans* (Leiden: Brill, 2002), 317-29.
[69]N. T. Wright, *The Climax of the Covenant: Christ and the Law in Pauline Theology* (Edinburgh: T&T Clark, 1991), 235. Cf. idem, *The New Testament and the People of God: Christian Origins and the Question of God* (Minneapolis: Fortress, 1992), 403-9.

Hafemann maintains that the real climax of the covenant envisioned in Romans 15 is Israel's future restoration for the sake of the nations:

> Our passage thus gives no ground for seeing Israel's identity and eschatological hopes reconfigured into Christ and/or the present Church, having been transformed by Paul into exclusively present realities. Redemptive history does not become abstracted into the "Christ-event" or personalized into an eschatological "community," but continues on after Christ's coming and establishment of the Church just as concretely and historically as it did before. The "climax of the covenant" remains Israel's future restoration for the sake of the nations. Moreover, it is precisely this climax to the covenant that secures the believer's salvific hope in the return of Christ. In light of God's promises to the patriarchs ([Rom] 15:8), the Messiah, as the servant to the circumcision, *must* come again to judge the nations in order to restore Israel and save the Gentiles ([Rom] 15:12; cf. 11:29).[70]

Significantly, Paul describes the future kingdom in Zionist terms in Romans 11:26, where he proclaims,

And so all Israel will be saved; as it is written,

"Out of Zion will come the Deliverer;
he will banish ungodliness from Jacob."

Based on this passage and Galatians 4:26-30 ("Be glad, barren woman" [NIV]), Horbury concludes in his seminal study "Jerusalem in Pre-Pauline and Pauline Hope," that

> Paul envisaged a coming messianic reign in the divinely prepared Jerusalem, bringing together the king with the city and the sanctuary on the Old Testament pattern.... Hints at a Jerusalem-centred messianic reign in both passages would be consonant with the eschatological importance of Zion or the land in Rom. 9.25-6.[71]

---

[70]Scott Hafemann, "The Redemption of Israel for the Sake of the Gentiles," in Rudolph and Willitts, *Introduction to Messianic Judaism*, 212-13. See Hafemann, "Eschatology and Ethics," 190-91; and Wagner, *Heralds of the Good News*, 329-40.

[71]Horbury, "Jerusalem in Pre-Pauline and Pauline Hope," 218. See James M. Scott, "'And Then All Israel Will Be Saved' (Rom 11:26)," in *Restoration: Old Testament, Jewish, and Christian Perspectives* (Leiden: Brill, 2001), 495-96, 524-25; and Kirk, "Why Does the Deliverer Come ἐκ Σιών (Romans 11.26)?," 91, 96-97. In Romans 15, Paul appears to view Jerusalem as the geographic center of the kingdom of God in an already-but-not-yet sense. This would explain why he describes his apostolic ministry as coming

Why does Horbury highlight this passage in Romans 9:25-26? It is because Paul quotes Hosea as saying,

> And *in the very place* where it was said to
> them, 'You are not my people,'
> *there* they shall be called children of the
> living God." (Hos 1:10, NRSV, emphases added)

Since the Greek word ἐκεῖ (translated "there" in Rom 9:26) does not appear in any known Septuagint version of Hosea, it would seem to suggest that Paul is placing an emphasis on this geographic location. What do the words "in the very place" and "there" point to? In the context of Hosea 1, these terms refer to the land of Israel. Moreover, the Hosea 1:10 text that Paul quotes is in the middle of the prophet's description of how the land and seed promises to the patriarchs are fulfilled in the eschaton. In Hosea, a messianic king is appointed and then possession of the land is restored. The context states:

> [Yet the number of the people of Israel shall be like the sand of the sea, which can be neither measured nor numbered]; and *in the [very] place* where it was said to them, "You are not my people," [*there*] they shall be called children of the living God. [The people of Judah and the people of Israel shall be gathered together, and they shall appoint for themselves one head; and they shall take possession of the land.] (Hos 1:10-11, NRSV)

W. D. Davies discusses this text in his monograph *The Gospel and the Land: Early Christianity and Jewish Territorial Doctrine*. Though Davies is known for his view that Paul regarded the land promise as "christified,"[72] when it comes to Hosea 1:10 (quoted by Paul in Romans 9:26), Davies concedes that Paul presents in this Romans passage a normative territorial view of Zion. He writes:

> What is illegitimate is to ignore the plain geographic emphasis of the text at Rom. 9:25-26 in favour of a generalized reference to the call of the Gentiles or

---

out of Jerusalem. He writes in Romans 15:19 that "from Jerusalem and as far around as Illyricum I have fully proclaimed the good news of Christ" (cf. Rom 15:25-26, 31; 1 Cor 16:3; Gal 1:18; 2:1).

[72]"'In Christ' Paul was free from the Law and, therefore, from the land." W. D. Davies, *The Gospel and the Land: Early Christianity and Jewish Territorial Doctrine* (Sheffield: Sheffield Academic Press, 1994), 220. For a recent reassessment of Davies's conclusions, see Forman: "This study of inheritance above has demonstrated that Davies is wrong to suggest that the concept of 'land' in Paul's writings is entirely spiritualized.... Against Davies, therefore, the present study has argued that Paul's language of inheritance continues in a geographical, physical direction *and that* using this kind of language in the first-century context was undeniably subversive of the message perpetuated by the powers of the day" (*Politics of Inheritance in Romans*, 234).

of lapsed Jews. The full weight of the doctrines which we dealt with in Part I are in favour of giving to Zion a geographic connotation. Zion or Jerusalem was for the Jew, Paul, the centre of the world, the symbol of the land itself and the focal point for the Messianic Age. The likelihood is that, at first at least, it occupied the same place in his life as a Christian. 2 Thess. 2, and possibly Rom. 11:26, and, probably Rom. 9:26 confirm this.[73]

In addition to these Pauline texts that uphold a territorial confirmation of Israel's promises, I would add 1 Corinthians 15 to the mix.[74] Horbury notes that:

> In the larger Pauline context the most important passage for the question is 1 Cor. 15.20-8. The present writer follows those who hold that in 1 Cor. 15 Paul envisages a Zion-centered Messianic reign, beginning with a second coming of Christ. As is shown in [1 Cor 15:]25-8 by the exposition of Pss. 110.1, 8.6 on the subjection of enemies, this reign involves the crushing victory over hostile forces granted to the king, God's son, in Zion, on the lines sketched in Pss. 2.6-9, 110.1-6. . . . In Christian sources this execution of foes in the messianic victory is pictured at 2 Thess. 2:8.[75]

All of this eschatological drama described in 1 Corinthians 15, centering on the death, resurrection *and bodily return of the Messiah*, takes place in the land of Israel.

The irrevocability of Israel's election. Paul writes in Romans 11:29 that "the gifts and the calling of God [to Israel] are *irrevocable* (ἀμεταμέλητα). While in English translations the word "irrevocable" usually appears at the end of the sentence, in the Greek text, ἀμεταμέλητα appears at the beginning, thus placing emphasis on this word, as though it were highlighted or had an exclamation mark attached to it. Paul's point is that Israel's general state of unbelief does not compromise its election, gifts or calling (cf. Rom 3:3-4 ["What if some were unfaithful? Will their faithlessness nullify the faithfulness of God? By no means!"] and the present-tense list of Israel's covenant privileges in Rom 9:1-6). God remains faithful to Israel despite Israel's unfaithfulness.

Paul makes the same point at the beginning of Romans 11 when he raises the rhetorical question, "I ask, then, has God rejected his people [or, in the marginalized

---

[73]Davies, *Gospel and the Land*, 196.
[74]See Seth Turner, "The Interim, Earthly Messianic Kingdom in Paul," *JSNT* 25, no. 3 (2003): 323-42; and L. Joseph Kreitzer, *Jesus and God in Paul's Eschatology* (Sheffield: JSOT Press, 1987), 131-64.
[75]William Horbury, "Land, Sanctuary and Worship," in *Early Christian Thought in Its Jewish Context*, ed. John Barclay and John Sweet (Cambridge: Cambridge University Press, 1996), 220.

reading, "his inheritance"]?" (Rom 11:1).[76] Here Paul does not go on to say: "Yes, God has rejected his people and transferred all of Israel's blessings to the church." On the contrary, he exclaims, "μὴ γένοιτο,"[77] which means, "Of course not!" (REB), "Absolutely not!" (NET), "Out of the question" (NJB), "By no means!" (NRSV), "Heaven forbid!" (CJB). The fact of the matter is that "if it can be concluded that God is unfaithful in his relationship to Israel, there is little reason to think that he should be otherwise in his relationship with the Christian Community."[78] Paul could not have been more loud and clear in affirming the irrevocability of Israel's election.

Conclusion

In this essay I have argued that Paul does *not* eliminate particularity for Israel and the land in his portrayal of salvation available for all the world, and that a compelling case can be made for particularity when we consider what Paul has to say about:

G The **Gifts** of Israel
U The **Uniqueness** of Israel
C The **Calling** of Israel
C The **Confirmation** of Israel's promises
I The **Irrevocability** of Israel's election

Paul does not undermine the particularity of the people or land of Israel in his teachings. Rather, he affirms the continuing election, gifts and calling of the Jewish people and spends considerable time in his letter to the Romans (at least five chapters!) to get this point across.

In Paul's view, particularity is part of the warp and woof of the kingdom of God, a kingdom that is manifest in a table fellowship of Jews and Gentiles who remain faithful to their calling as Jews and Gentiles in the Messiah. Paul's Isaianic vision of the world to come is best expressed in Romans 11 and 15, where Israel and the nations are described as worshiping God together in unity and diversity, in interdependence and mutual blessing. Paul sums it all up beautifully in Romans 15:10 when he says, quoting the Song of Moses, "Rejoice, O Gentiles, with his people."

---

[76]Forman, *Politics of Inheritance in Romans*, 136-71; Given, "Restoring the Inheritance in Romans 11:1," 89-96.

[77]Cf. Paul's use of μὴ γένοιτο in Romans 3:3-4. "The section [Romans] 2.25–3:4 therefore suggests that the Jew's election has not been annulled. There is value in being a Jew, and God has remained faithful even though Israel has not believed. Paul therefore does not hold to a substitution model here. God's election of Israel is unshakable." Bell, *Irrevocable Call of God*, 198.

[78]Bruce W. Longenecker, *Eschatology and the Covenant: A Comparison of 4 Ezra and Romans 1–11* (Sheffield: Sheffield Academic Press, 1991), 251. Cf. Markus Barth, *The People of God* (Sheffield: JSOT Press, 1983), 30. See Romans 11:20-22.

- PART THREE -

THEOLOGY AND ITS IMPLICATIONS

7

THEOLOGY AND THE CHURCHES

Mainline Protestant Zionism and Anti-Zionism

Mark Tooley

◆

An unlikely founder of American Christian Zionism was a zealous Methodist preacher and businessman named William Blackstone, who was a dispensationalist and restorationist, believing that biblical prophecy foresaw the Jews' return to the Promised Land. Although the notion may seem strange now, it was a natural link in the mid-nineteenth century, when mainline Protestants commonly assumed providential attention for nations and people groups, above all the American people, who were a sort of prototype of a New Zion. Methodists, with their fixation on constant moral reform, had a natural affinity for outreach to the long-displaced and frequently tormented Jewish people.

Much if not most of modern Christian Zionism in the United States originated primarily in mainline Protestantism when its institutions were still recognizably rooted in theological orthodoxy. As mainline denominations liberalized, Zionism often persisted, based no longer on particular biblical interpretations but in a Niebuhrian realism and humanitarian sympathy for Jewish suffering and statelessness. When utopianism and liberation theology displaced neo-orthodoxy in the 1960s and 1970s, mainline institutional support for Zionism receded rapidly. Eventually, after the close of the twentieth century, hostile mainline elites, typically indifferent to doctrinal parameters, were identifying Christian Zionism as uniquely heretical.

Christian Zionism in the United States has long since migrated from mainline Protestantism to evangelicalism. But some of the same theological trends and political assumptions that neutralized and stigmatized Zionism among mainline elites are now expanding among evangelicals. Preserving a robust Christian Zionism among evangelicals and others requires understanding what killed it in institutional mainline Protestantism. Without understanding this history, evangelical Zionists of today might follow the same trajectory as Methodists or Presbyterians during the twentieth century.

Blackstone's Memorial

In 1890 Blackstone hosted a conference on the "Past, Present and Future of Israel" at Chicago's First Methodist Episcopal Church, where mostly mainline Protestant church leaders and others implored the great powers, above all the Ottomans as custodians of the Holy Land, to return the Jews to their ancient homeland. In 1891 he launched the Blackstone Memorial, a petition urging American support for a Jewish homeland in Palestine, aimed at President Benjamin Harrison, an observant Presbyterian. It was signed by hundreds of notables, including soon-to-be-president William McKinley, a devout Methodist, and business moguls like John D. Rockefeller, J. P. Morgan and Cyrus McCormick, who were respectively Northern Baptist, Episcopalian and Presbyterian.[1]

Blackstone's letter to President Harrison explained,

> There seem to be many evidences to show that we have reached the period in the great roll of centuries, when the everlasting God of Abraham, Isaac and Jacob, is lifting up His hand to the Gentiles (Isa 49:22) to bring His sons and his daughters from far, that he may plant them again in their own land, Ezekiel 34, etc. Not for twenty-four centuries, since the days of Cyrus, King of Persia, has there been offered to any mortal such a privileged opportunity to further the purposes of God concerning His ancient people.[2]

The movement founded by Blackstone did not appreciably advance, but adherents often spoke on behalf of persecuted Jews, especially victims of pogroms in Russia. In 1916 Jewish leaders successfully urged Blackstone to revive his memorial, this time for another Presbyterian president, Woodrow Wilson. The

---

[1] Jerry Klinger, "Judge Brandeis, President Wilson and Reverend William E. Blackstone Changed Jewish History," *Jewish Magazine*, August 2010, www.jewishmag.com/146mag/brandeis_blackstone/brandeis_blackstone.htm.
[2] Jonathan Moorhead, "The Father of Zionism: William E. Blackstone?," *JETS* 53, no. 4 (2010): 792, www.etsjets.org/files/JETS-PDFs/53/53-4/JETS_53-4_787-800_Moorhead.pdf.

1916 Presbyterian Church in the U.S. General Assembly, citing Blackstone's Memorial, petitioned President Wilson, "in behalf of the persecuted Jews of Europe," to call "an international conference of the Powers" to consider "such measures as may be deemed wise and best for their permanent relief." Wilson later commented on his support for the Balfour Declaration, "To think that I, the son of the manse, should be able to help restore the Holy Land to its people," which a former Presbyterian Church (USA) official in 1990 said reflected Wilson's "subjective, sentimental understanding of Scripture."[3]

Zionism After World War I

Blackstone's Zionism comfortably melded with wider mainline Protestant interpretations of World War I as a divine instrument for chastening and reforming the nations, pushing them in the direction of God's ultimate kingdom. Bishop Samuel Spreng preached on the war's lessons in the summer of 1918 to the Oakwood Park Assembly outside Chicago. He was a bishop in the Evangelical Church, a denomination in which Orville and Wilbur Wright's father was also a bishop and which would decades later merge into the United Methodist Church in 1968.

The "cataclysm" of world war has brought suffering but also a "new birth," Bishop Spreng promised. "Above the battle's roar, and the cannon's thunder one can hear the voice of the Almighty saying, 'Behold I make all things new.'" He pronounced the war to be a judgment on the world and was confident that God, never intending that "one man should rule the world," would ensure that Germany's "war lord would fail too," with Germany ultimately freed from the "tyrant's yoke." Bishop Spreng celebrated the fall of Russia's czar and the "tyranny of the Greek Church," leaving Russia "now ready for the Gospel." Speaking prior to the Bolshevik takeover, which occurred a few months later, he enthused that Russia is "religiously free as a direct result of the war," and "this alone is worth all that the war has as yet cost in blood and life and treasure." He also rejoiced that with the fall of Turkey the "political significance of Islam will be broken." Spreng foresaw that "Mohammadan lands will be open to the Gospel as never before." Thanks to British arms, the "flag of a Christian nation" now floats above Jerusalem. Britain had promised a homeland for the Jews, which the bishop saw

---

[3]Paul Hopkins, "American Presbyterians and the Middle East Conflict," *American Presbyterians* 68, no. 3 (1990): 144, www.pcusa.org/resource/american-presbyterians-and-middle-east-conflict/.

as one of God's "miracles" emerging from the war. "War is the surgeon's knife in God's hand for the purpose of delivering the nations from their imperiling sins," Spreng suggested, adding that "Jehovah is a man of war." And this war is the "thunder and crash of the irresistible march of progress."[4]

Christian Zionism accelerated after World War I. A Baltimore Methodist minister in 1921 no doubt spoke for many when he preached on "Zionism—the Future of Israel," enthusing, "If the Jewish nation finds a spiritual center of its own, soundly based on industrious population, untrammeled, self-contained, inspired by memories of a splendid past, it may again produce fruits in the field of intellect for the enrichment of the world." He also suggested that Jews in Palestine would in "that land of prophets and heroes" likely "more carefully study the life and teachings of Him of whom the prophets wrote and will come to see Him as we who love and worship Him—the Messiah promised by God."[5]

The Federal Council of Churches helped host a pro-Zionist fundraiser for the "suffering" Jews of Palestine at a prominent New York City Methodist church in 1928, where the "historic kinship between Judaism and Christianity" was a theme. A church council official hailed the "new roads, new schools, better water supplies, the planting of forests and the increased productivity of the soil" by Palestine's Jews.[6]

There were voices of caution from liberal Protestants who were wary of Zionism, notably famed New York preacher and theological modernist Harry Emerson Fosdick, who in 1927 urged a "modified form of Zionism." He warned that the "Jew has got to stop his chauvinism" and "bring his ambitions down to a few concrete, definitely attainable objectives."[7]

But overshadowing appeals like Fosdick's were appeals from groups like the now ironically named Pro-Palestine Federation, which organized church leaders for Jewish return to Zion. (Palestine was universally then the term for what is now Israel.) In 1936 the group, including the Episcopal bishop of Washington, met the British ambassador, while claiming to represent "the consensus of enlightened Christian American opinion," to remind the British government that "God has bestowed upon England one of the greatest missions in human history—the salvation of Israel and restoration to its ancient patrimony."[8] Also

---

[4] Samuel P. Spreng, *The World-War and Its Lessons: A Sermon Preached at Oakwood Park Assembly on August 18, 1918* (Chicago: Oakwood Park Assembly, 1918).
[5] "Considers Palestine Hope of the Hebrew," *Baltimore Sun*, May 30, 1921, 3.
[6] "Christians Appeal for Palestine Fund," *New York Times*, September 16, 1929, 18.
[7] "Fosdick Sees Ruin Ahead for Zionism," *New York Times*, May 25, 1927, 8.
[8] "Americans Appeal for Jewish Refuge," *New York Times*, May 31, 1936, 14.

participating was liberal Methodist bishop Francis J. McConnell, a founder of the Methodist Federation for Social Action. Today, the Methodist Federation for Social Action is a leading proponent of anti-Israel divestment, but in the 1930s McConnell urged Britain "to fulfill its covenantal pledges" about a Jewish homeland in Palestine.[9]

CHRISTIAN REALISM AND ZIONISM

In the late 1930s a similar group, with some of the same church voices—"Christian Leaders, Clergymen and Laymen, on Behalf of Jewish Immigration into Palestine Federation"—declared that "the destiny of the Jews is a matter of immediate concern to the Christian conscience, the amelioration of their lot a duty that rests upon all that profess Christian principles." Joining prelates like Methodist bishop McConnell was an increasingly prominent German Reformed theologian at New York's Union Seminary named Reinhold Niebuhr. This group was "committed to the establishment of a Jewish commonwealth in Palestine in relation to the overall settlement in the postwar era" while "urg[ing] as immediate policy the admission now of Jewish exiles into other countries, including the United States, as well as Palestine." One of its seminary leaders, a Congregationalist, confidently exclaimed that "as soon as the British see that list of men on our stationery—Niebuhr, Tillich, McConnell, Albright, Sockman, and Poling—they'll open the gates of Palestine and let those Jewish refugees come pouring in. Then we'll disband the committee. It's as simple as that."[10]

Niebuhr's old publication, *Christian Century*, against which he turned for its pre–World War II pacifism, unsurprisingly disagreed with Niebuhr's Zionism. In 1950 it editorialized against Jews in the United States raising a bond for Israel with the headline, "A Billion to Make More Trouble." The editorial alleged the efforts would disrupt US attempts at peace in the Mideast.[11]

Many liberal Protestants in the early post–World War II years agreed with Niebuhr. In 1946 two Christian pro-Zionist groups merged into the American Christian Palestine Committee, whose membership was reportedly 20,000. It included prominent politicians and churchmen, both Catholic and Protestant,

---

[9]Paul Charles Merkley, *The Politics of Christian Zionism, 1891–1948* (Oxon, UK: Routledge, 1998), 113.
[10]Ibid., 154.
[11]"As We Were Saying: *Christian Century*'s Hopkins Playing Rough with Israel," *The American Israelite*, October 19, 1950, 1.

and helped push Congress to pass a Zionist resolution.[12] The group's New England chair, the editor of Methodism's *Zion's Herald*, in 1947 hailed a "righteous crusade for the establishment of peace and justice in the land which is holy in the great Judaic-Christian tradition."[13] More cautiously, in 1946 the Episcopal Church General Convention considered but referred for study an appeal to the Church of England on behalf of the "wretched remnant of the Jews left alive in Europe," that they be permitted to immigrate to Palestine, in compliance with the Balfour Declaration, which is the "will of God for the Jewish people."[14] In 1949 the Episcopal House of Bishops heard but declined to endorse an appeal for the internationalization of Jerusalem from the Anglican church in that city, whose representative warned against the "twin forces of a nationalistic Islam and a militant Zionism."[15]

New York Methodism in 1948 commended President Harry Truman for recognizing Israel and urged the United Nations to treat attacking Arab states as a "threat to world peace."[16] New York Methodist bishop G. Bromley Oxnam presented an award honoring newly formed Israel's "stand for dignity and equality of opportunity."[17] Methodist Council of Bishops president Fred Corson in 1953 joined others in urging President Dwight Eisenhower to denounce anti-Semitism in the Soviet Union.[18] In 1954, Missouri bishop Ivan Holt of the World Methodist Council and another bishop joined prominent officials in urging Arab states to resettle eight hundred thousand Arab (i.e., Palestinian) refugees from the 1948 war. Of the Palestinians, they declared, "Led into flight from their homes by Arab leaders, they are prevented from seeking permanent rehabilitation by these same leaders who use existence of the problem as a weapon against the West and against Israel."[19] The 1952 Episcopal General Convention considered but referred to study a resolution about the one million Arabs who in 1948 were "ruthlessly driven by the Israelis from their ancestral lands," having been "being reduced to utter degradation," an "evil situation" for which the

---

[12]"Christian Zionists Engaged in Educating Public on Palestine," *Jewish Advocate*, January 17, 1946, 1.
[13]"Palestine Topic of Talk by ACPA Chairman," *Jewish Advocate*, January 9, 1947, 14.
[14]*Journal of the General Convention of the Episcopal Church, Philadelphia, 1946* (New York: General Convention, 1947), 264.
[15]"Jerusalem Mandate Urged," *New York Times*, October 4, 1949, 17.
[16]"U.S. Lacks Plan, Methodists Find," *New York Times*, May 22, 1948, 3.
[17]"Oxnam Presents Israel Citation," *New York Times*, June 1, 1948, 4.
[18]"Eisenhower Move to Aid Jews Urged," *New York Times*, February 16, 1953, 1.
[19]"U.S. Asked to Back Big Mid-East Fund," *New York Times*, April 17, 1954, 3.

United Nations and United States bore a "heavy responsibility" and should strive to correct. Another motion, from the bishop of North Carolina, approved by the bishops but not the lay deputies, urged "permanent resettlement" for Arab refugees from Mandated Palestine.[20]

Prominent theologically radical Episcopal priest James Pike, later a bishop, was explicitly Zionist. In 1958, as dean of the Cathedral of Saint John the Divine in New York, he hailed Israel as an "oasis of freedom and democracy," explaining that the "heritage of Judaism—which is our heritage, too—is made more vivid by the restoration of Jewish life and culture in the place of its original development."[21]

Presbyterians typically were carefully impartial during the early years of Israel. The 1948 General Assembly of the Presbyterian Church in the U.S. urged "faithful devotion to the welfare, needs, and rights of both the Jewish and Arab peoples." They exhorted the United Nations to prevent the Palestine conflict from becoming the "tinderbox for world conflagration." The 1954 General Assembly repeated this call, citing 750,000 refugees. The 1967 assembly was similarly impartial in its "deep concern over the unrest and recent conflict in the Middle East, an area which contains much that is sacred to Christian, Jew, and Muslim alike, and it registers its wholehearted and prayerful support of individuals and nations who are seeking to bring peace and concord to that area of the world."[22]

Liberation Theology and Israel

By the 1970s, mainline Protestantism, no longer seeing Israel as the underdog after the 1967 victory and increasingly enthralled by liberation theology, which assumed that Western nations like Israel were de facto oppressors of Third World peoples, was shifting against Zionism. Some of the anti-Zionist sentiment originated earlier in the twentieth century with Protestant mission personnel active in Arab nations, especially Presbyterians and the antecedents of the United Church of Christ. These mission personnel inspired, among other initiatives, the founding of the Institute of Arab-American Affairs after World

---

[20] *Journal of the General Convention of the Episcopal Church, Boston, 1952* (New York: General Convention, 1952), 147.
[21] "Pike Hails Israel as Christian Link," *New York Times*, May 8, 1958, 16.
[22] "Survey of PCUSA General Assembly Resolutions on the Israeli-Palestinian Conflict," Israel Palestine Mission Network, accessed July 15, 2015, www.israelpalestinemissionnetwork.org/main/ipmndocuments/factsheet15.pdf.

War II to rebut Zionism. The Presbyterian Church in the U.S. Board of Foreign Missions complained in 1949 that resettled Jews had "displaced an equal number of Arabs from their ancestral homes, too often by high handed methods ... making missionary work very difficult."[23] But their influence receded, at least temporarily, after the excitement of Israel's 1948 founding as a new nation of Holocaust survivors.[24]

Despite this shift against Zionism by mainline Protestants, a report by the Task Force on the Middle East to the 1972 General Assembly of the United Presbyterian Church in the U.S.A. stressed that the "Abrahamic covenant is unconditional" and the "current conjunction of Land and People in the state of Israel may be viewed as a sign of the continuing relationship of God with the Jewish people" and allows the church to repent "its age-long antisemitism."[25] But such thoughts became increasingly rare among mainline Protestants.

Instead, liberal Protestant pronouncements reacting to the 1973 war, when Israel defeated a surprise attack by Egypt, were decidedly ambivalent. One United Methodist official declared, "The events of the last few years have tended to obscure the origin of the ongoing struggle in the Middle East. . . . Behind the big power conferences there are Israelis and Palestinians, two people who claim the same land, two people whose history in the twentieth century includes horror, war, resistance, and survival."[26] The 1973 Episcopal General Convention impartially prayed "earnestly for peace with justice" and affirmed United Nations' efforts for "peaceful negotiations."[27]

In 1974 the General Assembly of the Presbyterian Church in the U.S. affirmed that the "the right and power of the Jewish people to self-determination by political expression in Israel, based upon full civil liberties for all, should be recognized by the parties in the Middle East and by the international community" and that Middle East boundaries "should be mutually defined and accepted." It backed a "shared common authority for a unified Jerusalem," protecting the "legitimate national political interests of both Israel and the Palestinians."[28]

---

[23]Hopkins, "American Presbyterians and the Middle East Conflict," 149.
[24]Judith Hershcopf Banki, *Anti-Israel Influence in American Churches: A Background Report* (New York: American Jewish Committee, 1979), 2-3.
[25]Hopkins, "American Presbyterians and the Middle East Conflict," 157.
[26]"No Missionaries Believed Involved in Mideast War," *Newscope*, October 19, 1973, 1.
[27]*Journal of the General Convention of the Episcopal Church*, Louisville, KY, 1973 (New York: General Convention, 1952), 460.
[28]"Survey of PCUSA General Assembly Resolutions on the Israeli-Palestinian Conflict."

Zionism Equals Racism?

By 1974, Israel was boycotting a United Methodist panel on the Middle East held at the Church Center for the United Nations (located across the street from the United Nations headquarters in New York), alleging the program was biased toward Arabs.[29] In 1975, mainline Protestant officials mostly deplored the United Nations' declaration equating Zionism with "racism," although perhaps more out of concern for the United Nations than for Israel. Episcopalians of southern Ohio denounced the anti-Zionism resolution, which could "cause irreparable harm to the United Nations," while affirming "opposition to anti-Semitism in all its forms."[30] United Methodist, Episcopalian, Presbyterian and Lutheran leaders of southwest Pennsylvania denounced the United Nations for having "descended to a low point in its history."[31]

The president of the United Church of Christ was stronger, warning that the "sponsors of the resolution meant by [Zionism] Jews and Judaism as well as the State of Israel," recalling that "since the beginning of the biblical story, the history of humankind, the very souls of whole populations have been corrupted by the evil presence of those who would destroy the Jews." He insisted "there can be no peace and no justice until the continued existence of Israel is guaranteed and the Palestinian people has its own land and its own government." United Methodism's bishops also called the United Nations resolution "one-sided ... indefensible ... and irresponsible," for it adds "anguish to Jews ... endangers support for the United Nations ... [and] dulls the edge of hopes for combating racism wherever it exists."[32]

But even as many Protestants lamented the United Nations' equation of Zionism with racism, denominational statements became more outspoken against Israeli occupation policies. A statement from the Presbyterian Church in the U.S. General Assembly of 1975 cited the "very real and just claims of the Palestinian people that the government of Israel has too long neglected." It admitted the United States had a "commitment to help Israel as a nation to survive, but that this is not and must not be a commitment to support Israel in the defense of its present boundaries"[33]

---

[29]"Middle East Appraised by Church Leaders: Israelis Boycott Talks," *Newscope*, November 21, 1975, 1.
[30]"Episcopal Body Denounces UN Action on Zionism," *The American Israelite*, December 25, 1975, 1.
[31]"Church Leaders Protest United Nations' Anti-Zionism Action," *New Pittsburgh Courier*, November 22, 1975, 22.
[32]"Church Leaders in US Assail UN Resolution on Zionism," *Boston Globe*, November 27, 1975, 37.
[33]Hopkins, "American Presbyterians and the Middle East Conflict," 162.

In 1976, the United Methodist Church at its General Conference adopted its first official stance on the Middle East, which noted that Israeli Jews live with "insecurity" amid a "long history of oppression," culminating with the Holocaust. It also cited Palestinian "suffering," including "arrests, tortures, and expulsions" by Israelis. It affirmed "self-determination" for Jews and Palestinians, including a Palestinian state, while faulting the United States for ignoring Palestinian "aspirations." And it urged recognizing the Palestine Liberation Organization.[34]

Similarly, the 1977 United Presbyterian Church in the U.S.A. General Assembly reaffirmed its 1974 call for US commitment to Israel and for Palestinian self-determination. It also urged including the PLO in negotiations. In 1979 the Presbyterian Church in the U.S. deplored Palestinian raids into Israel and massive retaliation by Israel, while also condemning US arms sales to the region.[35]

A 1978 resolution from the National Council of Churches rejoiced over the Egypt-Israel peace treaty, which meant that Israel's "dream of peace and deliverance might be realized and the threat of annihilation diminished." But it also stressed Palestinian self-determination, the "principle of the inadmissibility of the acquisition of territory by force," and the need for participation by the "recognized representatives of the Palestinian people."[36]

The governing board of the National Council of Churches (NCC) in 1980 urged Israel to recognize the Palestine Liberation Organization (PLO) as the "only organized voice of the Palestinian people" and to "officially declare its recognition of the right of Palestinians to self-determination," while also specifying that the PLO must recognize Israel's right to exist as a Jewish state. Jewish groups denounced the NCC action, but an NCC official explained that the NCC "is trying to play some kind of bridge role between the two sides of the conflict."[37] In 1982 the NCC governing board implored the United States to begin dialogue with the PLO as "one means of moving toward" mutual recognition "between Israel and the representatives of the Palestinian people."[38] In 1991, in the aftermath of the Persian Gulf War, the NCC and US Reform Judaism together urged Arab states to recognize

---

[34] *The Book of Resolutions of the United Methodist Church 1976* (Nashville: United Methodist Publishing House, 1976), 129-32.
[35] "Survey of PCUSA General Assembly Resolutions on the Israeli-Palestinian Conflict."
[36] Hershcopf Banki, *Anti-Israel Influence in American Churches*, 13.
[37] "NCC Approves Middle East Policy Statement," Episcopal News Service, November 13, 1980.
[38] "Membership Bid and Peace with Justice NCC Focus," Episcopal News Service, May 20, 1982.

Israel and affirmed the right of Palestinians to choose their own representatives for negotiations with Israel, but did not mention a Palestinian state.[39]

In 1979 the Episcopal General Convention benignly hailed the peace treaty between Israel and Egypt, affirming the "right of Israel to exist as a free State within secure borders" and urging an "overall settlement and peaceful resolution to the issues and problems in the Middle East," including a "free and independent Palestinian state which recognizes the State of Israel" and a "solution" for Jerusalem that "would guarantee free and secure access to the Holy City by people of all faiths."[40]

The Episcopal General Convention in 1982 in a similar spirit urged "all parties to the conflict in the Middle East to lay down their arms, and to settle their dispute by direct negotiations and mutual recognition," while supporting the "right of Palestinian people to exercise responsibility for their political future, with the proviso that the Palestinians recognize the legitimacy of the State of Israel."[41]

In 1981 the United Presbyterian Church in the U.S.A. General Assembly joined with Lebanese Christian prelates to deplore Israel's "continued attacks on southern Lebanon." In 1982 the Presbyterian Church in the U.S. General Assembly urged Israel to "withdraw all of its forces from Lebanon immediately," for the PLO to "cease acts of violence against its neighbor" and for the United States to "enter into official contact" with the PLO when it "acknowledges the right of Israel to exist within secure and recognized boundaries."[42]

"Final Solution" of Palestinian Problem

More aggressively in 1982, a United Church of Christ Board for World Ministries executive wrote President Reagan, asserting that Israel "in some fashion planned and accomplished the assassination of [Lebanon's] president-elect Bashir Gemayel, because he would not allow Lebanon to remain a dependent client of Israel." He also suggested that Israeli policies in Lebanon caused its desire to "achieve a final solution of the Palestinian problem."[43]

---

[39]"Jewish Group, NCC Issue Postwar Statement," Episcopal News Service, April 29, 1991.
[40]*Journal of the General Convention of the Episcopal Church, Denver, 1979* (New York: General Convention, 1980), C-105.
[41]*Journal of the General Convention of the Episcopal Church, Denver, 1982* (New York: General Convention, 1983), C-129.
[42]"ACSWP Commentary," Presbyterian Church (USA), accessed February 2, 2016, http://index.pcusa.org/nxt/gateway.dll/SPCompilation/122/232/363/366?f=templates&fn=default.htm&vid=Publish:10.1048/Enu.
[43]James Franklin, "Religion & Politics: The Christian-Jewish Dialogue Picks up Static . . . ," *Boston Globe*, October 3, 1982, A23.

The 1983 assembly of the newly united Presbyterian Church (USA) urged the United States to stand against Israeli settlements on the West Bank by "denying all forms of aid to Israel as long as that nation persists in creating new West Bank settlements." The PCUSA General Assembly urged a Palestinian state in 1984, 1986 and 1987, commending talks between the United States and the PLO in 1984 and 1986.[44]

In 1985, the Episcopalians at their General Convention opposed moving the US Embassy from Tel Aviv to Jerusalem except "within the context of a broad resolution of Middle East problems" and "not by unilateral action by any one community, religion, race or nation."[45] Three years later the General Convention reiterated its "prophetic role by standing on the side of the oppressed," including Israel's existence within "secure borders" with "civic and human rights for all those who live within its borders," plus the Palestinians' right to "self-determination, including choice of their own representatives and the establishment of their own state."[46]

The 1988 PCUSA General Assembly denounced Israel's "systematic violation" of Palestinian human rights, specifically "administrative detention, collective punishment, the torture of prisoners and suspects, and the deportation of dissidents." It also demanded Israel end "practices of beatings and of food and fuel embargoes in the attempt to subjugate and break the will of the Palestinian population." The 1989, 1990 and 1991 PCUSA General Assemblies reiterated opposition to Israeli settlements.[47]

In 1989 the Episcopal Church's Executive Council denounced the "inhumane and untenable living conditions and lack of basic human rights endured by Palestinian refugees in Israel, the West Bank, Gaza and Jordan" and the "recent brutal treatment accorded Palestinians protesting their substandard quality of life," as well as the US role in "acquiescing in the continued oppression of this refugee people through a complicity of silence and continued provision of substantial material resources to the architects of the inhumane policies."[48]

---

[44]"Survey of PCUSA General Assembly Resolutions on the Israeli-Palestinian Conflict."
[45]*Journal of the General Convention of the Episcopal Church, Denver, 1985* (New York: General Convention, 1986), 130.
[46]*Journal of the General Convention of the Episcopal Church*, Denver, 1988 (New York: General Convention, 1989), 293.
[47]"Survey of PCUSA General Assembly Resolutions on the Israeli-Palestinian Conflict."
[48]Episcopal Church Executive Council Minutes, February 28–March 3, 1989, Fort Worth, 55.

The PCUSA General Assembly in 1990 asked the US Congress to make US aid to Israel contingent on ending further settlements and human rights violations, while asking the United States to designate 10 percent of US aid to Israel to benefit Palestinians in occupied territories.[49] A 1990 paper by a former PCUSA missions executive proclaimed: "Today the Palestinians have recognized the legitimacy of the State of Israel and are prepared to make peace with their enemy. All Presbyterians pray for the day when Israel will say with the prophet: 'Neither by force of arms nor by brute strength, but by my spirit! Says the Lord of Hosts.'"[50]

Episcopal Church presiding bishop Edmond Browning in 1990 denounced the settlement of twenty Jewish families in the Christian quarter of Jerusalem's Old City, asking President George H. W. Bush to "convey your displeasure to the Israeli government over this latest outrage and your concern that in providing American funds we free Israeli resources for such irresponsible use."[51] Several US Episcopal bishops participated in a protest march in Jerusalem against the Israeli settlers, complaining that the "intrusion by settlers during Holy Week upsets the ancient balance among the faith communities in Jerusalem and indicates the grave impediments created by the settlements to the way of peace." Bishop Peter Lee of Virginia said, "Thousands of these young people are growing up with the knowledge that American bullets are killing their friends. The long-term security of Israel rests on us working together for a peaceful settlement."[52]

Presiding Bishop Browning, still upset, wrote President Bush later in 1990 of his "profound distress" over the "tragic level of violence to which the Palestinian people have been subjected by the security forces of Israel," whose lack of restraint was "inexcusable." He insisted that American aid "can no longer be provided unconditionally to a state that is violating the fundamental human rights of an occupied people."[53]

---

[49] "1990 Statement," Presbyterian Church (USA), accessed February 2, 2016, http://index.pcusa.org/nxt/gateway.dll/SPCompilation/122/232/363/369?f=templates&fn=default.htm&vid=Publish:10.1048/Enu.
[50] Hopkins, "American Presbyterians and the Middle East Conflict," 164.
[51] "Jewish Settlement in Christian Quarter of Jerusalem Stirs International Protest," Episcopal News Service, April 26, 1990.
[52] "Episcopalians Join Protest March over Jewish Settlements in Christian Quarter of Jerusalem's Old City," Episcopal News Service, May 20, 1990.
[53] "Presiding Bishop Condemns Violence, Asks President Bush to Place Conditions on American Aid to Israel," Episcopal News Service, June 21, 1990.

After Iraq's invasion of Kuwait in 1990, the Episcopal House of Bishops declared that "no peace is possible in the Middle East without security for the State of Israel and self-determination in their own homeland for Palestinian people."[54]

More Directly Critical of Israel

By 1991, the Episcopal Church was becoming more directly critical of Israel. Its General Convention urged the United States to "assist" Israel to "secure the human rights" of Arabs in Israel by "stopping brutalities," "restricting the use of military force to measures and practices proportionate to the situation," pressing Israel to discontinue "administrative detention and collective punishment," reopening schools for Palestinians in occupied territories, and causing Israel to be "even handed and fair" in protection of Palestinian "personal safety, property rights, water rights, and rights of access to commercial markets."[55] The same convention also urged the United States to ensure no US aid facilitated Palestinian relocation from homes to new settlements in occupied areas, with "further relocations and new settlements to result in the immediate curtailment of aid."[56]

Perhaps self-aware of its accelerating criticisms of Israel, the 1991 Episcopal General Convention recognized "distinction exists between the propriety of legitimate criticism of Israeli governmental policy and action and the impropriety of anti-Jewish prejudice," while deploring "all expressions of anti-Jewish prejudice (sometimes referred to by the imprecise word "anti-Semitism"), in whatever form on whatever occasion, and urge its total elimination from the deliberations and affairs of the Episcopal Church."[57]

The 1992 PCUSA General Assembly called for an end to the US occupation of southern Lebanon, the West Bank and Gaza, plus the withdrawal of Syrian troops from Lebanon, while affirming protection for Palestinian rights in the face of new immigrants to Israel.[58]

In 1992 Episcopal Church presiding bishop Browning joined the NCC and officers of the Evangelical Lutheran Church in America, United Church of Christ, and Presbyterian Church (USA) in urging President Bush to deny Israel

---

[54]"Restore Security for Israel," Episcopal News Service, October 31, 1990.
[55]*Journal of the General Convention of the Episcopal Church, Denver, 1991* (New York: General Convention, 1992), 794.
[56]Ibid., 771.
[57]Ibid., 773.
[58]"1990 Statement," Presbyterian Church (USA).

housing-loan guarantees until Israel ends its settlements, which threaten "justice and self-determination for Palestinians."[59] Ten Episcopal bishops, meeting Palestinian representatives in Washington, D.C., added their support for Browning's stance because the settlements were "an enormous obstacle to this fragile peace process." A Palestinian official told the bishops that Palestinians were very grateful for their solidarity.[60]

Presiding Bishop Browning denounced Israel in 1993 for deporting to Lebanon 415 Palestinian Hamas militants, which was a "collective punishment" that was an "affront to decency" and a "violation of their human rights," he complained, pleading that they instead be returned to "their homes and families."[61] In 1994 Browning, after an Israeli settler massacred 69 Muslims in a mosque, demanded Israel disarm all settlers and suspend "any further loan guarantees to Israel." "The truth is that Israel has a shameful human rights record through its years of occupation," he declared.[62]

After visiting the Holy Land in 1994, Presiding Bishop Browning derided the "uneven approach" by the United States toward the "Israeli/Palestinian problem" and deplored the "uncritical support of many members of the U.S. congress for positions of the Israeli lobby" when Palestinians "are no less deserving of justice." He also lamented candidate Bill Clinton's affirmation of Jerusalem as Israel's capital, which was an "unfortunate capitulation to the Israeli lobby."[63]

The 1994 Episcopal General Convention affirmed the Israeli-Palestinian peace process and new Palestinian Authority while urging the United States to "condition aid" to the new Palestinian Authority on its "abandonment of violence as a tactic of struggle" and to likewise condition aid to Israel on its "abandonment of violence as a tactic of civilian control and on the release of all Palestinian political prisoners."[64] It also denounced Israeli settlements in the occupied territories as "illegal under international law and an obstacle to peace,"

---

[59]"U.S. Religious Leaders Urge Bush to Condition Israeli Loan on an End to Settlement Activity," Episcopal News Service, February 7, 1992.
[60]"Palestinian Negotiators Brief Episcopal Bishops During Washington Luncheon," Episcopal New Service, March 5, 1992.
[61]"Furor over Palestinian Deportees Fuels Call for Renewed Middle East Peace Talks," Episcopal News Service, January 15, 1993.
[62]"Browning Joins Condemnation of Hebron Massacre, Urges UN Protection for Palestinians," Episcopal News Service, March 10, 1994.
[63]"Easter Statement by Browning and Kafity on Peace and Justice in the Middle East," Episcopal News Service, April 4, 1994.
[64]*Journal of the General Convention of the Episcopal Church, Denver, 1994* (New York: General Convention, 1995), 283-84.

while urging the United States to "withhold funds equivalent to those used by Israel for any settlement activity."[65]

The 1995 PCUSA General Assembly opposed efforts to move the US embassy to Jerusalem and asked Israel to lift restrictions on travel to Jerusalem. The 1996 General Assembly focused on Palestinians living under the Palestinian Authority, where abuses by security forces, such as torture, were unsurprising, it asserted, since many Palestinian personnel suffered the same under Israeli treatment.[66]

In 1995 the Episcopal Church General Council reaffirmed opposition to Israeli settlements and commended delegations to the Holy Land organized through the Episcopal Peace and Justice Network and the Middle East Council of Churches.[67] Presiding Bishop Browning joined with the Evangelical Lutheran Church's top bishop, the US Greek Orthodox primate and the head of World Vision to implore President Clinton to stop Israeli construction in East Jerusalem, while faulting the administration for failing to "recognize and support Palestinian rights and interests in Jerusalem."[68]

Hamas Bombing

After Hamas terror bombings killed sixty-one people in 1996, Presiding Bishop Browning denounced the terror to President Clinton as "heinous acts" while urging a "dramatic, public witness to the irreversibility of the peace process," which cannot be extinguished by the violent hatred of a few."[69] Then Browning condemned Israel's "collective punishment . . . against the entire population of Palestinians" while regretting the peace process had been "broken by terrorist bombings, confiscation of land and blockage of access to work, education, and health care."[70]

---

[65]Ibid., 310.
[66]"1995 Statement," Presbyterian Church (USA), accessed February 2, 2016, http://index.pcusa.org/nxt/gateway.dll?f=templates&fn=default.htm&vid=Publish:10.1048/Enu; "1996 Statement," Presbyterian Church (USA), http://index.pcusa.org/nxt/gateway.dll?f=templates$fn=default.htm.
[67]Episcopal Church Executive Council Minutes, June 12-15, 1995, Bellevue, WA, 41.
[68]"Presiding Bishop Joins in Letter to President Clinton on Jerusalem," Episcopal News Service, March 16, 1995.
[69]"Christian Leaders Condemn Violence in Jerusalem, Pray for Peace," Episcopal News Service, March 7, 1996.
[70]"Presiding Bishop Criticizes Severity of Israeli Anti-Terrorist Moves Against Palestinians," Episcopal News Service, April 19, 1996.

In 1997 the Episcopal General Convention urged that Jerusalem serve as capital for Israel and Palestine and that East Jerusalem was an "integral part of the occupied territories," while insisting that Israel safeguard Palestinian homes and free access to Jerusalem and asking the United States to uphold "justice for Palestinians as it does for the security of the State of Israel."[71]

After returning from the Holy Land in 1997, Presiding Bishop Browning regretted the "perception that the United States is completely one-sided" in the Israeli-Palestinian conflict," which will "continue to frustrate a durable and just settlement."[72] He was "heartbroken at acts of terrorism against innocent Israelis committed by extremists opposed to the peace process," saying "great responsibility rests with President Arafat in combating terrorism from the Palestinian side." And he insisted "it is morally improper to demand that President Arafat not pursue dialogue with reconciliation with his Palestinian adversaries."[73]

In 1998, new Episcopal presiding bishop Frank Griswold asked President Clinton in an open letter to "redouble your efforts to achieve a negotiated peace" and "continue your principled stand for a Jerusalem that is shared by its two peoples and by three religious communities." The letter noted that Israel's creation and struggle "is seen by many in the United States as an incredible testimony to the human spirit," while the Palestinians suffered the "al Nakba," or Catastrophe, and have been a "pawn in a power game between nations within and outside the Middle East."[74]

The 1998 PCUSA General Assembly lamented that the Israeli-Palestinian peace process suffered thanks to the assassination of Prime Minister Yitzhak Rabin and "the policies of his successor Benjamin Netanyahu, plus internal struggles among Palestinians." It asked the United States to monitor Israel's fulfillment of the Oslo Accords for which US aid should be contingent.[75]

During the 2000 Palestinian Intifada, the Episcopal Church Executive Council reaffirmed the presiding bishop's appeal for Israel to refrain from "disproportional military response" and for the "withdrawal of Israeli forces from

---

[71] *Journal of the General Convention of the Episcopal Church, Denver, 1997* (New York: General Convention, 1998), 181.

[72] "Presiding Bishop Finds Growing Pessimism over Future of Mideast Peace Process," Episcopal News Service, April 3, 1997.

[73] "Presiding Bishop's Statement on Israeli/Palestinian Peace Process," Episcopal News Service, September 26, 1997.

[74] "Episcopal Church's Position on Middle East Issues Is Clear," Episcopal News Service, May 8, 1998.

[75] "ACSWP Commentary," Presbyterian Church (USA).

areas of tension in the territories," while warning that the "current crisis not be used as a pretext to continue the long and inhumane occupation."[76]

The 2003 Episcopal General Convention denounced Israel's demolition of Palestinian homes in the occupied territories and asked the United States to intervene.[77] It also denounced the Israeli security wall.[78]

In 2004 Episcopal presiding bishop Frank Griswold condemned Israeli military actions during its evacuation of settlements in Gaza that caused "grave human suffering." He said Israel's "legitimate need for self-defense against terrorism requires proportionality" and can't include "reckless killing of civilians." And he insisted the United States had a "moral responsibility to demand that Israel end these attacks on Palestinians while demanding that Palestinians also abandon violence and terror."[79]

Presiding Bishop Griswold wrote President George W. Bush in 2005 in advance of a visit by Israeli prime minister Ariel Sharon to protest "growth of settlements" that "undermine any possibility" of a "continuous Palestinian state" and to oppose Israel's separation barrier for its "devastating impact on the daily lives of Palestinians."[80]

In 2009 the Episcopal General Convention implored every Episcopalian to pray for the "Wall around Bethlehem and all other barriers to come down," anticipating that "crumbling walls herald the fall of all barriers that divide us."[81]

Opposing Divestment

The 2012 Episcopal General Convention, rejecting anti-Israel divestment, instead lamented the "lack of progress in negotiations between Israelis and Palestinians" and urged "positive investment in the Palestinian territories," including "healthcare, education, and social services without discrimination on the basis of religion, political ideology, gender, socioeconomic standing or national identity."[82]

---

[76]Episcopal Church Executive Council Minutes, October 24–27, 2000, Delavan, WI, 24-25.
[77]*Journal of the General Convention of the Episcopal Church, Denver, 2003* (New York: General Convention, 2004), 320ff.
[78]Ibid., 328f.
[79]"Presiding Bishop's Statement Regarding Israel," Episcopal News Service, May 20, 2004.
[80]"Presiding Bishop Affirms President's Recent Stance on West Bank Settlements; Barrier Concerns Underscored," Episcopal News Service, April 8, 2005.
[81]*Journal of the General Convention of the Episcopal Church, Anaheim, 2009* (New York: General Convention, 2009), 394-95.
[82]*Journal of the General Convention of the Episcopal Church, Anaheim, 2012* (New York: General Convention, 2013), 221-22.

Episcopal presiding bishop Katharine Jefferts Schori argued against divestment, having decried sanctions "and other divisive and punitive measures which seek to tear down, not to build up." The convention declined to heed a pro-divestment statement from South African archbishop emeritus of Cape Town Desmond Tutu, who declared, "Had the world not imposed sanctions on apartheid South Africa we might still be languishing under its oppression."[83] The American Jewish Committee commended the Episcopal Church's action for "its commitment to a negotiated resolution of the Palestinian-Israeli conflict and a rejection of unhelpful one-sided judgments aimed at Israel that do not advance the cause of peace."[84]

Bishops at the 2015 Episcopal General Convention helped ensure another defeat for anti-Israel divestment, rejecting a proposal to develop a list of firms that ostensibly facilitate Israel's occupation. "As Anglicans, we have the gift and ability to reach out to people on both sides in the conflict," explained Bishop Ed Little of Northern Indiana in his opposition to divestment. Southeast Florida bishop Leo Frade agreed, saying, "Palestinian jobs depend on investment, not on divestment." The bishops were also assured the Episcopal Church has no investments in firms negatively affecting Palestinians.[85] But others wanted more decisive action. A Diocese of California clergy deputy to the convention insisted, "Divestment is not about anti-Semitism, it's about justice.... The people of Palestine want action, not more talk. It should be clear that after 20 years of talk in the never ending peace process, our policy of positive investment has not worked.... To do nothing would also have an impact: It would put us on the side of oppression."[86]

Identifying Israel as the agent of "oppression" was the expanding theme of liberal Protestant political witness across the last four decades. Talk of Palestinian self-determination in the 1970s had, by the 1980s, led to mainline denominations funding pro-PLO advocacy groups in the United States, including one headquartered in the Interchurch Center in New

---

[83]Matthew Davies, "Israel-Palestine Issues Addressed at Legislative Hearing," Episcopal News Service, July 6, 2012.

[84]"American Jewish Committee Commends Church on Israel-Palestine," Episcopal News Service, July 12, 2012.

[85]Matthew Davies, "Bishops Overwhelmingly Oppose Divestment in Israel, Palestine," Episcopal News Service, July 2, 2015.

[86]Matthew Davies, "Israel and Palestine Issues Addressed at Legislative Hearings," Episcopal News Service, June 26, 2015.

York.[87] In the 1990s mainline Protestant church voices were increasingly loud in their denunciation of Jewish settlements and in urging reconsideration of US aid for Israel. In 1997 a United Methodist Volunteers-in-Mission official denounced Israel's crackdown in response to Palestinian suicide bombers, accusing Israel of "ethnic cleansing, racism, and the creating of a Jerusalem for Jews only." Dallas Methodist bishop William Oden, visiting the Middle East in early 2001, complained: "Israel is the only nation that buys arms from us from whom we do not require accountability."[88]

ZIONISM AS HERESY

By the start of the twenty-first century, liberal Protestantism had not only abandoned Christian Zionism; it was denouncing it as a heresy. In 2008, the National Council of Churches released a special brochure called "Why We Should Be Concerned About Christian Zionism" to warn its thirty-five member denominations.

"The danger of this ideology is that it is a manipulation of Christian scripture and teaching," fretted Antonios Kireopoulos, the NCC's interfaith spokesman. "Unfortunately it has influence in American churches, to the point where many well-meaning Christians are swayed to support particularly destructive directions in U.S. foreign policy with regard to the Middle East." Not typically concerned about upholding orthodox theology, the NCC even claims that Christian Zionists violate the "traditional teachings of the church."[89] As the NCC news release summarized: "'Christian Zionism' is a dangerous movement that distorts the teachings of the Church, fosters fear and hatred of Muslims and non-Western Christians, and has negative consequences for Middle East Peace."

A softer critique of Christian Zionism is offered by US evangelicals like Lynne Hybels and groups like World Vision and Telos, who urge a "Pro-Israeli, Pro-Palestinian, Pro-American, Pro-Peace" agenda. This perspective resents and often caricatures the ostensibly simplistic and unquestioning support that Christian Zionists give Israel. They understand that US evangelicals' historically pro-Israel views explain much of America's alliance with Israel. And they clearly

---

[87]Edmund W. Robb and Julia Robb, *The Betrayal of the Church* (Westchester, IL: Crossway, 1986), 229.
[88]Mark Tooley, *Methodism and Politics in the Twentieth Century* (Fort Valley, GA: Bristol House, 2011), 284.
[89]"Dangers of 'Christian Zionism' Are Cited in New NCC Brochure," National Council of Churches News Services, December 12, 2008, www.ncccusa.org/news/081202christianzionism brochure.html.

hope that persuading many evangelicals into a more neutral stance, if not openly partial to Palestinians, could have significant geopolitical repercussions.

SOFTER CRITIQUE OF ZIONISM

During the 2014 Gaza conflict, the head of Telos, Todd Deatherage, an Anglican in Virginia, blogged that a "ceasefire is needed immediately." Neither "acts of terrorism nor aggressive military campaigns" can displace the need for "addressing the fundamental issues underlying the years of violence," he noted, as "each side needs friends who will challenge them to do what is best for their own people, and, at the same time, who will encourage visionary leadership which realizes that the future of the two people is interconnected, that neither is going away, that the pain of grieving mothers is always the same, and that freedom and security for one people cannot be found at the expense of the other."[90] Similarly, a 2009 film aimed at evangelicals, *With God on Our Side*, faults Christian Zionism for Palestinian suffering, for US military adventurism and for impeding Christian witness and evangelism among Israel's Arab adversaries.

Articulating an old-style version of liberation theology, a former Southern Baptist who teaches at a United Methodist seminary, Miguel de la Torre, complaining about Netanyahu's 2015 reelection, succinctly explained, "My preferential option towards the Palestinians is because overall, they are the ones who are suffering economic and political oppression. As a liberation theologian, I must stand with Palestinians while remaining ready to also criticize their policies."[91]

In 2014, the Presbyterian Church (USA), before adopting anti-Israel divestment, published "Zionism Unsettled," which faulted Christian Zionism because it "fuses religion with politics, distorts faith, and imperils peace in the Middle East." Further, "in its liberal Christian manifestations, Zionism serves as a 'price-tag' theology providing Christians with a vehicle of repentance for the guilt accrued during centuries of European Christian anti-Semitism culminating in the Holocaust." In fact, "Israeli and American myths of origin are similar and derived from the same biblical sources." Since "the history and ideology of settler colonialism have been so central to the political history of the

---

[90]Todd Deatherage, "Can We Believe in the Mutual Flourishing of Israel and Palestine?," July 30, 2014, guest post on *LynneHybels.com*, www.lynnehybels.com/can-we-believe-in-the-mutual-flourishing-of-israel-and-palestine/.
[91]Miguel de la Torre, "Does Criticizing Israel Make Me an Anti-Semite?," *Our Lucha*, March 21, 2015.

United States[,] . . . it is not surprising the political and religious leadership in the US has been predisposed to uncritical support for the Zionist movement."[92]

Avoiding the Mainline Protestant Trajectory

At least the liberal Protestant hostility to Christian Zionism, guided by liberation theology for the last forty years, is concise and relatively consistent. The more recent evangelical left critique is more situational and therapeutic, claiming to be concerned about evangelism, which liberal Protestants decidedly are not. Meanwhile, a neo-Anabaptist twist to the ongoing critique of Christian Zionism, originally influenced by John Howard Yoder and Stanley Hauerwas, portrays it as an ideology of empire, war and domination, largely a particularly sinister manifestation of Constantinian church-state partnership, with Israel the prong of American militarism.

None of these critiques of Christian Zionism really understands or seriously addresses the original nineteenth-century American Christian Zionism that sought to restore a long-displaced and tormented people to their ancient homeland as an act of restorative justice and for their ongoing protection from persecution. It looked to a new Zion that would model political and economic justice to the world as well as serve as an ongoing witness of God's faithful fulfillment of his promises.

Blackstone and his earnest adherents, mostly mainline Protestants working with Jewish colleagues in an early manifestation of interfaith collaboration, offered a vision of spiritual and moral beauty that today's critics, whether harsh or therapeutic, cannot match. The mainline Protestant institutions that initially offered much of Zionism's early support through Blackstone and others no longer have confidence in Christian orthodoxy, in their own traditions or in their previous faith that nations and peoples, including America and the Jews of Israel, can be providential instruments of interest to Christians.

The anti-Zionist ideologies that now prevail in a now much-diminished mainline Protestantism are primarily interested in impersonal systemic injustice perpetuated by "empire," chiefly identified with Western civilization, patriarchy, militarism, capitalism and white racism, of which Israel is seen as the embodiment. Even though liberation theology as a religious tool for strategic

---

[92]"Survey of PCUSA General Assembly Resolutions on the Israeli-Palestinian Conflict," Israel Palestine Mission Network of the Presbyterian Church (USA), accessed July 15, 2015, www.israelpalestinemissionnetwork.org/main/index.php?option=com_content&view =article&id=256.

analysis faded with the end of the Soviet Union and the Cold War, its Marxist explanation of human struggle stubbornly persists in mainline perspectives on Israel's conflict with its hostile neighbors.

Official mainline Protestantism's outspoken hostility toward Israel and indifference to human rights abuses by far more repressive regimes reflects a divorce from ethical reality by religiously heterodox church bodies that have suffered continuous membership decline and reduced cultural influence for half a century. Evangelical leaders and institutions tempted to follow the mainline example should study its consequences.

8

THEOLOGY AND POLITICS

Reinhold Niebuhr's Christian Zionism

Robert Benne

◆

My intellectual awakening took place when the professor of a required course in Christian ethics at my small liberal arts college assigned Reinhold Niebuhr's *An Interpretation of Christian Ethics*. In that book Niebuhr offered a sharp critique of both liberal and orthodox Christian ethics and then applied his own approach to economic and political issues of the day. Deeply influenced by that encounter, I opted to study Niebuhr intensively when I arrived at the University of Chicago. The Chicago method was to read a few texts deeply. We were required to get so inside the thinking of our chosen theologian that we could actually think like him. I got so "inside" Niebuhr that I used his theological-ethical framework in the following years to develop arguments in a number of articles and books I wrote dealing with many social, economic and political issues. Not only did I think his was the most compelling theological-ethical vision; it also fit rather well with the Lutheran construal of theology and ethics that I as a Lutheran had learned along the way. Indeed, I thought his was the best exercise of Lutheran social-ethical thinking in the second half of the twentieth century.

When I was asked to write this chapter on Christian Zionism, I thought I would develop my own Niebuhrian argument for the support of Christian Zionism. After all, I could still think like Niebuhr. But before I did that, I thought I should check out what Niebuhr himself had to say about Israel and Christian

Zionism. I was astounded at how much he said and how well he said it.[1] I doubted whether I could improve on it much.

Moreover, as I got deeper into the discussion of Israel and Christian Zionism among Christians over many decades, I discovered that the arguments for and against really hadn't changed that much. Those Christians—including Niebuhr— who robustly supported Israel and Christian Zionism and those who opposed them employed pretty much the same arguments. There was a perennial feel to the arguments of both sides. Certainly the situations and the various players changed—the major threat was now Iran rather than Egypt—but the arguments were similar. So it made more sense to recover Niebuhr's persuasive arguments than to project my own.

Further, I found that long after his death Niebuhr's name had been resurrected to play a role in a contemporary debate about the Presbyterian Church (USA)'s program—titled *Zionism Unsettled*—that essentially undermines the legitimacy of Israel and debunks the great support that Niebuhr and his colleague, Paul Tillich, gave to the new state of Israel.[2] Rising to the occasion, Niebuhr's daughter and grandnephew offer a rousing defense of their forebear's Zionist sympathies.[3] Joining in the same debate, several rabbis offer appreciative remarks about Niebuhr's contribution to the Zionist cause and pose the plaintive question: Where is Niebuhr among mainstream Protestants when we need him?[4]

---

[1] I began to wonder why I had not seen the many articles he wrote about Israel. Most of his books, which I had read closely, were about other political issues. But he wrote copiously in many journals about Israel. Strangely enough, the many compilations of his journalistic articles did not contain the ones in which he dealt with Israel. Further, secondary literature about Niebuhr contained little discussion of his support for Israel. His principal biographer, Richard Fox, barely mentions the many efforts Niebuhr made on behalf of Israel. Most of these compilations do not even have *Israel* in their indexes. On further reflection, however, this dearth of references is not so strange. From the 1950s onward, many of Niebuhr's liberal and socialist friends gradually withdrew their support for Israel. This departure became a flood after the Six-Day War in 1967. For the mainstream Protestants who were Niebuhr's friends and students, his support for Israel was something of an embarrassment, and they simply did not include those writings in their compilations and commentaries.

[2] Don Wagner, "Time to End the Palestine/Israel Status Quo: 'Zionism Unsettled' Challenges Theological and Political Exceptionalism," *Mondoweiss*, May 27, 2014, www.mondoweiss.net/2014/05/palestineisrael-theological-exceptionalism.

[3] Gustav Niebuhr and Elisabeth Sifton, "Why Reinhold Niebuhr Supported Israel," *Huffington Post*, May 7, 2014, www.huffingtonpost.com/Gustave-nieburh/why-reinhold-niebuhr-supp_b_5280958.html.

[4] Jeffrey K. Salkin, "Reinhold Niebuhr, Where Are You Now?," *Martini Judaism* (blog), *Jewish Journal*, February 18, 2014, www//jewishjournal.com/martini_judaism/item/reinhold_niebuhr_where_are_you_now.

In the following I am going to outline and identify myself with the remarkable and admirable arguments that Niebuhr made in support of Israel and Christian Zionism. Toward the end I will offer my own additions to supplement Niebuhr's arguments. I call it "complementing his arguments," though I am not absolutely certain he would accept my effort. Niebuhr was curiously inattentive to the religious element in both the Jewish and Christian cases for a Jewish state. And he certainly did not take seriously enough the concern for the land deeply ingrained in the religious visions of many sorts of both Christian and Jewish Zionism. I want to add both concerns—the religious element and its concern for the land—to my overall argument.

NIEBUHR'S REMARKABLE RECORD

During his pastorate among working-class Germans in Detroit from 1915 to 1929, the young Niebuhr already supported the "Zionist approach to Palestine's ultimate settlement" and had "written sympathetically about the Jews in his regular Saturday night column in the *Detroit News*."[5] He also spoke out against the Ku Klux Klan, which was violently anti-Semitic and anti-Catholic. He argued in major magazines against assimilation as the sole strategy for the plight of the Jews, sharply criticizing the naive appeals to "brotherhood."[6]

When he arrived at Union Seminary in 1929, Niebuhr was invited to preach in the pulpit of the Community Church in New York City, pastored by a strong pro-Zionist pastor, John Hanes Holmes. By the early 1930s Niebuhr was fully aware of the problems German Jewry faced and wrote a seminal article in a May 1933 issue of the *Christian Century*, "Germany Must Be Told," in which he pointed to Palestine as a refuge for Jews fleeing Hitler's sadism. He denounced the Munich settlement in 1938 and called for supporting a national homeland for the Jews and not allowing it to fail.

---

[5]Carl Hermann Voss and David Rausch, "American Christians and Israel, 1948–1988," *American Jewish Archives* 40, no. 1, (1988): 52-53, http://americanjewisharchives.org/publications/journal/PDF/1988_40_01_00_hermann_rausch.pdf. This extensive essay by two pro-Zionist authors is a remarkable catalog of Christian responses to the founding and subsequent history of the state of Israel. It recounts some very surprising Christian responses, including virulent anti-Israel diatribes authored by evangelicals and mainstream Protestants soon after the founding of the state of Israel. But it is also a detailed account of the overwhelming support for Israel among fundamentalists and evangelicals and, early on, strong support by mainline Protestants and Catholics. However, it also chronicles from the 1960s onward the gradual disaffection of many of those mainline Protestants.
[6]Ibid.

In the early 1940s Niebuhr criticized the inequities of the British White Paper, which limited immigration to Palestine. He was a member of the American Palestine Committee from the early 1930s on and led in founding the Christian Council on Palestine in 1942. He was close friends with American Zionists for whom he spoke frequently. He was especially known for a set of articles in *The Nation* in 1942 titled "Jews After the War" in which he argued—to the consternation of his liberal and socialist friends—on behalf of the Zionist push for a state. The articles caused a great furor in the 1940s and were discussed widely for years thereafter. In them Niebuhr anticipated the Nazi plan for the complete "extermination of the Jews" and the Jews' need for a homeland as a refuge from the Nazis and other anti-Semitic tendencies in Europe. He also chastised the West for offering so little support for the Jews in their plight.

In 1941 he founded *Christianity and Crisis*, a journal in which he wrote many articles supporting Zionism and featured a considerable number by other authors, the most famous of which was one by Henry Atkinson titled "The Jewish Problem Is a Christian Problem" that appeared in 1943. It exposed the divisions among Christians that have persisted to the present day. Indeed, as the journal veered leftward and toward the pro-Palestinian line, Niebuhr left it, partly for health reasons but also for ideological reasons. The journal finally ended in 1993.[7]

In 1957 Niebuhr wrote an extremely influential article titled "Our Stake in the State of Israel" in *The New Republic*, another journal that he helped found. The article chastised the Western powers for their ambivalence toward Israel during the Suez Crisis. In the article, Niebuhr pronounced, "Equivocal words by us are highly improper. Life and death depend on clear policy."[8]

Even after a stroke in 1952 curtailed his activities, he was constant in his support of Israel. In 1969 the Hebrew University in Jerusalem awarded him an honorary degree, which he was unable to receive in person. In the only instance in its history, the president of the university left Israel to award the degree to Niebuhr in person. Niebuhr's response: "I am a friend of the Jewish people and have never ceased to be favorable to the state of Israel." Upon his death a distinguished party of Israeli officials came to his funeral, at which Abraham Joshua

---

[7]The preceding paragraphs draw material from Voss and Rausch, "American Christians and Israel," 53-54.
[8]Reinhold Niebuhr, "Our Stake in the State of Israel," *New Republic*, February 2, 1957, 6, https://newrepublic.com/article/our-sake-in-the-state-israel.

Theology and Politics

Heschel offered the eulogy. After Niebuhr's death in 1971, his wife, Ursula, continued his efforts in support of Israel even as many other mainline Protestants took quite a different tack.[9]

Niebuhr's Christian Zionist Arguments

Niebuhr was justly famous for the brilliant and persuasive "biblical anthropology" he developed in his *The Nature and Destiny of Man*, which he gave at the Gifford Lectures of 1939.[10] After developing that normative view of human nature early on in the first volume, *The Nature of Man*, he employed it in extended critiques of competing views of humankind in idealism, rationalism, pragmatism, Marxism and romanticism. In each case, he argued, a deficient view of human nature leads to faulty approaches to human problems, as well as to errant policies in domestic and international affairs.

He argued that humankind stands at the "juncture of nature and spirit," partaking of both animal nature and human distinctives. The "nature" pole breaks into both vitality (our biological desires and imperatives) and form (our genus, species, race, sex, ethnic group and mixtures of them in nations and civilizations). The "spirit" pole also breaks into two dimensions—form and vitality. Our forming capacity means our reason: our intellectual capacity to transcend, understand and reshape the world around us; our capacity to think clearly and coherently; and the capacity to guide our actions according to conscience. Spiritual vitality—the second pole on the "spirit" side—is the most precious human trait and sharply distinguishes us from the rest of creation. Spiritual vitality is the human capacity for self-transcendence. Humans can make an object of themselves, indeterminately reflecting on themselves, history and the world itself. Of all creatures, human beings alone can ask the meaning of themselves, history and the cosmos. It is an indeterminate freedom.

Such "indeterminate" freedom makes us anxious about ourselves—our mortality and fragility. It seeks some ultimate meaning and security. As Augustine put it: "Our hearts are restless until they rest in Thee." This spiritual vitality confounds rationalist and materialist anthropologies. They do not understand

---

[9]Caitlin Carenen, *The Fervent Embrace: Liberal Protestants, Evangelicals, and Israel* (New York: New York University Press, 2012), 155.
[10]Reinhold Niebuhr, *The Nature and Destiny of Man* (New York: Charles Scribner's Sons, 1941). The theological anthropology he developed was persuasive to many political theorists who did not share his Christian convictions. George Kennan, Hans Morgenthau and Arthur Schlesinger were so persuaded by it that they organized an "Atheists for Niebuhr" club.

spiritual hunger and freedom. Nor do they understand the stubbornness of natural vitalities that stem from humankind's embodiment in nature.

Individuals may try to assuage their spiritual hunger by immersing themselves in "mutable pleasures" of sensuality. Those pleasures can never completely satisfy the soul, even though they go to extremes—driven by their indeterminate freedom—to satiate themselves. Don Juans always want more women to conquer. The other path for anxious souls is pride, claiming superiority for themselves or attaching themselves to some powerful external entity.

In addition to this profound reading of the existential predicament of the individual, Niebuhr extends it to corporate life—economic, social, cultural, racial and political. Groups, he argues, have less reflective power but at the same time an exaggerated sense of vulnerability. Therefore they gather power to overcome their inchoate anxiety and employ all their means to exert their interest. The larger the group, the more inexorable the will to power. The largest of the groups—the national state—takes on a grandeur and majesty that mimics the divine. But such prideful propensities also pervade the organic entities of race, ethnic group and tribe. While human identity is always connected to these natural vitalities in important and wholesome ways, it is also likely to be magnified pridefully by the indeterminate spirit coursing through those natural vitalities. Idealists and rationalists, Niebuhr believed, often downplay these factors in the life of groups. They believe such vital interests can be overcome by rational persuasion, thus making them blind to their own power.

In such a world of competing wills to power, the best strategy is to balance powers. If large economic or political entities are balanced over against each other, a modicum of peace, order and even justice can be achieved. So from the realist point of view, the moral goal of international politics is to keep the largest powers in balance. In such a situation they fear that their rivals will be able to dominate them, or at least prevent them from winning. Such balancing, regardless of the relative moral quality of each claimant, is the way to keep the world from falling into disorder, violence and injustice wherein large and small nations lose their self-determination. This realist means to a moral end was practiced by earlier masters of *Realpolitik* such as Metternich. In recent years such strategies were pursued by the United States: for example, in the Cold War it supported China as resistance to the imperial aims of the Soviet Union. It also tried to balance nuclear capacities between the United States and the Soviet Union, achieving something of a "balance of terror."

This sort of realism cuts against the assumptions of rationalists and idealists, who think that the conflicts between great powers can be argued away by good-willed people of reason. Perhaps the leaders of the great powers can overcome the conflicts by friendly and reasonable private conversations. Realism doubts that. On the contrary, realism asserts that reason will serve at the behest of will to power. Powerful entities will spin out rationalizations and ideologies to mask and promote their will to power. Further, reasonable individuals cannot escape the inexorable corporate will to power that drives the nation. A political leader will inevitably have to represent the national interest even if it conflicts with his own predilections. The freestanding individual cannot make national policy.

Realism recognizes what is, not what ought to be or what might have been. Obsessing with those questions dissuades people from dealing with the practical means for grappling with what indeed is. They become so paralyzed with tending past grievances that they cannot move on to constructive solutions in the present.

Realism also assumes that large powers will use all sorts of power—economic, technical, political and military—to press their interests forward. In order for a modicum of justice to occur between and among nations, there must be a balance of power that includes military force to protect and project the self-interest of each nation. Such force must by matched by equal force from competing centers of power.

Niebuhr, along with other realists, gave support to Israel based on this sort of realism. He offered a number of arguments. First, he argued that the existence of Israel is a basic fact. Its existence cannot be wished away by arguments that the original agreements that established the state of Israel could somehow be reversed. Many opponents of Israel repeatedly lamented that its founding was unjust to the Palestinians and therefore should be nullified, and that Jews should be moved from Israel to some other place, perhaps the United States.[11] Niebuhr was unmoved by such concerns. Israel exists and therefore must be reckoned with.

Second, he contended that a stable and strong Israel was important to American national interest in order to counterbalance the Soviet influence that was increasingly being exerted among the Muslim Arab states, especially Egypt. In his 1957 article, "Our Stake in the State of Israel," he argued that the United

---

[11] Ronald Stone, *Professor Reinhold Niebuhr* (Louisville, KY: Westminster John Knox Press, 1992), 165; and Carys Moseley, *Nationhood, Providence, and Witness: Israel in Modern Theology and Social Theory* (Eugene, OR: Cascade, 2013), 57.

States had a strategic dimension in that stake: "For Israel is the only sure strategic anchor of the democratic world, particularly since Khrushchev and Nasser have proved that Islam is not as immune to Communism as had been supposed, but is, rather, an almost ideal ground for the growth of nationalism posing as Communism and Communism posing as nationalism."[12] In short, the United States wanted to balance Soviet ambitions and Arab nationalism with Israel's power, to which the United States had contributed.

Third, he insisted that the continued stability of Israel in a volatile area of the world was in the national interest. Israel is our "only secure bastion in this troubled area."[13]

Fourth, he argued that support of Israel contributed to the national interest not only by countering Soviet expansionism but by "establishing alternative routes for the vital oil," which Niebuhr thought could be transported across Israel to its ports.[14]

Fifth, his realism involved an affirmation of Israel's use of military force to defend itself against the intent and effort of her enemies to annihilate her. He broke with his early pacifism during the rise of the Nazis in the 1930s and argued against his brother, H. Richard Niebuhr, who believed that the United States should not enter World War II. By 1940 he elaborated a comprehensive argument that Christian political responsibility in a fallen world could not take the pacifist route.[15]

He therefore accepted the historic Christian teaching on just war. He saw "Israel's wars against its Arab neighbors as defensive wars against the intention to annihilate the Jewish state," and therefore Israel had every right to defend herself with lethal force.[16]

It is astonishing how the arguments remain the same even though the historic players and the arguers themselves change. There are still those—especially the Palestinians and their supporters—who refuse to accept practical solutions to their struggle with Israel by obsessing about the evil that was done to them in 1948. There are those who believe that support of Israel is not in our

---

[12]Niebuhr, "Our Stake," 4.
[13]Ibid., 6.
[14]Ibid.
[15]Reinhold Niebuhr, "Why the Christian Church Is Not Pacifist," first published by the SCM Press in Great Britain and included in *Christianity and Power Politics* (New York: Charles Scribner's Sons, 1940), chap. 1.
[16]Moseley, *Nationhood*, 41.

national interest. For many years they believed we had to soften our commitment to Israel in order to come to better terms with the suppliers of oil for the West. Or they believed we needed to dampen our relation with a small country in order to relate more constructively to a much larger set of nations and peoples. Lately they claim that in order to come to terms with Iran, to seduce it to change from a revolutionary state to a normal nation, we must risk the existence of Israel by making dubious agreements to slow down Iran's effort to become a nuclear state. There are those who still reject our support of Israel on the basis of pacifist objections to the use of military force. From the very beginning some liberal Protestants backed off their enthusiastic support when Israel mounted military resistance to the Arab armies at its founding in 1948. Pacifist leanings pried more liberal Protestants away from support when Israel used force against the Egyptians in the Suez Crisis of 1957; even more peeled away in the Six-Day War of 1967, and then in subsequent conflicts. Indeed, whenever Israel uses force, the pacifist predilections of the mainline Protestant elite exert themselves. Contemporary neosectarians such as Stanley Hauerwas condemn the use of military force in principle, even when the very existence of a nation or people is at stake.

Niebuhr would remain staunch in his realist arguments. But the realists who gravitate toward *Realpolitik* might find cynical reasons to withdraw their support for Israel. Indeed, over the years many have. It is a mistake, however, to align Niebuhr with such cynicism. As Paul Miller argues in his "What Realists Get Wrong About Niebuhr," Niebuhr's realist champions "fail to appreciate how his Christian faith informed his views on foreign affairs."[17] He goes on to note how Niebuhr's Christian commitments transcend the more cynical versions of realism. Niebuhr did not remain value neutral among the contending parties in any attempt to balance power. He definitely tipped for Israel in its contention with Arab states for many reasons, including Israel's commitment to democracy. It is to that "Christian" element in his realism that we now turn.

---

[17] Paul Miller, "What Realists Get Wrong About Niebuhr," *American Interest*, February 21, 2015, 1, www.the-american-interest.com/2015/02/21/what-realists-get-wrong-about-niebuhr/. In this article Miller successfully differentiates Niebuhr from the more hard-nosed realists of his day (George Kennan and Hans Morgenthau) and of today (Anatol Lieven, John Hulsman and Andrew Bacevich), who argue that Niebuhr would have been against the promotion of democracy in a world that has characterized certain neoconservative theorists. Miller shows that Niebuhr strongly supported America's promotion of democracy because democracy was a positive implication of the Christian movement in the West, though that promotion was always a measured one that took into account each nation's cultural and social constraints.

Christian Realism

Niebuhr successfully avoided both sentimental idealism and cynical *Realpolitik* in his approach to international relations and especially in his stance toward Israel. He did this by keeping the Christian notion of agape love in a dialectical relation to all historical achievement. We have already shown how his theological anthropology led to a realistic assessment of how will to power plays an inescapable role in the actions of large entities. This leads to a strategy of balancing powers so that a measure of justice (free self-determination of nations) will ensue.

But such balancing is not sufficient. More can be done in most historical situations. Moreover, the participants in the struggle for power can be distinguished by the quality of their moral and political commitments. Such relative distinctions are extremely important in the unfolding of history. The relatively good entity gains more favor for the Christian realist in the interplay of powers.

Already by 1934 Niebuhr had developed a Christian moral vision in which love plays an indirect but relevant role in political affairs. The ideal of agape love is articulated and realized most clearly in the teachings and life of Jesus of Nazareth. Agape is heedless of the needs of the self but focuses on the other, even to the extent of sacrificing the self. It goes out of itself to initiate care for the lost, the last and the least. It has a universal scope of respect for all those created in the image of God; every human being counts. It is strategically focused on the most vulnerable. It invites to mutuality, not keeping the recipient dependent. It is steadfast in its commitments. And, unsurprisingly, it involves suffering in a fallen world.[18]

The radical nature of this love, Niebuhr thought, made it an impossible possible. It was impossible to apply it directly to the interactions of worldly groups. If tried, it became a sentimental perfectionism which led to dangerous imbalances and then finally to disaster. Pacifism is a case of such perfectionism. But such love was possible because it was lived out in one life—that of Jesus as the Christ. Though that love ended on a cross, it is not completely defeated in history. The resurrection was God's yes to such Incarnate Love. Yet this love cannot be completely triumphant in history either. The persistence of sin precludes that.

---

[18]Niebuhr develops these characteristics of Christian love in "The Ethic of Jesus," in *Interpretation of Christian Ethics* (New York: Harper & Brothers, 1935), 43-62. The book was the further development of his Rauschenbusch Memorial Lectures, which were presented in 1934 at the Colgate-Rochester Divinity School.

Theology and Politics

However, this impossible-possible norm is relevant to political life, but only indirectly and dialectically. This "relevance of an impossible ethical ideal"[19] is exercised in four ways:

1. As indeterminate possibility and obligation. Love always "presents possibilities of action higher than the conventional and traditional habits and customs of men. . . . It always presents a challenge which stands vertically over every moral act and achievement."[20] Without this pull of love upon it, "justice degenerates into mere order without justice."[21] Thus, the transcendent norm of love is relevant when it presses toward a more imaginative achievement of human justice. "Imaginative justice leads beyond equality to a consideration of the special needs of the life of the other."[22]

2. As indiscriminate criticism and judgment. "Perfect love is the very ideal which discloses the imperfection of concrete moral achievement by revealing the alloy of egoism which expresses itself in every act of history, particularly in every collective act. . . . It prevents the pride, self-righteousness and vindictiveness of men that corrupts their efforts at justice. . . . It is both the fulfillment and negation of all achievement of justice in history."[23]

3. As a standard for discriminate decisions. The norm of love provides a vantage point for relative distinctions. Some formulations of human political arrangements are closer to the norm of love while others are farther. Some are ruled out as complete negations of the ideal. "Love universalism is not inimical to a discriminating social ethic."[24] For example, regimes that recognize human rights are closer to the ideal because they recognize the worth of each individual. Those that trample on those rights clearly negate the ideal of love.

4. As contrition and forgiveness. As humans encounter the agape love of God in Christ, they become aware of the contingent character of all human claims and the tainted character of all human pretensions, especially their own. They recognize the ambiguity in even the best of human actions. This spirit of contrition "lies at the foundation of what we define as democracy.

---

[19] Ibid., 101.
[20] Reinhold Niebuhr, *Niebuhr on Politics*, ed. Harry Davis and Robert Good (New York: Charles Scribner's Sons, 1960), 154.
[21] Ibid., 155.
[22] Niebuhr, *Interpretation*, 102.
[23] Ibid., 157.
[24] Ibid., 158.

For democracy cannot exist if there is no recognition of the fragmentary character of all systems of thought and value which are allowed to exist together within the democratic frame."[25]

CHRISTIAN REALISM AND ISRAEL

Niebuhr elevates realism to Christian realism regarding Israel in a number of crucial ways, which distinguish him as a Christian Zionist. He first elevates realism to Christian realism by having an extraordinary sensitivity to and compassion for the suffering of Jews across the world from the beginning of his ministry in the late 1920s. His moral vision leads from mere balances of power to a "consideration for the needs of the life of others," particularly Jews. In 1942, before there was any consensus on the reality of horrific Nazi plans for the Jews, Niebuhr was convinced that the Nazis were "bent on the extermination of the Jews.... Millions of Jews have been completely disinherited." In light of this, "it is a scandal that the Jews have had so little effective aid from the rest of us in a situation in which they are the chief victims."[26]

Moreover, the plight of the Jews will not be adequately alleviated when the war is over. It "is by no means the least of the many problems of post-war reconstruction." Presciently, Niebuhr noted that

> an impoverished Europe will not find it easy to reabsorb a large number of returned Jews, and a spiritually corrupted Europe will not purge itself quickly of the virus of race bigotry with which the Nazis have infected its culture. It must also be remembered that the plight of the Jews was intolerable in those parts of Europe which represented a decadent feudalism—Poland, pre-revolutionary Russia, and the Balkans—long before Hitler made their lot impossible in what was once the democratic world.[27]

Therefore, he believed that Jews—especially the poor Jews caught in those "decadent feudal" lands—should be allowed to immigrate freely to Palestine; he strongly opposed British efforts to limit immigration in the 1930s.

Because neither Europe nor America could handle the number of Jews disinherited by the upheaval of World War II, Christian compassion must neces-

---

[25]Ibid., 158.
[26]Niebuhr, "Jews After the War," in *Christianity and Crisis*, as reproduced in James Parkes, *End of an Exile: Israel, the Jews, and the Gentile World*, ed. Eugene Korn and Roberta Kalechovsky, 3rd ed. (Marblehead, MA: Micah Books, 2005), 219.
[27]Ibid.

Theology and Politics 233

sarily demand a homeland that will shelter oppressed Jews. That element of compassion led Niebuhr to another bold move—his promotion of a homeland for the Jews.

Christian realism—its love searching for higher possibilities—leads to establishing a homeland for the Jews. Not only could the mass of disinherited Jews not be accommodated in other countries, but there were good reasons why they should exist as a state. Even if individual Jews could be dispersed in many different countries, there would be an injustice involved in such a solution. For the Jews are unique. They have had the will to survive in many countries. "They have maintained some degree of integrity for thousands of years; they are a nationality scattered among the nations."[28] As a nationality there are many organic dimensions to their persistence—ethnic, racial, cultural and religious. Certainly, without the religious element the Jewish nationality could not have survived. All these elements gave Jews as a collective body a powerful will to survive.[29] They survived as nationalities within many nations, nearly always living in a precarious state and often the object of persecution. Their persistence as a nationality gives strength to their claim for a nation, a state.

Though Niebuhr was ambivalent about theological justifications for the Jews to return to the land promised them in the covenant, he did make some statements that pushed in that direction.[30] When he addressed the Zionist Organization of America in Cincinnati in September 1941, he said there was a special connection between diaspora Jews and the land of Israel. Justice, he argued, combines the Jewish desire for a state with the land of Israel because "there is no spirit without a body, and there is no body without geography."[31] Carys Moseley maintains that "this is the single most important Zionist statement Niebuhr made, because he connected the Land of Israel with creaturely embodiment and statehood, as they were in the Bible."[32] Further, she cites his remark that Israel's nationhood throughout the ages was "granted in a religious

---

[28] Ibid., 221.
[29] Niebuhr considered the "liberal idealists," who argued for complete assimilation, naive about the vital dimensions of nationalities, both among those who want to destroy Israel as well as the Jewish will to survive as a corporate entity. Collectivities are such a powerful combination of organic and spiritual vitalities that the idealist rarely comprehends their strength or their persistence.
[30] I shall have much more to say about his ambivalence about theological justification for Jewish return to the land of Israel later in this chapter.
[31] Niebuhr, cited by Charles Brown, *Niebuhr and His Age* (Edinburgh: T&T Clark, 2002), 142.
[32] Moseley, *Nationhood*, 38.

covenant experience."[33] Historically, such "covenant experience" involved the promise of land.

Because he believed in the exceptional nature of Jewish claims to a homeland in the land of Israel, he thought it was mistaken to conflate these claims with the nationalism of the time. He also observed that the Jews made Israel into a democratic state, and this made it unique among the nations of the Middle East.

This homeland should be a state with its own integrity. The state of Israel should be a Jewish state, an affirmation that went against the grain of many idealists and rationalists, who found that to be "racist." On the contrary, he thought that Israel's exceptionalism—the amalgam of religious, ethnic, racial and historical factors—warranted the establishment of a Jewish state. Moreover, Niebuhr supported a "two-state solution" over the idea of a binational state, which was popular among mainline Protestants as well as Jewish anti-Zionist intellectuals such as Martin Buber and Hannah Arendt.

A binational state would dilute and then eventually destroy the "Jewish-national" character of a state, especially since Arabs were vehemently against free immigration of the Jews into such a state.[34]

As a state Israel should have all functions assigned to a normal state, including the military capacity to defend itself.[35] That function would finally allow Jews in their own state and homeland an opportunity to overcome their perennial status as the object of someone else's action in their historical existence, and never as subjects of that action. As "nationalities" dispersed among the many nations, Jews were always vulnerable to anti-Semitic measures, including violent ones. In the more virulent forms of anti-Semitism, even "emancipated" Jews—secular and Christian—were the objects of such measures. Hitler, for example, spared no one who had Jewish blood from his deadly intentions.

---

[33] Ibid., 53. Moseley draws this quote from Niebuhr's *The Structure of Nations and Empires* (New York: Charles Scribner's Sons, 1959), 161-62.

[34] Moseley, *Nationhood*, 40-41, where she cites Niebuhr's argument in an article titled "The Partition of Palestine," *Christianity and Society* 13 (Winter 1948): 3-4.

[35] As noted earlier, many Protestants of a pacifist bent withdrew their support of Israel after it used force of arms to establish itself and then later to protect itself against those who wished to annihilate it. One of the more extreme forms of such a critique was that of Arnold Toynbee, who denounced Israel for its departure from the "way of gentleness." This extreme pacifism was rejected by Niebuhr in his essay "Christians and Jews in Western Civilization," in *The Essential Reinhold Niebuhr*, ed. Robert McAfee Brown (New Haven, CT: Yale University Press, 1986), 199. Moseley offers a critique of Stanley Hauerwas's neopacifism with regard to Israel in her *Nationhood*, 51-53. In her view, Hauerwas mistakenly rejects any theological-ethical framework that would support a state.

Theology and Politics 235

Because Jews in their new state had the capacity for self-determination, they had obtained a place where they "are not merely 'tolerated,' where they are neither appreciated nor condemned, but where they can be what they are, preserving their own unique identity without asking 'by your leave' of anyone else."[36] "A much weightier justification of Zionism is that every race finally has a right to a homeland where it will not be 'different,' where it will neither be patronized by 'good' people nor subjected to calumny by bad people."[37]

More aptly, the state of Israel could now legitimately defend itself in a way that the dispersed Jewish "nationalities" among many nations could not. Israel has used its military prowess to defend itself many times, which instances Niebuhr thought were justified. The Jews in Israel now are indeed subjects of history. The fact that they have defended their existence repeatedly has also had a down side, which may have more than a tinge of anti-Semitism in it. The Jews of Israel are no longer the oppressed. Because they have won, they are now viewed by some as oppressors. Somehow the Jews are different from other nationalities who defend themselves; they were much more attractive morally when they were oppressed. So Jews are exceptional in a perverse way: when they defend themselves successfully, they become oppressors, perhaps even taking on the characteristics of their one time destroyers, the Nazis.[38]

Niebuhr, on the other hand, believed not only that force was needed to establish and defend the new nation but also that the United States and Britain were right to use their power to impose a solution on the messy situation created by the establishment of Israel. "The Anglo-Saxon hegemony in the event of an Axis defeat will be in a position to see to it that Palestine is set aside for the Jews."[39] Later, in the Suez Crisis, Niebuhr criticized the attempted "even-handedness" of American foreign policy. He called for "unequivocal support" for Israel, including diplomatic and military support.[40]

Niebuhr rightly shrunk from the idea that Israel should be a religious state, a theocracy as it were. He sharply opposed the state being governed by religious authorities or the reinstitution of Orthodox legal norms. Such conflation of those responsible for the covenanted Jewish community with those

---

[36] Niebuhr, "Jews After the War," 224.
[37] Ibid., 229.
[38] One of my friends, in explaining to me why such sharp judgments are made on Israel's behavior, quipped: "They made the big mistake of winning."
[39] As cited by Richard Fox in *Reinhold Niebuhr: A Biography* (New York: Pantheon Books, 1985), 210.
[40] Niebuhr, "Our Stake," 6.

responsible for the policies of a state would lead to religionized politics and politicized religion, something Niebuhr was extremely wary of. The former gives politics an unwarranted sacrality that becomes dangerous in the hands of a powerful state, and the latter tends to undermine authentic religion, corrupting its transcendent claims by involving it too closely with political interests.

Such an identification of the Jewish faith with the state of Israel would lead to further problems. If the state of Israel were seen as the earthly religious model of upholding the divine law and of having its own messianic pretensions, excessively high expectations would be placed on it. Already at the time of its foundation, friendly supporters cast such expectations on it. A well-known liberal Protestant preacher, Harry Emerson Fosdick, expected the new state "to benefit mankind," and a distinguished Protestant of the Northeast elite, Adolf Berle Sr., expected it to "improve the world." Such idealistic notions were eschewed by Niebuhr, who knew that the state of Israel would be faced with all the ambiguities and difficulties of the life of any state. And in Israel's case, such projections were doubly dangerous because it was surrounded by fierce enemies who would provoke it to policies of survival that in other more secure circumstances would be viewed as problematic.[41]

Niebuhr was quite clear that establishing a homeland and state for the Jews would be an injustice to the Arabs residing there.

> Zionist leaders are unrealistic in insisting that their demands entail no "injustice" to the Arab populations since Jewish immigration has brought new economic strength to Palestine. It is absurd to expect any people to regard the restriction of their sovereignty over a traditional possession as "just," no matter how many other benefits accrue from that abridgment.[42]

He was genuinely sympathetic to the plight of dispossessed Arabs.

---

[41]Such obliviousness to the dangers that beset Israel continues among mainstream Protestants, who decry Israeli strategies of survival that are precipitated by alarming threats to her survival. For example, the Evangelical Lutheran Church in America advocates a program called "Peace Not Walls," which faults Israel for erecting walls between certain West Bank and Israeli communities; see www.elca.org/Our-Work/Publicly-Engaged-Church/Peace-Not-Walls. But such walls have nearly stopped the suicide bombings that wracked Israel during the intifadas. Admittedly, they are not pretty, and they do enact injustices on the nearby Palestinian population. But they are extraordinary measures taken against extraordinary threats. Another nation facing such threats would take perhaps even more extreme measures.

[42]Niebuhr, "Jews After the War," 230.

Early on he had some hope that the visceral reaction of the Arab population to Israel's founding could be assuaged by a "total settlement" in the Middle East that would also improve the lot of the Arab world, though not by absorbing the Jewish homeland into an essentially Arab federation.[43] By the time of the Suez Crisis he remarked that "the West did not reckon with the depth of the Arab spirit of vengeance, nor did it appreciate that this technically efficient democracy would exacerbate the ancient feud between the Jews and the Arabs."[44] He tried to parse this "spirit of vengeance" by noting that the Arabs thought the land was their soil and that the Jews' covenantal claim to the land ended hundreds of years ago with the fall of Jerusalem. Further, the fact that Arab countries would not take in the Arab refugees produced by the establishment of Israel was a constant source of anti-Israel animus in the region. Finally, and more profoundly, Niebuhr thought that

> the technical efficiency and democratic justice of Israel was a source of danger to the moribund feudal or pastoral economies and monarchical political forms of the Islamic world and a threat to the rich overlords of desperately poor peasants of the Middle East. It was also a threat to those Islamic religious people who delight in the "organic" quality of ancient life and who know that modern techniques would certainly destroy the old way of life in the process of lifting the burden on the poor.[45]

Little did he know how prescient he was in anticipating the sources of the continuing hostility of the Arabs to Israel.

Nevertheless, in spite of this continuing Arab refusal to come to terms with Israel, Niebuhr thought the violation of some of the "natural rights" of the Arabs were rightly overridden by the unique claims of the need for a Jewish homeland. The world will simply have to live with some of the intractabilities of this ongoing situation. Christian love's search for a higher justice for the Jews—its pressure toward indeterminate possibilities—led Niebuhr to conclude that establishing such a homeland was the higher justice. "It is a glorious and moral and political achievement."[46]

It is important to note here that although Niebuhr passionately supported a homeland (as a state) for the Jews, he promoted what he called a double strategy.

---

[43]Ibid.
[44]Niebuhr, "Our Stake," 4.
[45]Ibid.
[46]Cited by Fox in *Reinhold Niebuhr*, 199.

He thought the Jewish nationalities dispersed in many nations should continue to be welcomed and protected in those lands. The continued communal existence of the Jewish nationalities is a great blessing to every nation where they flourish. They have been great contributors to civilization—scientifically, technically, culturally, academically and religiously. Further, if Jewish communities and individuals wanted to be emancipated from their ancient nationalities, that too should be accommodated. They, too, have been great assets to civilization. "Any relaxation of democratic standards (to protect them) would also mean robbing our civilization of the special gifts which they have developed as a nation among nations."[47]

Christian Realism and Democratic Israel

"Man's capacity for justice makes democracy possible; man's inclination to injustice makes democracy necessary."[48] Or perhaps even more trenchant: "Democracy is finding proximate solutions for insoluble problems."[49]

These famous statements by Niebuhr follow from his biblical-theological insights into human nature. He thought that constitutional democracy was a direct result of Judeo-Christian teachings about humankind penetrating the culture and politics of the West. From his Christian point of view, the endorsement of democracy is one example of a "discriminate decision" (see our four points above) necessitated by the standard of love. While democracy in no way brings to earth the kingdom of God, it is relatively better than all other sorts of polities. It is an "approximation" of the kingdom, even though partial and fragile.[50]

Man's capacity for justice follows from the sense of original justice left in human nature after the fall. It is the law written on the heart that the apostle Paul affirms (Rom 2:15). It is further reinforced and enriched by the prodding of Christian love. On the other hand, human beings' inclination toward injustice follows from the pervasive sin that inevitably resides in the human will and is expressed by various sorts of pride, which are magnified in the life of groups.

Democracy has the best chance of all polities in harnessing both the capacity for justice and the inclination toward sin. Its foundation is anchored in the

---

[47]Niebuhr, "Jews After the War," 227-28.
[48]Reinhold Niebuhr, *The Children of Light and the Children of Darkness* (New York: Charles Scribner's Sons, 1944), xiii.
[49]Ibid., 18.
[50]*Niebuhr on Politics*, 162.

Judeo-Christian conviction that all humans are created in the image of God and are therefore sacred. This high status for humans is residually present in humankind's original justice but directly present in Jewish and Christian teaching. But given humanity's sin, how are the rights that flow from this deep foundation secured? It is first of all secured by balancing the centers of power—economic, political, ethnic, cultural, religious—that are present in the "natural equilibrium" that is one of the prerequisites for democracy to develop at all.[51] Without some sort of natural equilibrium, as is the case where the control of wealth is monopolized in a small elite, democracy is difficult to achieve. Likewise, democracy is unlikely to develop where there is a weak religious-cultural foundation for human rights, as is the case in many non-Western societies.

However, one cannot expect the natural equilibrium alone to achieve justice. The organizing center (the government) must make laws and policies that redress severe imbalances of power in which segments of society are oppressed. Democracies do this by relying on representative government and by the rule of law, constantly assessed by an independent judiciary. They also insist on consent of the governed and constitutional protections for minorities from the tyranny of a majority.

Niebuhr found these traits admirably embodied in Israel. He quotes Abraham Lincoln in his support (Niebuhr's) of Israel during the Suez Crisis: "We will not allow 'any nation so conceived and so dedicated . . . to perish from the earth.'"[52] He believed support for Israel was particularly demanded given the paucity of democracy in that part of the world. Since America was born "to exemplify the virtues of democracy and to extend the frontiers of the principles of self-government throughout the world," that extension to Israel was to be particularly cherished and supported.[53]

Israel has remained a stable democracy since its founding, something of a miracle considering the external strains under which she has lived. She has negotiated the claims of factions and parties of wildly different ideologies. Democratic practices over time have enabled the non-Jewish minorities within Israel gradually to gain economic and political power. Israel has continuously found "proximate solutions for insoluble problems." Niebuhr would have continued strongly to support the democratic commitments and development of Israel,

---

[51]Niebuhr, *Nature and Destiny of Man*
[52]Niebuhr, "Our Stake," 5.
[53]Reinhold Niebuhr, *A Nation So Conceived* (New York: Scribner, 1963), 123.

especially in a contemporary Middle East that is profoundly lacking in democratic ideals and practices.

> Christians are committed to democracy as the only safeguard of the sacredness of human personality. The opposition to a Jewish Palestine is partly based on the opposition of Arabs to democracy, Western culture, education and economic freedom. To support Arab opposition is but supporting feudalism and Fascism in a world at the expense of democratic rights and justice.[54]

Complementing Niebuhr

I have noted above that Niebuhr was ambivalent about assigning theological meaning to the establishment of Israel and its claim to the land. On the one hand, he came close to affirming the strong connection between the faith of Israel and the establishment of the state of Israel in the Holy Land. "The homeland could not have been established in Palestine except for religious memories."[55] In other places he observed that the land and the spirit have to go together, as they did in the Bible, and that the Jewish claim to the land was based on a "covenant religious experience."[56]

Generally, however, he eschewed theological justification. He mostly remained silent about it, but in one glaring place he seemed to agree with the Arab resistance to Israel when he offered this as a reason for their intransigence: "The West and the Jews may claim the previous Jewish right to the soil of Palestine, but we tend to forget that this right evaporated some thousands of years ago and that Arabs are not impressed by Old Testament prophecies, at least not by the political significance of these prophecies."[57] Niebuhr's reasons for support of Israel were similar to those of secular and liberal Jews.

There were several reasons for his ambivalence. First, he wanted to distance his position from that of the Social Gospel liberals on the one hand, and evangelicals and fundamentalists on the other. The Social Gospel liberals were postmillennialists who believed that the kingdom of God could be built on earth before the return of Jesus. Building the kingdom on earth was immeasurably advanced by the establishment of Israel as a democracy and beacon of Western civilization. Niebuhr thought the kingdom of God could never be built on earth

---
[54]Niebuhr, *Children of Light*, 84.
[55]Niebuhr, "Christians and Jews in Western Civilization," 199.
[56]Moseley, *Nationhood*, 53.
[57]Niebuhr, "Our Stake," 4.

because of the intransigence of human sin. Those who tried often did damage to both church and society. Many evangelicals and fundamentalists—influenced by dispensationalism—were premillennialists who saw the establishment of Israel and its subsequent victories as the fulfillment of biblical prophecy and as signs of the end times. The former were far too optimistic about the potentialities of history and the latter too literalistic about the Bible's visions. Niebuhr did not see biblical prophecy as a precise script for the end times.[58] He rejected both utopianism and dispensationalism.

A second reason for shunning a theological justification was that he thought that any such justification would involve a "sacerdotal state" in which political and religious power were conflated. He supported a secular state in Israel that would avoid the dangers of messianic politics, which had done so much damage in the twentieth century. Politics was about limited earthly possibilities, not about heavenly utopias. He thought that the Orthodox hegemony in Israel would not only lead to a form of messianic politics but would also submit Israel to "the legal norms which were handed down in tradition from a pastoral community thousands of years ago."[59] It was the gift of a secular democratic state to manage the claims of different sorts of Jews, religious and secular, leading in Niebuhr's opinion to the wise "abandonment of the plan of writing a constitution for the new state. It was a wise move because the chasm could not have been bridged by any legal arrangement but only by the pressures and creativities of actual history."[60] Such a democratic state could forge "proximate solutions to insoluble problems," both internal and external to Israel. A state that justified its existence and policies on theological grounds would have less capacity to arrive at such proximate solutions.

A third reason is central to what this book is about: supersessionism. In Niebuhr's case, however, it was a complex sort of supersessionism. On the one hand, it prevented him from openly and directly affirming the continuing covenant with Israel that includes a promise of the land as part of that covenant. The lingering supersessionist notion that after the coming of Jesus the covenant

---

[58]Niebuhr's own eschatology avoided both dispensationalist literalism as well as easy dismissal of the Bible's symbols. In the last chapter of *Nature and Destiny of Man*, he elaborated a profound interpretation of the end of history, which he judges will be cataclysmic because the capacities for evil grow along with the capacities for good in history. He concludes that "history cumulates rather than solves, the essential problems of human existence" (p. 318). When one adds technological advance to the mix, the likelihood of an apocalyptic end increases.

[59]Niebuhr, *Essential Reinhold Niebuhr*, 199.

[60]Niebuhr, "Our Stake," 3.

with Israel—and its promise of the land—was either suspended or ended led to his ignoring the whole subject. He generally ignored the issue of supersessionism but at times embraced a version of it.[61]

On the other hand, his was not the harsh supersessionism that completely replaces Israel as the covenanted people of God with the Christian church after the coming of Jesus as the Messiah. In this version Israel and its faith were no longer relevant. Nor was it the demonic sort of supersessionism that not only saw the covenant withdrawn from Israel but viewed the Jewish people as a malignant cancer in history and their age-long suffering as punishment for their refusal of the Messiah. This worse type was exemplified by the Nazis, who added to that suffering immeasurably and, in order to sanitize Jesus of his Jewishness, even claimed that biologically Jesus was an Aryan and not a Jew.

Niebuhr's was a milder sort of supersessionism, parts of which cannot be avoided, but parts of which can. Certainly Christians must, as an article of faith, believe that the Expected One was Jesus the Christ, who offered believers a new way into the covenant based on his life and work. In this sense, the coming of Jesus fulfilled the promises of God in the Hebrew Bible and reconciled humankind to God on the basis of faith in Jesus, not in fulfilling the Law. The early Christians, all of whom were Jews, believed this. Most, according to the scholars in this book, remained observant Jews even though they believed in Jesus as the Messiah. Yet, they believed that Jesus offered God's new way to salvation. It was God's new and decisive rescue mission: sending his own Son.

As a Christian, Niebuhr believed in such a sort of supersessionism, but he did so humbly and without putting Judaism down. After reflecting on the differences between the two religions—the identity of the Messiah, the relation of law and grace, and the relation of universality and particularity—he came to the conclusion that "the two faiths, despite their differences, are sufficiently alike for the Jew to find God more easily in terms of his own religious heritage than by subjecting himself to the hazards of guilt feeling involved in a conversion to a faith, which whatever its excellences, must appear to him as a symbol of an

---

[61]Carys Moseley argues that Niebuhr's reluctance to offer a theological justification for Israel's right to the land led to liberal Protestantism's view that the return of the Jews to the land was unjustified (*Nationhood*, 46). As I will argue in the conclusion, I believe that failure on Niebuhr's part was only a small piece of liberal Protestantism's diminishing support for Israel. His support for Israel in the late 1950s was already embarrassing to many of his liberal Protestant followers for other reasons. A theological justification would have done little to change their attitudes.

Theology and Politics 243

oppressive majority culture."[62] Thus, he was against missionary activity directed toward religious Jews.

Interestingly enough, when he discussed "particularity" he meant that the faith of Israel is sheltered by the state of Israel in Palestine, providing a home for the homeless. But he could not bring himself to connect that fact with the promises of God in the everlasting and continuing covenant with the Jews. However, if that covenant involved land, many sons and becoming a blessing to the nations, then there would have been good theological justification for him to connect the religious Jews of Israel to the land. He, like Paul, certainly did not argue that the covenant with the Jews ended with the coming of Jesus.

The earlier writers in this volume argue that the covenant with Israel continues, and that it involves the land, not only attested by the Old Testament prophets but also among the New Testament writers, as well as among many Jewish and Christian writers throughout the ages.

Had Niebuhr had the benefit of this new thinking about the relation of Christianity to Judaism that overcomes the more blatant forms of supersessionism—how both are encompassed in one covenant and how a continuing covenant with the Jews involves the land—I believe he would have moved toward such a theological justification for occupying the land. It would not have been a difficult step for him.

His other objections for refraining from such a justification would then fall by the wayside. His first objection—that the rationale for such a justification is offered only by dispensationalists on the one hand or Social Gospel liberals on the other—is confounded by the historical witness of many Christian and Jewish Zionists throughout history, as well as the writers in this volume. He himself was considered a Christian Zionist without resorting to either.

His second objection, that such a justification might lead to a sacerdotal state, has not come to pass, as he had already approvingly noted. The state of Israel is secular, providing a shelter for the covenanted people of Israel in the Holy Land, but also for many Jews, Arabs, Christians, Palestinians and other minorities. It cares for and provides access to Muslim holy sites. It is the most reliable protector of Christian holy places, which are so revered in Christian history, belying the claim that Christianity is purely "universal."[63] The state of Israel is the

---

[62]Niebuhr, "Christians and Jews in Western Civilization," 198.
[63]Robert Wilken, *A Land Called Holy* (New Haven, CT: Yale University Press, 1992). His book is a powerful demonstration that the Holy Land has been extremely important for Christians.

epicenter of Jewish particularity, guarding the land to which Jews believe the Messiah will come.[64]

Whether Niebuhr would have agreed to my complement to his argument is not utterly clear. However, given his support for Israel, his respect for Judaism and his admission that Judaism and a homeland in Israel were intimately connected, it seems that he might well have accepted it. If the apostle Paul testifies to the ongoing covenant with the Jews, and that the covenant involves the promise of the land, it is hard to believe that Niebuhr would have disagreed with Paul.

Conclusion

At the outset of this paper I admitted that Niebuhr had made most of the arguments I would have made in a putative Niebuhrian argument for Christian Zionism. If I would have made such an attempt—drawing on my mastery of Niebuhr's worldview—I would have had to footnote almost every reference. Why not just let him speak and assent to it? So I have just *complimented* him by my full identification with what he has said. I think I have also *complemented* him by adding a theological justification for his support of Israel, the Judaism that it protects and the land that is crucial to both. This addition strengthens his identity as a Christian Zionist, which was already secure.

When I elaborated his arguments, I was astonished at their power. His realism—accentuated by his *Realpolitik* admirers—has continuing relevance. Support of Israel is in our national interest. It is an island of needed stability in a turbulent part of the world. It helps us fend off militant Islam by its very presence and strength. It is a country that can represent and convey our power, including military power.

Israel adds an important element toward achieving a balance of power among competing centers—Sunni and Shia Muslims and the countries dominated by

---

Christianity is not simply a "spiritual" religion without sacred places. Israel's protection of Christian holy sites is a further reason to support Israel. Current Muslim hostility to Christianity would make it an untrustworthy trustee for such sites.

[64]There are difficult questions about who represents the covenanted people and what the perimeters of the land are. Who represents the Jewish side of the covenant, which Jewish tradition? How extensive is the land—greater or lesser Israel? I have no competence to answer those questions. They are as near to insoluble as I can imagine, but perhaps the answers to them have to be managed by a secular democratic state that offers "proximate solutions to insoluble problems." The "proximate solutions," of course, will have to be worked out not only in domestic arrangements but also with Israel's neighbors, some of whom are murderously bent on her annihilation, though there are others with whom she can deal constructively.

them, Chinese and Russian interests, and nuclear and nonnuclear regimes. It adds its weight to keep shifting balances of power from falling into outright tyranny or complete anarchy. It provides important resistance to the pretensions of imperial Iran, including its drive for nuclear weapons.

For Niebuhr, such realism was not enough. His was a Christian realism that commended compassion for the suffering of Jews worldwide. He was prescient in seeing that postwar Europe—even now extending into the twenty-first century—would not be a safe place for Jews. They needed a homeland. They still do. Christians should continue to support such a homeland wholeheartedly, partly out of sheer compassion but partly out of penitence for Christian complicity in the oppression of the Jews. Meanwhile, they should support the Jews in their homelands, both those in Jewish communities and those who have assimilated.

While most Western Christians—particularly German Christians—continue to have such compassion and a sense of penitence, their intensity has diminished. That is partly because the Jews of Israel have been able to go it alone when mortal danger faces them, and they have always won the decisive battles. For too many Christians the very fact that they can defend themselves changes their status as the oppressed to that of the oppressor, even though Israeli actions are always defensive. The Jews have made the mistake of winning too many battles. They have insisted on being the subjects of their own history, not only the objects surviving at the pleasure of others. This has led the purveyors of the distorted theologies of liberation to tip more toward the Palestinians and their malicious supporters than to Israel.

Niebuhr's defense of a homeland—the land of Israel—for the Jews has continuing relevance. The Jewish "nationalities"—an amalgamation of religious ethnic, racial and historical elements—are scattered throughout the nations, making great contributions to them. Their historical longevity and tenacity, but also their precariousness, as well as the stubborn particularity of Judaism itself, make them an exceptional case. Those Jewish nationalities need a homeland. Communal loyalty must be used as an instrument of survival. Even those who do not intend to move to that homeland support it. The case for Israel is unique. The world did right in allowing the establishment of the state of Israel and does right in supporting its continued existence. Adding to Niebuhr's argument, I have offered a theological justification for Israel's exceptional case: God has a continuing covenant with Israel that includes land and the promise of return.

These combined special claims override even the "natural rights" of the Palestinians to their lands, though it behooves Israel to accommodate them in some way yet to be found that is satisfactory to most. As we all know, this has been very difficult to do, mostly on account of the corrupt and intransigent Palestinian leaders and their malicious backers, such as Iran, but partly on account of neglect and bad policies by the Israelis themselves.

Here is where democratic Israel comes into play. The Jewish sense of justice in time has worked through the instruments of democracy to strengthen the human rights and political power of the Palestinians and other minorities. The prospects for Israeli minorities are increasing day by day. They would rather live in Israel than in Muslim lands. Many Palestinians in the West Bank would rather be Israeli citizens. But the danger of another Gaza emerging in the West Bank makes Israel reluctant to offer such opportunities or to give up military control over it. Further, like Niebuhr, Israel strongly resists a binational state in favor of a two-nation solution, though even that seems unlikely in the near future. Democratic Israel attempts to work through these conundrums, aiming at "proximate solutions for insoluble problems."

Israel's struggle with these continuing insoluble problems has not been met with patience by many factions in the world. For example, this painful search has led in too many cases to impatience and diminished support for Israel among American mainstream Protestant elites. Increasingly, the same attitudes have been exemplified in the American and European left. They claim that the establishment of Israel was merely a nineteenth-century manifestation of nationalism that should be sharply qualified along with other suspect nationalisms. They brand Israel an apartheid state. They obsess about the iniquities of Israel and turn a blind eye to the depredations of Muslim groups and states. They have tried to dictate how Israel ought to defend itself. They have even led campaigns to boycott companies that do business with Israel.

What is going on here? These are the same set of faulty arguments that Niebuhr had to combat. He called that set of arguments "liberal universalism," and those who hold them have always been skeptical of Israel. There are several components to this recurrent liberal universalism. First, its idealism blinds it to the mortal threats of millions of hostile people residing in many countries surrounding Israel. Because Israel has been successful in defending itself, liberal universalism thinks it will always be so. Israelis can relax a bit. Further, it underestimates the visceral hatefulness of both the leaders and the people of many

Theology and Politics

of Israel's enemies. Since it seems that Israel is secure, it is assumed that it always will be. Thus, sweet reason can reign. Chances can be taken. The Golden Rule can apply. In response, it is useful to quote this remark of Niebuhr made in 1942: "Thou shalt love thy neighbor cannot mean that I must destroy myself so that no friction may arise between my neighbor and myself."[65]

Liberal idealists underestimate the precariousness of Israel before its enemies, and thus have an inflated idea about the room that Israel has to negotiate. Therefore, it holds Israel to impossibly high standards of behavior.[66] The United Nations, throughout the years, has focused on Israel's "misdeeds" obsessively, with little attention given to far more serious violations by other countries around the world.[67] At home, liberal Lutheran elites criticize the erection of the wall between the West Bank and Israel proper, oblivious to the threat of suicide bombers who plagued Israel for the years of the intifadas, as well as to the fact that the wall stopped most of them.

Liberal idealism underplays the need for the corporate survival of a people compounded of historical, racial, ethnic and religious solidarities. When Israel exercises its will to survive as such a community, it is branded racist, even though it is far more diverse racially and culturally than its neighbors. The individualism of liberal universalism downplays such a drive for survival and seems to make the negotiation of contending survival impulses easier than it is. It reduces such negotiation to individual actors even as it assigns rights only to individuals. That leads it to downplay the threat to Israel's collective right for survival. Guaranteeing rights to individual Jews is as far as it wishes to go.

Above all, liberal universalism despises the claim of nations to be "exceptional." President Obama famously declared that America is exceptional in the same way that Greeks and Danes think their nation is exceptional. Yet Americans persist in seeing their nation as exceptional: one in which the American dream (equality of opportunity) is offered to all, and one that bears a special

---

[65] Niebuhr, "Jews After the War," 225.

[66] A college colleague offered a presentation about his visit to Israel in which he told of a mischievous action (one that could be interpreted as hostile) he took that intentionally drew the attention of Israeli plainclothes police. He thought that their response illustrated a hyperwatchfulness that was oppressive. However, it is doubtful whether he would have done such mischief in a Muslim country. He knew he would not be let off so easily.

[67] As David Gelernter has written, "But you *cannot* oppose Israel with a toxic ferocity reserved for it alone, lie about Israel casually and constantly, yet not be an anti-Semite." Gelernter, "Why Should a Jew Care Whether Christianity Lives or Dies," First Things, March 24, 2015 (emphasis original), www.firstthings.com/web-exclusives/2015/03/why-should-a-jew-care-whether-christianity-lives-or-dies.

democratic mission in the world. "A nation so conceived and so dedicated . . . should not perish from the earth." Lincoln's statement about America is what Niebuhr said about Israel, which he thought was exceptional: its role as a homeland for oppressed Jews who have long searched for return; its amalgam of ethnic, cultural and religious qualities; its unique democratic role in the Mideast; and, I would add, its role as a shelter for the covenanted people of God whose covenant includes the land.

Liberal universalists tend to be blind to claims of uniqueness, especially those of nations with religious identities. Rightly worrying about those identities being the source of conflict, they wrongly dismiss their ongoing validity as wholesome sources of cohesion. In doing so, they ignore the crucial way such unique vitalities contribute to the nature and destiny of nations and the world. Their vision of a "kingdom of ends" guided by universal reason floats like a phantasm over historical realities, neither understanding nor defending them when one or the other is called for.

Let Niebuhr have the last word:

> We ought to recognize that among the many illogical emergences of history (that is, configurations which do not fit into our logic) there is the strange miracle of the Jewish people, outliving the hazards of the diaspora for two millennia and finally offering their unique and valuable contributions to the common Western civilization as a state, particularly in the final stage of its liberal society. We should not ask that this peculiar historical miracle fit into any kind of logic or conform to some historical analogy. It has no analogy. It must be appreciated for what it is.[68]

Deep appreciation for this "miracle" defines Reinhold Niebuhr's Christian Zionism . . . and mine.

---

[68]Niebuhr, "Christians and Jews in Western Civilization," 201.

9

THEOLOGY AND LAW

Does the Modern State of Israel Violate Its Call to Justice in the Covenant by Its Relation to International Law?

Robert Nicholson

◆

The International Court of Justice (ICJ) could not have been clearer: "The construction of the wall being built by Israel . . . in the Occupied Palestinian Territory, including in and around East Jerusalem, and its associated régime, are contrary to international law."[1] The ICJ's 2004 ruling came in the middle of the Second Intifada in response to a query from the United Nations General Assembly about the legal consequences of Israel's attempt to stop Palestinian suicide bombers by building a separation barrier along the 1949 Israeli-Jordanian armistice lines.

The ICJ nimbly overcame various jurisdictional and evidentiary obstacles and condemned Israel's behavior in no uncertain terms. But the court did not stop there. It called on "all States," the "United Nations" and "especially" the United Nations Security Council to "consider what further action was required to bring to an end the illegal situation resulting from the construction of the wall and the associated regime."[2] In other words, the ICJ asked the nations of the world to punish Israel in the name of justice.

---

[1] "Legal Consequences of the Construction of a Wall in the Occupied Palestinian Territory (Request for Advisory Opinion): Summary of the Advisory Opinion 9 July 2004," International Court of Justice, The Hague, July 9, 2004, 70, www.icj-cij.org/docket/files/131/1677.pdf (henceforth cited as ICJ).
[2] Ibid.

The media cared little that the ICJ opinion was only advisory and not binding on anyone.[3] They took no notice of Judge Buergenthal's dissenting remarks about the court's failure to conduct a serious factual analysis befitting such harsh application of the law.[4] They passed over the court's failure to recognize that the wall was a response to armed attacks by nonstate actors (as was later pointed out by the court's top judge).[5] They paid no heed to the creeping politicization of the court's power or the court's break with the Permanent Court of International Justice—the ICJ's institutional forebear—in allowing advisory jurisdiction to be used as a backdoor to decide disputes over the jurisdictional objections of one of the parties.[6] From the global media's perspective, all that mattered was that a world court had found Israel guilty of violating world law.[7] The ICJ judgment was seen not as an advisory opinion but as a cosmic finding of Israel's intrinsic turpitude.

Yet the judgment was nothing new: national governments and international organizations have been accusing Israel of violating international law since 1948, and today international law remains the dominant mode of attacking the legitimacy of the Jewish state. In the first decade of its operation, the United Nations Human Rights Council issued no fewer than sixty-two condemnations of Israel based on international humanitarian and human rights law. Meanwhile the heinous human rights records of countries like Saudi Arabia, Iran, China, Sudan and Russia went entirely unnoticed. The Syrian regime of Bashar al-

---

[3]"It is of the essence of such opinions that they are advisory, i.e., that, unlike the Court's judgments, they have no binding effect." This is in the ICJ's self-description: "The Court: How the Court Works," accessed January 2, 2016, www.icj-cij.org/court/index.php?p1=1&p2=6#advisory.
[4]"Dissenting Opinion of Judge Buergenthal," International Court of Justice, July 9, 2004, posted in *Jewish Virtual Library*, www.jewishvirtuallibrary.org/jsource/Peace/dissent.html. See also Yoram Dinstein, *The International Law of Belligerent Occupation* (Cambridge: Cambridge University Press, 2009), 253; and Sean Murphy, "Self Defense and the Israeli Wall Advisory Opinion: An Ipse Dixit from the ICJ?," *American Journal of International Law* 99, no. 1 (2005): 62-76.
[5]Pieter Kooijmans, "The ICJ in the 21st Century: Judicial Restraint, Judicial Activism, or Proactive Judicial Policy," *International and Comparative Law Quarterly* 56, no. 4 (2007): 752.
[6]See Joel Tashjian, "Contentious Matters and the Advisory Power: The ICJ and Israel's Wall," *Chicago Journal of International Law* 6, no. 1 (2005): 427-37; and Michla Pomerance, "The ICJ's Advisory Jurisdiction and the Crumbling Wall Between the Political and the Judicial," *American Journal of International Law* 99, no. 1 (2005): 26-42.
[7]Christine Hauser and Greg Myre, "World Court Says Israeli Barrier Violates International Law," *New York Times*, July 9, 2004, www.globalexchange.org/news/world-court-says-israeli-barrier-violates-international-law; "U.N. Court Rules West Bank Barrier Illegal," World, *CNN.com*, July 9, 2004, www.cnn.com/2004/WORLD/meast/07/09/israel.barrier/; and Matthew Taylor, "International Court Rules Against Israel's Wall," *The Guardian*, July 9, 2004, www.theguardian.com/world/2004/jul/09/israelandthepalestinians.unitednations.

Assad, at the date of this writing responsible for killing two hundred thousand of his own citizens, received a mere fifteen condemnations. North Korea received only eight.[8] This says nothing of the innumerable declarations and speeches condemning Israel that are frequently leveled by governments, nongovernmental organizations, scholars, celebrities and public figures of all kinds.

Do the condemnations have basis in fact? If so, does the modern state of Israel violate the biblical covenant's call for justice by its violation of international law? These are good questions. Not enough Christians consider the legal ramifications of their theology, and many have even undergone what one scholar calls the "de-legalization of the Christian religious consciousness."[9] Some Christian Zionists find unthinkable the idea that Israel could be wrong in some of its policies.

This chapter argues first that the accusation most often made—that Israel violates the biblical covenant because it violates international law—is simply incoherent. International law and covenantal law are two very different things. Covenantal justice is more complex than most assume and operates in a domain quite removed from modern international law. Next I zero in on the most debated legal issue—the status of the disputed territories—and contend that Israel has not violated international law by virtue of its relation to those territories. The chapter ends with a brief word about how Christians can ensure their Zionism remains within biblical standards of justice.

Justice and the Land

Gary Burge writes, "The entire Old Testament links justice and the land."[10] Burge is right: the link between justice and the land in Scripture is evident and undeniable. Although God unilaterally and unconditionally promised the land of Canaan to Abraham as an everlasting inheritance, he also established a bilateral covenant between himself and Abraham's seed that subjected the land promise to a series of conditions (cf. Gen 17:1-21; Ex 19:1–24:11). Israel received irrevocable title to the land, but her possession was made contingent on covenantal

---

[8]The United Nations maintains a dedicated website called UNISPAL (United Nations Information System on the Question of Palestine) that contains over thirty thousand documents related to the "Question of Palestine," many of which are rooted in arguments and discussions surrounding international law. See unispal.un.org.

[9]Chaim Saiman, "Jesus' Legal Theory—A Rabbinic Reading," *Journal of Law and Religion* 23, no. 1 (2007): 127.

[10]Gary Burge, *Whose Land? Whose Promise? What Christians Are Not Being Told about Israel and the Palestinians*, rev. ed. (Boston: Pilgrim Press, 2013), 103.

performance. Indeed, the Pentateuch closes with Moses standing before the assembly and reciting a series of horrific curses for failure to obey those terms (Deut 28:15-68). Preeminent among those curses were expulsion from the land and exile among the nations.

Justice is a central component of the Mosaic covenant. Of course, justice is a pervasive biblical concept that extends far beyond the Mosaic covenant in describing "the order God seeks to reestablish in His creation where all people receive the benefits of life with Him."[11] This order, established in heaven and mandated for earth, is a dominant theme in Scripture that is directly linked to the character of God. The concept of a righteous Creator who executes justice among his creatures—and demands justice in their relations with each other—is an elemental principle that animates biblical history and distinguishes Israel's thinking from that of the surrounding pagan cultures.[12] The secondary concept of covenant—of a righteous God who makes promises and enters into formal relationships with human beings—is also unique. That God linked justice and covenant in forging his formal relationship with Israel is therefore hardly surprising.

But biblical justice is more than an abstract vision of heavenly order. Biblical justice is in fact profoundly concrete, particular and relational—a mode of living and decision making rather than just an ideal form. Justice stems from the character of God and reaches down into the mundane matters of daily life, seeking to restore society by ceaselessly recalling human equality before the leveling gaze of God.[13] In the context of the covenant, "Israel's life as a concrete social reality is to reflect the qualities already modeled by God in Israel's experience."[14]

Yet these ideas are still vague. If one wants to apply covenantal justice to the conduct of modern Israel, one must go beyond abstractions and look for the actual terms of the covenant. What exactly is demanded of Israel?

---

[11]Stephen Charles Mott, *Holman Bible Dictionary* (Nashville: Broadman & Holman, 1991), s.v. "justice."
[12]Walter C. Kaiser Jr., *Toward Old Testament Ethics* (Grand Rapids: Zondervan, 1983), 29-30.
[13]E. Clinton Gardner, *Justice and Christian Ethics* (Cambridge: Cambridge University Press, 1995), 48-53.
[14]Bruce C. Birch, *Let Justice Roll Down: The Old Testament, Ethics, and Christian Life* (Louisville, KY: Westminster John Knox, 1991), 177.

Due Process, Equal Treatment

The Pentateuch speaks frequently about what we now call due process. Indeed, the author or authors appear to have been just as concerned about justice as about the practical *administration* of justice.

> Appoint judges and officials for your tribes in all your towns the Lord your God is giving you. They are to judge the people with righteous judgment. Do not deny justice or show partiality to anyone. Do not accept a bribe, for it blinds the eyes of the wise and twists the words of the righteous. Pursue justice and justice alone, so that you will live and possess the land the Lord your God is giving you. (Deut 16:18-20 HCSB)[15]

The proper administration of justice in the courts was premised on equality of all people before the law; however, that equality depended on the uniform application of the *same* law to all people regardless of their lineage. Moses mentions this requirement no fewer than four times in the course of his writing. All inhabitants of Israel, whether natives or strangers, would be subject to the same legal standards in a dispute.[16]

This call for justice amidst diversity was necessary in the diverse setting of the ancient Levant. The Hebrews sat astride a complex ethnic and religious landscape on the shores of the Mediterranean Sea where many nations moved to and fro between Asia, Africa and Europe. It was imperative that these transient peoples take with them news of a nation that dealt justly with all those who passed through its borders.[17]

Indeed, concern for the rights of non-Hebrew "strangers" (*gērîm*, sing. *gār*) is a running theme throughout the Pentateuch. It is a concern based not only

---

[15]Cf. Zechariah 7:9-11; 8:16-17; Isaiah 1:17.

[16]In Exodus 12:49 (HCSB): "The same law will apply to both the native and the foreigner who resides among you." In Leviticus 24:22 (HCSB): "You are to have the same law for the foreign resident and the native, because I am Yahweh your God." In Numbers 15:15-16 (HCSB): "The assembly is to have the same statute for both you and the foreign resident as a permanent statute throughout your generations. You and the foreigner will be alike before the Lord. The same law and the same ordinance will apply to both you and the foreigner who resides with you." And in Deuteronomy 1:16 (HCSB): "I commanded your judges at that time: Hear the cases between your brothers, and judge rightly between a man and his brother or a foreign resident."

[17]"That concern for justice in its widest extent is to include just dealings with those who are outside the covenanted community altogether, who are not even sojourners (*gerim*) therein." Injustice prevents the Gentiles from appreciating the essential truth of the Torah and to embrace its principles as their own. David Novak, *Covenantal Rights: A Study in Jewish Political Theory* (Princeton, NJ: Princeton University Press, 2009), 91.

on God's egalitarian view of all humans but also on Israel's own experience as residents in Egypt.[18] It was a concern that even called for love:

> When a foreigner lives with you in your land, you must not oppress him. You must regard the foreigner who lives with you as the native-born among you. You are to love him as yourself, for you were foreigners in the land of Egypt; I am Yahweh your God. (Lev 19:33-34 HCSB)[19]

Put into practice, this love called for wealth redistribution in the form of agricultural surpluses left in the fields for the stranger and the impoverished to glean:

> When you reap the harvest of your land, you are not to reap to the very edge of your field or gather the gleanings of your harvest. You must not strip your vineyard bare or gather its fallen grapes. Leave them for the poor and the foreign resident; I am Yahweh your God. (Lev 19:9-10 HCSB)[20]

Deuteronomy called for fair judgment between the Hebrew and the *gār* along with the poor, the widow and the fatherless. Together, these communities formed a kind of protected class inside ancient Israel.[21] "Do not deny justice to a foreigner or fatherless child," Moses wrote, "and do not take a widow's garment as security. Remember that you were a slave in Egypt, and the LORD your God redeemed you from there. Therefore I am commanding you to do this" (Deut 24:17-18 HCSB). Any judge who perverted the judgment of the *gār* would be cursed (Deut 27:19). The Hebrew prophets would go on to repeat the call for minority justice for centuries after (see Jer 7:5-7; 22:3-9; Ezek 22:6-7, 29; Zech 7:10; Mal 3:5).

Yet while many commentators remark on how Moses took pains to protect the *gār*, few note that the concept of *gār* was limited. A *gār* was not just any non-Hebrew living in the land: he was a "resident alien," or "protected stranger." William Robertson Smith, in his classic *Lectures on the Religion of the Semites*, defined the *gār* as "a man of another tribe or district, who, coming to sojourn

---

[18]"You must not exploit a foreign resident or oppress him, since you were foreigners in the land of Egypt" (Ex 22:21 HCSB). "You must not oppress a foreign resident; you yourselves know how it feels to be a foreigner because you were foreigners in the land of Egypt" (Ex 23:9 HCSB).
[19]See also Deuteronomy 10:19.
[20]See also Leviticus 23:22; Deuteronomy 24:19; 26:12.
[21]"Because God's claim on his covenanted community is that they exercise their duty to deal justly with everyone, communally as well as individually, the greatest indictment of this community and its institutions by the prophets was their condemnation of the perversion of the rights of the most helpless members of the community by those with the societal power to do otherwise." Novak, *Covenantal Rights*, 90.

in a place where he was not strengthened by the presence of his own kin, put himself under the protection of a clan or a powerful chief."[22] Drawing on pan-Semitic sources, Smith saw in the ancient *gār* a posture of gratitude and fealty to the clan from which he sought refuge. Reverence for the clan's well-being was implied, and even reverence for the clan's god.[23]

Yet although the *gār* was a loyal resident who merited judicial equity, he did not necessarily enjoy social parity with Hebrew citizens. Employed mainly as laborers and craftsmen, *gērîm* occupied the working classes and rarely attained a position of wealth (Ex 20:10; 23:12; Deut 24:14-15). Hence the need to assign agricultural surpluses to maintain their well-being. While Moses commanded Israelites not to subject their brethren to slavery, he expressly permitted them to enslave the children of resident aliens (cf. Lev 25:39, 45-46). Some *gērîm*—notably Edomites, Egyptians, Ammonites and Moabites—faced generational restrictions on entrance to the congregation of the Lord (see Deut 23:4, 7-8).

Furthermore, while much attention has been paid to the *rights* of the *gār*, very little has been paid to his obligations. The Mosaic system demanded that the *gār* give as well as he got. *Gērîm* were required to observe the sabbath (Ex 20:10; Deut 5:14), practice ritual purification (Num 19:2-10), adhere to some food regulations (Lev 17:10-16) and observe religious festivals (Deut 16:11, 14), including fasting on the Day of Atonement (Lev 16:29). The *gār* was also expected to be loyal to Yahweh against the grain of local paganism (Lev 20:2).

However, there was another class of people in ancient Israel. This class, though non-Hebrews like the *gērîm*, was treated very differently under the law. These *zārîm* were, in a word, "foreigners" (see Ex 29:33). They retained their ties to their original home and sought to maintain their former political or social status. Moses permitted a Hebrew to charge usury from a foreigner but not from a fellow Hebrew (Deut 23:20). Moses also decreed that the periodic forgiveness of debts after seven years did not apply to the *zārîm* (Deut 15:3). Moses also pronounced a blanket prohibition on *zārîm* ever holding the throne (Deut 17:15).

Thus while Christian critics of modern Israel speak loosely of Israel's need to "protect the stranger," they neglect any serious inquiry into the covenantal law in question. Even a cursory reading of that law will show that the concept of

---

[22]William Robertson Smith, *Lectures on the Religion of the Semites* (London: Adam and Charles Black, 1894), 75-76.

[23]Indeed, we see Moses making room for *gērîm* to offer burnt offerings (Lev 17:8; 22:18; Num 15:14) and to sacrifice the Passover lamb if circumcised (Ex 12:48-49; Num 9:14). This suggests that *gērîm* often identified closely with Yahweh and actively worshiped him.

stranger is complex, carrying both rights and obligations and adhering to some non-natives and not to others. When applied to the modern state of Israel—as Israel's critics seem to think it should be—Israel in fact comes out far better than critics think. Commenting on this nuanced view of the stranger under the Mosaic law, Jewish theologian David Novak has suggested that critics need to hold non-Jewish residents in Israel to the same standard of covenantal law:

> The proper Jewish response to suffering at the hands of more powerful others is to extend justice to weaker others over whom Jews might have power. But, of course, in order for gentiles to receive full justice from Jews, they must become at least like a *ger toshav* by demonstrating they accept the basic moral norms the Jewish community regards to be binding on all humankind....
>
> Moreover, just as Jewish citizens of the state ought to acknowledge that the *raison d'être* of this Jewish state is to uphold the communal commandment to acquire the land of Israel and settle it (of which the establishment of a modern nation-state is the best means thereto), even if some individual citizens do not regard themselves to be personally bound by the commandments of the Torah, so too gentile citizens of the state ought to acknowledge the *raison d'être* of the Jewish state they have chosen to live in, even if they themselves do not regard themselves to be bound by [it].[24]

From the Jewish perspective, covenantal righteousness and justice remain immovable targets at which Israel's ethics and politics must be aimed.[25] Normative rabbinic Judaism presumes that the full letter of the Mosaic law, with all its 613 commandments, still applies and that the Jewish people are indeed obligated to execute the various provisions of the covenant with respect to Israel's non-Jewish minority.[26] Shlomo Riskin, the influential chief rabbi of Efrat, has written, "Our right to Israel is not so much a promise as a challenge."[27]

From the Christian perspective, however, things get more complicated. While justice is central to Christianity, and while Christians find themselves in a fallen world acting as agents of a coming kingdom where justice will roll down

---

[24]*Zionism and Judaism: A New Theory* (Cambridge: Cambridge University Press, 2015), 207.
[25]"Only if we establish a just society based upon compassionate righteousness and moral justice can we expect to inherit—and continue to possess—the Promised Land; only thus can we fulfill our purpose as God's covenantal nation, chosen to bring blessing to the world." Shlomo Riskin, *Torah Lights: Devarim—Moses Bequeaths Legacy, History and Covenant* (New Milford: Maggid, 2014), 11.
[26]See Alan Mittleman, *A Short History of Jewish Ethics: Conduct and Character in the Context of Covenant* (West Sussex, UK: Wiley-Blackwell, 2012); and Novak, *Zionism and Judaism*, 197-224.
[27]Riskin, *Torah Lights*, 12.

like waters, the Christian view of covenantal justice is expressly connected with the Christian view of the Mosaic covenant—that is, the Mosaic covenant after the advent of Jesus Christ.

The apostle Paul said the Mosaic law was still—even after the coming of Christ—holy, good and spiritual (Rom 7:12, 14). Yet the Mosaic sacrificial system that depended on temple sacrifices had been only temporary, serving a necessary but passing function until the arrival of a "better [version of the] covenant" (2 Cor 3:7, 11; Gal 3:23-24; Rom 10:4; Heb 8:13). Many Christian commentators have maintained a tripartite division of the Mosaic code into moral, civil and ceremonial law, preserving an enduring role for the moral law even after the coming of Christ.[28] Some see problems with this division—it makes little if any sense to the rabbinic tradition—yet still defend it.[29] Others find it arbitrary and propose more holistic approaches.[30]

But no matter how one treats the Law, the question of covenantal justice quickly becomes problematic from a Christian perspective. Any attempt to apply the standards of a Mosaic theocracy to a modern nation-state—even the state of Israel—will face serious problems. "Christians cannot ignore the law," write two scholars in a recent collection of essays, "but neither can they simply assume its direct, unfiltered relevance to contemporary concerns." The best course of action, they advise, is to "proceed gingerly."[31]

This caution should extend to the prophetic books and their recapitulations of Mosaic material. As two more scholars in the same volume point out,

> We believe it would be improper to read the prophetic literature as containing promises or judgments applicable to current or national world circumstances. In particular, we reject a reading of the Prophets as providing a religious basis for the claim that God has granted to any modern nation a unique role in human history that is akin to the nation of Israel.... We do not believe that any

---

[28]Thomas Aquinas, *Summa Theologica* 2.99.4; John Calvin, *Institutes of the Christian Religion*, trans. Henry Beveridge, vol. 2, 4.20.14 (Cambridge: James Clark, 1962), 663; and *Westminster Confession of Faith* 19.3-5. See also Tertullian, *An Answer to the Jews*, chaps. 2 and 5; and Augustine, *Against Faustus the Manichaean* 6.2.

[29]Walter Kaiser Jr., "The Weightier and Lighter Matters of the Law: Moses, Jesus and Paul," in *Current Issues in Biblical and Patristic Interpretation: Studies in Honor of Merrill C. Tenney*, ed. Gerald F. Hawthorne (Grand Rapids: Eerdmans, 1975), 176-92.

[30]David A. Dorsey, "The Law of Moses and the Christian: A Compromise," *JETS* 34 (1991): 321-34; and J. Daniel Hays, "Applying the Old Testament Law Today," *BSac* 158 (2001): 21-35.

[31]David Skeel and Tremper Longman III, "Criminal and Civil Law in the Torah: The Mosaic Law in Christian Perspective," in *Law and the Bible: Justice, Mercy and Legal Institutions*, Robert F. Cochran Jr. and David VanDrunen (Downers Grove, IL: InterVarsity Press, 2013), 80-83.

one country can be viewed as having a one-to-one relationship with the prophetic word. That word is now refracted through the gospel, where nationalistic boundaries are obliterated and one people of God is formed that is "neither Jew nor Greek" (Gal. 3:28). The prophets, therefore, cannot be read directly as promising blessings or curses on modern nations for particular behavior.[32]

Even if we do not accept the authors' unwillingness to see prophetic reference to modern Israel, we have to agree that the gospel did in fact change how we must interpret the ongoing covenant.

The issues and problems I have raised should make us consider some difficult questions before we make definitive judgments about covenantal justice in the Israeli-Palestinian conflict:

- What is the precise interrelationship between the unilateral Abrahamic and bilateral Mosaic covenants?[33]
- How much of the Mosaic covenant remains in force in the New Testament era? Which parts of it should apply? All of it? Or just the moral parts? How do we differentiate between moral and civil? Should Israel be observing the sabbath year? Should Israeli farmers be leaving the corners of their field uncut for Palestinians to glean?
- Assuming that the Mosaic covenant is still in force, how do the concepts of *gār* and *zār* apply in the context of modern Israel? What about in the disputed territories? Who would be considered *gērîm*? What about *zārîm*? What would be the proper standard of loyalty that would make non-Jews eligible to receive *gār* status? Assuming that the Palestinians qualify as *gērîm*, how would one go about applying to them the various rights and obligations enumerated in the text? What about Palestinians who reject the legitimacy of any Jewish sovereignty in the land of Israel?

Suffice it to say that there are serious hermeneutical and theological complexities that must be overcome before one can confidently declare Israel's breach of the Mosaic covenant for "oppressing the stranger." Covenantal justice is ambiguous, especially in the New Testament era and especially as it applies to a secular state and not a Hebrew theocracy. The tighter one seeks to grasp the concept of covenantal justice, the more slippery it becomes. Meanwhile, the stakes are incredibly high:

---

[32]Barbara A. Armacost and Peter Enns, "Crying out for Justice: Civil Law and the Prophets," in Cochran and VanDrunen, *Law and the Bible*, 132 passim.

[33]For more on these, see the introduction and first chapter of this volume.

Theology and Law

The moral issues posed by Israel's situation are among the most difficult that humans confront in our time since they involve conflicting rights as well as interests and the problem of a people who were committed for nearly 4,000 years to maintaining the highest of moral standards, even when exercising political power.[34]

These moral issues deserve our careful consideration and not hasty judgments based on sloppy readings of the Old Testament. Indeed, to "proceed gingerly" seems to be the only advisable and responsible course of action.

Christian Criticsism of Israel over International Law

Other chapters in this volume detail charges by Christian scholars and leaders that Israel has treated the Palestinian people unfairly. Some of these leaders have particularly focused on international law. For example, Anglican cleric and scholar Stephen Sizer has described Israel as "a materialistic and apartheid State practising repressive and dehumanizing measures against the Palestinians in flagrant disregard of the United Nations and UN declaration of human rights." After quoting Leviticus 18:24-28 and God's requirement to "keep my decrees and laws" (which for Sizer are expressed to some degree in international law) or face ejection from the land, Sizer writes, "On the basis of such a passage, the present brutal, repressive and apartheid policies of the State of Israel would suggest another exile on the horizon rather than a restoration."[35]

Palestinian Lutheran pastor Mitri Raheb goes much further. Unlike Sizer, who emphasizes the Jews' covenantal obligation to regard the stranger and alien to ensure possession of the land, Raheb argues that Jews are *themselves* the strangers and aliens. To hear Raheb tell it, it is the Palestinians who are the real Jews. Citing the controversial work of Shlomo Sand, Raheb argues that the Zionist "Jews" are nothing more than an artificial European nation contrived to secure colonial power in Palestine. "This is the crux of the problem: the natives of the land have been made strangers in order to make room for an invented people to occupy the land."[36]

Turning to the West Bank territories, where Raheb believes Israel has remained in violation of international law, he accuses Israel of designing an

---

[34]Daniel J. Elazar, "Introduction," in *Morality & Power: Contemporary Jewish Views*, ed. Daniel J. Elazar (Lanham, MD: University Press of America, 1990), 4.
[35]Stephen R. Sizer, "An Alternative Theology of the Holy Land: A Critique of Christian Zionism," *Churchman* 113, no. 2 (1999): 7.
[36]Mitri Raheb, *Faith in the Face of Empire: The Bible Through Palestinian Eyes* (Maryknoll, NY: Orbis, 2014), 29.

arbitrary system of control over land, people and resources merely for the sake of "expanding empire." Israel, like all empires in history, holds to an "imperial theology"—a higher logic in which "the violation of human rights needs to have something akin to divine purpose and to be set within an ideological and theological framework."[37]

Sizer and Raheb are among the legion of Christian and secular critics who have alleged that Israel violates international law. Most who make such allegations seem to assume that international law is clear and definitive, and that Israel's violation of it is consequently obvious. The facts of the matter, however, are quite different.

THE PECULIAR NATURE OF INTERNATIONAL LAW

International law is notoriously ambiguous. When religious leaders declaim about human rights, international resolutions and apartheid and use those terms as preludes to declarations that Israel violates international law, they suggest that international law is some kind of higher morality—a universal standard of human behavior written somewhere in the heavens. But this is myth, not fact. It has nothing to do with what international law actually is: namely, law *among* nations, not above them.[38]

And this law is quite different from the laws *of* nations with which most of us are familiar. Let me isolate some key features of international law and then explain them. International law is

- a mostly voluntary system of human rules that is
- largely unenforceable,
- developed over time,
- to some extent arbitrary,
- entered into by self-interested states and
- factually underdetermined.

Modern international law is *mostly voluntary*: that is, it is primarily composed of bilateral and multilateral agreements that states have freely entered into. These agreements, taken together with the ancient principle of *pacta sunt servanda* ("agreements must be kept"), are the bedrock on which international

---

[37]Ibid., 64.
[38]Gerhard von Glahn, *Law Among Nations: An Introduction to Public International Law* (London: Routledge, 2015).

law rests. Indeed, it would not be altogether incorrect to see international law as, first and foremost, an extension of the law of contracts. In recent decades, however, this *conventional law* of mutual agreements has been increasingly augmented by a large and amorphous body of *customary law*, or those practices that states follow from a sense of legal obligation. For example, the majority of states refrain from wars of unprovoked aggression even though they have not made a mutual agreement with neighboring states to so refrain. Taken together, conventional law and customary law constitute the bulk of modern international law.

International law is of different sorts, and not every sort is of equal weight. This is an important point to make at a time when many laypersons think any altruistic, globally directed standard (e.g., "Don't oppress developing countries") qualifies as law. The Dutch jurist Hugo Grotius (1583–1645) used the opening lines of his magnum opus, *The Rights of War and Peace*, to divide the law among nations into rules derived from (1) nature through reason, (2) divine or biblical commands, (3) custom and (4) tacit consent between sovereign governments. One of Grotius's goals in writing his work was to disentangle these various strands and explain how each applied to the modern world. Many of his predecessors had "without any Order, mixed and confounded together those Things that belong severally to the Law Natural, Divine, of Nations, Civil and Canon."[39] Additionally, modern international law makes a clear distinction between the laws of warfare and the laws of human rights—two substantive concepts that have their own intellectual, instrumental and institutional histories but are frequently confused by the uninitiated. Although one could point to various touch points between these legal regimes, none of them are entirely coterminous or ever have been.

The modern law of nations does not always track with morality. In fact, what is commanded or prohibited by international law may in fact violate deeper principles. Consider the following hypothetical: state A is systematically slaughtering its own people, neighboring state B has the power to stop state A, but the United Nations Security Council vetoes a military response. State B is not threatened in any way by the violence taking place next door. Does state B have an obligation to intervene in state A's affairs militarily in order to stop the killing? Or would such an intervention amount to the crime of aggressive war under the Charter of the United Nations? One can imagine different jurists providing

---

[39] Hugo Grotius, *The Rights of War and Peace*, ed. Richard Tuck (Indianapolis: Liberty Fund, 2005), 1:xxxviii.

different answers to this question, as indeed they do.[40] But the point stands: the paths of morality and international law do not always overlap.

In addition to being mostly voluntary, modern international law is also *mostly unenforceable*. That is to say, it lacks coercive power. Absent an overarching world government, states have no venue where they can obtain a dispassionate judgment. They can only self-help, using their instruments of national power (including their militaries) to secure their interests in a chaotic and dangerous world. While several international courts do exist, they lack the teeth to compel compliance with their rulings.[41]

International law has *developed gradually* over time; in other words, there is nothing primeval about it. It only appeared as a coherent concept in the late Middle Ages after having sprung from essentially Christian sources.[42] Yet only in the last century did international law really assume its current form; and only in the aftermath of World War II did it take on so many of the concepts we know so well today: Geneva Conventions, wars of aggression, human rights and genocide. Before World War II these ideas existed, but only afterwards did they become common coin. And it is likely that, with the passage of time, these rules will eventually be supplanted by new rules better suited to the times in which we live.[43] In other words, international law is far from fixed; it constantly evolves.

Much of modern international law is also to some extent *arbitrary*. Although some rules have an underlying moral impulse, the rules themselves are often as contrived as the conventions in which they are written. For example, the Law of Belligerent Occupation is relatively new, the product of the nineteenth- and twentieth-century international conventions. The idea that nations should regulate how their armies behave in the territories of their enemies did not occur to anyone, at least not in a significant way, for most of history. It was only in the aftermath of Napoleon's bloody crusade across Europe that states began to contemplate the benefits of rules. Therefore the Law of Belligerent Occupation as it is articulated in the

---

[40] See "Selected Reading on the Responsibility to Protect," *International Coalition for the Responsibility to Protect*, www.responsibilitytoprotect.org/index.php/component/content/article/628.
[41] Thomas M. Franck, "Legitimacy in the International System," *American Journal of International Law* 82 (1988): 712-59; and Louis Henkin, *How Nations Behave: Law and Foreign Policy*, 2nd ed. (New York: Columbia University Press, 1979), 13-27, 92-98.
[42] Lassa Oppenheim, *International Law: A Treatise* (London: Longman, Green, 1912), 1.i.i.1.
[43] For an insightful look at the potential future of the laws of war, see William C. Banks, ed., *New Battlefields/Old Laws: Critical Debates on Asymmetric Warfare* (New York: Columbia University Press, 2011).

Hague and Geneva Conventions is neither ancient nor immutable. The rules for when occupation starts and ends and how it should be managed are recent innovations devised by states wanting to protect themselves in the event that they lose a war. The misconception shared by many critics of Israel—that "occupation" is somehow, *ipso facto*, unlawful and even immoral—not only misrepresents this law but fails to understand its historical genesis.[44] Indeed, the notion is, as left-wing Israeli author Amos Oz has written, a "deceptively simple point of view."[45]

International law is also only as reliable as the *self-interested states* that adhere to it. Ever since ancient times, men have argued that kings abandon law whenever it is convenient or necessary.[46] In their 2005 study *The Limits of International Law*, Jack Goldsmith and Eric Posner argue that nations' engagement with international law is little more than a function of those nations' self-interest. Rather than being a check on states, compliance with international law—when, in fact, it is complied with—is itself a product of state interest.[47] Although Goldsmith and Posner have many critics, they would say their analysis reflects a realist view of the international system.

Lastly, outcomes of international law are *factually underdetermined*: they are only as good as the evidence available, which is often meager. One obvious problem is that of precedent. Because international law is so new, so fluid and so bereft of case law to address the entire range of human experiences, its "answers" always tend toward unhelpful abstraction and ambiguity. Rarely is there a case or situation directly on point.

Another problem is shortage of proximity. Justice carries a spatial quality that cannot be overlooked. The closer a judge sits to the locus of a case, the greater his odds of rendering perfect judgment. Knowledge of culture, context and locality is critical for determining an equitable result. In the international arena where judgments by definition are nonlocal and where concerns of politics, economics and security often discourage states from allowing outside actors to look for evidence, the odds of reaching a just outcome are proportionally and dramatically diminished.

---

[44]Yoram Dinstein, *The International Law of Belligerent Occupation* (Cambridge: Cambridge University Press, 2009), 2.
[45]Amos Oz, *Israel, Palestine and Peace: Essays* (Boston: Houghton Mifflin Harcourt, 1994), 86.
[46]See Thucydides, *History of the Peloponnesian War*; Cicero, *Pro Milone* 4.11; Lactantius, *The Divine Institutes* 5.xvi.3.
[47]Jack L. Goldsmith and Eric A. Posner, *The Limits of International Law* (Oxford: Oxford University Press, 2005).

None of this should be taken to mean that international law is inconsequential. On the contrary, it provides order, stability and a thin layer of morality that helps facilitate interstate relations. It also operationalizes deeper principles of natural and divine law that are embedded in the universe and the human spirit.

Neither does this mean that international law is not binding. States that are parties to these agreements expect other states to live up to their obligations, particularly those states that enter into them willingly and without coercion. However, failure to abide by these regulations should be seen as a breach of contract, not a breach of the cosmic order.

In light of the above, Christian critics of Israel who rely on international law as the linchpin of their critique should ask themselves, given the internal ambiguities and obstacles to enforcement, whether a judgment of guilt under international law is sufficiently conclusive to justify a public attack on Israel, especially on biblical grounds.

Analysis: The Palestinian Territories

The most complex and controversial legal questions surrounding Israel stem from its acquisition and control of several pieces of territory during the Six-Day War of 1967. And since most legal attacks against Israel begin here, any case in Israel's defense must do the same.

Critics hold that Israel's occupation of these territories is intrinsically unjust and the main reason why the Israeli-Palestinian conflict endures. They see Israel's presence on the West Bank—especially the presence of Jewish civilians who live as minorities in towns called settlements—as unlawful and unconducive to peace in the Middle East. The status of the territories—particularly the West Bank—remains the iron core of the legal argument against Israel and the issue most likely to give rise to penalties in international fora.[48]

---

[48] At the time of writing, the newly christened State of Palestine is bringing the Israeli occupation before the International Court of Justice. The Rome Statute, the treaty that gave birth to the International Criminal Court, was drafted with a unique provision designed to bring Israel under judgment should the opportunity present itself. Rome Statute, art. 8(2)(b)(viii) considers the following, among other items, to be a serious violation: "the transfer, directly or indirectly, by the Occupying Power of parts of its own civilian population into the territory it occupies, or the deportation or transfer of all or parts of the population of the occupied territory within or outside this territory" (www.icc-cpi.int/nr/rdonlyres/ea9aeff7-5752-4f84-be94-0a655eb30e16/0/rome_statute_english.pdf). Fourth Geneva Convention art. 49(6), www.icrc.org/applic/ihl/ihl.nsf/1a13044f3bbb5b8ec12563fb0066f226/523ba38706c71588c12563cd0042c407.

But maintaining that the occupation is unjust and that Jewish civilian presence in the West Bank is illegal under international law is to assert a conclusion without undertaking the necessary analysis. What really happened in the Six-Day War? What is the occupation, how did it start and what is the law that applies to it? What are the territories, and how are they controlled? Who controls them? Too many legal discussions start with the "1967 borders," the settlements or the separation barrier without understanding the history and nature of those borders and settlements. It would be comparable to thinking that the border between East and West Germany (in place between 1945 and 1989) was intended to be permanent without any consideration of the events that led up to the partition of 1945. So too with the Israeli-Palestinian conflict. It is impossible to understand any of these issues without understanding the larger military, political and legal contexts that gave birth to today's dilemmas. In the balance of this chapter I will identify and briefly explain eight essential elements of those contexts.

1. Israel's actions in the Six-Day War were conducted in self-defense in response to overwhelming aggression from surrounding Arab countries. Whether a war is aggressive or defensive makes a significant difference under international law. The Charter of the United Nations criminalized aggressive war. So if Israel launched the Six-Day War aggressively without genuine provocation, all its subsequent activity—including capture of the territories—would be unlawful.[49] If, however, Israel launched the war in anticipatory self-defense, the result is quite different. International law is, as always, unclear, but there seems to be substantial room to argue for the lawfulness of conquest in a defensive situation.[50]

There is no question that Israel fired the first shot of the Six-Day War. However, most experts agree that Israel fired that shot in response to overwhelming existential threats from the surrounding Arab states. In 1948, five Arab countries attempted to destroy the newborn nation. For two decades, the Arab world spewed hateful rhetoric against Israel, sponsored guerrilla raids into Israeli territory and vowed to eradicate the Jewish state from the Middle East. In May of 1967 this hostility reached a fever pitch. Egyptian president

---

[49]Charter of the United Nations, arts. 1, 2, 33, 39, www.un.org/en/charter-united-nations/. But see also art. 51.
[50]Stephen Schwebel, "What Weight to Conquest," in *Justice in International Law: Selected Writings* (Cambridge: Grotius, 1994), 521-25.

Gamal Abdel Nasser expelled the United Nations peacekeepers who had been stationed in the Sinai since 1956 to serve as a buffer force between Israel and Egypt. He piled up large military forces opposite Israel's border in the Sinai and closed off Israel's southern shipping route through the Red Sea. This last move was considered an act of war by all traditional standards. It was also a violation of the Convention on the Territorial Sea and the Contiguous Zone (1958), which called for free navigation for all "through straits used for international navigation between one part of the high seas and . . . the territorial sea of a foreign nation"[51] Nasser meanwhile solidified military pacts with Syria and Jordan, Israel's northern and eastern neighbors, and gave speeches that clearly indicated his hopes of provoking a conflagration that would result in Israel's destruction.[52]

Despite the flood of Arab military preparations and signals, some legal scholars have tried to prove that Israel did not act in self-defense but instead waged a war of conquest using Nasser's hostility as a pretext. John Quigley, the most well-known proponent of this view, dedicated an entire book to this thesis.[53] The book fails, however, because while it tells much about international perceptions, it virtually ignores perceptions inside Israel. The plain fact is that for two decades Israel had been surrounded by hostile Arab armies that openly advocated for its destruction. The Jordanians had been illegally occupying the West Bank since 1948, commanding the strategic ridgeline overlooking the entire population of Israel. The Egyptians had been illegally occupying Gaza during the same period, stationed just miles from Israeli population centers on the coast. Syria, Lebanon, Iraq and Saudi Arabia joined their voices in calling for the eradication of Israel. From Israel's perspective, Nasser's move to block

---

[51]Convention on the Territorial Sea and the Contiguous Zone, Geneva, April 29, 1958, art. 16(4): http://legal.un.org/ilc/texts/instruments/english/conventions/8_1_1958_territorial_sea.pdf.

[52]"Recently, we felt we are strong enough, that if we were to enter a battle with Israel, with God's help, we could triumph. On this basis, we decided to take actual steps. . . . Taking Sharm al Shaykh [and blockading Israeli ships] meant confrontation with Israel. Taking such action also meant that we were ready to enter a general war with Israel. . . . If Israel embarks on an aggression against Syria or Egypt the battle against Israel will be a general one and not confined to one spot on the Syrian or Egyptian borders. . . . Our basic objective will be to destroy Israel." Gamal Abdel Nasser, "Nasser Speech to Arab Trade Unionists" (May 26, 1967), in *The Israel-Arab Reader: A Documentary History of the Middle East Conflict*, ed. Walter Laqueur and Barry Rubin, 6th ed. (New York: Penguin, 2001), 99. For a more general background on the events leading up to the war, see Michael Oren, *Six Days of War: 1967 and the Making of the Modern Middle East* (New York: Random House, 2002).

[53]John Quigley, *The Six-Day War and Israeli Self-Defense: Questioning the Legal Basis for Preventive War* (Cambridge: Cambridge University Press, 2012).

Israel's southern sea passage, amass his forces along Israel's border and conclude a regional military strategy with Syria, Lebanon and Jordan signaled a plan to bring about, as he called it, "the hour of decision."[54] Completely encircled and outnumbered, the Israeli government decided to act first.

Israel's case for self-defense on its eastern front—that is, with respect to the West Bank and Jerusalem—is even stronger. Communicating through an intermediary, Israel promised to leave Jordan alone if Jordan stayed out of the fight. On June 5, Prime Minister Levi Eshkol sent King Hussein a message: "We are engaged in defensive fighting on the Egyptian sector, and we shall not engage ourselves in any action against Jordan, unless Jordan attacks us. Should Jordan attack Israel, we shall go against her with all our might."[55] King Hussein, however, was desperate to prove his Arab nationalist bona fides and fatefully initiated a full-scale attack on Israel that ultimately resulted in his loss of Jerusalem and the West Bank.[56]

Quigley tries, unconvincingly, to argue that Jordan's unprovoked attack on Israel should be considered lawful under the principle of "collective self-defense." In other words, Jordan's attack should be considered lawful because it was done in solidarity with Egypt, a country that, according to Quigley's thesis, was attacked first by Israel. Given the rather clumsy logic of the argument, the quickness with which Quigley disposes of it (less than two pages) and the centrality of the West Bank in all subsequent legal debates, the claim is weak and untenable in light of all known facts. The reality is that Jordan attacked Israel without provocation and in the face of pledges to remain at peace. But for this attack, both the West Bank and East Jerusalem might well have remained under Jordanian occupation until the present.[57]

As in many conflicts, people look at the same facts and see them differently. Israelis look back on June 1967 as an existential crisis that required decisive action to neutralize a relentless enemy bent on annihilation of the Jews. Arabs look back on June 1967 as an instance of unprovoked aggression on the part of foreign colonialists bent on seizing Arab land using whatever pretext they could

---

[54]For a more contemporary Israeli perspective see Abba Eban, "Speech at the Special Assembly of the United Nations" (June 19, 1967), in *The Israel-Arab Reader: A Documentary History of the Middle East Conflict*, ed. Walter Laqueur and Barry Rubin, 7th ed. (New York: Penguin, 2008), 105-10.

[55]*Israel's Foreign Relations: Selected Documents*, vols. 1-2, 1947-1974 (11.16, www.mfa.gov.il/mfa/foreignpolicy/mfadocuments/yearbook1/pages/table%20of%20contents.aspx.

[56]Oren, *Six Days of War*, 127-32.

[57]Quigley, *Six-Day War and Israeli Self-Defense*, 87-88.

find. Quigley himself recognizes the impassable gulf between these two positions. "The difference is not confined to what each side sees as desirable outcomes to the conflict but extends to factual disagreements over what has occurred at critical historical junctures," he explains. "This difference in perception of facts makes it difficult to describe events in a way that will not give rise to objection."[58]

2. The "Palestinian territories" that Israel captured in the war did not belong to anyone else under international law. It is not uncommon to hear people speak of Israel's seizure of Palestinian land in 1967; however, there was no sovereign Palestinian land to be taken, and, at any rate, former Mandate lands were a minority of the lands Israel actually captured. There were four pieces of territory seized from the control of three different states: the West Bank (Jordan), the Gaza Strip (Egypt), the Sinai Peninsula (Egypt) and the Golan Heights (Syria). In total Israel acquired 26,178 square miles of new territory. But the West Bank and Gaza Strip—the only conceivable "Palestinian land" in the mix—were already occupied by Jordan and Egypt, and no Palestinian state had ever existed. So the idea that Israel should return land to a Palestinian entity wrongly supposes there was such an entity to begin with.

The territories were not created equal. Prior to the war, the Sinai Peninsula and the Golan Heights had been under legitimate Egyptian and Syrian sovereignty. They had never been part of Mandatory Palestine, the 2.5 percent segment of the Ottoman Empire that the League of Nations had set aside to create a Jewish national home. Prior to the war, the only recognized sovereign over these territories was the Jewish people as determined by a line of international instruments.[59] While it was true that several plans had been proposed to partition Palestine between Jews and Arabs—including the most famous plan proposed by the United Nations General Assembly in Resolution 181 (1947)—none of those plans were binding or had actually been implemented. Because the Arab nations had immediately invaded the state of Israel on its declaration of independence in 1948 and tried their best to destroy it, seizing the West Bank

---

[58]John Quigley, *The Case for Palestine: An International Law Perspective* (Durham, NC: Duke University Press, 2005), xii.

[59]See the Smuts Resolution (January 30, 1919), interpreted in light of the Balfour Declaration (November 2, 1917), the Lloyd-Clemenceau Agreement (December 1, 1918) and the Weizmann-Feisal Agreement (January 3, 1919); the San Remo Resolution (April 25, 1920); the Franco-British Boundary Convention (December 3, 1920); the Mandate for Palestine (July 24, 1922); and the Anglo-American Convention Respecting the Mandate for Palestine (December 3, 1924).

and Gaza along the way, those partition plans were defunct. The reality on the ground was what the region looked like when the guns stopped shooting.

The upshot of this history is as follows: while many people today believe that Israel conquered Palestinian land in 1967, the reality is that Israel pushed Jordan and Egypt out of the original Mandate for Palestine, dislodging them from their own illegal occupation of Palestinian Arabs.

It is important to understand that the territories acquired in the war—the West Bank, Gaza Strip, Sinai and the Golan Heights—did not represent any ontological or political reality in and of themselves. None of them had ever constituted historic states; each had always been part of a larger state or empire. None were aspiring nations in 1967. Palestinian Arabs had no sense that the West Bank or the Gaza Strip was, in and of itself, anything significant. Their ambitions to sovereignty were aimed solely at razing Israel and erecting an Arab state on the entirety of the land. Neither did the so-called Green Line that separated Israel from its neighbors signify anything meaningful. Although in later years this line was dubbed the 1967 border, it was neither a border nor connected in any way with 1967. The Green Line marked nothing more than the farthest line of Arab aggression against Israel during the 1948 war and explicitly was "not to be interpreted as having any relation whatsoever to ultimate territorial arrangements affecting the two Parties."[60] It was to be held "without prejudice to future territorial settlements or boundary lines or to claims of either Party relating thereto."[61] As the British representative to the United Nations in 1967, Lord Caradon, later said, "[The lines] were just the places the soldiers of each side happened to be the day the fighting stopped in 1948."[62]

3. *Israel planned to exchange the captured territories for peace.* Israeli Prime Minister Eshkol voiced the unequivocal conclusion of Israel's leaders: "Be under no illusion that the State of Israel is prepared to return to the situation that reigned up to a week ago."[63] Their plan was to hold the captured territories,

---

[60] Israeli-Syrian Armistice Agreement (July 20, 1949) art. 5.1.
[61] Israeli-Jordanian Armistice Agreement (April 3, 1949) art. 6.9.
[62] Lord Caradon, interview in the *Daily Star* (Beirut), June 12, 1974, quoted in Steven Carol, *From Jerusalem to the Lion of Judah and Beyond: Israel's Foreign Policy in East Africa* (Bloomington, IN: iUniverse, 2012), 454.
[63] Levi Eshkol, "Statement to the Knesset," *Israel's Foreign Relations: Selected Documents*, vols. 1-2, 1947–1974 (11.23, www.mfa.gov.il/mfa/foreignpolicy/mfadocuments/yearbook1/pages/table%20 of%20contents.aspx. See also Abba Eban: "The Arab states can no longer be permitted to recognize Israel's existence only for the purpose of plotting its elimination. They have come face to face with us in conflict. Let them come face to face with us in peace." Eban, "Speech at the

defend them and exchange them for peace with the Arab states—and possibly with a self-governing Palestinian leadership—if at all possible.[64] Yet this desire was rejected by the Arab states at a meeting on September 1, 1967, in Khartoum, Sudan.

> The Arab Heads of State have agreed to unite their political efforts at the international and diplomatic level to eliminate the effects of the aggression and to ensure the withdrawal of the aggressive Israeli forces from the Arab lands which have been occupied since the aggression of 5 June. This will be done within the framework of the main principles by which the Arab States abide, namely, no peace with Israel, no recognition of Israel, no negotiations with it, and insistence on the rights of the Palestinian people in their own country.[65]

The Israelis saw Khartoum as an "Arab declaration of eternal hostility."[66] Suddenly Israel found itself stuck with lands it never intended to take, much less keep. As Gershom Gorenberg succinctly put it, "Accidentally, Israel had acquired an empire."[67] Faced with the prospect of endless hostility, Israel set out to govern that empire as best as it could, hoping that peace would eventually be possible. This course of action—holding onto territory in the wake of a conflict unless a treaty stipulated otherwise—is entirely typical under the ancient legal doctrine of *uti possidetis*.[68]

4. *The law of occupation may not actually apply to the West Bank and Gaza.* Israel officially maintains that the territories are disputed territories over which there are competing claims that should be resolved in peace talks. The difference between *disputed* and *occupied* is not just a matter of semantics; different bodies of law apply. Occupied territories are subject to occupation law while

---

Special Assembly of the United Nations" (June 19, 1967), in Laqueur and Rubin, *Israel-Arab Reader*, 7th ed., 110.

[64]On June 19, 1967, shortly after the war, the Israeli cabinet already voted secretly to exchange the Sinai and the Golan back to Egypt and Syria in exchange for peace treaties. Gershom Gorenberg, *Accidental Empire: Israel and the Birth of the Settlements 1967-2007* (New York: Henry Holt, 2006), 52-53.

[65]League of Arab States, Khartoum Resolution (September 1, 1967), *Council on Foreign Relations*, http://on.cfr.org/1fDcnqt.

[66]Gorenberg, *Accidental Empire*, 110.

[67]Ibid., 41.

[68]The doctrine of *uti possedetis*, handed down to international law from Roman law, was originally a "provisional remedy between two individuals based on possession and pending a final judicial determination as to ownership." In modern times the doctrine was applied to status of territorial gains at the conclusion of war. Suzanne Lalonde, *Determining Boundaries in a Conflicted World: The Role of Uti Possidetis* (Montreal: McGill-Queen's Press, 2002), 3. See also ICJ 1986 ICJ 554, paras. 20-26.

disputed territories are not. Under General Article 2 of the Geneva Conventions, the law of occupation applies to territory that formerly belonged to "a High Contracting Party." But because no country or people had any legally recognized claim to the territories, and because their possessors on the eve of the Six-Day War were themselves foreign occupiers, the territory may very well not fall within the scope of Geneva Conventions as the territory of a High Contracting Party.[69] If Israel did not occupy the territory of a foreign sovereign but merely repossessed the land that the Allied powers had designated through international legal instruments for a Jewish national home, then the legal analysis is quite different.

5. Israel has substantially performed its obligations as belligerent occupier. Notwithstanding Israel's argument that the law of occupation does not apply to the territories de jure, Israel has nevertheless applied that law de facto. Occupying powers must comply with a range of obligations under international law.[70] Foremost among these are maintaining law and order, ensuring public health and humanitarian well-being, protecting property and upholding, as much as possible, the legal status of the territories as they existed before the war.[71]

One of the most common charges leveled against Israel is that it maintains a two-tiered system of law in the West Bank that is tantamount to apartheid.[72] Christian critics are quick to point to passages in the biblical covenant like Exodus 12:49: "One law shall be to him that is homeborn, and unto the stranger that sojourneth among you" (KJV). They argue that maintaining separate legal

---

[69]Cession of Vessels and Tugs for Navigation on the Danube (August 2, 1921), *Reports of International Arbitral Awards* (United Nations, 2006). But see Dinstein, *International Law of Belligerent Occupation*, 20-25. Israeli Supreme Court also holds this view: HCJ 393/82 Jamait Askan v. IDF Commander of Judea and Samaria, Piskei Din 37:4, 792.

[70]See primarily the Hague Regulations: Laws of War: Laws and Customs of War on Land (Hague IV), October 18, 1907, arts. 42-56; and the Fourth Geneva Convention: Convention (IV) Relative to the Protection of Civilian Persons in Time of War, Geneva, 12 August 1949, part 1, arts. 27-34, 47-78.

[71]Hague Regulations, Hague IV, art. 43, state that the occupying power must "take all the measures in his power to restore, and ensure, as far as possible, public order and safety, while respecting, unless absolutely prevented, the laws in force in the country."

[72]The Rome Statute of the International Criminal Court defines apartheid as "inhumane acts . . . committed in the context of an institutionalized regime of systematic oppression and domination by one racial group over any other racial group or groups and committed with the intention of maintaining that regime," art. 7(2)(h). See also Jimmy Carter, *Palestine: Peace Not Apartheid* (New York: Simon & Schuster, 2006); Virginia Tilley, ed., *Beyond Occupation: Apartheid, Colonialism and International Law in the Occupied Palestinian Territories* (London: Pluto Press, 2012); and Richard Falk, "Situation of Human Rights in the Palestinian Territories Occupied Since 1967," United Nations General Assembly A/65/331 (August 2010).

systems in the territories—one for residents and another for Israeli citizens—is a violation of international law and, possibly, of the covenant.

The apartheid analogy fails in a number of respects, most notably in its misinterpretation of what the territories actually *are*. Apartheid activists talk about political and legal inequality for Palestinians who live there as if the territories are part and parcel of Israel. While after 1967 the status of the territories was ambiguous, since the Oslo Accords of 1993 and 1995 they have not been part of Israel proper. This is why Israeli citizens, both Jews and Arabs, get to vote in Israeli elections while Palestinians in the West Bank and Gaza do not. Those Palestinians who are not Israelis (more than one million Palestinians who live within Israel proper *are* citizens of Israel) do not enjoy the benefits of Israeli citizenship. Legally, politically and administratively the territories are distinct from Israel.

Palestinians who live in the territories fall under Palestinian, not Israeli, governance. Over 95 percent of them live within the legal and political jurisdiction of the Palestinian Authority, an indigenous Arab government created under the Oslo Accords and equipped with its own security forces, legal system and diplomatic corps. The longstanding feud between Fatah and Hamas does not invalidate this fact. As law professor Eugene Kontorovich has written, "It may be sometimes unclear whether the Palestinians are ruled from Ramallah or Gaza City, and their internal politics are far from democratic, but they are certainly not ruled from Jerusalem."[73]

Given that the vast majority of Palestinians are governed by Palestinians, it is hard to claim that Israel maintains an "institutionalized regime of systematic oppression and domination by one racial group." For one thing, Israelis are composed of many races, including black Ethiopian Jews and Arab citizens. Furthermore, for the purposes of statehood recognition, the Palestinian Authority argued to the world that its rule is sovereign and independent—threshold conditions for any would-be state. It goes without saying that the Palestinian Authority could not possibly be sovereign *and* suffering under the thumb of Israeli apartheid at the same time.[74] If Israel actually controlled the Palestinian

---

[73]Eugene Kontorovich, "The Apartheid Libel: A Legal Refutation," *The Tower* (June 2014), www.thetower.org/article/the-apartheid-libel-a-legal-refutation/.

[74]In his letter to the United Nations Secretary General seeking recognition, Abbas wrote, "After decades of displacement, dispossession and the foreign military occupation of my people and with *the successful culmination of our State-building program*, which has been endorsed by the international community . . . it is with great pride and honour that I have submitted to you an

Authority, the latter would not pursue and implement policies that conflict so obviously with those of the former.

It is true that the Israeli Supreme Court frequently applies Israeli jurisdiction to Israeli citizens living in the West Bank who are not Palestinians. But this should hardly be a surprise. The laws of occupation do not demand that an occupying power sacrifice itself or its citizens before the altar of the *status quo ante.* Yet when faced with a civil dispute between an Israeli and a Palestinian, the Supreme Court applies Israeli law to them both equally. "It is important to note that in many cases," a civil rights NGO found, "the application of Israeli law to Israeli employers of Palestinian employees benefits the workers and facilitates a better realization of their rights, due to the protections provided by Israeli labor laws and protective laws."[75] Furthermore, the Supreme Court, sitting as the High Court of Justice, maintains an open-door policy for Palestinians who seek to challenge the administrative policies and practices of state authorities. Israel is under no legal obligation to extend such a right, and is the only occupying power in history to do so. But it is an undisputed fact that she does.

Even many of Israel's left-wing critics reject the apartheid label. Menachem Klein, an Israeli political scientist and vehement opponent of Israeli policy in the territories, describes the situation there as "fundamentally softer and more multilayered" than apartheid.[76] South African jurist Richard Goldstone, author of perhaps the most scathing legal indictment of Israel in recent memory,[77] denies that the West Bank is under apartheid rule, calling the legal situation "more complex" than the situation inside Israel and noting the lack of requisite intent to oppress and continue oppressing on grounds of race. "This is a critical distinction," Goldstone wrote in 2011, "even if Israel acts oppressively toward Palestinians there." He further wrote, "The charge that Israel is an apartheid state is a false and malicious one that precludes, rather than promotes, peace and harmony."[78]

---

application for the admission of the State of Palestine to full membership in the United Nations." Application of Palestine for Admission to Membership in the United Nations, annex II, A/66/371 (September 23, 2011) (emphasis added).

[75]Limor Yehuda et al., "One Rule, Two Legal Systems: Israel's Regime of Laws in the West Bank," Association of Civil Rights in Israel (October 2014), 26, www.acri.org.il/en/wp-content/uploads/2015/02/Two-Systems-of-Law-English-FINAL.pdf.

[76]Menachem Klein, *The Shift: Israel-Palestine from Border Struggle to Ethnic Conflict* (New York: Columbia University Press, 2010), 18.

[77]Report of the United Nations Fact-Finding Mission on the Gaza Conflict, United Nations General Assembly A/HRC/12/48 (September 25, 2009).

[78]Richard Goldstone, "Israel and the Apartheid Slander," *New York Times*, October 31, 2011, A27.

6. The presence of Jewish civilians inside the West Bank does not constitute a war crime under the Geneva Conventions. Most arguments that "Israel violates international law" can be traced back to a single clause of the Fourth Geneva Convention, which states that an "occupying power shall not deport or transfer parts of its own civilian population into the territory it occupies." Critics often cite article 49(6) to indict Israel's policy of allowing Jewish civilians to live inside the West Bank and to build civilian settlements.

According to the official commentary of the International Committee of the Red Cross (1958), article 49 of the Fourth Geneva Convention was derived from the Tokyo Draft of 1934,[79] which prohibited the deportation of the inhabitants of an occupied country and was further inspired by the atrocities committed during World War II when "millions of human beings were torn from their homes, separated from their families and deported from their country, usually under inhumane conditions." Article 49 was "intended to forbid such hateful practices for all time," although "the Diplomatic Conference preferred not to place an absolute prohibition on transfers of all kinds, since some might up to a certain point have the consent of those being transferred." Ultimately the conference decided to allow voluntary population transfers implicitly, only prohibiting "forcible" transfers done without the consent of the transferees.

With respect to clause (6)—a clause that was "adopted after some hesitation"—the drafting committee

> intended to prevent a practice adopted during the Second World War by certain Powers, which transferred portions of their own population to occupied territory for political and racial reasons or in order, as they claimed, to colonize those territories. Such transfers worsened the economic situation of the native population and endangered their separate existence as a race.[80]

This clause was a direct response to the behavior of the Nazis and the Soviets during World War II in moving millions of human beings across national borders against their will. Unlike the Nazis and Soviets, however, Israel has never imported its citizens into the West Bank or Gaza against their will. As

---

[79]"Draft International Convention on the Condition and Protection of Civilians of Enemy Nationality Who Are on Territory Belonging to or Occupied by a Belligerent" (Tokyo, 1934), https://www.icrc.org/applic/ihl/ihl.nsf/Comment.xsp?action=openDocument&documentId=523BA38706C71588C12563CD0042C407.

[80]"Convention (IV) Relative to the Protection of Civilian Persons in Time of War, Geneva, 12 August 1949," Treaties and States Parties to Such Treaties, *Genève, Comité International de la Croix-Rouge*, www.icrc.org/ihl/COM/380-600056.

former Israeli ambassador Alan Baker writes, Israel has "consistently maintained a policy enabling people to reside voluntarily on land that is not privately owned."[81] Forcing transfer and enabling transfer are two very different ideas.

Former dean of Yale Law School and undersecretary of state Eugene Rostow wrote:

> The Jewish settlers in the West Bank are most emphatically volunteers. They have not been "deported" or "transferred" to the area by the Government of Israel, and their movement involves none of the atrocious purposes or harmful effects on the existing population it is the goal of the Geneva Convention to prevent.[82]

A plain reading of article 49(6) and its commentary, taken in conjunction with the historical circumstances from which it emerged, produces two key points: first, that the drafters were addressing states forcing movement of populations and not civilians voluntarily moving and, second, that they worried about evil intent, specifically "political and racial reasons" and colonization. The fact is that Jewish settlers (1) are civilians who (2) volunteer to live in the West Bank (sometimes with the blessing of the Israeli government, frequently against its wishes) (3) for a mix of religious or security reasons (4) who settle outside Arab population centers on public land[83] (5) in numbers so small that they hardly demonstrate malicious intent to de-Arabize the territory. Using the maximum available estimates, Jewish settlers compose only around 12 percent of the population in the territories; Arabs constitute around 88 percent. Drawing analogies from this relatively small movement of civilian homesteaders to massive Nazi deportations in World War II is to miss the meaning of article 49(6).[84]

---

[81] Alan Baker, "The Settlements Issue: Distorting the Geneva Convention and the Oslo Accords," *Jewish Political Studies Review* 23, nos. 3-4 (2011): 35.

[82] Eugene W. Rostow, "Historical Approach to the Issue of Legality of Jewish Settlement Activity," *New Republic*, April 23, 1990.

[83] In a seminal 1979 case, the Israeli Supreme Court found it unlawful for the state to permit Jews to live on private Palestinian land. See HCJ 390/79 Duweikat v. Government of Israel, aDin 34:1 (October 22, 1979). See also archival documents surrounding the case, commonly called the Elon Moreh case, at the website of the Israel State Archives (in Hebrew), www.archives.gov.il/ArchiveGov/pirsumyginzach/HistoricalPublications/ElonMore/.

[84] International law jurist Julius Stone found it absurd that article 49(6), which had been "designed to prevent repetition of Nazi-type genocidal policies of rendering Nazi metropolitan territories *judenrein*," should be applied in a way so as to ensure the West Bank "must be made *judenrein* and so must be maintained, if necessary by the use of force by the government of Israel against

This does not mean that Israel should pursue expansion of Jewish settlements in the West Bank. Asking whether settlements are illegal and whether they are imprudent are two very different questions. And although the state of Israel has consistently answered the first question in the negative, it has more than once answered the second in the affirmative. After signing a peace treaty with Egypt in 1979, Israel began evacuating the entire Sinai Peninsula, including eighteen Jewish settlements containing 1,400 Jewish families. In 2005, in an effort to revive the peace process, Israel unilaterally evacuated from the Gaza Strip (which contained twenty-one settlements) and a small section of the West Bank (which contained four). All told, the 2005 disengagement forcibly relocated approximately 10,000 Jews from their homes. In 2008, Israeli prime minister Ehud Olmert offered Palestinian president Mahmoud Abbas approximately 99.3 percent of the territory that composed the so-called 1967 borders—a move that, if accepted (which it was not), would have entailed the evacuation of tens of thousands of Jews from the West Bank.[85] Between 2010 and 2011 Israeli prime minister Benjamin Netanyahu conducted secret peace negotiations with Syria based on the premise that Israel would completely withdraw from the Golan Heights.[86] Here, too, Jewish towns would necessarily be evacuated.

These evacuations and proposed evacuations all stemmed from Israel's belief that these particular territories and settlements would have to go for the sake of peace. Yet that is not the same as Israel believing that Jewish residence in those settlements was ipso facto contrary to international law.

7. Israel has substantially performed its obligations under United Nations Security Council Resolution 242. In November of 1967, just a few months after the Six-Day War, the United Nations Security Council—which, unlike the United Nations General Assembly, carries the power to bind under international law—passed Resolution 242, which called in its core provisions for:

1(i) Withdrawal of Israeli armed forces from territories occupied in the recent conflict;

---

its own inhabitants." Stone, *Israel and Palestine: Assault on the Law of Nations* (Baltimore: Johns Hopkins University Press, 1981), 179.

[85]Elliott Abrams, *Tested by Zion: The Bush Administration and the Israeli-Palestinian Conflict* (Cambridge: Cambridge University Press, 2013), 290.

[86]Shimon Shiffer, "Netanyahu Agreed to Full Golan Heights Withdrawal," *Yedioth Ahronoth* (December 10, 2012), www.ynetnews.com/articles/0,7340,L-4291337,00.html.

Theology and Law

(ii) Termination of all claims or states of belligerency and respect for and acknowledgment of the sovereignty, territorial integrity and political independence of every State in the area and their right to live in peace within secure and recognized boundaries free from threats or acts of force.

This "land for peace" formula in which Israel would withdraw from territories occupied during the war and, in return, be released from all Arab claims and be recognized as a legitimate state has been the bedrock on which all Arab-Israeli peace efforts have been built since. Israel, Egypt and Jordan accepted the idea in principle (although neither Egypt nor Jordan softened its insistence that all of Palestine belonged to the Arabs). The Palestinians, meanwhile, through their Palestine Liberation Organization (PLO), utterly rejected the concept of land for peace until Yasser Arafat signed the Oslo Declaration of Principles in 1993.[87]

Much attention has been paid to the wording of Resolution 242, especially with respect to Israel's need to withdraw from "territories" rather than "*the* territories," implying that the drafters envisioned a continued Jewish presence in some parts of the occupied territories.[88] Indeed, it appears based on statements

---

[87] The Palestinian Arabs never wavered in their demand for all of Palestine—not some of it—starting in the Mandate period and continuing until the end of the twentieth century. The idea of receiving the West Bank and Gaza as their own state has been fundamentally inconsistent with the Palestinian cause for most of its history. These territories carried no significance as being more Palestinian than the rest of the land. *All* of Palestine needed to be liberated, from the river to the sea. The original Palestine National Charter (1964) stated that "the Partitioning of Palestine in 1947 and the establishment of Israel are illegal and false" and that "the destiny of the Arab Nation and even the essence of Arab existence are firmly tied to the destiny of the Palestine question; from this firm bond stems the effort and struggle of the Arab Nation to liberate Palestine. The People of Palestine assumes the vanguard role in achieving this sacred national goal." The Palestinian National Charter (1968) restated the centrality for armed liberation of all of Palestine on the original draft constitution for the Palestine Liberation Organization (PLO), which stated that "all the Palestinians are natural members in the Liberation Organization exercising their duty in their liberation of their homeland in accordance with their abilities and efficiency." Yasser Arafat's Fatah party released its "Seven Points" in 1969, stating that "Fatah, the Palestine National Liberation Movement, categorically rejects the Security Council Resolution of 22 November 1967 and the Jarring Mission to which it gave rise." In 1974, the Palestine National Council reaffirmed its objection to Resolution 242, "which obliterates the national right of our people and deals with the cause of our people as a problem of refugees," and "therefore refuses to have anything to do with this resolution at any level, Arab or international, including the Geneva Conference." Speaking even more explicitly, the "PLO: Six Point Program" (1977) stated, "We reaffirm our rejection of Security Council resolutions 242 and 338." Laqueur and Rubin, *Israel-Arab Reader*, 215.

[88] See Eugene Kontorovich, "Resolution 242 Revisited: New Evidence on the Required Scope of Israeli Withdrawal," *Chicago Journal of International Law* 127 (2015), http://papers.ssrn.com/sol3/papers.cfm?abstract_id=2534179; Ruth Lapidoth, "The Misleading Interpretation of Security Council Resolution 242 (1967)," in *Israel's Rights as a Nation-State in International Diplomacy*, ed.

from the resolution's drafters that this wording was intentional and that few people expected Israel to completely withdraw from the captured lands.[89]

More interesting, however, is how sweeping Israel's withdrawal from those territories has actually been. Whether Resolution 242 had read "territories" or "the territories," the fact is that Israel has evacuated from almost every inch and offered the remainder in exchange for peace. A simple look at the numbers drives the point home.

Israel captured 26,178 square miles in the Six-Day War. By the end of the 1980s, under the terms of a peace agreement with Egypt, Israel withdrew from the Sinai Peninsula, or 88.4 percent (23,166 sq. mi.) of the 1967 territories. Under the Oslo Accords, when the PLO finally agreed to accept Resolution 242's land-for-peace formula, Israel ceded sovereignty to Areas A and B of the West Bank and Gaza (566.28 sq. mi.), making it a total of 86.5 percent that was relinquished. Then in 2005, Israel vacated Gaza, bringing the total to 87 percent (139 sq. mi.).

In various negotiations post-Oslo, Israel offered the Palestinians virtually all the rest of the 1967 territories in exchange for peace: at Camp David/Taba in 2000/2001, Israel offered somewhere between 92 and 97 percent of the West Bank;[90] in 2008, Israel offered about 99.3 percent (including sovereignty over the Old City of Jerusalem, safe passage between Gaza and the West Bank, and the resettlement of thousands of refugees).[91]

If these offers had been accepted, Israel would have given back 97 percent of all the territories taken in the Six-Day War, with only the Golan—the territory of a self-described enemy state—remaining. And yet Israel has sought to return the Golan to Syria in exchange for peace as well, most recently in 2010 under Prime Minister Benjamin Netanyahu.[92] (Furthermore, although unrelated to the

---

Alan Baker (Jerusalem: Jerusalem Center for Public Affairs, 2011), 85-95; and Alan Dershowitz, *The Case for Israel* (Hoboken, NJ: John Wiley & Sons, 2003), 95-99.

[89] Arthur J. Goldberg, "U.N. Resolution 242: Origin, Meaning and Significance," *National Committee on American Foreign Policy* (April 2002), www.mefacts.com/cache/html/arab-countries/10159.htm; and Eugene V. Rostow, "The Future of Palestine," *Institute for National Strategic Studies*, McNair Paper 24, National Defense University, Washington, DC (November 1993), http://mercury.ethz.ch/serviceengine/Files/ISN/23476/ipublicationdocument_singledocument/a5adb139-2930-415c-ab16-f49b619a7716/en/mcnair24.pdf.

[90] See Dennis Ross, *The Missing Peace: The Inside Story of the Fight for Middle East Peace* (New York: Farrar, Straus & Giroux, 2004).

[91] Elliott Abrams, *Tested by Zion: The Bush Administration and the Israeli-Palestinian Conflict* (Cambridge: Cambridge University Press, 2013), 290.

[92] Isabel Kershner, "Secret Israel-Syria Peace Talks Involved Golan Heights Exit," *New York Times*, October 12, 2012, A4, www.nytimes.com/2012/10/13/world/middleeast/secret-israel-syria-peace-talks-involved-golan-heights-exit.html?_r=0.

Six-Day War, it should not be forgotten that Israel unilaterally withdrew its troops from southern Lebanon in 2000, demonstrating yet further resolve to evacuate territories in the name of peace.)

Historically and mathematically speaking, there is no argument that Israel stands in violation of Resolution 242 or refuses to make concessions for the cause of peace. Indeed, Israel has gone so far as to forcibly remove its own Jewish citizens when the prospect of peace seemed within reach.[93]

8. Palestinians have legal and political autonomy. The most ignored fact about the territories is that, for the first time in history, Palestinian Arabs now hold sovereignty over large swaths of their homeland and control the vast majority of the Arab population inside the Green Line. While the Turks, Jordanians and Egyptians made no effort during their reigns to give Palestinians any kind of autonomy, Israel has done just that. The Palestinian Authority today has its own systems of law, finance, tax, security, governance, education, media, culture and business. It has a seat at the United Nations, diplomatic recognition and embassies around the world. It also collects billions of dollars in international aid. And yet critics of Israel act and speak as if this Palestinian government is just a farce, a legal fiction created by Israel to hide its ongoing oppression.

The idea that Israel is occupying the West Bank and Gaza under the Geneva Convention's meaning of that term is tenuous to say the least. The existence of a self-governing, indigenous Palestinian state (or, at the very least, a proto-state) complicates any application of international law to the territory. The fact that Palestinians can say and do anything they want inside their zone of sovereignty (at least from an Israeli perspective) greatly undermines accusations that Israel is an apartheid state running roughshod over noncitizen Arabs, stealing their land and eating off their dishware. The truth is that Israel has given back huge pieces of land to entities that spent decades trying to destroy it. Israel did not have to do that. But Israel did.[94]

Conclusion

We have seen that the biblical covenant's call for justice is complex. It treats strangers within the land differently from foreigners and stipulates that both of them have obligations. We have also seen that international law is quite different

---

[93]In 1982, Israel forcibly removed about 2,500 Jews living in the Sinai settlement of Yamit. In 2005, it removed over 9,000 Jews from Gaza and four small settlements in Samaria.
[94]Robert Nicholson, "Oslo Accords Unequal? You Bet," *Times of Israel* (blog), August 26, 2013, http://blogs.timesofisrael.com/oslo-accords-unequal-you-bet/.

from biblical justice. It is far more ambiguous, evolutionary and unenforceable. When it is nonetheless applied to the current conflict in Israel/Palestine, an objective reading of the situation must conclude that Israel has in fact complied with international law. That Israel is routinely thought to be in violation stems more from ignorance of the laws involved and prejudice against Israel than the facts on the ground.

Should Israel and her supporters sit back in self-congratulation and ignore the ongoing demands of biblical justice? Of course not. Injustice is a fact of life, given the human condition, so the need to redress injustice is never-ending. Therefore the government of Israel should continue to try to work with those Palestinian leaders who want a separate state and are willing to live in peace with the Jewish state—though at this writing it is not clear if such leaders exist.[95] Israel should continue to prosecute Israeli citizens who do violence to Palestinian people and property. The state should continue to make available to Israeli Arabs high-quality healthcare and education. She should also teach her own citizens (who are Arab, Jewish and other ethnic/religious groups) in the public square and in her schools that Palestinians are created by God in his image and are entitled to respect and the fullness of human rights. Let us hope and pray that Palestinians do the same.

---

[95]The present leaders continue to glorify as "martyrs" terrorists who have purposely maimed and killed innocent Israeli elderly, women and children.

10

THEOLOGY AND MORALITY

*Is Modern Israel Faithful to the Moral Demands
of the Covenant in Its Treatment of Minorities?*

Shadi Khalloul

◆

The Bible calls for justice and morality in the covenant. In this chapter I want to consider whether modern Israel is violating the biblical principle that a political state ought to be just, upholding basic principles of morality. My question, then, can be stated as follows: is modern Israel faithful to the moral demands of the covenant in its treatment of Palestinians and other non-Jews, like the Arameans?

To understand the issue, it is important to show that the original Christians of Israel are in fact not Arabs or Palestinians but Arameans, who have deep roots in the region and who are related to Israel and its people ethnically, culturally, linguistically and religiously. Before answering the question of the morality of the Jewish state, I will therefore explain these common roots and how they are related to the question I have just posed.

The Arameans are a Semitic people, native to the area that includes parts of today's Israel, Jordan, Lebanon, Syria, Iraq and Turkey.[1] The ancient Arameans strode onto the world stage in the second millennium BC and later established kingdoms such as Aram Naharayim, Paddan Aram, Aram Tzova and Aram Damascus, which are mentioned in the Bible and other Jewish sources. For

---

[1] See Herbert Niehr, ed., *The Aramaeans in Ancient Syria* (Leiden: Brill, 2010); and Sebastian Brock, *The Hidden Pearl: The Syrian Orthodox Church and Its Ancient Aramaic Heritage* (Rome: Trans World Film Italia, 2001).

example, the Bible tells the story of Hazael, whose name means "God has seen" and who was the king of Aram Damascus in the ninth century BC. According to the story in 1 Kings, God ordered the prophet Elijah to anoint Hazael king over Aram Damascus, even though he was not an Israelite.[2]

After their dominance ended, the Arameans lived under a succession of empires—Assyrian, Babylonian, Persian, Greek, Roman, Arab and Turkish. In the late seventh century BC Aramaic became the lingua franca of the whole region. It was adopted by the Jews in the sixth century BC as a parallel tongue to Hebrew and used in some of the biblical books as well as parts of the Talmud. It fell into widespread disuse only after the Arab conquests of the seventh century AD. The Ktuba, a Jewish wedding prayer, is still in Aramaic.

Among the first Christians in Antioch there were Aramaic-speaking Jews, who were more traditional and conservative than the Greek-speaking hellenized Jews.[3] There were also Arameans, whom later historians called Syrians (since the Greek Seleucid Empire conquered the region and applied the Greek name Syria to the land of Aram).[4]

The Aramaic (Syriac) liturgy—still used by many Aramaic churches, especially the Syriac Orthodox Church of Antioch and the Syriac Maronite Church of Antioch—is one of the oldest existent liturgies. Significantly, it contains Jewish customs and patterns that demonstrate the connections between the Jewish people and Aramaic culture. For example, there is deep emphasis on the Old Testament in the liturgy, as seen in the repeated intonation of important Jewish luminaries such as Abraham, Isaac, Jacob (Israel), Moses, David, the Jewish prophets, Job and Daniel. There is also heightened emphasis on the sac-

---

[2]"Then the LORD said to him, 'Go, return on your way to the wilderness of Damascus; when you arrive, you shall anoint Hazael as king over Aram'" (1 Kings 19:15). According to the biblical text, Hazael and his predecessor Ben-Hadad call the God of Israel "Lord": "Elisha went to Damascus while King Ben-hadad of Aram was ill. When it was told him, 'The man of God has come here,' the king said to Hazael, 'Take a present with you and go to meet the man of God. Inquire of the LORD through him, whether I shall recover from this illness'" (2 Kings 8:7-8).

[3]For the ancient Christian community in Antioch see Magnus Zetterholm, *The Formation of Christianity in Antioch: A Social-Scientific Approach to the Separation Between Judaism and Christianity* (London: Routledge, 2003); Cynthia White, *The Emergence of Christianity* (Westport, CT: Greenwood, 2007); and James Carleton Paget, *Jews, Christians and Jewish Christians in Antiquity* (Tübingen: Mohr Siebeck 2010).

[4]There is evidence, from both Syriac church fathers and ancient historians, that the peoples called Syrians are in fact what I am calling Arameans. For example, Flavius Josephus writes in his *Jewish Antiquities*: "Aramus ruled the Aramaeans, whom the Greeks term Syrians." Josephus, *Jewish Antiquities*, in *Josephus: In Nine Volumes*, trans. Henry St. J. Thackeray (Cambridge, MA: Harvard University Press, 1961), 4:71.

rificial act. Even the interior architecture points to Jewish roots: in Syriac (Aramean) churches there is an ark with a veil and candle to hold the Scripture (similar to the ark in a synagogue that holds the Torah) and a seat for the bishop, which represents the seat of Moses. According to Louis Bouyer, "The old Syrian church appears as a Christianized version of a Jewish synagogue," to which the Eucharist service as a modified temple rite was added.[5]

I am an Israeli Christian of Aramean descent. Since Aramaic culture has been so heavily shaped by Jewish roots and Jewish ways of thinking, we Arameans consider the fathers of Israel to be our fathers too. So I will go to these fathers and try to explain their perspective on the land in order to explain my Aramaic culture. This will help readers understand how my community in Israel—a non-Jewish community—understands the question of morality and justice for non-Jews in today's Israel.

Israel as God's Beloved Child: The Relationship Binding God, People and Land

Throughout the Tanak (the Hebrew word for the Old Testament) and New Testament, a relationship of universal importance is described: that between God and Israel. God's love for his chosen people is a pervasive theme of the Scriptures:

> It was not because you were more numerous than any other people that the LORD set his heart on you and chose you—for you were the fewest of all peoples. It was because the LORD loved you and kept the oath that he swore to your ancestors, that the LORD has brought you out with a mighty hand, and redeemed you from the house of slavery, from the hand of Pharaoh king of Egypt. Know therefore that the LORD your God is God, the faithful God who maintains covenant loyalty with those who love him and keep his commandments, to a thousand generations. (Deut 7:7-9)

The Bible tells us that the establishment of Israel and the birth of the Messiah emerged from this relationship. Through his covenant with Abraham, Isaac and Jacob, God established a nation for himself that included a land and people.

> Reside in this land as an alien, and I will be with you, and will bless you; for to you and to your descendants I will give all these lands, and I will fulfill the oath that I swore to your father Abraham. I will make your offspring as

---

[5]Louis Bouyer, *Eucharist* (Notre Dame, IN: Notre Dame University Press, 1968), 25. See also Benjamin D. Williams and Harold B. Anstall, *Orthodox Worship: A Living Continuity with the Synagogue, the Temple and the Early Church* (Minneapolis: Light and Life, 1990).

> numerous as the stars of heaven, and will give to your offspring all these lands; and all the nations of the earth shall gain blessing for themselves through your offspring. (Gen 26:3-4)

God chose Abraham, Isaac and Jacob because of his everlasting love and faithfulness. These men were sinners who nevertheless trusted God's promises, and, in doing so, they became the fathers of a people who carried God's love and word throughout the world of the ancient Near East. Because of God's love, Abraham was brought to a land where he and his descendants could live and prosper. According to Scripture, it was "a land flowing with milk and honey" (Deut 26:9). Just as a father wants his children to be safe, God sent Abraham to a land that would be his, safe for the development of a people and a faith.

So God linked the people of Israel to a certain territory. The land became a holy (lit., "set apart") land because God chose it to be the land for his holy (again, "set apart") people. Hence, the people of Israel were connected to the land of Israel by God's decision. When they were delivered from Egyptian captivity, God gave them his law and brought them to this Promised Land where they could live out that law.

Later, on this holy soil, King David united his people to be a God-serving nation. They fell from this faith many times and were disciplined by their loving Father by two bitter experiences of exile. But through those many centuries they kept returning to their heavenly Father and his law. It was also on this holy soil where a descendant from the house of David was born to reconcile all humankind with God: the Messiah or, as we say in Aramaic, *Mashiach*—whom the New Testament identifies as Jesus of Nazareth.

We Christians know that it was this Messiah who brought salvation for the whole world. If this is true, how can we fail to love Israel, the land and the people? Shouldn't we love, honor and respect the descendants of Abraham, Isaac and Jacob?

In the last two thousand years, the children of Israel have faced the greatest tragedies imaginable. Christians have killed hundreds of thousands—perhaps even millions—of Jews. Jews have been hounded out of countries and forced from their livelihoods. Yet through it all, God has demonstrated his faithfulness. No other ancient people has survived such exiles and persecutions and returned to its ancient land to establish a nation.

The amazing persistence of Israel is powerful evidence that the Tanak is still valid and Israel is still God's partner in the covenant. How could this regathering of the Jewish people to today's Israel occur without the intervention of God, who fulfills his oath and promises? We Arameans believe that these remarkable events in our own lifetimes attest to the biblical testimony that it was not their decision but God's will that the children of Abraham, Isaac and Jacob live in that land and that Jerusalem is their holy city. As Jeremiah wrote two and a half millennia ago, God promised to keep Israel as his people through all the vicissitudes of history.

> Thus says the LORD,
> who gives the sun for light by day
>   and the fixed order of the moon and the stars for light by night,
> who stirs up the sea so that its waves roar—
>   the LORD of hosts is his name:
> If this fixed order were ever to cease
>   from my presence, says the LORD,
> then also the offspring of Israel would cease
>   to *be a nation before me forever*. (Jer 31:35-36; emphasis added)

We Arameans believe that only because of God's faithfulness to his people "being a nation before me forever" could this people have resisted elimination and assimilation for more than three thousand years.

ARAMI OVED AVI: THE ARAMEAN FATHERS OF ISRAEL

In ancient times, when the firstfruits were brought to the temple, Jews recited the following words from Deuteronomy 26:5: *Arami Oved Avi*, which means "My father was a wandering Aramean." Since it was common for first-century Jews to bring the firstfruits to the temple, we can be sure that Jesus said these words when he visited the temple every year: *Arami Oved Avi*.

But to whom does the Bible refer when it says *Arami Oved Avi*? Who was the father who was a wandering Aramean? Or, as it could also be rendered, the father who was a "suffering/homeless/lost Aramean"? Let us look at the larger passage in which this statement is contained.

> When you have come into the land that the LORD your God is giving you as an inheritance to possess, and you possess it, and settle in it, you shall take some of the first of all the fruit of the ground, which you harvest from the land

that the Lord your God is giving you, and you shall put it in a basket and go to the place that the Lord your God will choose as a dwelling for his name. You shall go to the priest who is in office at that time, and say to him, "Today I declare to the Lord your God that I have come into the land that the Lord swore to our ancestors to give us." When the priest takes the basket from your hand and sets it down before the altar of the Lord your God, you shall make this response before the Lord your God: "A wandering Aramean was my ancestor; he went down into Egypt and lived there as an alien, few in number, and there he became a great nation, mighty and populous. When the Egyptians treated us harshly and afflicted us, by imposing hard labor on us, we cried to the Lord, the God of our ancestors; the Lord heard our voice and saw our affliction, our toil, and our oppression. The Lord brought us out of Egypt with a mighty hand and an outstretched arm, with a terrifying display of power, and with signs and wonders; and he brought us into this place and gave us this land, a land flowing with milk and honey. So now I bring the first of the fruit of the ground that you, O Lord, have given me." You shall set it down before the Lord your God and bow down before the Lord your God. Then you, together with the Levites and the aliens who reside among you, shall celebrate with all the bounty that the Lord your God has given to you and to your house.

When you have finished paying all the tithe of your produce in the third year (which is the year of the tithe), giving it to the Levites, the aliens, the orphans, and the widows, so that they may eat their fill within your towns, then you shall say before the Lord your God: "I have removed the sacred portion from the house, and I have given it to the Levites, the resident aliens, the orphans, and the widows, in accordance with your entire commandment that you commanded me; I have neither transgressed nor forgotten any of your commandments: I have not eaten of it while in mourning; I have not removed any of it while I was unclean; and I have not offered any of it to the dead. I have obeyed the Lord my God, doing just as you commanded me. Look down from your holy habitation, from heaven, and bless your people Israel and the ground that you have given us, as you swore to our ancestors—a land flowing with milk and honey." (Deut 26:1-15)

This passage suggests that only Jacob, whom God gave the name *Israel* and appointed to be the father of a new nation, can be meant. The prayer that was to be uttered at the temple claims that God is the creator and founder of the people of Israel and that *God made Israel out of another struggling people, the Arameans.*

Jacob was Aramean, we are told here, just as his forefathers Abraham and Isaac were. The wives of the patriarchs were also Arameans:

> Then Isaac called Jacob and blessed him, and charged him, "You shall not marry one of the Canaanite women. Go at once to Paddan-aram to the house of Bethuel, your mother's father; and take as wife from there one of the daughters of Laban, your mother's brother. May God Almighty bless you and make you fruitful and numerous, that you may become a company of peoples. May he give to you the blessing of Abraham, to you and to your offspring with you, so that you may take possession of the land where you now live as an alien—land that God gave to Abraham." Thus Isaac sent Jacob away; and he went to Paddan-aram, to Laban son of Bethuel the Aramean, the brother of Rebekah, Jacob's and Esau's mother. (Gen 28:1-5)

Isaac forbade Jacob to marry a woman who was not Aramean. We believe that this shows the deep connection between Israel and the Arameans. I think it shows two other things as well: God's control of history and the difference between Arameans and Jews. God changed the natural course of history and determined it through his decision and hand. Instead of leaving Jacob within the natural borders of an existing people (the Arameans), he created a new people for himself, a people who were to follow his will and establish his law on earth. He gave them the name he himself chose: Israel. The prayer begins with the saying "my father was a wandering Aramean" in order to make clear that it was a direct act of God that transformed one people into another and that created the people of Israel apart from the ordinary development of existing tribes and peoples.

This passage shows still a third principle: Israel is specially connected to God because he established its name and nation. There is no Israel without God. He appointed Israel to be a holy (again, it means "set apart"), God-serving nation. We Arameans believe the name Israel itself is holy because it comes from God; theologically, we think it is therefore important to bless this name and the people called by this name. There is no other people of this kind—created by God's direct intervention in history. By creating the people and linking it to a certain territory, Scripture makes clear that this people is a part of God's everlasting plan for the salvation of humanity. This is why he rescued his people from captivity in Egypt and brought them to the land that he promised they would have forever.

These are some of the theological reasons that we Arameans support Israel. We believe that we have close ethnic and religious ties with them. We even sometimes call our sons Israel, showing our connection to God's chosen people.

Civil Rights

But if we feel connected to the land of Israel and its Jewish people, how does Israel feel about us? Or more importantly, how does Israel *treat* us as a non-Jewish minority? And, as it is often asked today, how does Israel treat Palestinians and other non-Jews? They represent about 24 percent of the Israeli population and consist primarily of Arabic-speaking groups. Israel claims the Torah in some sense, despite its being a secular state, and the Torah calls for justice and morality in its covenant. Does Israel seek to uphold what most of us would say is just and moral in its treatment of these minorities? These are the questions I seek to address in the remainder of this chapter.

Israel's declaration of independence (formally known as the Declaration of the Establishment of the State of Israel, proclaimed on May 14, 1948) guarantees "full social and political equality of all its citizens without distinction of race, creed and sex."[6] My answers to the questions above are essentially affirmative. While no state is perfect, and Israel has its own share of imperfections, it nevertheless seeks to uphold the ideal stated in this declaration. Its attempts to provide for the civil rights of minorities are remarkable, especially when compared to the other nations of the Middle East.

Among Israel's imperfections is its recent treatment of the Maronites, a Christian community of ten thousand Israeli citizens. Their loyalty to Israel has been evident for many decades. Their leaders spoke out in the early twentieth century against persecution of Jews in both Germany and Palestine. In 1937 the Christian Maronite patriarch, who had settled in Lebanon, met with Jews at their synagogue in Beirut and explained his plan under the French mandate to allow Jews to settle in Lebanon. He told them that Jews and Maronite Christians share common origins and similar languages—Aramaic and Hebrew. Arab Muslims held many demonstrations in Damascus and Beirut to protest the patriarch's support for Jews. Maronites also helped hide Jews who were escaping Europe during World War II so that they could pass through Lebanon to Jewish

---

[6]"Establishment of Israel: The Declaration of the Establishment of the State of Israel," *Jewish Virtual Library*, accessed January 13, 2016, www.jewishvirtuallibrary.org/jsource/History/Dec_of_Indep.html (author's translation).

settlements in Israel. In 1976 the Israeli Foreign Affairs office published a UNSCOP (United Nations Special Committee on Palestine) recommendation of the Syriac Aramaic Maronite Church that Israel and Lebanon be recognized as the Jewish and Christian states, respectively, that were havens for persecuted minorities in the Middle East.[7]

But there is a stain on the record of Israel's treatment of this loyal minority, many of whose citizens serve in the IDF (Israel Defense Forces). In 1948 residents of the Aramaic Maronite village of Kfar Baram in northern Israel were told by Jewish fighters to leave for two weeks, with the promise that they could return when fighting subsided. The Jews were afraid that these Christians might join the Arab war against them. The two weeks have turned into sixty-seven years (at this writing), and the Maronites are still waiting. These Maronites feel the sting, especially because Israel has built villages on the hills of Galilee for Arab citizens who sometimes turn against them, but the Maronite community has always been loyal.[8]

This and other situations notwithstanding, Israel has made great strides in social and religious equality for minority communities. We Arameans were officially recognized by the state of Israel in September 2014 as a distinct ethnic and religious group. This means that Israel recognized the existence of a Christian people within its borders. The Jewish state supports us and gives us the legal right to exist and develop ourselves as a Christian minority. This is unprecedented in today's Middle East. It demonstrates a level of justice that is not accorded to any religious minority by any other country in the Middle East.

Yet the state of Israel is doing more than simply giving recognition of the existence of minorities. It has initiated and continues to maintain a wide variety of social and cultural programs to support minority communities. Even though the majority of Muslim Arab Palestinians do not want to integrate and be part of Israel, viewing this country as their enemy, Israel still supports their interests by preserving their cultural heritage, language and religion. For example, the Arab-speaking minority has a representative in a special department of the Israeli Ministry of Education responsible for the promotion

---

[7] For this history, see Edmund Meir, "The Maronites: With Special Regard to the Political Development Since 1860," June 24, 1942, *Central Zionist Archive* (Jerusalem), S25/6639. Meir shows that "the Maronites are direct descendants of the Syrian-Aramaic population who inhabited Syria at the time of the Moslem conquest in the seventh century" (ibid., 2).

[8] Ryan Jones, "Israeli Christians Urge Israel to Rebuild Their Village," *Israel Today*, May 27, 2014, www.israeltoday.co.il/NewsItem/tabid/178/nid/24642/Default.aspx?article=related_stories.

of the identity, roots, language and religion of the Arabs in the country. The state develops programs, together with representatives from the Palestinian Arab community, to teach Arabic and Islamic history. At the same time that Israel is (unjustifiably) accused of ethnic cleansing and other crimes, it strengthens and preserves the culture of those who want to wipe out the state. Israel does not force its Arab minority to join the defense forces, while Jews and Druze sacrifice three years of their lives to protect their fellow citizens, Arab and Aramean and Jewish. (Critics will charge—falsely—that IDF soldiers do not protect non-Jews, but they forget that terrorism and war have killed Jews and non-Jews alike.)

Readers might be surprised to learn that the government of Israel has affirmative action programs for Arabs.

> Affirmative action policies initiated under Ehud Olmert were accelerated during the Netanyahu administration. These prioritized economic development, including allocating funds for joint industrial parks in Arab and Jewish towns. Subsidies helped firms hire Arab labor and expanded transportation infrastructure, which allowed Arabs to reach employment sites. These ventures were so successful that the government began setting up industrial parks and employment offices exclusively in Arab towns. In addition, the Israeli government developed a five-year plan for improving Arab education and established a special unit in the prime minister's office to promote economic development in the Arab community.[9]

I have personally experienced social equality as a minority in Israel. When I was nineteen years old, as a young paratrooper lieutenant, I led almost one hundred Jewish soldiers in the field. I was in charge, responsible for all their needs. The IDF trusted my loyalty by putting into my hands the precious lives of one hundred young soldiers fresh out of high school. I acted as their father when we were away from home for most of their three years of military service. Fifteen hundred Christian soldiers are receiving the same care today from young Jewish Zionist officers. Since I retired from the military, I have had many different positions in business and society in Israel, enjoying freedom and job opportunities like any Israeli who wishes to have a successful career.

---

[9]Robert Cherry, "Netanyahu and the Israeli Arabs: The Untold Story," *Mida*, July 9, 2015, http://mida.org.il/2015/07/09/netanyahu-and-the-israeli-arabs-the-untold-story/.

More importantly, Israel protects the political rights of its minorities, and this is unique in the Middle East. The state guarantees its non-Jewish citizens all the rights and privileges of Israeli citizenship. When the first elections to the Knesset (Israel's parliament) were held in 1949, Israeli Arabs were given the right to vote and to be elected. Today, Israel's non-Jewish minorities are granted full political rights and are entitled to complete participation in Israeli society. They are active in Israeli social, political and civic life and enjoy representation in the Knesset, Foreign Service and judicial system.[10] As I already mentioned, many of us join the IDF. Last year I ran for a seat in the Knesset.

We minorities also get to enjoy nearly free medical care in one of the best medical systems in the world. We have full economic freedom to start a business and participate fully in one of the most vibrant economies in the world, and certainly the healthiest economy in the Middle East. Our children get free education in excellent schools, and we Christians can send them to schools that reinforce our faith. We feel privileged indeed.

Yet even more important than all these civil rights is religious freedom, which is—once again—a rare commodity in the Middle East. Benjamin Netanyahu has his critics, but he was accurate when he said the following:

> Israel's minorities, including over one million citizens who are Arabs, always have full civil rights. Israel's government will never tolerate discrimination against women. Israel's Christian population will always be free to practice their faith. This is the only place in the Middle East where Christians are fully free to practice their faith. They don't have to fear; they don't have to flee. In a time where Christians are under siege in so many places, in so many lands in the Middle East, I'm proud that in Israel Christians are free to practice their faith and that there's a thriving Christian community in Israel.[11]

CHRISTIANS IN ISRAEL

This is one of many ways in which Christians flourish in Israel. News media regularly report that Christians are fleeing the Middle East because of ethnic cleansing perpetrated by radical Muslims, and most recently by the Islamic State. But what has gone unreported by most of the media is that there is one place in

---

[10]"Minorities in Israel," *Israel Record*, Anti-Defamation League, accessed January 13, 2016, http://archive.adl.org/israel/record/minorities.html.

[11]"People: Minority Communities," *Israel Ministry of Foreign Affairs*, accessed January 13, 2016, www.mfa.gov.il/mfa/aboutisrael/people/pages/society-%20minority%20communities.aspx.

the Middle East where the Christian population has steadily risen for six decades—Israel proper (that is, outside of the West Bank, which is not controlled by Israel). Today there are 1.5 million Arabs who are descended from those who stayed in Israel after 1948. In addition, there are 160,000 Arabic-speaking Christians of Aramaic-Syriac roots whose families go back to the land long before Islamic occupation in the seventh century.

Their lives in Israel today differ markedly from those of Christians who have lived for centuries in dhimmitude (second-class) status under Arab-Islamic regimes or secular nations with an Arab or Islamic majority. They also differ markedly from the pitiful lives of Christians today in Iraq, Syria, Egypt and Lebanon. Their numbers have been decreasing since the last century, and now many are facing rape, massacres and forced Islamization. The contrast with life in Israel could hardly be greater: Christians here are increasing in numbers, enjoying democracy in all of its best aspects—freedom of religion, movement and speech. People from all genders and religions enjoy a higher quality of life than in most developed nations and even in some Western social democracies.

Civil Rights Even for Enemies

If Israel provides civil rights for all of its citizens—Jewish and non-Jewish— there is something even more remarkable. Many of its citizens treat the state as its enemy, and yet the state continues to provide these same rights to them. This too is unheard of in the Middle East.

The irony is that there are Arab members of the Knesset who have full rights as citizens even though they do not show loyalty to the state and curse it at every opportunity. Israel supports and protects the people, culture, language and religion of those who want to destroy it. These extreme circumstances prove that Israel is faithful to its moral values even when it is provoked in extreme circumstances.

That has been its history with its neighbors. Israel has always wanted peace with its neighbors but has been provoked into war repeatedly. Like most nations, Israel wants peace and prosperity. Its citizens hate violence and death. But sadly, its neighbors and even some of its own citizens seem to prefer violence and death. As Golda Meir once lamented, "When peace comes we will perhaps in time be able to forgive the Arabs for killing our sons, but it will be harder for us to forgive them for having forced us to kill their sons."[12]

---

[12]Golda Meir, statement at a press conference in London 1969, as quoted in *A Land of Our Own: An Oral Autobiography*, ed. Marie Syrkin (New York: Putnam, 1973), 242.

It is not enough to want peace for there to be an end to violence and war. Not if the other party hates you, for dark theological reasons (which I will mention below), and wants to wipe you out. Again Golda Meir's comment was insightful: "Peace will come to the Middle East when the Arabs love their children more than they hate us."[13]

This actually underlines Israel's morality. She gives full civil rights to citizens who hate her and sometimes act in cooperation with forces bent on her destruction. Israel also showed her commitment to morality in its 2014 summer war with Hamas in Gaza. According to the High Level International Military Group, a consortium of some of the world's leading military experts, Israel went out of its way to minimize civilian casualties and observe international law during the crackdown in Gaza, even to the point of costing the lives of its own soldiers and citizens. Despite a daily barrage of rockets, often launched from schools, mosques and hospitals within Gaza, Israel went to great lengths to follow laws governing armed conflict after launching Operation Protective Edge on July 8, 2014. The fighting was sparked by daily rocket and tunnel attacks mounted from Gaza, as well as the kidnapping and murder of three Israeli teens by Hamas operatives, and lasted for seven weeks, leaving more than two thousand dead. "Israel not only met a reasonable international standard of observance of the laws of armed conflict, but in many cases significantly exceeded that standard," states the report, sponsored by the Friends of Israel Initiative.[14]

General Klaus Naumann, former chief of staff of the German armed forces, observed, "A measure of the seriousness with which Israel took its moral duties and its responsibilities under the laws of armed conflict is that in some cases Israel's scrupulous adherence to the laws of war cost Israeli soldiers' and civilians' lives."[15]

DOUBLE STANDARDS

Unfortunately, Israel's morality is invisible to much of the world because of the double standards that are applied by other states and world media. Consider the following strange anomalies.

---

[13]Golda Meir (1957), as quoted in *Midstream* 25 (1979): 58.
[14]"Key Preliminary Findings of the High Level International Military Group on the Gaza Conflict," *UN Watch*, June 15, 2015.
[15]Ibid.

1. In 1947 Israel's first prime minister, David Ben-Gurion, said he wanted Arab citizens to feel at home in Israel: "If the Arab citizen will feel at home in our state . . . if the state will help them in a truthful and dedicated way to reach the economic, social, and cultural level of the Jewish community, then Arab distrust will accordingly subside and a bridge will be built to a Semitic, Jewish-Arab alliance."[16] His hope was that Arabs would be fully integrated and feel welcomed. What Muslim state or leader says this to its non-Muslim citizens? The answer is none. Why does the media not report this?

2. Israel works hard to integrate our minority group of Arameans and other minority groups into Israel's larger society, but I doubt that Iran or any other Muslim state has a single program that benefits Christians or other minority groups, with the purpose of sustaining their identity. Why is this not noticed?

3. Palestinians in Israel have more freedom of speech and religion than in any other Arab country in the Middle East. King Hussein massacred thousands of Palestinians during the Black September of 1970 for protesting against him, and all the Arab states backed him. Hamas in Gaza slaughtered almost one thousand Fatah Palestinians in order to consolidate its own rule, and the Arabs kept silent. Israel allows its Arab citizens to practice their democratic rights, to protest and even curse the state and still enjoy freedom from the Zionist state. Why are these anomalies never cited when Israel is routinely excoriated in the media?

4. Israel allows Christians many rights that other Christians in Arabs countries can only dream of. In Israel, a Christian lieutenant can lead young Jewish soldiers to any mission and be in charge. Israeli Christians are well respected and well treated, and the majority of them want to identify themselves as Israelis rather than as Palestinians. According to a census done by Open University sociologist Sammy Smooha among Israeli Arabs, "60% of Israeli Christians, 90% of Druze, and 48% of Muslims in Israel see themselves as Israelis and not as Palestinians."[17] Why is this rarely reported?

5. In Israel, a Christian or even a Muslim can be elected as prime minister. Only in Israel can you find members of parliament (the Knesset) siding with

---

[16] Quoted in Efraim Karsh, *Fabricating Israeli History: The "New Historians"* (London: Frank Cass, 1997), 67.
[17] Sami Smooha, "Relationship Between Jews and Arabs in Israel as a Jewish Democratic State" (Sociology Department, Open University, 2001), 288. http://soc.haifa.ac.il/~s.smooha/download/arabsandjewsrelations.pdf.

enemies of the country without facing threats from the government. They side with terrorists and are protected by Israeli law and security forces. But if they or their families traveled a few miles to the West Bank and publicly condemned the Palestinian Authority, they could be killed.[18] There is no other state in the Middle East where it is possible to speak so publicly against the state and not be attacked, thrown into prison, tortured or killed. Where is the media report on this anomaly?

6. When there are reports of Israeli killings of Palestinian civilians during war (which are rarely if ever intentional), thousands of Jewish people in Israel protest against the government. This shows the moral feeling that Jews have even for their enemies. But when a bus with Jews is blown up by Palestinian terrorists, Arabs often dance in the streets or name their children or parks after suicide bombers, and honor the murderers as martyrs. Why are the Israelis and not the Arabs vilified in the courts of world opinion?

7. The current Palestinian Authority religious leader, Mufti Muhammad Hussein, said that the killing of Jews by Muslims is a religious goal. At an event celebrating the founding of Fatah, he cited a Hadith (collections of sayings of Muhammad) saying that the Hour of Resurrection will not come until Muslims fight all Jews and kill them: "The Hour will not come until you fight the Jews. The Jew will hide behind stones or trees. Then the stones or trees will call: 'Oh Muslim, servant of Allah, there is a Jew behind me, come and kill him.'"[19] Why do world leaders not condemn these hateful and genocidal statements?

8. Many Muslim Arab leaders deny the Holocaust, and some supported it.[20] While much of the world demonizes Israel for its supposedly immoral

---

[18]Shadi Khalloul, "Israeli Christians: Don't Place 'Christ at the Checkpoint,'" *Israel Today*, March 11, 2014, www.israeltoday.co.il/NewsItem/tabid/178/nid/24495/Default.aspx?hp=readmo.

[19]"PA Mufti: 'Kill a Jew, Go to Heaven,'" *InvestmentWatch* (blog), January 17, 2012, http://investmentwatchblog.com/pa-mufti-kill-a-jew-go-to-heaven-youtube-tell-the-truth-get-your-account-suspended/.

[20]For example, the following was published in a leading Egyptian newspaper: "With regard to the fraud of the Holocaust. . . . Many French studies have proven that this is no more than a fabrication, a lie, and a fraud!! That is, it is a 'scenario' the plot of which was carefully tailored, using several faked photos completely unconnected to the truth. Yes, it is a film, no more and no less. Hitler himself, whom they accuse of Nazism, is in my eyes no more than a modest 'pupil' in the world of murder and bloodshed. He is completely innocent of the charge of frying them in the hell of his false Holocaust!! The entire matter, as many French and British scientists and researchers have proven, is nothing more than a huge Israeli plot aimed at extorting the German government in particular and the European countries in general. But I, personally and in light

treatment of its minorities, of whom I am one, we see little condemnation of terror attacks against innocent Jews or Christians and their symbols in Israel and surrounding Arabs countries, either by the media or the international community. While Israel has been condemned and targeted by more than sixty-five United Nations resolutions and has its own agenda item (#7) at the United Nations Human Rights Council, no other United Nations member state, including egregious human-rights violators like North Korea, Syria, Iran and Sudan, gets its own agenda item. When has the United Nations blamed the Grand Mufti or other Islamic leaders for their hateful speeches that have led to thousands of Israeli casualties? Why does the United Nations not protect persecuted minorities like Christians and Yazidis from terrorism in the Middle East conducted by Muslim powers (like ISIS) or states (Syria)?

9. Israel is routinely charged with violation of international law for its supposed occupation of the West Bank. When was the last time the United Nations condemned Turkey for its illegal occupation of one-third of Cyprus for forty-one years and its deployment of forty thousand Turkish troops there? Or China's brutal occupation of Tibet? Where are the United Nations resolutions condemning present and past genocides by Muslims against Jews and Christians in the Middle East? A Palestinian journalist exclaims, "It is a scandal of global proportions that the UN in general and UNRWA in particular—as well as the EU—ignore the hundreds of thousands of killed and maimed and the millions of refugees desperately in need of aid in the neighboring Arab countries."[21]

This powerful set of double standards is why the proximate justice and imperfect-but-real commitment to morality that Israel displays are invisible to most of the world. The media are obsessed with Israel and its imagined injustices and have blinded themselves to enormous injustices perpetrated by other states, especially those of Israel's neighbors. If one were to judge from the silence of the media about them and their incessant harping about Israel, Israel's neighbors

---

of this imaginary tale, complain to Hitler, even saying to him from the bottom of my heart, 'If only you had done it, brother, if only it had really happened, so that the world could sigh in relief [without] their evil and sin.'" Fatima Abdallah Mamhoud, "Accursed Forever and Ever," *Al-Akhbar*, April 29, 2002, quoted in Ibn Warraq, *Defending the West: A Critique of Edward Said's Orientalism* (Amhert, NY: Prometheus, 2007), 253.

[21]Bassam Tawil, "Western Scandals in the Middle East," *Gatestone Institute*, July 9, 2015, www.gatestoneinstitute.org/6126/western-scandals-middle-east.

can do no wrong and Israel can do no right. That's why my attempts to point to Israel's relative morality will have a difficult time being heard.

And as I said earlier in relation to the Maronites, Israel is not perfect. It has not always treated its minorities morally. The former soldiers of the SLA (Southern Lebanese Army) and their families are another case in point. They fought alongside the IDF during its first war in Lebanon in 1982 and then off and on until 2000, when the IDF withdrew from southern Lebanon. SLA soldiers brought their families into Israel, where they have struggled ever since. They have had a difficult time trying to integrate into Israeli society because they have had a hard time speaking Hebrew. Some have lost their Christian identity, especially the children who have studied in Jewish schools where they are taught nothing about their own history and culture. Most of the parents have not been able to find good jobs and cannot afford to buy their own homes. They are glad they were able to escape the Islamic terror group Hezbollah, but many are depressed. They expected Israel to do more to help them integrate.

Now I must admit that the Israeli strategy of putting these soldiers and their families into the middle of Israeli society rather than in a separate all-Lebanese village was smart long-term. This is the best way for their children to learn to speak Hebrew without an accent and get the education they will use to fully integrate themselves. But I also sympathize with their parents, who wish Israel would do more to help *them*.

So is Israel living up to the moral demands of the covenant? Not perfectly. It has a lot more to do. But it is doing far better morally than any of its neighbors.

THE MORALITY OF MINORITIES

Since this essay is about morality, it might be instructive to reflect on the morality of the other actors in this debate. What of the morality of the media that always blame and demonize Israel, even when Israel makes serious efforts to behave morally in ways that few other states do, such as in the summer 2014 Gaza war? Is it moral for the international community to demonize Israel in their treatment of this war?

What about the morality of the minority communities in Israel? Israel tries to promote the idea of civil service by non-Jews, but Arab Palestinians categorically reject the thought of this. They choose against taking any responsibility for the society that supports and protects them. Jewish mothers send their sons and daughters away from home at a young age to defend the country's borders, fighting against brutal and immoral enemies, enemies who say that death is better than life and who glory in suicide attacks on civilians. Israeli soldiers, on the other hand, are not permitted to leave base without finishing a course in ethics. They are taught to avoid civilian deaths if at all possible and to go after only combatants who are clearly targeting them or others. What is the moral contrast here?

What is the morality of church leaders who betray the Christian message by serving Islamic propaganda against our country, Israel? It is disturbing to see Christian leaders participating in anti-Israel political conferences like Christ at the Checkpoint because they engage in dishonesty at such conferences.[22] These Christians enjoy full rights and freedom, even the freedom to publicly slander the state without fear. But they suggest otherwise in their public statements at conferences like these, often because of pressure from their Muslim countrymen. Therefore these Christian leaders do not represent the real Christian voices of this land. If they felt free to speak without reprisal from their Muslim neighbors, most Arabic-speaking Aramaic Christians would say they disagree with those Christian leaders who publicly condemn Israel.

The moral question, therefore, should also ask about the approach of minorities in Israel toward the state. How do minorities view Israel and its Jewish majority? It is a human responsibility to support a state that tries to protect the rights and freedoms of its citizens. Israel is our homeland, and the Jews are our brothers. We minorities have a duty as citizens to share the same responsibilities and difficulties that our Jewish fellow citizens bear. That means that we too should serve in the defense forces or civil services. We should not demand our rights without giving anything back. This matter of duty should be part of any discussion of the morality of the Jewish state, especially when treating the issue of non-Jewish minorities.

Then there is the question of the morality of Islamist ideology. It is not new but can be found among Muslims before the establishment of the state of Israel in 1948. Even before that date, there were intifadas against Jews. The Grand Mufti at that time met with Adolf Hitler to develop plans for the extermination of Jews in the land of Israel.[23]

---

[22]Paul Wilkinson, "The Church at Christ's Checkpoint," *Christian Witness Ministries*, August 10, 2013, www.cwm.org.au/3/11-61/39-the-church-at-christ-s-checkpoint.

[23]Germany, Auswärtiges Amt., *Documents on German Foreign Policy, 1918–1945, from the Archives of the German Foreign Ministry*, series D, vol. XIII, no. 515 (Washington, DC: US Government Printing Office, 1949), 881-85.

So the moral question for Palestinians is this: how can they live in a country, enjoy all types of freedoms and rights, benefit from the system, and still be its enemy from their deepest hearts? This position is immoral, to say the least. It reveals that the hatred of Israel and the Jews has little to do with how the state treats Arabs or any other minority but suggests that a certain Islamist theology animates many.

This is not true for all Arab Muslims in Israel. There are many who know that living in Israel has been good for them and want nothing more than to live in peace with their Jewish neighbors. Bassem Eid, for example, is a Palestinian Muslim and human rights activist who decries the BDS (Boycott, Divest, Sanction) movement that is popular on American university campuses. It calls on American corporations to stop doing business with Israeli companies that operate in Israel and the West Bank. Eid thinks this is shortsighted.

> BDS spokespeople justify calling for boycotts that will result in increased economic hardships for the Palestinians by asserting that Palestinians are willing to suffer such deprivations in order to achieve their freedom. It goes without saying that they themselves live in comfortable circumstances elsewhere in the world and will not suffer any such hardship. It would seem, in fact, that the BDS movement in its determination to oppose Israel is prepared to fight to the last drop of Palestinian blood. As a Palestinian who actually lives in east Jerusalem and hopes to build a better life for his family and his community, this is the kind of "pro-Palestinian activism" we could well do without. For our own sake, we need to reconcile with our Israeli neighbors, not reject and revile them.[24]

So it is not only Christian minorities but Muslim Arabs also who want to live in peace with Israel and recognize the benefits of living in Israel.

The Way to Peace

I have tried to show that the state of Israel is not fundamentally unjust in the ways that it treats its minorities. It is not perfect. There have been injustices, just as there have been many American injustices in its treatment of minorities. But since its founding nearly seventy years ago, Israel has been committed, legally and in other ways, to just treatment of its minorities.

---

[24]Bassem Eid, "The Palestinian Case Against BDS," *Fikra Forum*, Washington Institute for Near East Policy, June 25, 2015, www.washingtoninstitute.org/policy-analysis/view/the-palestinian-case-against-bds.

Many Palestinians are committed to a story that says that Jews stole Palestine from Arabs in 1948, and they will never forgive Israel for that, no matter what the Jewish state does to make them feel like equal citizens. I do not think that story is true. Not by a long shot. But this is not the place for me to argue that historical question, and I would refer my readers to good historians such as Benny Morris.[25]

Those who believe that false narrative will never be convinced that Israel could possibly be just or moral. When they criticize Israel, therefore, they are not driven by concern for minority communities like mine or even Muslim communities. What drives them is simply hatred for the Jewish state.

How, then, can we make peace? First of all, we need to bring a halt to the cynical use of local Christians as pawns in the Palestinian cause or other Arab efforts to destroy Israel as a democratic Jewish state. In other words, those who say that Christians in Israel are being treated unjustly by the state are not speaking for me or any other Christian communities in Israel.

Second, Arab Palestinians must stop the killing and their attempts to exterminate the Jews. They must recognize the right of the Jewish people to live in their original land. Arab Palestinians also have rights to land. But while the Israeli state has shown repeatedly that it is willing to share the land, the Palestinian leadership has repeatedly spurned serious offers that would have enabled them to create their own state.[26] That continues to this day. As Palestinian journalist Khaled Abu Toameh writes,

> No Palestinian leader has a mandate to reach an everlasting peace agreement with Israel. No leader in Ramallah or the Gaza Strip is authorized to end the conflict with Israel. Any Palestinian who dares to talk about concessions to Israel is quickly denounced as a traitor. Those who believe that whoever succeeds Abbas will be able to make real concessions to Israel are living in an illusion.
>
> There are two main reasons why Palestinians will not sign a real and meaningful peace agreement with Israel—at least not in the foreseeable future.
>
> The first is a total lack of education for peace. The second is related to the absence of a leader who is authorized—or has the guts—to embark on such a risky mission.

---

[25]Benny Morris, *One State, Two States: Resolving the Israeli/Palestine Conflict* (New Haven, CT: Yale University Press, 2009).
[26]See ibid.

Americans and Europeans who keep talking about the need to revive the stalled peace process in the Middle East continue to ignore these two factors. They continue to insist that peace is still possible and that the ball is in Israel's court.

The Americans and Europeans fail to acknowledge that in order to achieve peace, the leaders must prepare their people for compromise and tolerance.[27]

Third, the Palestinians and other Arabs must eliminate their religious hatred for Jews, Christians or other minorities.

Finally, all the minorities of Israel must support the only state in the region whose favorite system is democracy, tries to treat minorities fairly and allows them legal equality and the fullest range of freedoms. Only then can Arabs be friends of Israel. Only then will come the peace that Ben-Gurion hoped for.

---

[27] Khaled Abu Toameh, "Why Palestinians Cannot Make Peace with Israel," *Gatestone Institute*, July 13, 2015, www.gatestoneinstitute.org/6142/palestinians-peace-israel.

- PART FOUR -

THEOLOGY

AND

THE FUTURE

11

HOW SHOULD THE NEW CHRISTIAN ZIONISM PROCEED?

Darrell Bock

◆

Christian Zionism is not an oxymoron; it is an appeal in an era of narratives to get the story right about God, his character and his promises. Whether one thinks theologically, morally, historically, politically or legally, the way one views Israel is also a reflection of how one thinks about God. This discussion is a big deal because the character of God, his faithfulness and his promises are in view. Seeing Israel in the program of God says God keeps his promises to those he originally addressed. That story also is rooted in reconciliation, an important detail that gets lost when one dismisses the ongoing significance of Israel.

I am reminded of a song from *Porgy and Bess* when I hear some discuss Israel: "It Ain't Necessarily So." The narratives we generally hear about this people and the land give me pause since they typically leave out what the essays in this book show is Israel's role in God's program according to the scriptural narrative. As the song puts it, "It ain't necessarily so . . . the things dat yo' li'ble to read in the Bible, it ain't necessarily so." But if the usual narratives about Israel should give us pause, then how should we think about this people and land in a very troubled region of the world? Let me start by reviewing where we have been, and suggesting where we might go. Then I will discuss what the next steps might be.

SUMMARY OF THE ESSAYS

My review will be brief but important because it suggests that Israel matters to God and should matter to us.

Gerald McDermott argues that Christian Zionism is not a recent phenomenon, nor did it come from one denomination or theological tradition. It goes back hundreds of years and has had distinguished proponents such as Reinhold Niebuhr and Karl Barth in the twentieth century.

In his essay on hermeneutics, Craig Blaising points out that Israel has an ongoing presence in the New Testament. Nothing about the presentation of Jesus as Messiah as the center of the New Testament message needs to exclude God's commitments to Israel as a people or nation. The Christification of promise does not mean the nullification of hope for Israel. Promises of restoration after proclamations of judgment are rooted in God's speech acts in the Torah *and* in the New Testament.

Joel Willitts contends that the nation of Israel is not a moot question for Matthew. Matthean scholars recognize how the people of Israel are a concern for Matthew but often understate the national dimensions of this focus. Support for this view comes at multiple levels: the early Jewish context, the geographical perspective, the Davidic messianism, the "turfed" kingdom, the presentation of Jerusalem and the temple, atonement theology of the blood of the innocents pointing to restoration and the allusions to eschatological hope, including the tribes and the land.

Mark Kinzer makes a similar claim for Luke–Acts: Those two books point to a restoration in Luke's "until" language in texts like Luke 21:24 and Acts 3:21. To this may be added Luke 13:34-35, a text shared with Matthew that looks at judgment on the nation until she says, "Blessed is the one who comes in the name of the Lord." That text also points to restoration hope. Even the geographical design of Luke and Acts points to restoration and a return to Jerusalem. Acts ends with a story to be continued that looks toward a return to Jerusalem, which is a cycle common to Acts.

Finally, David Rudolph shows how particularity for Israel and the land is not absent in Paul's epistles. A focal point of promise is Israel's election, a major concern of Romans 9–11. This is a text that cannot be about a "new" Israel since Paul opens it with remarks about how he wishes he were accursed for the sake of those he is discussing, by whom he means those in Israel who have rejected Jesus. The discussion closes with remarks about grafting back in those grafted out, a clear reference to the same group of Jews who reject Christ at the start of Romans 9. Paul thinks those who are currently opposing Jesus will be more receptive to him when the Deliverer comes from Zion. He also points to reconciliation, present in such texts as Ephesians 2:11-22, a theme to which I will return.

Turning to politics, Mark Tooley adds to the narrative of how deep, wide and long the support for Israel has been in American theology from the late nineteenth century and well into the twentieth. Theologians from the time of Benjamin Harrison's presidency through Harry Truman's time were supportive. Only since the 1970s has there been a shift in this approach to Israel with a wider embrace of a kind of supersessionism.

Robert Benne takes a closer look at Reinhold Niebuhr's strong theological-ethical case for supporting the state of Israel. While Niebuhr emphasizes the political implications of his theological-ethical case—Israel provides order in the region, a haven for an unjustly persecuted people and a shining beacon of democracy among authoritarian regimes—the heart of his argument is that the Jewish people are something "exceptional" and "unique" in human history and that the world should recognize and support the state that shelters them. Benne adds a further note that God's ongoing covenant with that special people involves the promise of land.

Robert Nicholson observes that the vague nature of international law in these areas and the application of concerns about covenantal injustice do not have enough clarity, and so do not reach levels to disqualify either Israel's right to the land or her legitimacy to be a nation. Whether one thinks of the issues tied to 1948, the 1967 acquisition of land during the Six-Day War or recent events, nothing points to Israel's violations to an extent that would undermine its right to exist or that cancels previous international recognition of such a position.

Shadi Khalloul argues as an Aramaic Christian that Israel's treatment of religious minorities, such as the one to which he belongs, is much better than the treatment minorities receive in the rest of the region. This shows the moral and democratic character of Israel and therefore an element of important consistency with the moral demands of the biblical covenant.

These last three chapters show that in matters of justice, Israel has a defensible track record. The hostility often projected at Israel for her seemingly excessive actions tied to claims of injustice is largely the product of legitimate security concerns that Israel has to constantly deal with because national neighbors and some inhabitants seek her extinction. What nation does not retain the right to protect and defend her own people?

These essays make a case for Israel's theological right to exist in a land given to her by God. They also suggest that, as a nation within a world of nations, she has the right to protect her own people, who often have faced extreme persecution and live under constant threats to her security. The world has a short memory. Even in this era after the Holocaust, there are large numbers who never were told, or have forgotten, that Israel as a people was nearly wiped off the map of Europe not so long ago. With new threats looming and the need for Christians to gain or renew a vision of biblical Israel, the question is where Christian Zionists should go from here. In one sense, all the term Christian Zionism means in the end is that Israel has a right to exist with the same human rights and security guarantees that other nations receive. But of course Christian Zionism is also more than that, for it makes a *theological* case for that right to exist, beyond a merely prudential one.

Important Distinctions

Let me start with an important distinction. The Christian Zionism that we are proposing is not merely a hope for individual ethnic Jews. Some Christian theologians argue for a future for Israel as a dispersed people with anticipation of a future in which many will recognize Jesus. Many see this faith as bringing those believers into the church. This aspect of hope is widespread, but it is not what Christian Zionism focuses on. Christian Zionism argues that Israel has a *corporate* future in God's plan and as a nation has a right to land in the Middle East. Israel also has a right to function as a nation and be recognized as such in the world. That is the first key distinction the New Christian Zionism makes—the difference between individual hope for Jews and a corporate place for the nation.

The second key distinction is that national Israel is not the same thing as believing Israel. Yet the existence of believing Israel (whether conceived as only messianic Jews in distinction from Gentile believers in churches or as Jewish believers as a part of the larger church) in distinction from national Israel does not mean exclusion of national or corporate Israel from God's program, or the hope that unbelieving Jews one day will come to faith in God's Messiah. Unbelieving Israel has a right to the land because God gave it to all the nation and seed of Abraham initially as an act of his grace when he called Abraham to form a nation even before the patriarch trusted God. This future for Jewish people can be affirmed alongside the idea that Christ is also the heir of all promises, including promises about rule of the earth. This combination of ideas about hope means that although Christ is the center of the realization of promise, fulfillment in him does not nullify previous commitments God has made to ethnic Israel, which God will complete through the Christ. Christ comes as one who fulfills national goals for Israel as well as those he fulfills for all the world. Israel's current unbelief does not disqualify her from the covenant but makes her subject to covenant discipline from the Messiah—even if she does not recognize it. This can be seen in Jesus' declaration that Israel's house will be desolate *until* she recognizes the one who comes in the name of the Lord (Lk 13:34-35; Mt 23:37-39). This remark about the house could be about the temple and not the nation, but the judgment on the temple symbolizes the spiritual status of the nation. This exilelike discipline is for covenantal unfaithfulness in not recognizing the divinely sent Messiah (Lk 19:41-44), but it does not mean forfeiture of ultimate promise, hope and realization. The essays by Blaising, Willitts, Kinzer and Rudolph all contend that large portions of the New Testament maintain this sense of national hope despite the remarks of Jesus about discipline for the nation and despite his presence as the one in whom covenant promises are realized. Discipline is not disqualification but censure.

This second distinction has several implications. The first is that Israel is still responsible to God for how she responds to covenant obligations. To endorse Israel and a national place for the nation is *not* to give her carte blanche for everything she does. Christian Zionism is not a blind endorsement for Israel. It does not give the nation a pass on issues of justice or moral obligations. She is still called to live responsibly as a nation like other nations. Rather, Christian Zionism merely makes an affirmation that Israel has a right to a secure homeland, which she should govern and occupy morally and responsibly.

It also means there is no room for a two-covenant view of Israel that says Gentiles are saved through Jesus but Israel is saved through the Torah. Jesus' ministry to his own people in his own time makes no sense of a dual track to salvation that argues that the Jews have one way of salvation and Gentiles have Jesus. The ministry of the apostles to the synagogues in the book of Acts underscores the same point. Jesus is the Messiah of all, both Jew and Gentile. And the gospel is for all, "to the Jew first and also to the Greek" (Rom 1:16-17).

Important Emphases for the Future

As Christian Zionism makes its case, there are certain emphases it needs to stress in order to bring balance to its position. Five of these are theological emphases; one is more historical. First, *inclusion should not become exclusion.* To point to Israel having a national future is not to deny the centrality of Jesus to the promises of God. As already noted, the case for Israel in the land is tied to speech acts of God made to the nation as a whole before and in anticipation of Jesus' coming. Ultimately the blessing for this gift of land is realized in the Messiah, who is also Israel's Messiah. Even if those blessings are shared with others, as some argue, it does not exclude the original recipients. In other words, even if the land ultimately is Christ's and those who believe, whether Jew or Gentile, share in it because Jesus is their Messiah too, that does not exclude Israel's claim to the land and Israel's right to exist as a political people. More than this, Jesus' own remarks about the nation and her future show she has not fallen off God's radar or program. When those who reject a national future for Israel argue that the promises belong only to Jesus, or that national Israel has disqualified herself from access because of her refusal of the Messiah, they fail to account for these other features of Jesus' and the New Testament's teaching. I have in mind texts like the "until" texts of Luke 13:34-35 and 21:21-24 and Matthew 23:37-39, as well as the continued expectation of hope for the nation expressed in Acts 1:6-7 and 3:18-22. Acts 3 is especially important here because it refers to the Hebrew Scripture as still telling us what is to come for Israel and the world when Messiah returns. Therefore, to exclude Israel from God's program misses the biblical mark by ignoring the ways that Scripture articulates Israel's hope as an identifiable people alongside the nations, even as it discusses the hope of their being included among the blessed in Christ.

But at the same time, Christian Zionists need to do better work theologically. Christian Zionists need to articulate more clearly how to put into proper relationship the following: fulfillment in Christ, current covenantal discipline for Israel, Israel's responsibility to be just and the nation's rights. Explaining how all these themes combine to make a coherent divine program requires more detailed exegetical, hermeneutical and theological response than simply waving the label "replacement theology" at those who disagree. What is labeled replacement theology by those who defend Israel's existence is seen as fulfillment theology by those who say fulfillment of promises is only in Christ and in his church. They claim that Israel no longer has a place at the table of blessing. The essays in this volume begin to address this need by noting issues such as covenantal discipline on the model of exilelike judgment and by pointing to texts in both testaments that see a national Israel in the mix. But exactly how these themes cohere needs more detailed work. By this I mean that we need to put all these themes on the table together and think hard about how they fit together—rather than highlighting just one or two at the expense of the others.

Let me illustrate. How, for example, does the destruction of the temple in AD 70 cohere with a future for national Israel? If it was not a symbol for the rejection of Israel as a nation, what was it? Or consider another example. If all promises are fulfilled in Jesus, and that includes land commitments that God made, then how could there still be a role for national Israel? Here is a third. If there is a universal church, why would there be a need for a national Israel? As I have noted, some of the essays in this volume suggest the ways some of these questions might be answered. But more exegetical and theological work is needed.

The key point to be made is that Gentile inclusion does not mean Israelite exclusion. To expand the promise to others or to include others who had been more indirectly alluded to as present in earlier forms of the promise does not require that the promise be constricted to the exclusion of the original primary recipients. This was implied all the way back in Genesis 12, where we read that the world would be blessed through Abraham's seed. The expansion of hope to all was built into the promise from the start. Then, in both the Old Testament and New Testament, the seed is treated as both Israel and the Messiah. For example, Israel is numbered as the dust of the earth and the stars in the sky in both Genesis (13:16; 15:5) and Acts (3:25). Christ as the seed is seen most powerfully in Galatians 3. These lines running through the biblical canon are important pieces of the puzzle that remains to be finished.

A second key to a biblical understanding of Israel is the canon's repeated appeal to *God's faithfulness*. This form of biblical reasoning needs to be applied to these questions. Could God have made a promise to Abraham and his seed, with a corporate-national element from the start, and then later exclude the nation that originally received that promise? This question needs to be pressed and developed. God keeps his commitments to those with whom he makes them originally. The Christian Zionist argument is that this is precisely the supposition behind Paul's defense of hope for Israel in Romans 9–11.

Yet some argue that the promise was fulfilled in ways that excluded the original recipients of the promise. They appeal to the promise of Genesis 12 I have just mentioned, focusing on the promise to include the world but strangely detaching it from the promise to Abraham and his Jewish descendants.[1] Those of us who find this inadequate need to demonstrate what makes it less than compelling. One of the ways to do this is to show how Israel, whether in belief or unbelief, is still in view in most of these texts and still is tied to the original hope and promise as a result. We also need to highlight the biblical theme of God's faithfulness to his promises and show the linguistic and semantic roots that lie at the base of this theme. In sum, we need to argue that God means what he says to those to whom he made the promise originally. Speech acts to an original audience identify the beneficiaries—all of them. The veracity and faithfulness of God are at stake when some of them are excluded from the biblical story of blessings promised and fulfilled.

Third, the case for Christian Zionism is *not as nationalistic* as some within the movement make it out to be and as some outside the movement perceive it to be. In fact, more needs to be said about this than these essays were able to express. This is because the hope of life for Israel in the end as Scripture depicts it is not only for the land to be a haven of peace for Jews but also for it to be a place of peace and reconciliation that permeates all of creation. It is a place where all nations will come to share in the worship of the one true God (Is 2:2-4). The land may be Israel's, but all share in what it represents—a good, gracious and promise-keeping God who brings peace to those who turn to him. It is this vision of eschatology that should guide how we view the land in the present. This region is one that all the world senses belongs to it in one way or another.

Critics of Christian Zionism often ask why the New Testament does not talk about the land more, or more directly, than it does. It is a fair question. Let me proffer two answers. First, the nation was in the land when the New Testament was being written, so there was no need to make a point about it. It was a given at the time. Second, in a time of peace and unity, such as the eschatological hope for the land foresees, borders matter less. Think of the difference between crossing the German-French border in 1943 during World War II and crossing it today as part of the European Union. Think also of the fact that today one can

---

[1]The list of scholars who hold such views is large today as it is probably the most widely held view in Reformed circles and has been made popular by an array of interpreters from a variety of traditions who are deservedly respected for their general contributions to biblical studies. Among those on this list are N. T. Wright, Christopher Wright, Bruce Waltke, John Stott, Gary Burge, Stephen Wellum and Peter Gentry. Other more popular speakers are also known for this view, though the case they make for it is peppered with excessive rhetoric that does not help these conversations. Among this group are Stephen Sizer and Colin Chapman.

be European and at the same time German or French. This is the result of reconciliation, which is integral to the biblical vision and should be a part of any biblical Christian Zionism. Where there is reconciliation, there can be unity and particularity without hostile rivalry. In fact, in maintaining a sense of particularity one is also reminded of the beauty of reconciliation and unity. What was formerly hostile and torn asunder is now brought together, not in homogeneity but as a blending in variety with respect given to each part. Seen in this light, the land becomes on the one hand a testament to God's faithfulness to his original people and on the other hand a witness to God's concern for all people. With this vision of prospective peace, presence in the land is less nationalistic.

Fourth, this is why we Christian Zionists need to put more emphasis on the *hope of reconciliation*. We have already seen that this element of hope permeates the vision for Israel's place in the land. But the necessity for making this point is underscored when Palestinian Christian believers who live in the land ask legitimate questions of Christian theologians about where they fit in a theology of Christian Zionism. They rightly ask, Where is justice for us? Are we equal partners or only water carriers? The answer, in short, is that they share in the promises and benefits tied to the Messiah whom they share. All the New Testament language about Gentiles as coheirs of promise means that this question of justice needs to be addressed.

Here I have in mind developing the theological implications of texts like Ephesians 2:11-22, where unity and distinction exist to display the abiding presence of reconciliation. Those who enter into blessing through the Messiah Jesus share the promise and union with each other but still retain some identity as Jew and Gentile reconciled. So in one sense, as a result of salvation, there is no Jew or Gentile (Gal 3:28-29). Participants in Christ share the same savior, salvation and benefits. Nevertheless, there is also the recognition in other New Testament texts that while God has brought Jew and Gentile into this new entity he has created, the one new man, the evidence of the reconciliation is that Jew and Gentile function side by side but with slightly differing practices, as texts like Romans 14–15 contend and the book of Acts illustrates. Homogeneity is not the goal; ethnic respect without tribalism is. Reconciliation is an important feature of our vision for God's people in God's land at the end. We need to reflect on it more.

But if *justice* is addressed, it must be discussed in *nondiscriminatory* fashion. This is a fifth emphasis a new Christian Zionism must make. If there are injustices from Israel that need attention, so are there injustices that come from those who oppose her with hostility and hatred. It is the one-sided way in which claims of injustice are thrown around that has provoked reaction among not only those in Israel but also among Christian Zionists. When the public charges and votes in international proceedings are one-sided, one wonders if concerns about anti-Semitism may in fact be valid. Justice needs to be invoked carefully, in a balanced way, taking into account all the factors that have led to loss of rights, property, health and life. It is here where the essays of Nicholson and Khalloul are important.

One of the realities that makes this discussion of justice so complex is that the Christian values of compassion for outsiders, grace and love for enemy, which are usually part of messianic and Christian Palestinian discussions, are not as prominent in discussions among Jews and Muslims. This is because these values are not so prominent in their traditions. Yet the Old Testament's concern for the treatment of aliens, based on sensitivities Jews have had since the exodus in Egypt, does mean that much more Jewish concern exists in this area and gives us cause for hope. On the Muslim side, the Qur'an is split between texts of compassion and those of hostility to outsiders, with the hostile texts coming later and unfortunately dominating much Islamic discourse today. Those who respect human life and dignity, whether for religious or secular reasons, could be able to tap into and appreciate the positive values noted, even if they do not share all of them.

This consideration is important because the majority populations in the region come from these other faiths—and those majorities are substantial in number on each opposing side. Their animosity for each other and distrust fuel the inability to work toward any peace. The few Christians in the region, whether Jewish, Arab or Palestinian in ethnicity, are caught in this crossfire. Yet as Christians there is the possibility (1) of showing the potential for reconciliation among those messianics, Arabs and other minorities who share a Christian faith and (2) of introducing the potential that Christian values can add to the discussion in working toward a resolution. I am not so naive as to think this is easy, but the past patterns clearly do not work. Only the addition of new and fresh perspectives has a chance of changing the current equation.

The sixth and final emphasis that is needed in the future is the careful articulation of the *international and legal right* Israel has to the land and to nationhood. This is a story that is mostly left untold. It is important because of all the feelings that exist about what took place in 1948. It is especially important to those for whom religious argument means little or nothing. There was a very developed international process that led to Israel being in the land and that has led to its being accepted in the United Nations as a recognized state. The history behind things like the Balfour Declaration and the process of United Nations recognition of Israel need to be told in careful detail. People need to understand that history and appreciate what it meant for all her neighbors to be slow (and in some cases still hesitant) to accept Israel's right to be a nation. Some reject her right to be a state emphatically and hold positions that call for her extermination. Even some in the land bear arms in the hopes of eliminating her. All of this reality complicates the current situation, but establishing her international status on international legal and secular grounds is an important base from which to work.

We now have generations of people who do not know this story and history. It needs to be told carefully and in detail. It also needs to face up to the complexity of the story for those who ended up displaced. The ways in which law and justice have interacted also constitute a complex narrative with competing plot lines and emphases. That is yet another reason to tell this story with detail, sensitivity and care. The Nicholson essay is a start here, but more detail is needed because what one meets in the literature is an array of competing views of what took place and why.[2]

So these are some of the emphases Christian Zionism needs to make its case heard. What more is needed?

Making the Case for Christian Zionism

The emphases just noted are not shared by all Christian Zionists, not even by all Christians. So one needs to make the case for these ideas in books and serious

---

[2]This is a difficult area of historical study. Even the historiography of the period from Israeli historians shows a wide range of views and approaches. Many points of contention exist. I am not sure a definitive study exists. Rather, what one has to do is look at an array of studies and take note of the angle each pursues. Here is a short list reflecting this variety: Abba Eban, *My People* (London: Random House, 1984); Benny Morris, *1948* (New Haven, CT: Yale University Press, 2009); Gudrun Krämer, *A History of Palestine* (Princeton, NJ: Princeton University Press, 2008); Joan Peters, *From Time Immemorial* (New York: Harper & Row, 1984); Paul Johnson, *A History of the Jews* (New York: Harper & Row, 1987); Martin Gilbert, *Israel* (New York: Doubleday, 2008); Alan Dershowitz, *The Case for Israel* (Hoboken, NJ: John Wiley & Sons, 2003); and Jonathan Schneer, *The Balfour Declaration* (New York: Random House, 2010). To this might be added the theological study of essays edited by Salim Munayer and Lisa Loden, *The Land Cries Out* (Eugene, OR: Wipf & Stock, 2012), which is written primarily from an Arab-Palestinian Christian point of view.

articles that dive into the details of what I have time only to sketch in an essay of this size. Treatments from the variety of angles pro and con could be investigated.

But even with detailed and careful treatment, this will not be enough. For our society is not one of readers, as statistics show. A surprising percentage of people today do not read a single book in a year, and a significant number read only one or two.[3]

So although books speak to a segment of our society and are appreciated by some, we will need to tell the story in other ways as well. Ours is a digitized and visual society. Documentaries and other media are needed where we present the issues and *show* the case rather than simply making textual arguments. People will need to get the picture about the facts, not just engage with printed facts. They will need to hear stories of lives lived in the region, on all sides. They will need to appreciate the complexity of what is being debated and contemplated. Hence, more will need to be done than just writing analyses and presenting theological, legal or political cases in print.

There also will be a need for more conferences like the one that generated the essays for this book.[4] Some, like this volume and the conference that stands behind it, should present a single point of view. Others, however, will need to represent a greater diversity of views, where there can be real give and take between speakers with fundamentally different positions. Some private discussions, where there is less opportunity for public grandstanding, are very important. As Mark Tooley pointed out, since the 1970s voices standing against Israel have become more numerous and more prominent in the public square. Those voices need direct engagement, as does their argument in venues where all sides are heard.

Conclusion

In this book we have presented an outline of a case for Israel as a nation in the land. That case is theological, moral, historical, biblical, political and legal. But this book has put its greatest emphasis on the biblical and theological case to be

---

[3] According to statista.com, about 16 percent of people in the United States in 2014 did not read a single book. If one adds to this readers of only one or two books, that percentage exceeds 30 percent. See "How Many Books Do You Read in an Average Year?," *Statista: The Statistics Portal*, www.statista.com/statistics/262631/number-of-books-read-by-us-adults-per-year/.

[4] "People of the Land: A Twenty-First Century Case for Christian Zionism," hosted by The Institute on Religion and Democracy, Georgetown University Conference Center, Washington, DC, April 17, 2015. Proceedings can be seen at http://christiansandisrael.org.

made. The writers are convinced that this story needs to be heard. They believe that Christian Zionism is not an oxymoron. We are convinced it is a sound humanitarian and theological position. I close with a play on the words from the *Porgy and Bess* song with which I opened. As we look to make the case as Christians that Israel has a right to the land, we also tell our story with a plea and appeal to get the story right. Christian Zionism is bigger than any denomination, theological tradition or period. It focuses on the character of God and the teaching of Jesus and the apostles. Those at the start of the Christian faith argued that God will keep his promises to Israel. This confidence also provides a basis for assurance about his promises to us. Those promises point to a reconciliation God has worked through his Messiah for the life and the shalom of the world. Given that hope, I close with this refrain:

> It ain't necessarily so
> ......
> The things with which you trifle
> That you read in the Bible,
> It ain't necessarily so.
> The land and the nation
> in Messiah's closing story
> show God's wondrous glory
> if to the entire story we go.

12

IMPLICATIONS AND PROPOSITIONS

Gerald R. McDermott

◆

This book has tried to unfold a new vision for the relationship between the church and Israel. It has argued that the old Christian Zionism was married to premillennial dispensationalism—for better or for worse. Traditional dispensationalists exhibited a certain theological ingenuity that rightly insisted, against many cultured despisers, that God's covenant with Israel had not been severed. They were right about that. But we are proposing a New Christian Zionism that departs from traditional dispensationalism in some important ways, as I have already explained in the introduction. Now it is time to think about what difference this new approach to Israel and the church might make. First I will look at the implications of this new vision for a number of theological disciplines: biblical exegesis and hermeneutics, historical theology, systematic theology, theological reflection on the Israeli-Palestinian conflict and Jewish-Christian dialogue. Then I will close with five propositions that I think should be intrinsic to future thinking about the church and Israel.

Exegesis and Hermeneutics

First and foremost, it will change the way scholars and others translate and interpret the biblical text (exegesis). To start with a simple but far-reaching change, it would help English readers if the word *Christ* in the New Testament were sometimes (or often!) translated as *Messiah*. Not only is this the genuine meaning of the Greek word *christos*, but it also helps readers realize the intimate connection in the minds of the New Testament authors to their Jewish background.

Second, we have all been told that the kingdom of God was at the center of Jesus' preaching. But what if that kingdom was not simply hidden in the hearts of men and women but was also envisioned by Jesus to be an earthly reality in the future, with territorial Israel at its center? That would change the way we understand the prophecies of a future kingdom in the Old Testament and the numerous discussions of the kingdom in the New Testament.

It would also change the way we think of the relationship between the two testaments, as Craig Blaising argues in chapter three. If the New Testament is as thoroughly Jewish as we suggest, and if Israel as a people and land will continue to have theological significance until the end of time, then we Christians should take the Jewish Bible (the Old Testament)—which tells of this people and land—more seriously. In other words, it is not only the backdrop to the New Testament, and it not only prepares a people and consciousness for the revelation of the Messiah, but according to Christ's own testimony (Lk 24:25-27) it is the key to unlocking the mysteries of the Messiah. The rabbis said that the book of Leviticus is the most important book of all the Tanak because it is the deepest revelation of the character of the God of Israel as the Holy One, and the most particular blueprint for how his elect people were to maintain communion with him.[1] Since the Tanak was Jesus' Bible, which he said he embodied (Jn 1:1, 14; 5:46; 8:58), then the book of Leviticus is the most necessary. It provides the clearest way in to the holy of holies where Jesus is revealed. Ironically, most Christians think Leviticus is the most impenetrable of all the books of the Bible and read it the least. That might be a sign and even one of the causes of the profound misunderstanding the church has had of Judaism, and therefore a warning of how far we need to go to see the God of Israel—who, we need to be reminded, is the true God—with sufficient clarity.

Augustine famously pronounced, "In the Old Testament the New Testament is concealed; in the New Testament the Old Testament is revealed."[2] The New Christian Zionism sheds a bit more light on this truth. Not only is the Old Testament revealed in the New Testament, but the meaning of that revelation is further clarified: Israel is not just a memory in the New Testament, nor is she

---

[1] For a contemporary rabbinic estimation of Leviticus as "the key text of Judaism," see Jonathan Sacks, "Leviticus: The Democratisation of Holiness," 1-3, accessed July 7, 2015, www.rabbisacks.org/wp-content/uploads/2015/02/CCVayikraPreview.pdf.
[2] Augustine, *Quaestiones in Heptateuchum* 2.73.

simply an unwitting witness to the Messiah, as Augustine argued.[3] Rather than merely a voice from the past, she is a living presence in the church and will be the center of the world to come.

Once translators and readers of the Bible are convinced that Israel is not merely past but also present and future, they might see things in the biblical text that were always there but they somehow missed. For example, they might be newly struck by the intimate connection between Jewish history and its land. The Old Testament text reveals how Jewish laws and customs are based on the land and its climate and how its festivals are linked to events on the land. Passover, for example, is the annual celebration of the original divine gift of the land, and Hanukkah is the annual festival commemorating the rededication of the temple on the land.[4] But it is not only the Bible's historical festivals that mark events on the land. Its agricultural festivals follow the seasons of the land: the seven-day springtime festival of Unleavened Bread, around the barley harvest; the early summer festival of harvest, when the wheat ripens (Weeks or Shavuot, hence Pentecost); and the autumn festival of ingathering, when olives, grapes and other fruits were harvested (Tabernacles). Even when Jews were living in exile, they pined for the land:

> By the rivers of Babylon—
> there we sat down and there we wept
> when we remembered Zion. (Ps 137:1)

This is why Jews have said for millennia that they can live as Jews with the greatest integrity only when they are on the land.

Once they catch this vision, readers might also see for the first time that according to the biblical text, people and land suffer and prosper together: Obedience brings "prosperity . . . in the fruit of your ground in the land that the LORD swore to your ancestors to give you" but disobedience makes "the sky over your head . . . bronze, and the earth under you iron" (Deut 28:11, 23).

Readers might then realize that their previous assumptions about Israel and the land—that its importance was temporary, just like that of the sacrificial system or what Christians have called the "ceremonial law"—were wrong. On closer examination of the biblical text, which always brings new understandings

---

[3]Paula Fredriksen, *Augustine and the Jews: A Christian Defense of Jews and Judaism* (New Haven, CT: Yale University Press, 2010).
[4]Of course the rededication of the temple is recorded in 2 Maccabees, which is typically not included in Protestant Bibles.

of God, they would see that while the Mosaic law—with its "ceremonial" commands about worship—was a *sign* of the covenant, the land was part of the covenant *itself*. This is what Hebrews 8:13 means when it says the first covenant has been made "obsolete." It refers to the sacrificial system revealed through Moses, which Rome's destruction of the temple in AD 70 brought to an end.[5] But the land was the principal gift of God in the master covenant with Abraham in Genesis, and its promise was never revoked.[6]

Scripture never puts the land on the same level as Mosaic law. If the latter is binding on Jews but not Gentiles in the same way, and the church is overwhelmingly Gentile, in one sense Gentiles can say that it has become obsolete (but not irrelevant) for them. But they can never say that about the people of Israel or the land of Israel. The Gentiles of faith have been grafted into the olive tree of the people of Israel. And the land of Israel is God's "holy abode" (Ex 15:13). As the earlier chapters have shown, the New Testament authors believed the land *continued* to be God's holy abode.

The New Christian Zionism also suggests that we should put away our old assumptions about the Old Testament dispensation of law and its legalistic treatment of the land. As several authors in this book have shown, it is true that Israel's *enjoyment* of the land was conditional: they were exiled when they disobeyed the terms of the Mosaic covenant. But just as the original gift of the land was *un*conditional and forever, so too the return to the land was a gift of grace. Repentance did not precede it. The Scriptures suggest instead that repentance and full spiritual renewal will take place *after* return and restoration. In Ezekiel's vision of the resurrection of the dry bones, first God says he will take the people of Israel and "bring them to their own land," then at some point which seems to come later, he "will make them one nation in the land," and at what might be a still later point he "will cleanse them" (Ezek 37:21, 22, 23). So the relationship between Israel and the land, if seen through eyes that are not veiled by supersessionism, is one of unconditional grace *as well as* conditional law. It takes a new orientation to Israel and land to see these things.

---

[5]Hebrews moves directly from its statement of the first covenant being obsolete to a discussion of the tabernacle in the wilderness where "sacrifices are offered that cannot perfect the conscience of the worshiper" (Heb 9:1-2, 9). It is clear from this that by "covenant" the text means the Mosaic sacrificial system, not the master covenant cut with Abraham.

[6]Jesus spoke of the "blood of *the* covenant" (Mt 26:28; Mk 14:24, emphasis added), suggesting there was only one fundamental (Abrahamic) covenant and that the Mosaic law was an aspect of but not the same as that fundamental covenant.

HISTORICAL THEOLOGY

We saw in the introduction that for most of the last eighteen hundred years the Great Tradition has not expressed in the best or fullest way the truth of God's covenant with Israel or the place of the land in that covenant. There have been notable exceptions, but most of the great theologians have been bitten by the bug of supersessionism. As a result, their representations of God's covenant, the relation between the two Testaments, relations between law and grace or gospel, the meaning of Judaism and the people of Israel, their eschatology and—most critically—the meaning of Jesus have all been flawed.

Historical theology therefore has work to do. Its work on the great theologians needs to include analysis of how supersessionism has affected the ways the great theologians and their eras have treated these critical topics. Historical theologians ought to consider how a biblical view of Israel's people and land might provide new perspective on each of these topics. To take just one of many examples, how did Chrysostom's view of the Jewish covenant influence his sermonic invective against Jews? How did that invective shape Jewish-Christian relations in the fourth and fifth centuries and beyond? What if he had been convinced that the people and land of Israel were central to the eschaton? Would that have made a difference? Of course counterfactuals like this are often unsatisfying because they are speculative. But they draw attention to the need for deeper analysis to be done in historical theology on what impact this negation of the covenantal people and land had on theology and history.

Historical theologians could also look at the creeds. It is noteworthy that the two greatest creeds, the Apostles' and Nicene, jump from creation and fall to redemption through Jesus Christ without explicit (it is implicit in "the prophets") mention of the history and people of Israel.[7] This is an example of Soulen's structural supersessionism—the suggestion that Israel is not needed for salvation. Yet Jesus said "salvation is from the Jews" (Jn 4:22), and Mary spoke of her Son's redemption in terms of salvation for and through Israel.[8] What might

---

[7] I am not recommending changing what is already in the creeds; rather, I suggest that the church consider supplementing by teasing out in a phrase or two the implication of "I believe in the Holy Spirit . . . who has spoken through the prophets" (Nicene Creed). This would be an example of what John Henry Newman meant by the development of doctrine that the Holy Spirit has led through all the history of the church.

[8] In the Magnificat she says God "has helped his servant Israel . . . according to the promise he made to our ancestors" (salvation for Israel) and "from now on all generations will call me blessed . . . [because of this fulfillment of the promise made to] Abraham and to his descendants forever" (salvation through Israel to all the world) (Lk 1:48, 54-55).

historical theology do to understand the reason for this lacuna in the creeds and what impact the creeds had on later supersessionism?

The same sort of work could be done by liturgical theologians. Why were Old Testament readings left out of the lectionary readings for Sunday worship for so many centuries? Why do some still omit Old Testament readings? How have these omissions affected Christian attitudes toward Jews, Israel and the land? Why are so few sermons devoted to Old Testament texts? These are some of the questions that scholars of liturgy and homiletics should ask.

Systematic Theology

The New Christian Zionism is a challenge to systematic theologians. It suggests that anti-Zionism in Christian theology is supersessionist because it leaves the God of Israel, with his great promise to his particular people, behind. In most systematic theology today, Israel is only a propaedeutic or beginning instruction that prepares the way for its displacement—a kingdom of God in which the people and land of Israel have been replaced by a Trinity strangely removed from Israel's greatest promise. Even those theologians who acknowledge that somehow God's covenant with the people of Israel remains typically leave no room for what is at the heart of that covenant, the land. For these theologians, the people and land of Israel, which are central and distinctive in the Jewish Scriptures, are lost in a sea of Gentile sameness.

Most systematic theology today, when it treats Israel, betrays a modernist bent. As Peter Ochs suggests, anti-Zionist theology flies with one wing.[9] It tries to fly with the wing of universalism but without a corresponding wing of particularity. This was the hallmark of modernity, starting with Lessing's "ugly, great ditch" between universal reason and the particulars of history that he and most Enlightenment thinkers after him thought could not be jumped.[10] Hence, despite the fact that God made clear in his First Testament that he saves the world (the universal) through the particular (Israel), much of Christian theology today treats the Second (New) Testament as if it also rejects the diversity of the particular for the homogeneity of the universal. No longer is Jew different from Gentile in most Christian theologies; nor is the land of Israel of any sig-

---

[9]Peter Ochs, *Another Reformation: Postliberal Christianity and the Jews* (Grand Rapids: Baker Academic, 2011), 28.
[10]Gotthold Ephraim Lessing, "On the Proof of Spirit and Power," in *Lessings's Theological Writings*, ed. and trans. Henry Chadwick (repr., Stanford University Press, 1957), 51-56. See Ochs, *Another Reformation*, 28, 30, 254.

nificance—even though, as this book has shown, the New Testament authors held the land and people of Israel to be of future significance. The result is a strange universality in eschatology, where there is no interrelationship among different peoples or nations in the eschaton. Instead, there is the dominance of eternal abstractions—submission to a non-Jewish deity by myriads of human beings without national or ethnic distinctions. This is Gnostic and Docetic eschatology, in which matter is absent (Gnostic) or blandly undifferentiated and therefore only *seemingly* important (Docetic). All these eschatologies have a kind of geometric beauty, perhaps, but they lack the nonsymmetrical beauty of biblical eschatology.

Another way that this prevailing eschatology reveals its modernist character is its individualism. It is redemption of individual souls without nations or people groups. Somehow modern eschatology omits the "tribes and peoples and languages" that the book of Revelation describes (Rev 7:9). Even though many contemporary theologians decry disembodied eschatologies of yesterday by teaching the new heavens and new earth to come, they typically strip the new earth of the distinctive nationalities and the centrally placed nation depicted in the Bible. It is akin to giving the resurrected body of an individual a nondistinctive face so that it could not be distinguished from the myriads of other faces in the world to come.

Covenant theologians also need think through the implications of the New Christian Zionism. They have recently published scores of books and articles on how God's covenant with humanity included a covenant with the wider creation, especially the physical earth.[11] We humans were called to be priests and stewards of the physical environment of the earth, they rightly say, not simply guardians of our souls on a journey to a disembodied heaven. Yet theologians generally ignore the corollary: if God's covenant with humanity was not detached from the whole earth, why would the God of Israel's covenant with the people of Israel be detached from the land that he promised to them? They might consider the corollary to the apostles' teaching that Jesus' bodily resurrection was a proleptic (anticipatory) sign of the general bodily resurrection to come: the return and restoration of Israel in the last century might be a proleptic sign of the renewal of the nations to come. They

---

[11]They are right to find this throughout the Bible, including the Pauline literature. Paul speaks of the "groaning" of all creation as it awaits its future liberation from its "bondage to decay" (Rom 8:18-25).

should recall that Ezekiel's vision of dry bones coming to life is a vision not of individuals but of a whole nation coming back to life.[12] Both the prophets and the book of Revelation speak of the nations in the world to come, not simply a swarm of undifferentiated individuals. And at the center of the nations in that world is the nation of Israel. Theologians need to come to terms with that.

Theology Reflecting on Israel and Palestine

This New Christian Zionism has three implications for theologians reflecting on the relative justice of the Israeli-Palestinian conflict. First, it suggests that Jews and Arabs both need to "share responsibility for the bitterness."[13] Another way of putting it is to say that humility is needed on both sides. Jews can accurately say that they bought land fairly from Arabs starting in the nineteenth century, turned huge arid tracts into productive soil, and brought enormous material advantages to Arab populations. But they should acknowledge that in the wars of 1948 and 1967, land that was previously owned and controlled by Arabs passed over into Jewish hands. Jews have legitimate reasons for thinking that these transfers were for the most part conducted fairly, either by free financial exchange or after wars started by Arabs. But they should also concede that Arabs lost dignity and ownership of much, and Jews won.

Arabs need to acknowledge that while they had rights to land before wars and terrorism, these two kinds of tragedy have displaced some of those rights. I say "some" of those rights because Arabs still own and control much land in Israel proper, and the Palestinian Authority still controls much if not all of the West Bank. Hamas, an Arab government, owns and controls all of Gaza. Lands that have passed from Arab to Jewish ownership have done so, for the most part, because of wars started and lost by Arabs. Other lands have been lost by Arabs because of the fence (more popularly known as "the wall") that has been built between the West Bank and portions of Israel. It was built to stop terrorist strikes coming from the West Bank to attack civilians in Israel, and it has been largely successful.

---

[12]See Jon D. Levenson, *Resurrection and the Restoration of Israel: The Ultimate Victory of the God of Life* (New Haven, CT: Yale University Press, 2006), 156-65.
[13]James Parkes, *End of an Exile: Israel, the Jews and the Gentile World*, ed. Eugene B. Korn and Roberta Kalechofsky (Marblehead, MA: Micah, 2004), 43.

Sometimes Christians who seek to apply their theology to questions of justice in this conflict do so with more heat than light. Here are some facts that are little known but which should inform any evaluation of the dispute.

1. During the 1948 war, Jordan invaded the part given to Arabs and occupied it, calling the area its (Jordan's) West Bank. The Arab world did not recognize a separate Palestinian people for twenty years. In the meantime Jordan called the people who lived on the West Bank Jordanians, while Syria called them Syrians because Palestine had been considered part of southern Syria for centuries during the Ottoman Empire.

2. After the 1948 war there was an exchange of refugees throughout the Middle East. Jews lost at least as many homes as Arabs did. While Israel absorbed most of the 800,000 Jewish refugees who fled Arab and Muslim lands where they had lived for hundreds and even thousands of years, Arab nations refused to give new homes to incoming Arab refugees (725,000) and chose to keep them in refugee camps to use as a propaganda tool against Israel.

3. In the 1978–1979 peace treaty with Egypt, Israel returned 90 percent of the occupied territory it gained after the 1967 Six-Day War. Most of this was in the Sinai.

4. "The wall" has cut through Palestinian settlements, hurt Palestinian farmers by cutting them off from their orchards and farms, and in some cases reduced them to poverty. The Jewish state has taken in more territory. But at the same time, the wall has cut off more than twelve hundred acres of Jewish land around Jerusalem that was bought by Jews before 1948.[14]

5. Muslim theology contributes to the conflict, for the Qur'an prophesies that Jews will live in dispersion, poverty and misery.[15] Israel's prosperity therefore appears to pious Muslims to be a contradiction that is puzzling at best and damnable at worst. At the same time, the Qur'an testifies that God gave the land of Israel to the Jews: "Pharaoh sought to scare them [the Israelites] out of the land [of Egypt]: but We [Allah] drowned him [Pharaoh] together with all who were with him. Then We [Allah] said to the Israelites: 'Dwell in this land [the Land of Israel]. When the promise of the hereafter [End of Days] comes to be fulfilled, We [Allah] shall assemble you [the Israelites] all

---

[14]*Israel Today* (February 2007), 11, cited in David W. Torrance and George Taylor, *Israel God's Servant: God's Key to the Redemption of the World* (London: Paternoster, 2007), 19.

[15]For example, Q Baqarah 2:61: "And they were covered with humiliation and poverty and returned with anger from Allah [on them]" (Sahih International).

together" (Q Isra 17:103-104). One contemporary sheikh takes it at face value: "The Qur'an recognizes the Land of Israel as the heritage of the Jews and it explains that, before the Last Judgment, Jews will return to dwell there. This prophecy has already been fulfilled."[16]

A third implication of the New Christian Zionism for our understanding of this conflict is that there is a good reason why this conflict engages the whole world. The Bible suggests that the fate of the nations is bound up with Israel.[17] In Isaiah 19:23-25 Egypt and Assyria are blessed because of Israel, and Zechariah 12 prophesies that God makes Jerusalem a "cup of reeling" for the surrounding nations. In other words, not only is Israel a witness to the nations (Is 43:10) but God deals with the nations *through* Israel. In their relationship to Israel, the nations in some mysterious way come into contact with the God of Israel. They respond to God and are judged by God in this secret relationship.

We must confess immediately that there is much that we don't know about this. It certainly does not mean that Israel is always right or that it has never been unjust in its dealings with other nations. Nor does it mean that Christian theology must always take Israel's side against other nations, particularly when Israel is clearly wrong. But Scripture makes clear that God rules the nations and that Israel as a people and land is still within his secret providence—not only when God deals with Jews and Gentiles as individuals, but also when he judges the nations qua nations. They must beware of being like Job's friends, who made false accusations against Job and faced God's wrath.

Jewish-Christian Dialogue

Today we often hear that it is not anti-Semitic to criticize Israel. We agree. So do most Israelis, who criticize their own government much of the time. But there is a disproportionate criticism of Israel when, for example, Christian churches publish statements criticizing Israel for its alleged acts of injustice while giving a pass to Palestinian terrorism against Israel and oppression of fellow Palestinians by the Palestinian Authority and Hamas, Syria's killing thousands of its own citizens with chemical weapons, Iran's political murders of thousands of Iranians, North Korea's brutality toward its own people and mass murders com-

---

[16]Shaykh Professor Abdul Hadi Palazzi, "What the Qur'an Really Says," reprinted from *Viewpoint*, Winter 1998, accessed July 8, 2015, www.templemount.org/quranland.html. Palazzi is the secretary general of the Italian Muslim Assembly and the Khalifah for Europe of the Qadiri Sufi Order.

[17]Torrance and Taylor, *Israel God's Servant*, 28, 62.

mitted by Boko Haram and ISIS. They typically ignore Muslim persecution of Arab Christians *within* Israel, the West Bank and Gaza and are oblivious to the dangers that Arab Christians face when they mention this persecution in public. It was this kind of inconsistency that led Martin Luther King Jr. to say, shortly before he was assassinated, "When people criticize Zionists, they mean Jews; you are talking anti-Semitism."[18]

The New Christian Zionism suggests that when Christians dialogue with Jews, Christians need to enter the dialogue with humility. Not only do we need to be mindful that the church has been complicit in the oppression and murder of myriads of Jews. We also need to remember that we have much to learn from Jews who know and love their tradition, for it is a treasure of wise and pious reflection on God and Scripture, most of which is Jewish and not *explicitly Christian*. So we should enter the dialogue with the intent of learning and not just professing or teaching. It might also enhance our appreciation for such dialogue to recall that the humanity God took into the Godhead was Jewish humanity, and that the flesh that is now at the right hand of the Father is Jewish flesh. Therefore we should tell ourselves on this side of the dialogue that if our church does not see and explore its Jewish roots, it loses touch with its God and Lord.

FIVE PROPOSITIONS

We close this book with five propositions that we think should guide the church in its thinking about Israel and itself. These points will help Christians keep joined together what Christian theology has often separated: Israel and the church.

1. Israel shows us who we are and who God is. God called Israel to represent all the peoples of the world. She shows us who we are before God, at both our best and our worst. Israel demonstrates God's creation of human beings with capacity to trust in him, and the human predilection to reject God. The New Testament hints, paradoxically, that Israel was chosen to reject Jesus' messianic claim, but it also implies that this sin represents all human sin against God. If Israel rejected Jesus, so did we. As the Lutheran Lenten hymn "Ah, Holy Jesus" asks,

> Who was the guilty? Who brought this upon thee?
> Alas, my treason, Jesus, hath undone thee.
> 'Twas I, Lord Jesus, I it was denied thee:
> I crucified thee.

---

[18]Seymour Martin Lipset, "The Socialism of Fools: The Left, the Jews and Israel," *Encounter*, December 1969, 24.

Yet Scripture also indicates that Israel had not just a representative but a special election: that her blindness led to the world's gaining sight. Both Jesus and Paul said (Mk 4:12; Rom 11:8) that God used Israel's stubbornness to redeem the world, just as the Egyptians learned about the God of Israel because Joseph's brothers sold him into slavery. So we can say that Israel was elected to bear the glory and pain of bringing salvation to the world. We need to acknowledge that the world owes Israel a debt. This is true in the secular realm, for most of the last century's great scientific advances were gained by Jews. But it is also true religiously, as Jesus told the Samaritan woman: "Salvation is from the Jews" (Jn 4:22).

Therefore we need Israel to know God. Israel shows us that we live by grace, just as she has survived millennia of pogroms and holocausts only by the grace of God. The church bears witness to this grace and mercy, while Israel has also borne witness to God's judgment.[19] But only if the church learns from the judgment Israel has suffered will she be able to know God's mercy.

2. Sacred history is not over. Jean Cardinal Daniélou observed that biblical prophecy "is the announcement of the fact that, at the end of time, God will accomplish works still greater than in the past."[20] This means that we can expect that in the latter days the unfolding of sacred history will continue. Unusual and remarkable events are to be anticipated, if biblical prophecy is not simply spiritual exhortation but actually refers in part to future events in the history of salvation.

Therefore we can trust that God is still lovingly confronting the nations through Israel and that Israel is still God's servant for the redemption of the world in some mysterious way. Through her, God is still saying to the nations, "Just as you did it to one of the least of these who are members of my family, you did it to me" (Mt 25:40). Some might say that Israel with her military might cannot be considered "one of the least of these," but at this time in history Israel is threatened daily with extinction by her neighbors and hostility from much of the rest of the world. She often feels alone and small.

---

[19] Torrance and Taylor, *Israel God's Servant*, 126.
[20] Daniélou, "The Sacraments and the History of Salvation," in *Letter and Spirit: The Authority of Mystery, The Word of God and the People of God*, ed. Scott Hahn and David Scott (Steubenville, OH: St. Paul Center for Biblical Theology, 2006), 211.

Israel continues to be a vessel of revelation. Her deliverance from the Holocaust and her restoration in the land reveal God's faithfulness to his covenantal promises. Her survival demonstrates to all with ears to hear that God is the Lord of history.[21]

Israel's continued survival and recent emergence as a people on the land show that sacred history is ongoing. Pannenberg wrote that the church is a provisional sign of the end time but not the consummation itself.[22] So too Israel today is a provisional sign of the end time that in its restoration points to the eschatological restoration of creation to come. Prophetic fulfillment has not come to an end.

3. Eschatological fulfillment is both revealed and hidden. Luther is famous for his dictum that God in Jesus Christ is both revealed and hidden, and Barth made that a major theme of his *Church Dogmatics*. The same is true of eschatology, particularly in relation to Israel.

God called Israel to be both a nation (*ethnos*) and a people (*laos*) set apart for him. We and they (the people of Israel) must live with the tension between those two callings. The first requires an army and security apparatus to protect Israel from near annihilation again. The second requires Israel to trust in God and not her arms. Like every other part of the people of God, Israel's balance between the two is often flawed. For this reason, among others, the fulfillment of the biblical promises of Israel's restoration often seems questionable. Just as, I might add, the promise that the church in all of its brokenness and dysfunction is really the body of Christ also seems questionable at times.

Much of eschatology is wrapped in mystery. Scripture clearly teaches that God chose Israel, but it never explains *why* Israel was chosen. We are told that God uses Israel to demonstrate his power and glory, just as he delivered Israel from Egypt and raised up Pharaoh for this very purpose (Ex 9:16). But Paul warns us not to "argue with God" about his sovereign decisions and teaches us that such divine ways and judgments are "unsearchable" (Rom 9:20; 11:33).

The same applies to these present stages of fulfillment for eschatological Israel. *That* the emergence of modern Israel is a fulfillment of prophecy seems plain, as we have argued in this book. But *how* all this is working out, and will work out, is a mystery we must not think we can penetrate with any precision.

---

[21]Torrance and Taylor, *Israel God's Servant*, 70.
[22]Wolfhart Pannenberg, *Systematic Theology* (Grand Rapids: Eerdmans, 1998), 3:476.

4. *This fulfillment is not in its final stage.* We cannot know the unfolding of the end times with any precision, but we can know that this stage of fulfillment is not the final one. We have already referred to the prophecy of Israel's resurrection in Ezekiel 37. It is significant that in this classic prophecy the resurrection proceeds in stages. First the bones came together, bone to bone. Then God put sinews and flesh and skin on the dry bones. Next he told Ezekiel to prophesy to them. Finally, the breath came into them, they came to life and they stood up. In another version of the process, Ezekiel said God would open their graves, then bring them up from their graves and then they would live. After that, he would place them on their own soil. Either at that point or after (it is not clear in the Hebrew) they would know that "I, the Lord, have spoken and will act" (Ezek 37:14). Besides showing that spiritual renewal seems to come *after* return to the land, this classic account of Israel's return suggests that the restoration of Israel to the land takes place in stages.

It is not apparent to the outside world if spiritual renewal is now taking place in the land. Informal reports suggest that it is, but few religious Zionists would say that it approaches the degree of religious renewal that the prophets predicted. Others recognize that Israel is still a long way from the full vision of the prophets.

> Only a part of the Jewish people has gathered together into a Jewish state, and only in certain areas of the country. Only some of the returnees observe the precepts of Torah. Political and military strife has not vanished from the land. Peace is elusive and morality compromised. Universal redemption seems even more remote than before. In short, the concrete fulfillment wrought by Zionism remains relative and contingent, stopping well short of the absolute terms of the classical vision. As the rabbis said, the End of Days continues to "tarry."[23]

The New Christian Zionism would note two things. First, there is always tension between promise and fulfillment of any prophecy, and we need to live with that tension. As I have noted several times, we already live with that tension in the church, believing it is the body of Christ despite its many spots and wrinkles and blemishes (Eph 5:27). Second, the final coming that we await is not a perfect Israeli people or state but that of the Son of Man.

---

[23]Aviezer Ravitsky, *Messianism, Zionism, and Jewish Religious Radicalism* (Chicago: University of Chicago Press, 1996), 2.

5. Israel and the church are integrally joined. The New Christian Zionism suggests that the relationship between the people of Israel and the church is parallel to the relationship between Scripture and the church. The Great Tradition holds that Scripture illuminates the church just as the church in its faith-seeking understanding sheds new light on Scripture. It is a dialectical relationship. So too, we would propose, Israel in its millennia of reflection on the Torah and the Prophets has much to teach the church about the God of Israel who is also the Father of Jesus Christ. And, to complete the dialectic, the church can teach Israel about its final fulfillment in Messiah and his kingdom.

But this integral joining goes beyond understanding. It includes communion. If the church has communion with the saints of the Old Testament, as it has proclaimed for two thousand years in the creeds, then it also has communion with the Israel of God in whom those saints live and move and have their being. If Christians worship the God of Israel, then in some way we have communion with Jews who also worship the God of Israel and are in communion with him. This begins with messianic Jews. We don't know how or when nonmessianic Jewish believers will be joined self-consciously with Israel's Messiah, but we believe that God will bring that about in his perfect way and time.

We have already observed that Christian theology teaches, without often putting it this way, that God took Jewish flesh up into his inner life when he raised Jesus' body to his right hand. We affirm as well that this is part of the mystery of the Eucharist. Here Christians participate in the covenant God made with Jewish flesh, communing with the Jewish body and blood of the Messiah. This is difficult for some Christians to swallow—but no more difficult than it was for Jesus' disciples, many of whom "turned back and no longer went about with him" after he told them that they must "eat the flesh of the Son of Man and drink his blood" (Jn 6:66, 53). This was a "hard saying."

This is another example of the scandal of particularity. Although the objection has been around for millennia, the eighteenth-century deists first raised this protest in the modern world by complaining that a God for the whole world would never restrict his revelation to certain peoples and certain times. Nor would he have chosen just one people in an isolated part of the world. All revelation would be universal, they asserted, and any revelation that was restricted to a particular people and particular land cannot also be universal. Therefore it cannot be true.

The New Christian Zionism proposes that the scandal of Zionism is the twenty-first-century version of the scandal of particularity. Just as he did thousands of years ago, God comes to the world universally through a particular people and a particular land. He has done that for millennia, and he continues to do that today.

LIST OF CONTRIBUTORS

Robert Benne (PhD, University of Chicago), Jordan-Trexler Professor of Religion Emeritus at Roanoke College and founder of its Center for Religion and Society. He is the author of twelve books, including *Good and Bad Ways to Think About Religion and Politics* (Eerdmans, 2010).

Craig Blaising (PhD, University of Aberdeen), Jesse Hendley Chair of Biblical Theology, and executive vice president and provost of Southwestern Baptist Theological Seminary. Among his many writings, he has published "The Future of Israel as a Theological Question," "Then You Will Know That I Am the Lord: The Revelatory Significance of the Return of the Jews to Zion in Christian Non-Supersessionist Theology," and coedited *Psalms 1-50*, Ancient Christian Commentary on Scripture (IVP Academic, 2008).

Darrell Bock (PhD, University of Aberdeen), senior research professor of New Testament Studies at Dallas Theological Seminary, and executive director of cultural engagement at its Hendricks Center. A member of the board of Chosen People Ministries, Darrell has edited or written several books and articles tied to the role of Israel in Scripture, including the recently released book *The People, the Land, and the Future of Israel* (Kregel, 2014).

Shadi Khalloul (BS, University of Nevada), Israeli Christian Maronite, paratrooper captain (reserve) in the Israeli Defense Forces, and chair of the Aramaic Christian Association.

Mark S. Kinzer (PhD, University of Michigan), senior scholar and president emeritus of Messianic Jewish Theological Institute; rabbi, Congregation Zera Avraham, Ann Arbor, Michigan. He is the author of *Postmissionary Messianic*

Judaism: Redefining Christian Engagement with the Jewish People (Brazos, 2005) and *Israel's Messiah and the People of God* (Cascade, 2011).

Gerald R. McDermott (PhD, University of Iowa), Anglican Chair of Divinity, Beeson Divinity School; and associate pastor, Christ the King Anglican Church, Birmingham, Alabama. He is the author, coauthor or editor of eighteen books, including *A Trinitarian Theology of Religions* (Oxford University Press, 2014) and *God's Rivals* (IVP Academic, 2009).

Robert Nicholson (JD, Syracuse University), executive director of the Philos Project, New York City. He promotes positive Christian engagement with Israel and the wider Middle East. He also holds an MA (Middle Eastern History) from Syracuse University and a BA in Hebrew Studies from SUNY Binghamton.

David Rudolph (PhD, University of Cambridge), is the director of Messianic Jewish Studies and professor of New Testament and Jewish Studies at The King's University in Southlake, Texas. His recent publications include *Introduction to Messianic Judaism: Its Ecclesial Context and Biblical Foundations*, coedited with Joel Willitts (Zondervan, 2013), and *A Jew to the Jews: Jewish Contours of Pauline Flexibility in 1 Corinthians 9:19-23* (Mohr Siebeck, 2011).

Mark Tooley (BA, Georgetown University), president, Institute on Religion and Democracy. He has authored three books, including *Methodism and Politics in the 20th Century* (Bristol House, 2012), and has written for numerous publications, including *Wall Street Journal*, *Christianity Today*, *World*, *American Spectator*, *Weekly Standard* and *Time*.

Joel Willitts (PhD, University of Cambridge), professor, Biblical and Theological Studies, North Park University. He is coeditor and contributor to *Paul and the Gospels* (T&T Clark, 2011) and *Jesus, Matthew and Early Christianity* (T&T Clark, 2013).

NAME INDEX

Abbas, Mahmoud, 276
Abrams, Elliott, 276, 278
al Azm, Haled, 22
Allison, Dale C., 128, 137, 149
Alon, Gedaliah, 17, 36
Amaru, Betsy, 114-15
Anderson, Gary A., 11, 14, 73-74
Aquinas, Thomas, 257
Arafat, Yasser, 277
Arameans, 281-83, 285-88
Arendt, Hannah, 234
Aruel, Yaakov, 47
Augustine, 38, 56, 74, 257, 320-21
Bader-Saye, Scott, 39
Baker, Alan, 275
Bale, John, 58
Balthasar, Hans Urs von, 13
Banki, Judith Hershcopf, 204, 206
Banks, William C., 262
Barth, Karl, 11, 42, 45, 71-73
Barth, Marcus, 42
Bauckham, Richard, 91, 146
Baur, F. C., 171
Beale, Greg, 81
Beaton, Richard, 120-21
Bede, 57
Bell, Richard H., 183-84
Ben Gurion, David, 25, 294
Bengel, Johann Albrecht, 72
Bicheno, James, 65
Bielfeldt, Dennis, 39
Birch, Bruce C., 252
Blackstone, William, 197-99, 218
Blaising, Craig, 43, 320
Blomberg, Craig L., 79
Blumhart, Christoph Friedrich, 72
Blumhart, Johann Christoph, 72
Bockmuehl, Markus, 53, 187
Booth, Roger P., 179

Borgen, Peder, 115
Bouyer, Louis, 283
Boyarin, Daniel, 36, 123, 180-81
Brakel, Wilhelmus à, 61, 62
Brawley, Robert L., 145
Brightman, Thomas, 59, 61
Brooke, George J., 127
Browning, Edmond, 209-13
Brueggemann, Walter, 111, 115, 184
Buber, Martin, 69, 234
Buchanan, George Wesley, 115-16, 177
Buell, Denise K., 181
Bunyan, John, 58
Burge, Gary, 28, 46-47, 51, 83, 114-15, 141-42, 153-54, 164, 171-72, 177, 251, 312
Bush, George H. W., 209
Bush, George W., 214
Burnett, Fred, 138
Burrell, David, 57
Caird, G. B., 100
Calvin, John, 39, 56, 257
Campbell, William S., 170, 180, 185
Carenin, Caitlin, 225
Carleston, Charles E., 109-10
Carter, Jimmy, 271
Carter, Warren, 137
Chae, Young Sam, 123
Cherry, Robert, 290
Chrysostom, John, 38
Cohen, Aharon, 21
Cohen, Hillel, 22
Collins, Raymond F., 178
Contreras, Elvira Martin, 17
Conzelmann, Hans, 154
Cook, Michael J., 186
Cotton, John, 61
Cowgill, Benjamin, 49, 50
Cranfield, C. E. B., 42
Culver, Douglas J., 57

Daniélou, Jean Cardinal, 330
Davies, Matthew, 215
Davies, W. D., 42-43, 81, 115, 128, 137, 192-93
de Vos, J. Cornelis, 115-16
Dershowitz, Alan, 278, 315
Dinstein, Yoram, 263
Donaldson, Terrence L., 185
Dorsey, David A., 257
Draxe, Thomas, 58
Dunn, James D. G., 171, 177, 179, 184
Eban, Abba, 267, 269, 315
Edwards, Jonathan, 62-65
Ehle, Carl F., Jr., 56
Ehrensperger, Kathy, 181
Eid, Bassem, 299
Eisenbaum, Pamela, 180-81
Eisenhower, Dwight, 202
Elazar, Daniel J., 259
Enns, Peter, 258
Eshkol, Levi, 267, 269
Evans, Craig A., 109-10, 127
Faithful, George, 71
Falwell, Jerry, 47
Feinstein, Rabbi Moshe, 20
Felsenstein, Frank, 65
Fiedler, Peter, 130
Finch, Henry, 60-61
Forman, Mark, 175-76, 187, 194
Fosdick, Harry Emerson, 200, 236
Foxe, John, 58
France, R. T., 128-29
Franck, Thomas M., 262
Fredricksen, Paula, 38, 180, 321
Gardner, E. Clinton, 252
Gelernter, David, 247
Gillet, Lev, 68-69
Glahn, Gerhard von, 260
Griswold, Frank, 214
Goldman, Shalom, 18-19, 47, 68
Goldsmith, Jack L., 263
Goldstone, Richard, 273
Goremberg, Gershom, 270
Graetz, Heinrich, 170
Granott, Abraham, 22
Grotius, Hugo, 261
Gundry-Volf, Judith M., 180-82
Gurtner, Daniel M., 108, 128-29
Hafemann, Scott, 179, 190-91
Hagee, John, 47
Hagner, Donald A., 84, 108
Hamilton, Catherine Sider, 130, 132-33
Hardin, Justin K., 180

Harink, Douglas, 168
Harvey, Richard, 14
Hastings, Adrian, 16
Hauerwas, Stanley, 218, 234
Hauser, Christine, 250
Hays, Richard, 52, 116, 155
Hazony, Yoram, 25
Hechler, William, 68
Heil, Christopher, 125, 136-37
Henkin, Louis, 262
Herder, Johann Gottfried, 15-16
Hertzberg, Arthur, 64
Herzl, Theodore, 16, 18, 25, 47, 68
Heschel, Abraham Joshua, 224-25
Hildegard of Bingen, 56
Himmelfarb, Martha, 189
Hinlicky, Paul, 39
Hobsbawm, Eric J., 15
Hodge, Caroline Johnson, 178
Hoehner, Harold, 108
Hopkins, Paul, 199, 209
Horbury, William, 138, 177, 183-84, 191-93
Horner, Barry E., 62, 97, 172
Horrell, David G., 178
Horsley, Richard A., 180
Hsieh, Nelson, 173
Huizenga, Leroy Andrew, 117
Hussein, Abdullah (king of Jordan), 22, 267
Hussein, bin Tallal (king of Jordan), 294
Hussein, Mufti Muhammad, 295, 296
Hume, David, 41
Hurst, L. D., 86
Huxley, Julian, 57
Hvalvik, Reidar, 186
Hybels, Lynne, 216
Irenaeus, 37-38, 54
Jenson, Robert, 11, 14
Joachim of Fiore, 56
Johnson, Paul, 17-18, 315
Jones, Ryan, 289
Joseph of Arimathea, 57
Josephus, 115, 183-84, 282
Justin Martyr, 36-38, 54, 167
Kaiser, Walter, 79, 252, 257
Kalechovsky, Roberta, 16
Kant, Immanuel, 41
Karsh, Efraim, 294
Katanacho, Yohanna, 174
Kershner, Isabel, 278
Khalloul, Shadi, 295
King, Martin Luther, Jr., 329
Kinzer, Mark S., 14, 148

Name Index

Kirk, J. R. Daniel, 186, 191
Klawans, Jonathan, 179
Klein, Menachem, 273
Klinger, Jerry, 198
Konradt, Matthew, 110-11, 118, 120-22, 138
Kontorovich, Eugene, 272, 276
Kook, Rabbi Abraham Isaac, 20
Koonijmans, Pieter, 250
Kreitzer, L. Joseph, 193
Lalonde, Suzanne, 270
Lapidoth, Ruth, 276
Lerner, Robert E., 56
Lessing, Gotthold Ephraim, 324
Levenson, Jon D., 326
Lewis, Donald, 48, 58, 66, 99
Lipset, Seymour Martin, 329
Loden, Lisa, 315
Longenecker, Bruce, 172, 194
Longman, Tremper, III, 257
Luter, A. Boyd, 173
Luther, Martin, 39, 58
Lux, Richard C., 109, 184
Luz, Ulrich, 130-31, 137
Maimonides, 19-20
Manji, Irshad, 23, 23n
Manuel, Frank E., 40-41
Marcion, 24, 62
Marshall, I. Howard, 145
Martens, Elmer, 48
Martin, Oren R., 171
Martin, Troy W., 180
Martyn, J. Louis, 180
Mather, Increase, 61
Mattox, Mickey, 39
McDermott, Gerald, 63
McKnight, Scot, 43, 125
Mede, Joseph, 60
Meier, John P., 43
Meir, Edmund, 289
Meir, Golda, 292-93
Mendels, Doron, 174
Merkley, Paul, 68, 70
Miller, Paul, 229
Milman, Henry Hart, 67
Milton, John, 60
Mittelman, Alan, 256
Mitternacht, Dieter, 187
Moorhead, Jonathan, 198
Morris, Benny, 22, 300, 315
Mosely, Carys, 71-73, 227, 233, 240-42
Moule, C. F. D., 184
Munayer, Salim, 315

Murray, Iain H., 98
Nahmanides, 20
Nanos, Mark D., 180, 185-86
Nasser, Gamal Abdel, 266
Naumann, Klaus, 293
Netanyahu, Benjamin, 276, 278, 290
Newman, John Henry, 66, 323
Newton, Isaac, 65
Nicholson, Robert, 279
Niebuhr, Gustav, 222
Niebuhr, H. Richard, 228
Niebuhr, Reinhold, 11, 28-29, 201, 221-48
Niehr, Herbert, 281
Nolland, John, 108, 129-31
Novak, David, 253, 256
Oberman, Heiko, 56-57
Ochs, Peter, 324
Oepke, Albrecht, 151, 163
Oliver, Isaac W., 146
Olmert, Ehud, 276
Olmstead, Wesley G., 127
Oppenhein, Lassa, 262
Oren, Michael, 266-67
Origen, 38, 55, 167
Osborne, Grant R., 7
Oz, Amos, 263
Palazzi, Abdul Hadi, 328
Pannenberg, Wolfhart, 331
Parkes, James, 16, 18, 326
Pennington, Jonathan, 125, 136
Perkins, William, 58
Peterman, Gerald, 186
Philo, 115, 183-84, 189
Pike, James, 203
Poliakov, Léon, 16
Pomerance, Michla, 250
Posner, Eric A., 263
Puskas, Charles B., 158
Quigley, John, 266, 267, 268
Quine, Willard Van Orman, 82
Rabin, Chaim, 16
Rabinowitz, Noel, 27
Rad, Gerhard von, 48
Raheb, Mitri, 259
Rausch, David, 223
Ravitsky, Aviezer, 18-19, 332
Reeves, Marjorie, 56
Richardson, Peter, 36
Riskin, Schlomo, 256
Robb, Edmund W., 216
Robb, Julia, 216
Ross, Dennis, 278

Rostow, Eugene, 275
Rousseau, Jean-Jacques, 15, 16
Rudolph, David J., 172, 177, 180, 188
Runesson, Anders, 129, 188
Saiman, Chaim, 251
Sacks, Jonathan, 320
Saddington, James A., 70
Saladrini, Anthony, 113-14
Salkin, Jeffrey, 222
Sanders, E. P., 43, 179
Sanders, James, 53
Schechter, Jack, 51
Schiffer, Shimon, 276
Schleiermacher, Friedrich, 41-42
Schlink, Mother Basilea, 70-71
Schori, Katherine Jefferts, 215
Schwebel, Stephen, 265
Scott, James M., 96, 115, 174, 191
Scott, Thomas, 65, 67
Shaftesbury, Lord Ashley, 48, 66-67
Silva, Moisés, 79
Simeon, Charles, 66
Simon, Marcel, 36
Sizer, Stephen, 47, 259, 312
Skarsaune, Oskar, 36, 37
Smith, Robert O., 48, 58, 61, 71
Smith, William Robertson, 254-55
Smooha, Sami, 294
Snodgrass, Klyne, 126-27
Soulen, R. Kendall, 34, 36, 41, 82, 83, 168, 170, 182-83, 186
Stanley, Christopher D., 181
Stanton, Graham, 117-18
Stendahl, Krister, 42
Stone, Julius, 275-76
Stone, Ronald, 227
Stowers, S. K., 172
Stuhlmacher, Peter, 42, 123
Tannehill, Robert C., 150, 152, 160-61
Tapie, Matthew A., 168
Tashjian, Joel, 250
Tawil, Bassam, 296
Taylor, Justin, 158-59
Taylor, Matthew, 250
Tertullian, 55, 257
Thiselton, Anthony C., 178
Ticciati, Susannah, 185

Tilley, Virginia, 271
Tillich, Paul, 222
Timmerman, Kenneth, 21
Toameh, Khaled Abu, 300-301
Tomson, Peter J., 147, 178
Tooley, Mark, 216
Toon, Peter, 98
Torrance, David W., 327, 330-31
Trigg, Joseph W., 38
Truman, Harry, 11, 70, 202
Tuchman, Barbara W., 57
Tucker, J. Brian, 188
Turner, Seth, 193
Tutu, Desmond, 215
Tyson, Joseph, 154, 161
Vahrenhorst, Martin, 111, 115, 125
VanGemeren, Willem A., 62
Vanlaningham, Michael G., 168, 177, 186
Visscher, Gerhard, 172-73
Vlach, Michael J., 168
von Rad, Gerhard. *See* Rad, Gerhard von
Voss, Carl, 223
Wagner, Don, 222
Wagner, J. Ross, 190
Walker, Peter W. L., 83, 174
Weaver, Dorothy Jean, 112
Weber, Timothy P., 47
White, Cynthia, 282
Wilberforce, William, 66
Williamson, Paul R., 176
Willitts, Joel, 109-10, 114, 115, 120, 122-23
Wilken, Robert, 43-44, 55, 142, 175, 243
Wilkinson, Paul, 298
Wilson, Woodrow, 198-99
Winter, Bruce W., 189
Wolfe, David L., 82
Wood, Charles M., 81
Woods, David B., 180
Wright, N. T., 43, 81, 149, 168-71, 177, 190, 312
Wyschogrod, Michael, 107, 139, 169-70, 188
Yehudah, Limor, 273
Yoder, John Howard, 218
Zakai, Avihu, 39, 64-65
Zangenberg, Jürgen K., 110, 118, 120, 125
Zetterholm, Magnus, 282
Zoccali, Christopher, 178, 186

SUBJECT INDEX

amillennialism, 56, 74
apartheid, 22-24, 272
apokatastasis, 53-54, 151, 162-63
atonement in Matthew, 132-35
Babylon, return of Jews from, 52, 99, 101-2
Balfour Declaration, 66, 199, 315
Bar Kokhba, 16, 36
Barnabas, epistle of, 36
Calvinism, role of in Zionism, 57
Christian Century, 201, 223
civil rights in Israel for minorities, 292-93
Dabru Emet, 44
Damascus Blood Libel, 67
Declaration of Independence of the State of Israel, 24, 288
deists, 39, 63
dispensationalism, 11, 13-15, 26, 27, 46-48, 67-68, 71, 74-75, 108, 241
    progressive, 14-15
Docetism, 29, 325
England, eschatological singularity of, 57, 66
Federal Council of Churches, 200
Geneva Bible, 58
Geneva Conventions, 262-63, 271, 274, 279
gnostic tendency of supersessionism, 325
Hague Regulations, 271
International Court of Justice, 249-50
international law, 249-80
    Law of Belligerent Occupation, 262-63
Israel
    calling of, 188-89
    gifts of, 182-85
    hardening of, 94, 97
    irrevocability, 43, 73, 97, 183-84, 185, 188, 193-94
Jerusalem
    heavenly or future, 35, 44, 52-57, 59, 62, 64-65, 67, 70, 85-86, 91, 128-32

    pivot for Luke–Acts, 143-53
kabbalah, 17
law of return, 24-25
League of Nations, 21
liberation theology, 197, 203-4
Mandatory Palestine, 268-69
Maronites, 288-89
millennium, 54, 56, 62, 64-65
Mishnah, 17, 114
National Council of Churches, 206
nationalism, 15-18
    nationhood, 71-73, 245-46, 312, 325, 331
new Israel, 38, 43, 62, 83, 185, 306
occupied territories, 264-70
Oslo Accords, 213, 272, 278
Palestine Liberation Organization (PLO), 206
Pietists, 66
pollution, 133-34
postmillennialism, 65-67, 75
premillennialism, 11, 45-46, 48, 66-68, 70, 74-75, 241
Puritans, 58-59, 62, 64, 74
replacement theology. *See* supersessionism
scandal of particularity, 40, 333-34
Social Gospel, 240-41
supersessionism, 26-28, 60, 62, 127, 168-70, 241-42
    history of, 34-44
tabernacle, 85
Talmud, 18-20
telos, 216-17
temple, 17, 19, 47, 52-53, 55, 62, 84, 101, 128-32, 311
theocracy, 24-26
transference theology. *See* supersessionism
two covenant view, 309
United Nations, 12, 21-22, 205-7, 250-51, 265, 268, 279, 289, 296, 315
    Resolution, 242, 276-79

War of 1948, 22
West Bank, 21, 29. *See also* occupied territories
Zionism
    as heresy, 216-17

political, 16, 74
and racism, 205-7
spiritual, 69-70
Zionist Congress, 18, 69

SCRIPTURE AND ANCIENT WRITINGS INDEX

OLD TESTAMENT

Genesis
1–11, *73*
1:27-28, *181*
2:24, *181*
10, *72*
12, *126, 311*
12:3, *67, 102*
12:7, *173*
13:14-18, *93*
13:15, *173*
13:16, *311*
15, *126*
15:5, *173, 311*
17, *126*
17:1-21, *251*
17:5, *173*
17:8, *93, 173*
22, *35*
22:17-18, *176*
23, *51*
23:2, *51*
26, *35, 126, 176*
26:2-5, *176*
26:3-4, *284*
27:29, *89*
28, *35, 126*
28:1-5, *287*
35:11-12, *177*
49:10, *89*

Exodus
3:13-17, *103*
3:15, *103*
3:16-17, *100*
4:22-23, *188*
6:2-8, *103*
9:16, *331*
12:48-49, *255*
12:49, *253, 271*
15:13, *322*
19:1–24:11, *251*
19, *189*
19:5-6, *189*
20:10, *255*
22:21, *254*
23:9, *254*
23:12, *255*
25:40, *85*
29:33, *255*
32:15, *184*

Leviticus
16:29, *255*
17:8, *255*
17:10-16, *255*
18:24-30, *73*
18:24-28, *259*
19:9-10, *254*
19:33-34, *51, 254*
20:2, *255*
22:18, *255*
23:22, *254*
24:22, *253*
25:39, *255*
25:45-46, *255*

Numbers
9:14, *255*
13, *74*
15:14, *255*
15:15-16, *253*
19:2-10, *255*
30:2, *138*
33:53, *20*

Deuteronomy
1:16, *51, 253*
4:23, *93*
4:29-31, *97*
4:37-40, *93, 97*
4:40, *93*
5:14, *255*
5:23, *138*
7:6, *189*
7:7-9, *283*
10:19, *254*
11:31-32, *19*
11:31, *19*
12:10, *93*
14:2, *189*
14:28-29, *51*
15:3, *255*
15:4, *93*
16:11, *255*
16:14, *255*
16:18-20, *253*
17:15, *255*
19:8-9, *51*
19:10, *93*
19:14, *93*
21:1-9, *133*
21:23, *93*
23:4, *255*
23:20, *255*
23:7-8, *255*
24:4, *93*
24:14, *51*
24:14-15, *255*
24:17, *51*
24:17-18, *254*
24:19, *254*
25:19, *93*
26:1-15, *286*

26:5, *285*
26:5-11, *183*
26:9, *284*
26:12, *51, 254*
26:18, *189*
27:19, *51, 254*
28:11, *321*
28:15-68, *252*
28:23, *321*
30, *105*
32:43, *172*

Joshua
8:33-35, *51*
9, *51*
10:6-8, *51*

2 Samuel
5:2, *122*
7:8-16, *90*
7:11, *132*
7:13-18, *100*
23:8-39, *23*

1 Kings
4:17-19, *138*
19:15, *282*

2 Kings
8:7-8, *282*

1 Chronicles
11:2, *122*
11:10-47, *23*
17:7-15, *90*
17:11-14, *100*
17:12, *132*
17:14, *124*
27:16, *138*
27:16-22, *138*
28:5, *124*
29:23, *124*

2 Chronicles
9:8, *124*
13:8, *124*
18:16, *122*
30:25, *51*
36:23, *70, 73*

Ezra
1:1, *70*

2:2, *138*
6:17, *138*
8:35, *138*

Nehemiah
7:7, *138*

Psalms
2, *87, 89-90, 104, 173*
2:6-9, *193*
2:8, *90*
8:6, *193*
14:7, *96*
22, *173*
37, *136-37, 174*
37:11, *135-36*
47, *173*
72, *126, 173*
72:17-20, *89*
105:7-11, *93*
110:1, *86, 91, 193*
110:1-6, *193*
110:4, *86*
128:6, *140*
137:1, *321*

Isaiah
1:17, *253*
2:1-4, *173*
2:2-4, *312*
5:1-7, *85*
5:2, *127*
6, *154, 158-59*
8:23-9:1, *120*
9:1, *121*
9:6-7, *90*
11, *190*
11:10, *89-90, 190*
11:11-12, *190*
11:12, *52*
19:18-25, *173*
19:19-25, *89*
19:23-25, *328*
25, *126*
25:6-8, *89*
27, *190*
27:9, *96*
35:10, *153*
40–66, *95*
40, *156, 158*
40:1, *156*
40:4-5, *156*

40:5, *156, 158*
41:8-10, *97*
43:1-7, *97*
43:10, *328*
45:3, *97*
48:2, *128*
48:12, *97*
49, *157-58*
49:5-6, *157-58*
49:6, *154*
49:6-7, *90, 173*
49:22-23, *126*
49:22, *198*
52:1, *128*
52:7-10, *173*
53, *71*
54, *130*
54:1-2, *131*
54:1-3, *176*
54:6-8, *97*
54:7, *131*
55:3-5, *173*
56:7, *52*
56:7-8, *52*
59, *53, 97, 190*
59:20-21, *43, 96*
60:21, *43*
66:23, *173*

Jeremiah
7:5-7, *254*
16:14-15, *52*
16:15, *54, 151*
22:3-9, *254*
23:1-7, *122*
23:8, *52*
24:6, *54, 151*
25, *99, 101*
29-33, *97*
29:7, *74*
29:14, *92*
30:3, *92*
30:17-18, *92*
31, *97*
31:9, *188*
31:23, *92*
31:31-34, *13*
31:31-37, *100*
31:33-34, *96*
31:33-37, *97*
31:35-36, *285*
31:35-37, *97*

Scripture and Ancient Writings Index

32:37-44, *92*
33:7-9, *92*
33:11, *92*
33:15-16, *90*
33:26, *92*
50:19, *54*

Ezekiel
20:42, *103*
22:6-7, *254*
22:29, *254*
34, *122-23, 198*
34:21, *123*
36–37, *85*
36:22-38, *103*
36:36, *103*
37, *122, 134, 332*
37:14, *332*
37:21, *322*
37:22, *322*
37:23, *322*
39:25, *103*
39:25-29, *92*
39:28, *103*

Daniel
7, *123*
9, *101*
9:20-27, *90*
9:24, *128*
9:27, *149*
11:31, *149*
12:11, *149*

Hosea
1, *192*
1:10, *192*
1:10-11, *192*
6:6, *179*
6:11, *92*
11:1, *188*
11:11, *54, 151*

Joel
2:32, *104*
3:1, *92*

Amos
9:11, *131, 139*
9:11-12, *173*
9:11-15, *89-90*
9:13-15, *92*

Micah
4:1-3, *89*
5:2, *122*
5:4-5, *89*

Habakkuk
1:12–3:16, *103*

Zephaniah
3:9-10, *173*
3:20, *89, 92*

Haggai
2:4-5, *100*

Zechariah
1:1-6, *104*
2:10-12, *89*
7:9-11, *253*
7:10, *254*
8:16-17, *253*
10:9, *52*
12–14, *164*
12, *328*
12:3, *102, 150*
12:7, *53*
12:10, *53*
13:7, *123*
14:2-5, *163*
14:8-9, *165*
14:9, *173*

Malachi
3:5, *254*
3:7, *104*

Apocrypha

Tobit
13:9, *128*

Judith
11:19, *122*

Sirach
44:19, *173*
44:21, *173*

2 Baruch
14:13, *174*
44:12, *137*
51:3, *174*
57:2, *137*

1 Maccabees
1:11-15, *189*

2 Maccabees
3:1, *128*

Psalms of Solomon
8:4, *128*
17:21-24, *150*

New Testament

Matthew
1:1–4:11, *120*
1:1, *111-13, 137*
1:2, *112*
1:2-16, *112*
1:6, *133*
1:16, *112*
1:17, *112-13*
1:18, *112*
1:21, *84, 132*
1:22, *113*
2:1-12, *143*
2:6, *113, 121-22*
2:15, *113*
2:17, *113*
2:20-21, *113, 117, 120, 125*
2:21, *107, 112*
2:22, *120*
2:23, *113*
3:9, *112*
4:5, *113, 128*
4:8, *137*
4:12, *120*
4:12-17, *120*
4:12–18:35, *120*
4:12–19:1, *118*
4:13, *117*
4:15-16, *120*
4:18–18:35, *120*
5:3, *111*
5:5, *125, 135, 137-38*
5:13, *125*
5:14, *125*
5:16, *125*
5:17, *27*
5:18, *137*
5:21, *113*
5:35, *128*
6:1-18, *113*
6:10, *124*

8:11, *124, 126*
8:28-34, *113*
9:36, *122*
10:1-4, *121*
10:1-5, *122*
10:5-6, *84, 113, 121, 187*
10:6, *123*
10:23, *130*
11:29, *136*
13:3-9, *126*
13:18-23, *126*
13:23, *124*
14:32, *137*
15:22, *113*
15:24, *84, 113, 121, 123, 187*
19:1–28:15, *118*
19:1-9, *113*
19:1, *117*
19:4, *137*
19:8, *137*
19:28, *53, 113, 122, 135, 137-38*
21–22, *127*
21:5, *136*
21:9, *130*
21:13, *128*
21:18-22, *113*
21:28-32, *127*
21:33-46, *127*
21:33-43, *127*
21:43, *124, 127*
21:45, *127*
22:1-14, *127*
23, *113*
23:34-36, *148*
23:35, *132*
23:37-39, *53, 84, 113, 128, 147, 309-10*
23:37, *44, 130*
23:38, *131*
23:39, *44, 129*
24:20, *113*
24:29–25:13, *130*
24:30, *53*
24:31, *131*
24:35, *137*
25:31-32, *123*
25:31-36, *84*
25:40, *330*
26:28, *130, 132, 322*
26:31-32, *123*
27:11, *130*

27:24-25, *132*
27:25, *130*
27:53, *113, 128*
27:62-66, *113*
28:11-15, *113*
28:15, *112*
28:16-20, *118, 123*
28:16, *123*
28:18-20, *111*
28:18, *84*
28:19-20, *135*
28:20, *112*

Mark

2:17, *180*
4:12, *330*
5:1-17, *113*
7:15, *180*
7:27, *187*
11:11-19, *113*
11:17, *52*
13, *149*
13:14-20, *148*
14:24, *322*

Luke

1:5-23, *143*
1:26-38, *90*
1:32-33, *43, 90*
1:48, *323*
1:54-55, *34, 90, 323*
1:68, *151*
1:68-79, *151*
1:71, *151*
1:72, *151*
1:72-73, *90*
1:73, *151*
1:74-75, *90*
1:77, *151*
1:79, *151*
2:1-20, *143*
2:22-38, *143*
2:25, *90, 151, 156*
2:29-32, *156*
2:31-32, *90*
2:32, *157, 158*
2:38, *53, 151*
2:41-51, *143*
3, *143*
3:4-6, *156*
3:23-38, *33*
9, *143*

9:51–18:14, *144*
9:51, *143-44*
13:22, *144*
13:31-33, *147*
13:34-35, *53, 306, 309-10*
13:34, *147*
13:35, *152, 160, 164*
17:11, *144*
19:38, *164*
19:41-44, *148, 152, 164, 309*
21, *150*
21:5-36, *148*
21:20-24, *149*
21:21-24, *310*
21:23, *150*
21:24, *150, 158, 162, 306*
21:24-28, *53*
22:20, *100*
22:30, *137*
23:27, *148*
23:28-31, *148*
24, *91*
24:21, *91*
24:25-27, *320*
24:25, *91*
24:27, *91*
24:44-49, *91*
24:44, *91*
24:49, *144*
24:53, *144*

John

1:1, *320*
1:14, *320*
2:19-21, *84*
2:21, *52*
3:3-8, *84*
3:5, *85*
4:13-14, *84*
4:21-24, *85*
4:22, *323, 330*
5:46, *320*
6:30-65, *85*
6:53, *333*
6:63, *85*
6:66, *333*
7:37-39, *84*
8:58, *320*
15, *85*
15:1-17, *85*
18:36, *85*

Acts

1, *93, 142, 153*
1:3, *91*
1:6, *53, 154, 162-63*
1:6-7, *310*
1:6-8, *91, 142-43, 153-55, 162, 164*
1:7-8, *163*
1:8, *142, 144-46*
1:9-12, *163*
1:11, *163*
1:12, *163*
2, *91*
2:5, *146*
2:9-11, *146*
2:21, *104*
2:36, *104*
2:46, *53, 144*
3, *92-93, 150, 162-63, 310*
3:1-10, *144*
3:17-26, *93*
3:17-21, *150, 162*
3:18-22, *310*
3:19, *92*
3:19-21, *152, 160*
3:21, *53, 92, 105, 151, 162, 306*
3:25, *92, 311*
3:25-26, *187*
3:26, *92*
4:1-2, *144*
4:12, *104*
5:12, *144*
5:20-21, *144*
5:42, *144*
8:1, *144*
8:4-25, *144*
9:1-2, *144*
9:1-19, *155*
9:10, *144*
9:19, *144*
9:26-29, *145*
10, *144, 155*
11, *144*
11:2, *145*
11:4-18, *155*
11:19, *144*
11:27-30, *145*
13, *158*
13:1-3, *144*
13:4-14:26, *144*
13:16-41, *154*
13:19, *92, 97*
13:42-43, *154*
13:46, *187*
13:46-47, *154, 157*
13:47, *155*
15, *88*
15:2, *145*
15:7-9, *155*
15:13-19, *139*
16:9-10, *144, 155*
17, *72*
18:5-7, *155*
18:22, *145*
21, *172*
21:17-26, *172*
21:17–23:11, *145*
22:6-16, *155*
26:12-18, *155*
26:22-23, *157*
28, *154, 158-59, 161*
28:14, *92*
28:16-31, *158*
28:17-20, *161*
28:17, *145, 159*
28:20, *84, 159*
28:23-31, *153*
28:23-25, *159*
28:25-28, *154*
28:25-27, *159*
28:28, *153-56, 159*
28:31, *92*

Romans

1:16, *187*
1:16-17, *309*
2-3, *174*
2:9-10, *188*
2:15, *238*
2:25–3:4, *194*
2:25, *186*
2:29, *38*
3:1-2, *186*
3:3-4, *193, 194*
3:4, *73, 190*
3:30, *185*
4, *88, 168-69, 173, 184*
4:4, *184*
4:9, *185*
4:11-12, *181*
4:12, *185*
4:13, *87, 169, 171-73, 175-77, 189*
4:14, *189*
4:16, *184, 189*
4:17-18, *173*
4:20, *189*
4:21, *189*
5-8, *167-68*
5:1-5, *168*
5:12, *168*
7:1–8:11, *168*
7:12, *257*
7:14, *257*
8:12, *168*
8:18, *168*
8:18-25, *325*
9-11, *42, 90, 93, 158, 171, 174, 182-83, 306, 311*
9, *34, 183, 306*
9:1-6, *193*
9:2, *34*
9:3-5, *93, 182*
9:3, *168*
9:4-5, *182, 184*
9:4, *34, 94, 172, 184-85, 188-90*
9:6, *190*
9:8-9, *189*
9:20, *331*
9:25-26, *192*
9:26, *191, 193*
10:1, *185*
10:4, *257*
10:10-12, *180*
10:12-13, *104*
11, *26, 34, 42-43, 58, 69, 97, 183, 185, 187, 193-94*
11:1, *187, 190, 194*
11:1-2, *94, 187*
11:1-10, *94*
11:2, *42*
11:8, *94, 330*
11:11, *190*
11:11-14, *186*
11:11-32, *172, 185*
11:12, *94, 99, 186*
11:13, *181, 185, 189*
11:15-16, *94*
11:15, *43, 186*
11:17, *95, 185, 186*
11:18, *37*
11:20-22, *194*
11:21, *185*
11:23, *95*
11:24, *95, 185*
11:25, *94, 96*
11:25-26, *185-86, 191*
11:25-29, *95*

11:26, *43*, *53*, *62*, *65*, *96*, *183*, *186*,
    191, *193*
11:28, *97*, *183*, *187*
11:28-29, *35*, *185*
11:29, *43*, *97*, *183-84*, *188*, *191*, *193*
11:30-31, *186*
11:30-32, *97*
11:31, *43*
11:33, *331*
14–15, *313*
15, *171*, *190-91*, *194*
15:7-27, *172*
15:8, *184*, *189-91*
15:8-9, *35*
15:10, *172*, *194*
15:12, *190*, *191*
15:16, *189*
15:19, *192*
15:25-26, *192*
15:27, *186*

1 Corinthians
3:5-7, *178*
3:16, *172*
6:19, *172*
7:1-40, *172*
7:17, *189*
7:17-18, *188*
7:17-20, *188*
7:17-24, *188*
7:18, *188-89*
7:19, *177-79*
7:20, *188-89*
11:1-16, *181*
14:34, *181*
15, *193*
15:20-28, *193*
15:25-28, *193*
16:3, *192*

2 Corinthians
3:6-11, *179*
3:7, *257*
3:8, *179*
3:9, *179*
3:11, *179*, *257*
6:16, *172*
11:2, *172*
12:11, *178*

Galatians
1:18, *192*
2–4, *168*
2:1, *192*
2:3, *181*
2:12, *181*
2:14, *181*
2:15, *185*
3–4, *184*
3, *180*, *311*
3:14, *35*
3:16, *35*
3:23-24, *257*
3:28, *45*, *87-88*, *180-81*, *258*
3:28-29, *313*
3:29, *35*
4:26-30, *191*
4:27, *176*
5:3, *186*
5:6, *177-78*
6:15, *178*

Ephesians
2:11-22, *307*, *313*
2:11–3:17, *87*
2:14-18, *180*
2:21-22, *172*
5:21-33, *172*
5:22-24, *181*
5:27, *332*

Philippians
3:2, *168*

Colossians
3:11, *185*
3:18, *181*
3:18-19, *172*

2 Thessalonians
2, *193*
2:4, *172*
2:8, *193*

1 Timothy
2:12, *181*

2 Timothy
3:16, *172*

Hebrews
1, *104*

2:5, *86-87*
6:17-18, *86*
7:18–10:18, *100*
8:5, *86*
8:13, *322*
9:1-2, *322*
9:9, *322*
9:11, *86*
9:24, *86*
11, *87*
11:9, *86-87*
11:10, *86*
11:13, *87*
11:14, *86*
12:27, *86*
12:28, *87*
13:14, *86-87*

Revelation
1:7, *58*
7:9, *325*
11:2, *128*
14:1, *54*
16:12, *59*
21:1-2, *128*
21:2, *54*
21:3, *89*
21:12, *35*, *54*
21:22–22:5, *89*

PSEUDEPIGRAPHA

1 Enoch
5:7, *174*
45:4-5, *137*
91:16, *137*

Testament of Judah
25:1-2, *138*

Testament of Benjamin
10:7, *138*

Letter of Aristeas
234, *180*

Jubilees
17:3, *175*
22:11, *174*
22:14, *174-75*
22:15, *174*
32:19, *174-75*

Scripture and Ancient Writings Index

Dead Sea Scrolls

CD
I, 7-8, *175*
III, 7, *175*
III, 10, *175*
V, *133*
XIII, 21, *175*

1QM (War Scroll)
II, 1-3, *138*
XIX, 4-5, *175*

4Q171 (4QpPsa)
II, 9-12, *136*

4Q400
3, II, 2, *138*

4Q403
1, I, 1, *138*
1, I, 10, *138*
1, I, 21, *138*
1, I, 26, *138*

11QT
57, 11-15, *138*

Finding the Textbook You Need

The IVP Academic Textbook Selector
is an online tool for instantly finding the IVP books
suitable for over 250 courses across 24 disciplines.

www.ivpress.com/academic/